Kaplan Publishing are constantly finding new ways to make a difference to your studies and exciting online resources really do offer something different to students looking for exam success.

This book comes with free MyKaplan online resources so that you can study anytime, anywhere. **This free online resource is not sold separately and is included in the price of the book.**

Having purchased this book, you have access to the following online study materials:

CONTENT	AAT	
	Text	Kit
Electronic version of the book	✓	✓
Progress tests with instant answers	✓	
Mock assessments online	✓	✓
Material updates	✓	✓

How to access your online resources

Kaplan Financial students will already have a MyKaplan account and these extra resources will be available to you online. You do not need to register again, as this process was completed when you enrolled. If you are having problems accessing online materials, please ask your course administrator.

If you are not studying with Kaplan and did not purchase your book via a Kaplan website, to unlock your extra online resources please go to www.mykaplan.co.uk/addabook (even if you have set up an account and registered books previously). You will then need to enter the ISBN number (on the title page and back cover) and the unique pass key number contained in the scratch panel below to gain access. You will also be required to enter additional information during this process to set up or confirm your account details.

If you purchased through Kaplan Flexible Learning or via the Kaplan Publishing website you will automatically receive an e-mail invitation to MyKaplan. Please register your details using this email to gain access to your content. If you do not receive the e-mail or book content, please contact Kaplan Publishing.

Your Code and Information

This code can only be used once for the registration of one book online. This registration and your online content will expire when the final sittings for the examinations covered by this book have taken place. Please allow one hour from the time you submit your book details for us to process your request.

Please scratch the film to access your MyKaplan code.

tybR-4pdj-WxsM-6UQw

Please be aware that this code is case-sensitive and you will need to include the dashes within the passcode, but not when entering the ISBN. For further technical support, please visit www.MyKaplan.co.uk

KAPLAN

PUBLISHING

AAT

AQ2016

FOUNDATION CERTIFICATE IN ACCOUNTING

Synoptic Assessment

EXAM KIT

This Exam Kit supports study for the following AAT qualifications:

AAT Foundation Certificate in Accounting – Level 2

AAT Foundation Diploma in Accounting and Business – Level 2

AAT Foundation Certificate in Bookkeeping – Level 2

AAT Foundation Award in Accounting Software – Level 2

AAT Level 2 Award in Accounting Skills to Run Your Business

AAT Foundation Certificate in Accounting at SCQF Level 5

KAPLAN
PUBLISHING

British Library Cataloguing-in-Publication Data

A catalogue record for this book is available from the British Library.

Published by:

Kaplan Publishing UK

Unit 2 The Business Centre

Molly Millar's Lane

Wokingham

Berkshire

RG41 2QZ

ISBN: 978-1-78740-283-6

© Kaplan Financial Limited, 2018

Printed and bound in Great Britain.

CONTENTS

Features in this exam kit

In addition to providing a wide ranging bank of real exam style questions, we have also included in this kit:

- unit-specific information and advice on exam technique

- our recommended approach to make your revision for this particular unit as effective as possible.

You will find a wealth of other resources to help you with your studies on the AAT website:

www.aat.org.uk/

Quality and accuracy are of the utmost importance to us so if you spot an error in any of our products, please send an email to mykaplanreporting@kaplan.com with full details, or follow the link to the feedback form in MyKaplan.

Our Quality Co-ordinator will work with our technical team to verify the error and take action to ensure it is corrected in future editions.

SYNOPTIC ASSESSMENT SPECIFICATION

AAT AQ16 introduces a Synoptic Assessment, which students must complete if they are to achieve the appropriate qualification upon completion of a qualification. In the case of the Foundation Certificate in Accounting, students must pass all of the mandatory assessments and the Synoptic Assessment to achieve the qualification.

As a Synoptic Assessment is attempted following completion of individual units, it draws upon knowledge and understanding from those units. It may be appropriate for students to retain their study materials for individual units until they have successfully completed the Synoptic Assessment for that qualification.

All units within the Foundation Certificate in Accounting are mandatory. Four units are assessed individually in end of unit assessments, but this qualification also includes a synoptic assessment, sat towards the end of the qualification, which draws on and assesses knowledge and understanding from across the qualification.

- Bookkeeping Transactions – end of unit assessment
- Bookkeeping Controls – end of unit assessment
- Elements of Costing – end of unit assessment
- Work Effectively in Finance – assessed within the synoptic assessment only

Note that Using Accounting Software is a unit assessment only and is not assessed as part of the synoptic assessment. Note also that Work Effectively in Finance is assessed in the synoptic assessment only.

Summary of learning outcomes from underlying units which are assessed in the synoptic assessment

Underlying unit	*Learning outcomes required*
Work Effectively in Finance	LO1, LO2, LO3, LO4
Bookkeeping Transactions	LO2, LO3, LO4, LO5
Bookkeeping Controls	LO3, LO4, LO5
Elements of Costing	LO2, LO3

KAPLAN PUBLISHING

FORMAT OF THE ASSESSMENT

The specimen synoptic assessment comprises seven tasks and covers all four assessment objectives. Students will be assessed by computer-based assessment. Marking of the assessment is partially by computer and partially human marked.

In any one assessment, students may not be assessed on all content, or on the full depth or breadth of a piece of content. The content assessed may change over time to ensure validity of assessment, but all assessment criteria will be tested over time.

The synoptic assessment will ask students to apply knowledge and skills gained across the qualification in an integrated way, within a workplace context. Scenarios will change over time to ensure the validity of the assessment.

The following weighting is based upon the AAT Qualification Specification documentation which may be subject to variation.

	Assessment objective	Weighting
AO1	Demonstrate an understanding of the finance function and the roles and procedures carried out by members of an accounting team	24%
AO2	Process transactions, complete calculations and make journal entries	24%
AO3	Compare, produce and reconcile journals and accounts	34%
AO4	Communicate financial information effectively	18%
	Total	100%

Time allowed

2 hours

PASS MARK

The pass mark for all AAT assessments is 70%.

 Always keep your eye on the clock and make sure you attempt all questions!

DETAILED SYLLABUS

The detailed syllabus and study guide written by the AAT can be found at:

www.aat.org.uk/

ASSESSMENT OBJECTIVES

The synoptic assessment objectives are based upon the learning outcomes of four of the units which are subject to individual unit assessment. Note that not all of the content of those units is assessable in the synoptic assessment. Note also that content from Using Accounting Software is not part of the assessment objective.

To perform this synoptic assessment effectively you will need to know and understand the following:

Assessment objective 1	Demonstrate an understanding of the finance function and the roles and procedures carried out by members of an accounting team
Related learning outcomes	**Work Effectively in Finance** LO1 Understand the finance function within an organisation LO2 Use personal skills development in finance LO3 Produce work effectively LO4 Understand corporate social responsibility (CSR), ethics and sustainability within organisations
Assessment objective 2	Process transactions complete calculations and make journal entries
Related learning outcomes	**Bookkeeping transactions** LO2 Process customer transactions LO3 Process supplier transactions LO4 Process receipts and payments LO5 Process transactions through the ledgers to the trial balance
Assessment objective 3	Compare, produce and reconcile journals and accounts
Related learning outcomes	**Bookkeeping Controls** LO3 Use control accounts LO4 Use the journal LO5 Reconcile a bank statement with the cash book **Elements of Costing** LO2 Use cost recording techniques LO3 Provide information on actual and budgeted costs and income
Assessment objective 4	Communicate financial information effectively
Related learning outcome	**Work Effectively in Finance** LO3 Produce work effectively

KAPLAN PUBLISHING

INDEX TO QUESTIONS AND ANSWERS

EXAM TECHNIQUE

- **Do not skip any of the material** in the syllabus.

- **Read each question** *very* carefully.

- **Double-check your answer** before committing yourself to it.

- Answer **every** question – if you do not know an answer to a multiple choice question or true/false question, you don't lose anything by guessing. Think carefully before you **guess**.

- If you are answering a multiple-choice question, **eliminate first those answers that you know are wrong.** Then choose the most appropriate answer from those that are left.

- **Don't panic** if you realise you've answered a question incorrectly. Getting one question wrong will not mean the difference between passing and failing.

Computer-based exams – tips

- Do not attempt a CBA until you have **completed all study material** relating to it.

- On the AAT website there is a CBA demonstration. It is **ESSENTIAL** that you attempt this before your real CBA. You will become familiar with how to move around the CBA screens and the way that questions are formatted, increasing your confidence and speed in the actual exam.

- Be sure you understand how to use the **software** before you start the exam. If in doubt, ask the assessment centre staff to explain it to you.

- Questions are **displayed on the screen** and answers are entered using keyboard and mouse. At the end of the exam, in the case of those units not subject to human marking, you are given a certificate showing the result you have achieved.

- In addition to the traditional multiple-choice question type, CBAs will also contain **other types of questions**, such as number entry questions, drag and drop, true/false, pick lists or drop down menus or hybrids of these.

- In some CBAs you will have to type in complete computations or written answers.

- You need to be sure you **know how to answer questions** of this type before you sit the exam, through practice.

KAPLAN'S RECOMMENDED REVISION APPROACH

QUESTION PRACTICE IS THE KEY TO SUCCESS

Success in professional examinations relies upon you acquiring a firm grasp of the required knowledge at the tuition phase. In order to be able to do the questions, knowledge is essential.

However, the difference between success and failure often hinges on your exam technique on the day and making the most of the revision phase of your studies.

The **Kaplan Study Text** is the starting point, designed to provide the underpinning knowledge to tackle all questions. However, in the revision phase, poring over text books is not the answer.

Kaplan Pocket Notes are designed to help you quickly revise a topic area; however you then need to practise questions. There is a need to progress to exam style questions as soon as possible, and to tie your exam technique and technical knowledge together.

The importance of question practice cannot be over-emphasised.

The recommended approach below is designed by expert tutors in the field, in conjunction with their knowledge of the examiner and the specimen assessment.

You need to practise as many questions as possible in the time you have left.

OUR AIM

Our aim is to get you to the stage where you can attempt exam questions confidently, to time, in a closed book environment, with no supplementary help (i.e. to simulate the real examination experience).

Practising your exam technique is also vitally important for you to assess your progress and identify areas of weakness that may need more attention in the final run up to the examination.

In order to achieve this we recognise that initially you may feel the need to practice some questions with open book help.

Good exam technique is vital.

THE KAPLAN REVISION PLAN

Stage 1: Assess areas of strengths and weaknesses

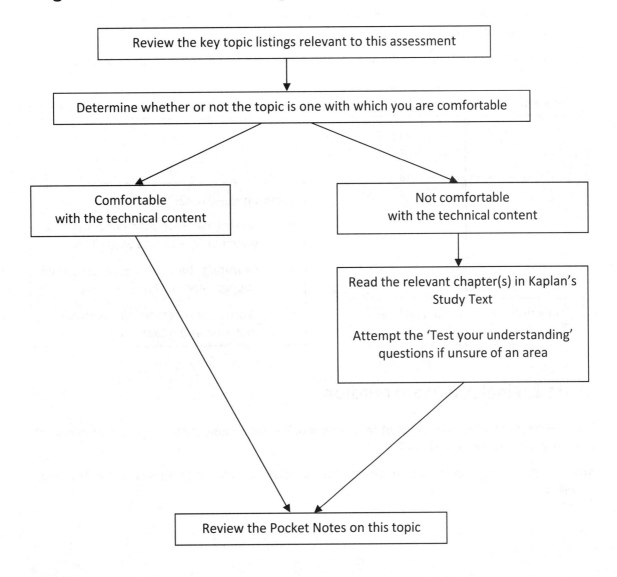

Stage 2: Practice questions

Follow the order of revision of topics as presented in this Kit and attempt the questions in the order suggested.

Try to avoid referring to Study Texts and your notes and the model answer until you have completed your attempt.

Review your attempt with the model answer and assess how much of the answer you achieved.

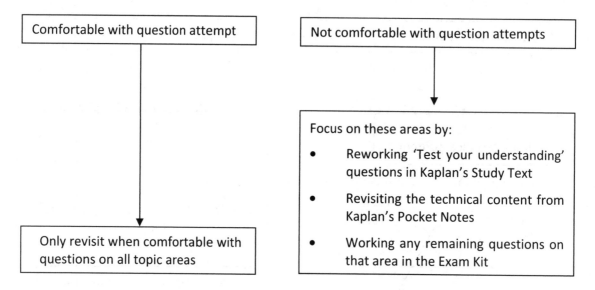

Stage 3: Final pre-exam revision

We recommend that you **attempt at least one mock examination** containing a set of previously unseen exam-standard questions.

Attempt the mock CBA online in timed, closed book conditions to simulate the real exam experience.

Section 1

PRACTICE QUESTIONS

ASSESSMENT OBJECTIVE 1

LO1 UNDERSTAND THE FINANCE FUNCTION WITHIN AN ORGANISATION

1   POLICIES AND PROCEDURES

Select THREE policies and procedures from the following list which are likely to apply to the accounting function:

A   Data Protection Act

B   Health and Safety at Work

C   Curriculum policy

D   Authorised signatory procedure

E   Kitchen Hygiene policy

F   Administration of substances policy

2   DOCUMENTS

The accounts department of an organisation receives documents and information from other departments.

Match the department with the ONE document they would send to the accounts department:

Department	Document
Purchasing Department	(a) Bank interest charged
	(b) Copy of Purchase order
HR Department	(c) Sales Commission
	(d) New employee forms
Payroll Department	(e) Statutory Sick pay forms
	(f) Customer invoice

3   DEPARTMENTS

Match the following departments to ONE information type it would normally use:

Department	Information
Sales Dept	Health and Safety guidelines.
Accounts Dept	List of all new employees for the period.
Payroll Dept	Cheque book stubs.
	Commission payable to sales staff.
	Employee car registration numbers.

4   PRINCIPLES

Select THREE principles from the list below that are not a part of the Data Protection Act 1998.

- Data processed fairly and lawfully.
- Information obtained for personal use.
- Historic information that is not up to date.
- Not kept longer than necessary.
- Transferred to other countries without authorisation.

5   DATA SECURITY

(a)   Which ONE item would be the best method to back up data from your computer?

- printing out paper copies of everything and filing them away
- make a copy on a removable storage device e.g. DVD, external hard drive
- keep a second copy of the data on your hard disk

(b)   Where should data back-ups from your computer be kept?

- in a separate locked room or off site
- in a drawer near the computer
- on the computer's hard disk

(c)   Which ONE of the following is less likely to damage or delete data?

- archiving
- a virus
- system breakdown

(d)   State three features of a secure password.

- Feature 1
- Feature 2
- Feature 3

(e)   Which ONE of the following is not a physical control to protect data?

- Restricting access to an office
- Installing an alarm system
- Passwords

6   INFORMATION

(a)   **Identify the FOUR key characteristics of useful information from the list below:**

- understandable
- accurate
- legible
- complete
- timely
- credible
- fit for purpose

(b)   **Identify whether each of the following statements is TRUE or FALSE.**

- Only information stated in monetary terms is useful to accountants

– True/False

- Non-financial information is useful information to individuals who make decisions

– True/False

7   SERVICE PROVISION

Which TWO of the following services are staff in the finance function most likely to provide to staff in the sales department?

- Conducting job interviews
- Preparing sales brochures
- Budget report analysis
- Photocopier servicing
- Marketing new products
- Payment of sales commission

8   STAKEHOLDERS

Identify which TWO of the following stakeholders a trainee in the finance function is most likely to communicate with.

- People living in houses close to the organisation's Head Office
- The local MP
- H M Revenue & Customs
- The Head teacher of the local school
- Receivables
- An AAT examiner

9   REPORTING LINES

A business employs 2 Directors, 3 Managers and 6 Assistants.

Identify who each person should report to by selecting from the picklist. You may use an item more than once.

Person	Should report to the following
Sales and Purchase Ledger Assistant	
Administration Assistant	
3 Sales Assistants	
Payroll Assistant	
Accounting Department Manager	

Picklist: Managing director, Finance director, Sales manager, Accounts department manager, General manager

10   PERSON AND ROLE

Match which ONE person each role must report to:

Role	Reports to
Accounts assistant	Payroll manager
Sales Ledger clerk	Finance director
Machine operator	HR manager
	Factory manager
	Accounting department manager
	Marketing assistant

11   COMPLIANCE AND SOLVENCY

Select TWO actions that will ensure the legal compliance and two actions that will help the solvency of a business

Action	Legal Compliance	Solvency
Ensure financial statements are filed on time.		
Improve credit control procedures.		
Maintain a petty cash book.		
Create and maintain a cash budget.		
Ensure the work place is a safe environment for staff and visitors.		

12 THE ACCOUNTING FUNCTION

The Accounting function is an essential part of the business.

Select TWO actions for each of the columns. Actions should only be selected once:

Actions	Efficient running of the business	Solvency of the business	Legal Compliance
Monitor cashflow.			
Provide quotation to customer.			
Ensure Sales Tax is paid to HMRC on time.			
Regularly chase outstanding receivables.			
Ensure inventory is ordered when it falls to the minimum level.			
Ensure members of staff are first aid trained.			
Regular maintenance of machinery.			
Produce a staff rota for tea making.			

13 ISSUES

Some issues should be referred to a manager if they are unable to be resolved easily by an employee.

Which TWO of the following issues would you try to resolve yourself?

- The paper for the photocopier keeps running out without a new order being placed.
- You suspect a colleague is being harassed by another colleague.
- Your manager has requested you complete a task you do not have sufficient knowledge to complete.
- Somebody in the office continues to prop the fire door open.

14 PETTY CASH

Identify the most likely effect on the organisation if you were unable to complete the petty cash reconciliation on time.

- Your colleagues would be unable to complete their work on time.
- Fraudulent activity may have taken place and go undetected.
- Petty cash will be withdrawn, replaced with invoicing for small purchases.

15   CONFLICT

Some issues may lead to conflict in the workplace.

Indicate which issues can be resolved by you and which should be referred to your line manager.

Issue	Resolve myself	Refer to line manager
Your manager has asked you to complete a Statement of Financial position; however you do not have the accounting knowledge to do this.		
You suspect your colleague knows your computer password.		
You suspect an expenses form which has been passed to you has non-business expenses on it and the form has been submitted by a manager.		

LO2 USE PERSONAL SKILLS DEVELOPMENT IN FINANCE

16   CPD

(a)   **Identify TWO of the following activities that count towards an employee's Continuing Professional Development requirements.**

- Attend a client lunch meeting to discuss improving services offered.

- Complete a course to further relevant knowledge.

- Arrive at work one hour earlier every day during busy times.

- Read articles online related to the trade in which the employee works.

(b)   **Identify the Strength, Weakness, Opportunity and Threat from the information listed below.**

	Strength	Weakness	Opportunity	Threat
Attend a time management course.				
Leaves filing to the end of the week.				
Excellent customer service.				
Insufficient staff members to cover time off for courses.				

17 PERFORMANCE

Your manager has reviewed your performance over the past 6 months and the following has been noted.

Strengths	*Weaknesses*
Excellent computer skills.	Lack of confidence with clients.
Enthusiasm for learning.	Little double entry knowledge.

Indicate which TWO courses would be appropriate for you to attend:

- Bookkeeping course.

- Online computer studies course.

- Communication and presentation skills.

- Nail art evening classes.

- Kick boxing classes.

Identify whether each of the following statements is TRUE or FALSE.

A qualified accountant does not need to attend Continued Professional Development courses – True/False

CPD must be undertaken for a minimum of 1 day per month – True/False

18 WEAKNESSES

(a) Your manager has assessed that you have the following weaknesses:

(1) Poor communications skills.

(2) Poor timekeeping.

(3) Inadequate technical accounting skills.

Which of the following 3 courses of action could address each of the weaknesses identified?

- Attend a bookkeeping course.

- Learn to drive.

- Buy new accounting software.

- Adopt a new clock in and out system for the office.

- Attend a 'how to communicate in an office' course.

- Go on a sky dive course.

(b) **Identify whether each of the following statements is TRUE or FALSE.**

All accountants, qualified and unqualified must complete CPD – True/False

CPD must be carried out on an annual basis by unqualified members – True/False

CPD must be carried out on an annual basis by qualified members – True/False

19 APPRAISAL

Identify whether each of the following statements is TRUE or FALSE.

An employee performance appraisal is designed to focus solely upon weaknesses problems experienced by an employee during the appraisal period.   – True/False

There is a benefit in an employee undertaking a self-appraisal exercise even if their employer operates a system of annual appraisal.   – True/False

An appraisal is a 'backward looking process' that concentrates solely upon what has happened during the previous year.   – True/False

An appraisal process should allow an employee the opportunity to identify and discuss aspects of their work that they have either performed very well or performed less well during the previous year.   – True/False

An effective appraisal process should result in objectives or goals to be achieved during the following year.   – True/False

20 SELF-DEVELOPMENT

You currently work in the financial accounting department of your organisation and have identified the need for some self-development activities.

Identify the development activity from the picklist below that will help you to meet each of your self-development needs.

Self-development need	Development activity
To improve your practical experience of using the purchase ledger management system used by your organisation	
To develop a better understanding of financial accounting theory, principles and techniques	
To improve your knowledge of the goods and services provided by your organisation	
To improve your knowledge and understanding of how the management accounting department compiles product costings	
To improve your communication and presentation skills in meetings	

Picklist: Study for a professional accountancy qualification, Attend practical course, Secondment to another department, Product catalogue review, Work shadowing,

LO3 PRODUCE WORK EFFECTIVELY

21 **(a)** **REGIONAL SALES**

Regional sales made by a business for the three months ended 31 March 20X2 were as follows:

Eastern region	£200,000
Western region	£180,000
South	£150,000
North	£160,000

(a) What was the total sales figure for the quarter?

(b) What percentage of the total sales was made by the North (round your answer to 2 decimal places)?

(c) What percentage of total sales was made by the Eastern and Western regions (round your answer to 2 decimal places)?

(b) **WIGGINS LTD**

Below are the sales figures of Wiggins Limited for the six months ended 31 August 20X4:

20X4	Sales – (£)
March	456,123
April	459,578
May	461,591
June	465,837
July	468,149
August	472,298

(a) What were the total sales for the first 3 months?

(b) What was the percentage increase from March to April?

(c) What will sales be in September 20X4 if they are 5% higher than August 20X4?

(d) How much higher (in £) are sales in June than March?

Note: (round all answers to 2 decimal places).

22   BOB

You are the manager of an accountancy firm (bob – bob@accountancyfirm.co.uk)

You want to discuss the exam performance of the AAT trainees with the training manager, Ally Mckoist (ally@accountancyfirm.co.uk) tomorrow afternoon. One student in particular (John Barnes) has performed poorly.

Draft an email to Ally Please to request a meeting tomorrow afternoon to discuss exam performance of the AAT trainees, particularly that of John Barnes. Hopefully we will be able to support John to improve things.

From: bob@accountancyfirm.co.uk

To:

Subject:

23   K KIPLING

Draft an email which confirms an appointment with a client, Mr K Kipling (kk@cakes4tea.org.uk), to take place at his premises on Monday at 2.30 pm to discuss the business plan for the forthcoming year with Mrs Anna Howes.

From: AATstudent@Kaplan.co.uk

To:

Subject:

24 JOSHUA VALENTINE

The following is a partially completed email to inform Joshua Valentine (jvalentine@atoz.org.uk), Carmel Jenton (cjenton@atoz.org.uk) and Dane Wheeler (dwheeler@atoz.org.uk) of a conference on Thursday at 10am in the King's Hotel. The conference is being held to cover the issue of recycling within organisations. **Please complete as appropriate.**

From:	AATstudent@atoz.org.uk
To:	_____
	_____
Subject:	_____

Hello All,

This conference is being held at _____ on _____ at _____am.

The conference will be held regarding the issue of recycling within organisations.

Please confirm your attendance.

Regards,

AAT Student

25 PURCHASE OF LAPTOPS

Your employer, K.P. Little has a surplus of cash in October 20X8 and it has decided to approve the purchase of 6 new laptops for the sales team.

The total cost approved for the laptops is £6,000.

Draft an email, dated 2 October 20X8, to Joe Wriggle (j.wriggle@kplittle.co.uk) the sales manager to make him aware of this news.

You need to ensure that Joe lets the sales team know that they will be provided with the new laptops.

Your name is Bernie Coalie and your email address is: (b.coalie@kplittle.co.uk).

To:
From:
Subject:
Date:

26 WORK SCHEDULE

Below is your work scheduled to be completed this week. You work part time from 8 am to 4 pm Monday to Wednesday and you have an hour for lunch at 12.30 pm. There is the weekly planning meeting on Monday at 8.15 am which lasts for 45 minutes.

You routine tasks for the week are:

Daily

Open and distribute the post	9 am (takes 1 hour)
Frank post and take to the post office	3.30 pm (takes 30 mins)

Monday

Process Sales invoices onto Sage	10 am (takes 1 hr 30 mins)

Tuesday

Process Purchase invoices onto Sage	10.30 pm (takes 1 hr 30 mins)

Wednesday

Prepare bank and petty cash reconciliations	1 hour

You have been requested to assist the Payroll Manager on Monday afternoon to calculate the Salesmen's bonuses for the period which must be processed on Tuesday at 2 pm to ensure these are paid at the end of the week.

Complete your to-do list for Monday in order of task completion.

(1)

(2)

(3)

(4)

(5)

27 WORK PLANNING

Your workload for the coming week is shown below. You work from 9am to 5pm and take a lunch break from 12:30 – 1:30pm every day.

Task	Tasks to be completed by:		Task Duration
	Day	*Time*	
Process payroll.	Friday	11am	2 hrs
Bank reconciliations.	Every day	4.30pm	1 hr
Wages reconciliation.	Thursday	2pm	3 hrs
Overtime calculation.	Wednesday	12pm	2 hrs
Team meeting.	Thursday	10am	1 hr
Cash to bank.	Every day	5pm	½ hr

You receive the following email from your line manager on Wednesday at 5pm:

> Hi,
>
> Tomorrow I will be leaving the office at 3pm to meet a potential new customer. I will need to check the wages reconciliation before I go so that the staff are paid on Friday.
>
> Thanks

Tomorrow is Thursday. Please list the order in which you are to complete these tasks:

Process payroll	(1st, 2nd, 3rd, 4th, 5th, 6th)
Bank reconciliation	(1st, 2nd, 3rd, 4th, 5th, 6th)
Wages reconciliation	(1st, 2nd, 3rd, 4th, 5th, 6th)
Overtime calculation	(1st, 2nd, 3rd, 4th, 5th, 6th)
Team meeting	(1st, 2nd, 3rd, 4th, 5th, 6th)
Cash to bank	(1st, 2nd, 3rd, 4th, 5th, 6th)

28 FEEDBACK

50 feedback forms have been sent out by e-mail to the delegates following a training course. The results are shown in the table below:

	Response	
Question	Yes	No
Was the course content relevant to your job role?	15	5
Did the presenter explain the purpose of the training?	20	1
Would you recommend the course to others?	18	2
Was the venue easy to find?	6	15

Select TWO conclusions from the list below that could be drawn from the feedback:

- The course was not relevant to the delegates' job role.

- Most delegates found the venue difficult to find.

- The course was not very successful.

- The course was relevant to the delegates' job role.

Select TWO items from the list below which should be investigated:

- Why did we send the staff on the course?

- Why was there so little feedback received?

- Look for a different venue.

- Do we need to use a different presenter?

29 SURVEY

The following survey was recently carried out at a company.

	Number of staff that agreed	Number of staff that disagreed	Number of staff that did not answer
Are you happy with your work/life balance?	12	45	3
Are you satisfied with your current pay?	34	24	2
Do you believe you have strong promotion prospects in your current role?	5	55	0

(a)　How many people were asked each question?

(b)　In terms of work/life balance, are staff happy/unhappy?

(c)　In terms of current pay/are most people happy/unhappy?

(d)　Do the majority of people agree that there are good promotion prospects – yes/no?

30 REPORT CONTENT

What information is usually contained within the areas of a report listed below?

	Introduction	Appendices
Information regarding what the report is based upon.		
Supporting calculations for figures contained within the body of the report.		

LO4 CORPORATE SOCIAL RESPONSIBILITY, ETHICS AND SUSTAINABILITY

31 PRINCIPLES

The fundamental code of ethics set out five principles that a professional accountant is required to comply with. Two principles are objectivity and professional competence/due care.

Select TWO other ethical principles from the list below.

A　Confidence

B　Integrity

C　Truthfulness

D　Confidentiality

Section 2

PRACTICE QUESTIONS

ASSESSMENT OBJECTIVE 2

47   HLB WHOLESALE

On 1 Feb Painting Supplies Ltd delivered the following goods to a credit customer, HLB Wholesale.

Painting Supplies Ltd **19 Edmund St** **Newcastle, NE6 5DJ**	
Delivery note No. 46589 01 Feb 20XX	
HLB Wholesale 98 Back St Consett DH4 3PD	**Customer account code:** HLB24
20 tins of white paint, product code SD19	

The list price of the goods was £15 each plus VAT. HLB Wholesale are to be given a 10% trade discount and a 4% discount if they pay within 4 working days.

(a)   Complete the invoice below.

Painting Supplies Ltd
19 Edmund St
Newcastle, NE6 5DJ
VAT Registration No. 402 2958 02

HLB Wholesale
98 Back St
Consett
DH4 3PD
Date: 1 Feb 20XX

Customer account code:

Delivery note number:

Invoice No: 298

Quantity	Product code	Total list price £	Net amount after discount £	VAT £	Gross £

Painting Supplies Ltd offer a discount of 10% if their customers buy from them.

(b) **What is the name of this type of discount?**

Picklist: bulk discount, prompt payment discount, trade discount

48 MASHED LTD

On 1 Aug Hickory House delivered the following goods to a credit customer, Mashed Ltd.

Hickory House
22 Nursery Road
Keighley, BD22 7BD

Delivery note No. 472
01 Aug 20XX

Mashed Ltd   **Customer account code:** MA87
42 Moorside Court
Ilkley
Leeds, LS29 4PR

20 flower pots, product code P10

The list price of the goods was £5 per flower pot plus VAT. Mashed Ltd is to be given a 10% trade discount and a 4% early payment discount.

(a) **Complete the invoice below.**

Hickory House
22 Nursery Road
Keighley, BD22 7BD

VAT Registration No. 476 1397 02

Mashed Ltd   **Customer account code:**
42 Moorside Court
Ilkley   **Delivery note number:**
Leeds, LS29 4PR

                                                        Date: 1 Aug 20XX
Invoice No: 47

Quantity of pots	Product code	Total list price £	Net amount after discount £	VAT £	Gross £

Hickory House offers each customer a discount if they buy over a certain quantity of goods.

(b) **What is the name of this type of discount?**

Picklist: Bulk discount, prompt payment discount, trade discount

49 SDB

Sales invoices have been prepared and partially entered in the sales day-book, as shown below.

(a) **Complete the entries in the sales day-book by inserting the appropriate figures for each invoice.**

(b) **Total the last five columns of the sales day-book.**

Sales day-book

Date 20XX	Details	Invoice number	Total £	VAT £	Net £	Sales type 1 £	Sales type 2 £
31 Dec	Poonams	105	3,600				3,000
31 Dec	D. Taylor	106		1,280		6,400	
31 Dec	Smiths	107	3,840		3,200		3,200
	Totals						

50 WILLIAM & SAMMY LTD

The account shown below is in the sales ledger of Hickory House. A cheque for £668 has now been received from this customer.

William and Sammy Ltd

Date 20XX	Details	Amount £	Date 20XX	Details	Amount £
1 June	Balance b/f	4,250	2 June	Bank	4,250
23 June	Sales invoice 255	1,876	15 June	Sales returns credit note 98	1,208
30 June	Sales Invoice 286	2,459			

(a) **Which item has not been included in the payment?**

Picklist: Balance b/f, Sales invoice 255, Sales invoice 286, Bank, Sales returns credit note 98

An invoice is being prepared to be sent to William and Sammy Ltd for £3,890 plus VAT of £778. A prompt payment discount of 4% will be offered for payment within 10 days.

(b) **What is the amount Hickory House should receive if payment is made within 10 days?**

£

(c) **What is the amount Hickory House should receive if payment is NOT made within 10 days?**

£

51 PIXIE PAPERS

A supply of paper has been delivered to Alpha Ltd by Pixie Paper. The purchase order sent from Alpha Ltd, and the invoice from Pixie Paper, are shown below.

Alpha Ltd

121 Baker St

Newcastle, NE1 7DJ

Purchase Order No. PO1792

To: Pixie Paper

Date: 5 Aug 20XX

Please supply 50 boxes of A4 paper product code 16257

Purchase price: £10 per box, plus VAT

Discount: less 10% trade discount, as agreed.

Pixie Paper

24 Eden Terrace, Durham, DH9 7TE

VAT Registration No. 464 392 401

Invoice No. 1679

Alpha Ltd
121 Baker St
Newcastle, NE1 7DJ
9 Aug 20XX

50 boxes of A4 paper, product code 16257 @ £10 each	£500
VAT	£100
Total	£600

Terms: 30 days net

Check the invoice against the purchase order and answer the following questions.

Has the correct product been supplied by Pixie Paper?	Y	N
Has the correct net price been calculated?	Y	N
Has the total invoice price been calculated correctly?	Y	N
What would be the VAT amount charged if the invoice was correct?	£_____	
What would be the total amount charged if the invoice was correct?	£_____	

52 FREDDIE LTD

Purchase invoices have been received and partially entered in the purchases day-book of Freddie Ltd, as shown below.

(a) **Complete the first two entries in the purchases day-book by inserting the appropriate figures for each invoice.**

(b) **Complete the final entry in the purchases day book by inserting the appropriate figures from the following invoice.**

Novot & Co
5 Pheasant Way, Essex, ES9 8BN
VAT Registration No. 453 098 541

Invoice No. 2176

Freddie Ltd

9 Banbury Street

Sheffield

31 July 20XX

10 boxes of product code 14212 @ £400 each	£4,000
VAT	£800
Total	£4,800
Payment terms 30 days	

Purchases day-book

Date 20XX	Details	Invoice number	Total £	VAT £	Net £	Product 14211 £	Product 14212 £
31 July	Box Ltd	2177			800	800	
31 July	Shrew Ltd	2175		2,400		12,000	
31 July	Novot & Co	2176					
	Totals						

53   HOLLY LTD

The account shown below is in the purchase ledger of AD Wholesale. A cheque for £4,770 has now been paid to this supplier.

Holly Ltd

Date 20XX	Details	Amount £	Date 20XX	Details	Amount £
			5 Jan	Balance b/f	1,500
15 Jan	Purchase return 251	540	19 Jan	Purchase invoice 3658	2,360
31 Jan	Purchase return 286	360	27 Jan	Purchase invoice 2987	1,450

(a)   Which item has been not been included in the payment, causing it to be overstated?

```
                                                         
```

Picklist: Balance b/f, Purchase invoice 3658, Bank, Purchase returns 286, Purchase invoice 2987

An invoice has been received from Rickman Repairs for £860 plus VAT of £172. A prompt payment discount of 10% will be offered for payment within 30 days.

(b)   **What is the amount we should pay, if we meet the 30 days requirement?**

£

(c)   **How much VAT is payable if the payment is NOT made in 30 days?**

£

(d)   **What is the amount we should pay if payment is NOT made within 30 days?**

£

54   EP MANUFACTURERS

Shown below is a statement of account received from a credit supplier, and the supplier's account as shown in the purchases ledger of EP Manufacturers.

KLP Ltd

19 Mussell Street, Newcastle, NE4 8JH

To: EP Manufacturers
19 Edmund St
Newcastle, NE6 5DJ

STATEMENT OF ACCOUNT

Date 20XX	Invoice number	Details	Invoice amount £	Cheque amount £	Balance £
1 Jan	468	Goods	5,200		5,200
3 Jan	458	Goods	3,600		8,800
8 Jan		Cheque		1,400	7,400
19 Jan	478	Goods	800		8,200
21 Jan		Cheque		6,500	1,700
28 Jan	488	Goods	4,350		6,050

KLP Ltd

Date 20XX	Details	Amount £	Date 20XX	Details	Amount £
8 Jan	Bank	1,400	1 Jan	Purchases	5,200
21 Jan	Bank	6,500	3 Jan	Purchases	3,600
31 Jan	Bank	1,200	19 Jan	Purchases	800

(a)   **Which item is missing from the statement of account from KLP Ltd?**

Picklist: cheque for £1,200, invoice 468, Invoice 478, Cheque for £6,500, Invoice 488, Cheque for £1,400

(b)   **Which item is missing from the supplier account in EP Manufacturers' purchases ledger?**

Picklist: Invoice 468, Invoice 472, Invoice 478, Invoice 488, Purchase return £900, Cheque for £2,500

(c)   **Once the omitted items have been recorded, what is the agreed balance outstanding between EP Manufacturers and KLP Ltd?**

£

55 STANNY LTD

Ringo's Rings sends out cheques to suppliers on the last day of the month following the month of invoice. Below is an extract from the purchases ledger of Ringo's Rings.

Stanny Ltd

Date 20XX	Details	Amount £	Date 20XX	Details	Amount £
13 Feb	Purchases returns credit note 198	650	1 Feb	Balance b/f	4,650
19 Feb	Purchase return credit note 154	1,250	10 Feb	Purchases Invoice 694	2,300
28 Feb	Bank	4,650	11 Feb	Purchase invoice 658	3,640

(a)   **Complete the remittance advice note below.**

Ringo Rings

37 Parker Lane

Stoke SK1 0KE

REMITTANCE ADVICE

To: Stanny Ltd   **Date:** 31 Mar 20XX

Please find attached our cheque in payment of the following amounts.

Invoice number	Credit note number	Amount £
Total amount paid		

(b)   **Are these two statements true or false?**

A remittance note is for ours and the supplier's records   T   F

A remittance note is sent by a supplier confirming amounts received from them   T   F

56   TOYWORLD

Shown below is a statement of account received from a credit supplier, and the supplier's account as shown in the purchases ledger of Hickory House

Toyworld

18 Landview Road

Skipton

BD27 4TU

To: Hickory House

22 Nursery Road

Keighley, BD22 7BD

STATEMENT OF ACCOUNT

Date 20XX	Invoice number	Details	Invoice amount £	Cheque amount £	Balance £
1 Jan	207	Goods	2,500		2,500
8 April	310	Goods	900		3,400
9 June		Cheque		3,400	0
17 Aug	504	Goods	500		500
18 Aug	505	Goods	4,000		4,500

Toyworld

Date 20XX	Details	Amount £	Date 20XX	Details	Amount £
9 June	Bank	3,400	1 Jan	Purchases	2,500
25 June	Bank	500	8 April	Purchases	900
			17 Aug	Purchases	500

(a)   **Which item is missing from the statement of account from Toyworld?**

   Picklist: Invoice 207, Invoice 310, Invoice 504, Invoice 505, Cheque for £3,400, Cheque for £500

(b)   **Which item is missing from the supplier account in Hickory Houses' purchases ledger?**

   Picklist: Invoice 207, Invoice 310, Invoice 504, Invoice 505, Cheque for £3,400, Cheque for £500

(c)   **Assuming any differences between the statement of account from Toyworld and the supplier account in Hickory Houses' purchases ledger are simply due to omission errors, what is the amount owing to Toyworld?**

   £

57 GREY GARAGES

Grey Garages makes payments to suppliers by BACS on the 25th of every month and includes all items that have been outstanding for more than 10 days.

Below is a pre-printed remittance advice slip taken from a statement of account received from a supplier, Mulberry Motors, showing all items outstanding.

Complete the remittance advice ready for the next payment to Mulberry Motors.

Remittance advice			
To: Mulberry Motors			
From: Grey Garages			
Payment method:		**Date of payment:**	
Items outstanding			Tick if included in payment
Date 20XX	Details	Amount £	
23-Jun	Invoice 213	740	
06-Jul	Credit note 14	120	
13-Jul	Invoice 216	620	
19-Jul	Invoice 257	870	
Total amount paid		£	

58 ERRICO

The two invoices below were received on 5 June from credit suppliers who offer prompt payment discounts.

Invoices:

Giacomo
VAT registration 446 1552 01
Invoice number 1923

To: Errico	4 June 20XX
	£
4 product code 45 @ £14.50 each	58.00
VAT @ 20%	11.60
	————
Total	69.60

Terms: 3% prompt payment discount if payment is received within 7 days of the invoice date.

Gaetani
VAT registration 446 4742 01
Invoice number 4578

To: Errico	4 June 20XX
	£
3 product code 42a @ £11.50 each	34.50
VAT @ 20%	6.90
	————
Total	41.40

Terms: 5% prompt payment discount if payment is received within 5 days of the invoice date.

Calculate the amount to be paid to each supplier if the prompt payment discount is taken and show the date by which the supplier should receive the payment.

Supplier	£	Date by which the payment should be received by the supplier
Giacomo		
Gaetani		

59   LADY LTD

Given below is the purchases day book for Lady Ltd

Date	Invoice No.	Code	Supplier	Total	VAT	Net
1 Dec	03582	PL210	M Brown	300.00	50.00	250.00
5 Dec	03617	PL219	H Madden	183.55	30.59	152.96
7 Dec	03622	PL227	L Singh	132.60	22.10	110.50
10 Dec	03623	PL228	A Stevens	90.00	15.00	75.00
18 Dec	03712	PL301	N Shema	197.08	32.84	164.24
			Totals	**903.23**	**150.53**	**752.70**

You are required to:

* Post the totals of the purchases day book to the general ledger accounts given

* Post the invoices to the payables' accounts in the subsidiary ledger given.

General ledger

Purchases ledger control account

	£			£
			1 Dec Balance b/d	5,103.90

VAT account

	£			£
			1 Dec Balance b/d	526.90

Purchases account

	£		£
1 Dec balance b/d	22,379.52		

Subsidiary ledger

M Brown

	£			£
			1 Dec Balance b/d	68.50

H Madden

	£			£
			1 Dec Balance b/d	286.97

L Singh

	£		£
		1 Dec Balance b/d	125.89

A Stevens

	£		£
		1 Dec Balance b/d	12.36

N Shema

	£		£
		1 Dec Balance b/d	168.70

60   SPARKY LTD

The following credit transactions all took place on 31 July and have been entered into the sales returns day-book of Sparky Ltd as shown below. No entries have yet been made in the ledgers.

Sales returns day-book

Date 20XX	Details	Credit note number	Total £	VAT £	Net £
31 July	Clarkson Ltd	150C	1,680	280	1,400
31 July	Kyle & Co	151C	720	120	600
	Totals		2,400	400	2,000

(a)   **What will be the entries in the sales ledger?**

Sales ledger

Account name	Amount £	Debit ✓	Credit ✓

Picklist: Net, Purchases, Purchases ledger control, Clarkson Ltd, Purchases returns, Sales, Sales ledger control, Sales returns, Kyle & Co, Total, VAT

(b)   **What will be the entries in the general ledger?**

General ledger

Account name	Amount £	Debit ✓	Credit ✓

Picklist: Kyle & Co, Net, Purchases, Purchases ledger control, Purchases returns, Sales, Sales ledger control, Sales returns, Clarkson Ltd, Total, VAT

61   LOUIS LTD

The following transactions all took place on 31 Jan and have been entered into the sales day book of Louis Ltd as shown below. No entries have yet been made into the ledger system.

Date 20XX	Details	Invoice number	Total £	VAT £	Net £
31 Jan	Sheep & Co	1400	3,840	640	3,200
31 Jan	Cow Ltd	1401	11,760	1,960	9,800
31 Jan	Chicken & Partners	1402	6,720	1,120	5,600
31 Jan	Pig Ltd	1403	14,496	2,416	12,080
	Totals		36,816	6,136	30,680

(a)   **What will be the entries in the sales ledger?**

Account name	Amount £	Debit ✓	Credit ✓

Picklist: Sheep & Co, Purchases, Sales ledger control, Cow Ltd, Purchases returns, Sales, Chicken & Partners, Purchases ledger control, Sales returns, VAT, Pig Ltd

(b)   **What will be the entries in the general ledger?**

Account name	Amount £	Debit ✓	Credit ✓

Picklist: Purchases ledger control, Sales, Sales ledger control, Purchases, VAT

62   THOMAS & TILLY

The following credit transactions all took place on 31 Jan and have been entered into the purchase returns day-book of Thomas & Tilly as shown below. No entries have yet been made in the ledgers.

Purchase returns day-book

Date 20XX	Details	Credit note number	Total £	VAT £	Net £
31 Jan	May Ltd	230C	1,920	320	1,600
31 Jan	Hammond & Co	231C	1,200	200	1,000
	Totals		3,120	520	2,600

(a)   **What will be the entries in the purchases ledger?**

Purchase ledger

Account name	Amount £	Debit ✓	Credit ✓

Picklist: Net, Purchases, Purchases ledger control, May Ltd, Purchases returns, Sales, Sales ledger control, Sales returns, VAT, Hammond & Co, Total.

(b)   **What will be the entries in the general ledger?**

General ledger

Account name	Amount £	Debit ✓	Credit ✓

Picklist: May Ltd, Net, Purchases, Purchases ledger control, Purchases returns, Sales, Sales ledger control, Sales returns, Hammond & Co, Total, VAT

63   JESSICA & CO

The following credit transactions all took place on 31 Dec and have been entered into the purchases returns day-book as shown below. No entries have yet been made in the ledgers.

Purchases returns day-book

Date 20XX	Details	Credit note number	Total £	VAT £	Net £
31 Dec	Iona Ltd	4763	1,680	280	1,400
31 Dec	Matilda Ltd	2164	4,320	720	3,600
	Totals		6,000	1,000	5,000

(a) **What will be the entries in the purchases ledger?**

Purchases ledger

Account name	Amount £	Debit ✓	Credit ✓

Picklist: Iona Ltd, Matilda Ltd, Net, Purchases, Purchases ledger control, Purchases returns, Sales, Sales ledger control, Sales returns, Total, VAT

(b) **What will be the entries in the general ledger?**

General ledger

Account name	Amount £	Debit ✓	Credit ✓

Picklist: Iona Ltd, Matilda Ltd, Net, Purchases, Purchases ledger control, Purchases returns, Sales, Sales ledger control, Sales returns, VAT, Total

64 HORSEY REACH

The following transactions all took place on 31 July and have been entered into the discounts allowed day book of Horsey Reach as shown below. No entries have yet been made into the ledger system.

Date 20XX	Details	Credit note number	Total £	VAT £	Net £
31 July	Ashleigh Buildings	145	36.00	6.00	30.00
31 July	143 WGT	146	54.00	9.00	45.00
31 July	McDuff McGregor	147	43.20	7.20	36.00
31 July	Cameron Travel	148	93.60	15.60	78.00
	Totals		226.80	37.80	189.00

(a) **What will be the entries in the general ledger?**

Account name	Amount £	Debit ✓	Credit ✓

Picklist: 13 WGT, Ashleigh Buildings, Cameron Travel, Discounts Allowed, Discounts Received, McDuff McGregor, Purchases, Purchases ledger control, Sales, Sales ledger control, VAT

(b) **What will be the entries in the subsidiary ledger?**

Account name	Amount £	Debit ✓	Credit ✓

Picklist: 143 WGT, Ashleigh Buildings, Cameron Travel, Discounts Allowed, Discounts Received, McDuff McGregor, Purchases, Purchases ledger control, Sales, Sales ledger control, VAT

65 BUTTERFLY BEES

These are the totals from the discounts received book of Butterfly Bees at the end of the month.

Total £	VAT £	Net £
427.20	71.20	356.00

(a) **What will be the entries in the general ledger?**

Account name	Amount £	Debit ✓	Credit ✓

One of the entries in the discounts received day book is for a credit note received from Bella Bumps for £20 plus VAT.

(b) **What will be the entry in the purchases ledger?**

Account name	Amount £	Debit ✓	Credit ✓

66 OLIVIA ROSE BRIDAL SUPPLIES

These are the totals from the discounts allowed book of Olivia Rose Bridal Supplies at the end of the month.

Total £	VAT £	Net £
226.80	37.80	189.00

(a) **What will be the entries in the general ledger?**

Account name	Amount £	Debit ✓	Credit ✓

One of the entries in the discounts allowed day book is for a credit note sent to Bridezilla for £45 plus VAT.

(b) **What will be the entry in the sales ledger?**

Account name	Amount £	Debit ✓	Credit ✓

67 CHUGGER LTD

The following transactions all took place on 31 July and have been entered in the credit side of the cash-book as shown below. No entries have yet been made in the ledgers.

Cash-book – Credit side

Date 20XX	Details	VAT £	Bank £
31 July	Stationery	16	96
31 July	Photocopier repair	40	240

(a) **What will be the entries in the general ledger?**

General ledger

Account name	Amount £	Debit ✓	Credit ✓

Picklist: Stationery, Insurance, Repairs, Purchases ledger control, Sales ledger control, VAT

The following transactions all took place on 31 July and have been entered in the debit side of the cash-book as shown below. No entries have yet been made in the ledgers.

Cash-book – Debit side

Date 20XX	Details	Bank £
31 July	Balance b/f	6,350
31 July	BBG Ltd	7,200
31 July	EFG Ltd	5,000

(b) **What will be the TWO entries in the sales ledger?**

Sales ledger

Account name	Amount £	Debit ✓	Credit ✓

Picklist: Balance b/f, Sales ledger control, BBG Ltd, Purchases ledger control, EFG Ltd, Bank

(c) **What will be the entry in the general ledger?**

General ledger

Account name	Amount £	Debit ✓	Credit ✓

Picklist: Balance b/f, EFG Ltd Purchase ledger control, Sales ledger control, VAT, Bank, BBG Ltd

68 ITALIAN STALLIONS LTD

The following transactions all took place on 31 Jan and have been entered in the credit side of the cash-book of Italian Stallions Ltd as shown below. No entries have yet been made in the ledgers.

Cash-book – Credit side

Date 20XX	Details	VAT £	Bank £
31 Jan	Printer repair	32	192
31 Jan	Paper	16	96

(a) **What will be the entries in the general ledger?**

General ledger

Account name	Amount £	Debit ✓	Credit ✓

Picklist: Repairs, Office supplies, Purchases ledger control, Sales ledger control, VAT

The following transactions all took place on 31 Jan and have been entered in the debit side of the cash-book as shown below. No entries have yet been made in the ledgers.

Cash-book – Debit side

Date 20XX	Details	Bank £
31 Jan	Balance b/f	5,100
31 Jan	AAG Ltd	4,000
31 Jan	HLG Ltd	3,000

(b) **What will be the TWO entries in the sales ledger?**

Sales ledger

Account name	Amount £	Debit ✓	Credit ✓

Picklist: Balance b/f, Sales ledger control, AAG Ltd, Purchases ledger control, HLG Ltd, Bank

(c) **What will be the entry in the general ledger?**

General ledger

Account name	Amount £	Debit ✓	Credit ✓

Picklist: Balance b/f, EFG Ltd Purchase ledger control, Sales ledger control, VAT, Bank, BBG Ltd

69   FRED'S FISH

The following transactions all took place on 31 Dec and have been entered in the debit side of the cash-book as shown below. No entries have yet been made in the ledgers.

Cash-book – Debit side

Date 20XX	Details	Bank £
31 Dec	Balance b/f	4,280
31 Dec	K and D Ltd	8,200

(a)   What will be the entry in the sales ledger?

Sales ledger

Account name	Amount £	Debit ✓	Credit ✓

Picklist: Balance b/f, Bank, Purchases ledger control, K and D Ltd, Sales ledger control

(b)   What will be the entry in the general ledger?

General ledger

Account name	Amount £	Debit ✓	Credit ✓

Picklist: Balance b/f, Bank, Purchases ledger control, K and D Ltd, Sales ledger control

The following transactions all took place on 31 Dec and have been entered in the credit side of the cash-book as shown below. No entries have yet been made in the ledgers.

Cash-book – Credit side

Date 20XX	Details	VAT £	Bank £
31 Dec	Stationery	20	120
31 Dec	Postage		800

(c)   What will be the entries in the general ledger?

General ledger

Account name	Amount £	Debit ✓	Credit ✓

Picklist: Bank, Postage, Stationery, Purchases ledger control, Sales ledger control, VAT

70 ABC LTD

There are five payments to be entered in ABC Ltd's cash book.

Receipts

Received cash with thanks for goods bought. From ABC Ltd, a customer without a credit account.		Received cash with thanks for goods bought. From ABC Ltd, a customer without a credit account.		Received cash with thanks for goods bought. From ABC Ltd, a customer without a credit account.	
Net	£180	Net	£220	Net	£530
VAT	£36	VAT	£44	(No VAT)	
Total	£216	Total	£264		
S. Lampard		S Bobbins		Penny Rhodes	

Cheque book counterfoils

Henley's Ltd (Purchase ledger account HEN002) £4,925 000372	Epic Equipment Maintenance (We have no credit account with this supplier) £480 (incl VAT at 20%) 000373

(a) **Enter the details from the three receipts and two cheque book stubs into the credit side of the cash-book shown below and total each column.**

Cash-book – credit side

Details	Cash	Bank	VAT	Payables	Cash purchases	Repairs and renewals
Balance b/f						
S. Lampard						
S. Bobbins						
Penny Rhodes						
Henley's Ltd						
Epic Equipment Maintenance						
Total						

There are two cheques from credit customers to be entered in ABC Ltd's cash book:

D. Davies   £851

E. Denholm   £450

(b)   Enter the above details into the debit side of the cash-book and total each column.

Cash book – debit side

Details	Cash	Bank	Receivables
Balance b/f	1,550	7,425	
D Davies			
E Denholm			
Total			

(c)   Using your answers to (a) and (b) above calculate the cash balance.

£

(d)   Using your answers to (a) and (b) above calculate the bank balance.

£

(e)   Will the bank balance brought down calculated in (d) above be a debit or credit balance?

Debit/Credit

71   BEDS

There are five transactions to be entered in Beds' cash book.

Receipts

Received cash with thanks for goods bought.	Received cash with thanks for goods bought.	Received cash with thanks for goods bought.
From Beds, a customer without a credit account.	From Beds, a customer without a credit account.	From Beds, a customer without a credit account.
Net £590	Net £190	Net £230
VAT £118	VAT £38	(No VAT)
Total £708	Total £228	
A. Blighty Ltd	R Bromby	Roxy Bland

Cheque book counterfoils

Burgess Ltd	Fast Equipment Repairs
(Purchase ledger account BUR003)	(We have no credit account with this supplier)
£2,400	£96 (inc VAT at 20%)
No. 000101	No. 000102

(a) Enter the details from the three receipts and two cheque book stubs into the credit side of the cash-book shown below and total each column.

Cash-book – credit side

Details	Cash	Bank	VAT	Payables	Cash purchases	Repairs and renewals
Balance b/f						
A. Blighty Ltd						
R Bromby						
Roxy Bland						
Burgess Ltd						
Fast Equipment Repairs						
Total						

There are two cheques from credit customers to be entered in Beds' cash book:

A. Barnett   £698

H. Connelly   £250

(b) Enter the above details into the debit side of the cash-book and total each column.

Cash book – debit side

Details	Cash	Bank	Receivables
Balance b/f	1,175	3,825	
A Barnett			
H Connelly			
Total			

(c) Using your answers to (a) and (b) above calculate the cash balance.

£

(d) Using your answers to (a) and (b) above calculate the bank balance.

£

(e) Will the bank balance brought down calculated in (d) above be a debit or credit balance?

Debit/Credit

72   HICKORY HOUSE

Hickory House maintains a petty cash book as both a book of prime entry and part of the double entry accounting system. The following transactions all took place on 31 Dec and have been entered in the petty cash-book as shown below. No entries have yet been made in the general ledger.

Petty cash-book

Date 20XX	Details	Amount £	Date 20XX	Details £	Amount £	VAT £	Postage £	Motor expenses £	Office expenses
31 Dec	Balance b/f	210.00	31 Dec	Stapler	6.72	1.12			5.60
31 Dec	Bank	90.00	31 Dec	Stamps	15.00		15.00		
			31 Dec	Parking	14.88	2.48		12.40	
			31 Dec	Stationery	19.20	3.20			16.00
			31 Dec	Balance c/d	244.20				
		300.00			300.00	6.80	15.00	12.40	21.60

What will be the FIVE entries in the general ledger?

General ledger

Account name	Amount £	Debit ✓	Credit ✓

Picklist: Balance b/f, Balance c/d, Bank, Stationery, Stapler, Motor expenses, Parking, Office expenses, Petty cash-book, Stamps, Postage, VAT

73   MESSI & CO

Messi & Co maintains a petty cash book as a book of prime entry; it is not part of the double entry accounting system. The following transactions all took place on 31 Dec and have been entered in the petty cash-book as shown below. No entries have yet been made in the general ledger.

Petty cash-book

Date 20XX	Details	Amount £	Date 20XX	Details £	Amount £	VAT £	Postage £	Motor expenses £	Office expenses £
31 Dec	Op balance	100.00	31 Dec	Paper	27.33	4.55			22.78
			31 Dec	Stamps	4.50		4.50		
			31 Dec	Biscuits	6.60	1.10			5.50
			31 Dec	Parking	9.60	1.60		8.00	
			31 Dec	Cl balance	51.97				
		100.00			100.00	7.25	4.50	8.00	28.28

What will be the FIVE entries in the general ledger?

General ledger

Account name	Amount £	Debit ✓	Credit ✓

Picklist: Balance b/f, Balance c/d, Bank, Motor expenses, Paper, Parking, Petty cash control, Office expenses, Petty cash-book, Stamps, Postage, VAT

74   YUMMY CUPCAKES

Yummy Cupcakes maintains a petty cash book as a book of prime entry; it is not part of the double entry accounting system. The following transactions all took place on 31 July and have been entered in the petty cash-book as shown below. No entries have yet been made in the general ledger.

Petty cash-book

Date 20XX	Details	Amount £	Date 20XX	Details £	Amount £	VAT £	Sundry expenses £	Business travel £	Postage
1 July	Op balance	150.00	31 July	Parking	15.00	2.50		12.50	
			31 July	Tea & Coffee	12.00	2.00	10.00		
			31 July	Travel	39.44	6.57		32.87	
			31 July	Stamps	4.00				4.00
			31 July	Cl balance	79.56				
		150.00			150.00	11.07	10.00	45.37	4.00

What will be the FIVE entries in the general ledger?

General ledger

Account name	Amount £	Debit ✓	Credit ✓

Picklist: Postage, Balance c/d, Bank, Fuel, Balance b/f, Motor repair, Sundry expenses, Petty cash-book, VAT, Business Travel

75   BROOKLYN BOATS

The following two accounts are in the general ledger of Brooklyn Boats at the close of day on 31 Dec.

(a)   Insert the balance carried down together with date and details.

(b)   Insert the totals.

(c)   Insert the balance brought down together with date and details.

Electricity

Date 20XX	Details	Amount £	Date 20XX	Details £	Amount £
01 Dec	Balance b/f	870			
12 Dec	Bank	350			
	Total			Total	

Picklist: Balance b/d, Balance c/d, Bank, Closing balance, Opening balance, Purchases ledger control

Discounts received

Date 20XX	Details	Amount £	Date 20XX	Details £	Amount £
			1 Dec	Bal b/f	500
			15 Dec	Purchase ledger control	100
	Total			Total	

Picklist: Balance b/d, Balance c/d, Bank, Closing balance, Opening balance, Sales ledger control

76   CRAZY CURTAINS

The following two accounts are in the general ledger of Crazy Curtains at the close of day on 31 Jan.

(a)   Insert the balance carried down together with date and details.

(b)   Insert the totals.

(c)   Insert the balance brought down together with date and details.

Electricity expense

Date 20XX	Details	Amount £	Date 20XX	Details £	Amount £
01 Jan	Bal b/f	200			
22 Jan	Bank	250			
	Total			**Total**	

Picklist: Balance b/d, Balance c/d, Bank, Closing balance, Opening balance, Electricity Expense

Rental income

Date 20XX	Details	Amount £	Date 20XX	Details £	Amount £
			01 Jan	Balance b/f	400
			28 Jan	Bank	600
	Total			**Total**	

Picklist: Balance b/d, Balance c/d, Bank, Closing balance, Opening balance, Sales ledger control

77   SMITH & SON

Below is a list of balances to be transferred to the trial balance of Smith & Son at 31 Dec.

Place the figures in the debit or credit column, as appropriate, and total each column.

Account name	Amount £	Debit £	Credit £
Fixtures and fittings	8,250		
Capital	18,400		
Bank overdraft	4,870		
Petty cash control	350		
Sales ledger control (SLCA)	42,870		
Purchases ledger control (PLCA)	23,865		
VAT owed to tax authorities	10,245		
Inventory	9,870		
Loan from bank	22,484		
Sales	180,264		
Sales returns	5,420		
Purchases	129,030		
Purchases returns	2,678		
Discount allowed	2,222		
Discount received	3,432		
Heat and Light	1,490		
Motor expenses	2,354		
Wages	42,709		
Rent and rates	10,600		
Repairs	3,020		
Hotel expenses	1,890		
Telephone	2,220		
Delivery costs	1,276		
Miscellaneous expenses	2,667		
Totals			

78   EXPIALIDOCIOUS LTD

Below is a list of balances to be transferred to the trial balance of Expialidocious Ltd as at 31 July.

Place the figures in the debit or credit column, as appropriate, and total each column.

Account name	Amount £	Debit £	Credit £
Capital	25,360		
Petty cash control	250		
Loan from bank	11,600		
Sales ledger control (SLCA)	159,242		
Purchases ledger control (PLCA)	83,682		
Motor vehicles	35,900		
Inventory	28,460		
Bank overdraft	10,063		
VAT owed from tax authorities	15,980		
Purchases	343,014		
Purchases returns	1,515		
Wages	56,150		
Motor expenses	2,950		
Interest income	400		
Sales	532,900		
Sales returns	5,760		
Stationery	1,900		
Light & heat	6,500		
Discount received	200		
Discount allowed	2,160		
Interest paid on overdraft	550		
Travel	1,800		
Marketing	650		
Telephone	1,510		
Miscellaneous expenses	2,944		
Totals			

Section 3

PRACTICE QUESTIONS

ASSESSMENT OBJECTIVE 3

79   INTREPID INTERIORS

(a)   Intrepid Interiors has started a new business, Intrepid Exteriors, and a new set of accounts are to be opened. A partially completed journal to record the opening entries is shown below.

Record the journal entries needed in the accounts in the general ledger of Intrepid Exteriors to deal with the opening entries.

Account name	Amount £	Debit ✓	Credit ✓
Cash at bank	7,250		
Bank loan	5,000		
Capital	10,625		
Motor vehicles	4,750		
Insurances	575		
Stationery	300		
Sundry expenses	225		
Motor expenses	135		
Advertising	990		
Rent and rates	1,400		
Journal to record the opening entries of new business			

(b)   **From the list below, select which one of the following transactions would be recorded in the journal.**

Picklist: Credit sale, contra, electricity expense, reimbursement of petty cash

80   DOWN & OUT

Down & Out pays it employees by cheque every month and maintains a wages control account. A summary of last month's payroll transactions is shown below:

Item	£
Gross wages	8,542
Employer's NI	1,025
Employees' NI	940
Income tax	1,708
Trade union fees	425

Record the journal entries needed in the general ledger to:

(i)   Record the wages expense

(ii)   Record the HM Revenue & Customs liability

(iii)   Record the net wages paid to the employees

(iv)   Record the trade union liability.

(i)

Account name	Amount £	Debit ✓	Credit ✓

(ii)

Account name	Amount £	Debit ✓	Credit ✓

(iii)

Account name	Amount £	Debit ✓	Credit ✓

(iv)

Account name	Amount £	Debit ✓	Credit ✓

Picklist for each: Bank, Employees NI, Employers NI, HM Revenue and Customs, Income Tax, Net wages, Trade union, Wages control, Wages expense.

81   RHYME TIME

Rhyme Time pays its employees by cheque every month and maintains a wages control account. A summary of last month's payroll transactions is shown below:

Item	£
Gross wages	10,130
Employers' NI	1,185
Employees' NI	1,006
Income tax	2,835
Employer's pension contributions	600
Employee's Pension contributions	550

Record the journal entries needed in the general ledger to:

(i)   Record the wages expense

(ii)   Record the HM Revenue and Customs liability

(iii)   Record the net wages paid to the employees

(iv)   Record the pension liability.

(i)

Account name	Amount £	Debit ✓	Credit ✓

(ii)

Account name	Amount £	Debit ✓	Credit ✓

(iii)

Account name	Amount £	Debit ✓	Credit ✓

(iv)

Account name	Amount £	Debit ✓	Credit ✓

82   BEDROOM BITS

A credit customer, ABC Ltd, has ceased trading, owing Bedroom Bits £2,400 including VAT.

Record the journal entries needed in the general ledger to write off the net amount and the VAT.

Account name	Amount £	Debit ✓	Credit ✓

Picklist: Irrecoverable debts, ABC Ltd, Bedroom Bits, Purchases, Purchases ledger control, Sales, Sales ledger control, VAT.

83   CHESTNUT

On 1 December, Chestnut had a balance of £46,000 on its SLCA and £31,000 on its PLCA. It also sold goods to Cook Ltd, one of its main suppliers for £4,000. Cook was owed £12,000 for goods it had sold to Chestnut.

Perform a contra and balance off the ledger accounts below. Dates are not required.

SLCA

Details	Amount £	Details	Amount £

PLCA

Details	Amount £	Details	Amount £

84 BEANZ

This is a customer's account in the sales ledger.

Beanz Co

Details	Amount £	Details	Amount £
Balance b/f	4,530	Payment received	2,100
Invoice SD4564	3,210	Credit note	420

The customer has now ceased trading.

Record the journal entries needed to write off the receivable, including VAT.

Account name	Amount £	Debit ✓	Credit ✓

Picklist: Irrecoverable debts, Beanz Co, Purchases, Purchases ledger control, Sales, Sales ledger control, VAT.

85 RENT ERROR

An entry to record a bank receipt of £500 for rent has been reversed.

Record the journal entries needed in the general ledger to:

(i)   remove the incorrect entry

(ii)   record the correct entry.

(i)

Account name	Amount £	Debit ✓	Credit ✓

(ii)

Account name	Amount £	Debit ✓	Credit ✓

Picklist for all above: Bank, Cash, Rent Received, Purchases, Purchases ledger control, Sales, Sales ledger control, Suspense, VAT.

86   GAS ERROR

An entry to record a gas expense of £300 was made correctly in the bank but was posted to electricity expenses instead of gas expenses.

Record the journal entries needed in the general ledger to record the correction.

Account name	Amount £	Debit ✓	Credit ✓

87   BUILDING ERROR

An entity purchased a new building for £400,000. This amount was debited to the buildings account, but £40,000 was credited to the bank account.

Record the journal entries needed in the general ledger to record the correction.

Account name	Amount £	Debit ✓	Credit ✓

88   SALES ERROR

A credit sale of £12,000 including VAT has been made. The full £12,000 has been debited to the SLCA and credited to sales.

Record the journal entries needed in the general ledger to record the correction.

Account name	Amount £	Debit ✓	Credit ✓

89   CB INTERIORS

CB Interiors' initial trial balance includes a suspense account with a balance of £8,640.

The error has been traced to the purchases day-book shown below.

Purchases day-book

Date 20XX	Details	Invoice number	Total £	VAT £	Net £
30 Jun	Able Paints Ltd	2,763	2,400	400	2,000
30 Jun	Matley Materials	2,764	3,120	520	2,600
30 Jun	Teesdale Parts	2,765	4,080	680	3,400
	Totals		960	1,600	8,000

Identify the error and record the journal entries needed in the general ledger to

(i)   remove the incorrect entry

(ii)   record the correct entry

(iii)   remove the suspense account balance.

(i)

Account name	Amount £	Debit ✓	Credit ✓

(ii)

Account name	Amount £	Debit ✓	Credit ✓

(iii)

Account name	Amount £	Debit ✓	Credit ✓

Picklist for all above: Able Paints Ltd, Matley Materials, Teesdale Parts, Purchases, Purchases day-book, Purchases ledger control, Purchases returns, Purchases returns day-book, Sales, Sales day-book, Sales ledger control, Sales returns, Sales returns day-book, Suspense, VAT.

90   ROGER DODGER

Roger Dodger's initial trial balance includes a suspense account with a balance of £360.

The error has been traced to the purchase returns day-book shown below.

Purchase returns day-book

Date 20XX	Details	Note number	Total £	VAT £	Net £
30 Jun	Dennis Designs Ltd	421	1,200	200	1,000
30 Jun	XYZ Ltd	422	1,920	320	1,600
30 Jun	Denby Prints	423	4,800	800	4,000
	Totals		7,920	1,680	6,600

Identify the error and record the journal entries needed in the general ledger to:

(i)   remove the incorrect entry

(ii)   record the correct entry

(iii)   remove the suspense account balance.

(i)

Account name	Amount £	Debit ✓	Credit ✓

(ii)

Account name	Amount £	Debit ✓	Credit ✓

(iii)

Account name	Amount £	Debit ✓	Credit ✓

Picklist for all above: Dennis Designs Ltd, XYZ Ltd, Denby Prints, Purchases, Purchases day-book, Purchases ledger control, Purchases returns, Purchases returns day-book, Sales, Sales day-book, Sales ledger control, Sales returns, Sales returns day-book, Suspense, VAT.

91 BUCKLEY DRAINS

Buckley Drains' trial balance was extracted and did not balance. The debit column of the trial balance totalled £336,728 and the credit column totalled £325,923.

(a) **What entry would be made in the suspense account to balance the trial balance?**

Account name	Amount £	Debit ✓	Credit ✓
Suspense			

(b) The error has been traced to an unpaid invoice for advertising, which was recorded correctly in advertising expenses but nowhere else.

Record the journal entries needed in the general ledger to record the correction.

Account name	Amount £	Debit ✓	Credit ✓

(c) **Show one reason for maintaining the journal**

	✓
To correct errors only	
To correct errors and record transactions that have not been recorded in any other book of prime entry	
To record transactions from every other book of prime entry.	

92 MENDONCA

Mendonca's trial balance was extracted and did not balance. The debit column of the trial balance totalled £643,475 and the credit column totalled £641,495

(a)   What entry would be made in the suspense account to balance the trial balance?

Account name	Amount £	Debit ✔	Credit ✔

(b)   The error has been traced to the posting of the wages payment. The total payment made was £3,200. This was incorrectly made in both the wages and bank account. The amount recorded in wages was £2,300, with a credit to the bank of £320 shown.

Record the journal entries needed in the general ledger to record the correction.

Account name	Amount £	Debit ✔	Credit ✔

93 BEASANT

Beasant's trial balance was extracted and did not balance. The debit column of the trial balance totalled £630,000 and the credit column totalled £615,000.

(a)   What entry would be made in the suspense account to balance the trial balance?

Account name	Amount £	Debit ✔	Credit ✔
Suspense			

(b)   The error has been traced to a late credit sale. The full amount of the sale (including VAT) was correctly recorded in the SLCA but no other entries were made.

Record the journal entries needed in the general ledger to record the correction.

Account name	Amount £	Debit ✔	Credit ✔

(c)   Show one reason for maintaining the journal

	✔
To detect fraud	
To record non-regular transactions	
To record goods sold on credit	

94   HEARN

On 30 June Hearn extracted an initial trial balance which did not balance, and a suspense account was opened. On 1 July the following errors were noted:

1   A rent payment of £430 had been correctly included in the bank, but included within rent expenses as £340.

2   An irrecoverable debt of £600 plus VAT had been credited correctly credited to the SLCA, but the only debit entry was £600 to irrecoverable debts.

Complete the journal to correct the errors, and re-draft the trial balance by placing figures into the debit or credit column. You re-drafted trial balance should take into account the journal entries you have made.

Journal entries

Account name	Debit £	Credit £

	Balances extracted on 30 June £	Balances at 1 July	
		Debit £	Credit £
Sales ledger control	34,560		
Purchases ledger control	21,420		
VAT owing to HM Revenue and Customs	3,412		
Capital	50,000		
Sales	201,327		
Sales returns	1,465		
Purchases	87,521		
Purchase returns	252		
Plant and equipment	15,200		
Motor expenses	4,310		
Office expenses	10,321		
Rent and rates	21,420		
Heat and light	8,920		
Wages	53,205		
Irrecoverable debt	1,450		
Office equipment	42,030		
Bank overdraft	4201		
Suspense account (debit balance)	210		
Totals			

95 RODMAN

On 30 June Rodman extracted an initial trial balance which did not balance, and a suspense account was opened. On 1 July the following errors were noted:

1   A VAT refund of £1,250 received from HMRC was recorded in the bank, but no other entry was made.

2   A wages payment of £4,300 was credited to both the bank and wages.

Complete the journal to correct the errors, and re-draft the trial balance by placing figures into the debit or credit column. You re-drafted trial balance should take into account the journal entries you have made.

Journal entries

Account name	Debit £	Credit £

	Balances extracted on 30 June £	Balances at 1 July	
		Debit £	Credit £
Sales ledger control	38,070		
Purchases ledger control	20,310		
VAT owed from HM Revenue and Customs	2,510		
Capital	70,000		
Sales	153,488		
Sales returns	2,135		
Purchases	63,261		
Purchase returns	542		
Plant and equipment	17,319		
Motor expenses	3,214		
Office expenses	6,421		
Rent and rates	17,414		
Heat and light	6,421		
Wages	45,532		
Irrecoverable debt	1,532		
Office equipment	35,313		
Bank overdraft	2,152		
Suspense account (debit balance)	7,350		
Totals			

96 LUXURY BATHROOMS

On 28 April Luxury Bathrooms received the following bank statement as at 24 April.

SKB Bank plc
68 London Road, Reading, RG8 4RN

To: Luxury Bathrooms   Account No: 55548921   24 April 20XX

Statement of Account

Date 20XX	Detail	Paid out £	Paid in £	Balance £	
03 April	Balance b/d			17,845	C
03 April	Cheque 120045	8,850		8,995	C
04 April	Bank Giro Ricketts & Co		465	9,460	C
04 April	Cheque 120046	2,250		7,210	C
05 April	Cheque 120047	64		7,146	C
08 April	Cheque 120048	3,256		3,890	C
14 April	Direct debit AMB Ltd	2,265		1,625	C
14 April	Direct debit D Draper	2,950		1,325	D
14 April	Cheque 120050	655		1,980	D
22 April	Paid in at SKB bank		2,150	170	C
22 April	Bank charges	63		107	C
23 April	Overdraft fee	25		82	C

D = Debit   C = Credit

The cash book as at 24 April is shown below.

Cash book

Date	Details	Bank	Date	Cheque	Details	Bank
01 April	Balance b/d	17,845	01 April	120045	R Sterling Ltd	8,850
19 April	Olsen & Lane	2,150	01 April	120046	Bert Cooper	2,250
22 April	Frith Ltd	685	01 April	120047	Hetko & Sons	64
22 April	Hodgetts & Co	282	02 April	120048	Barrett Ltd	3,256
			02 April	120049	K Plomer	542
			08 April	120050	I&E Brown	655
			08 April	120051	T Roberts	1,698
			14 April		AMB Ltd	2,265

Details column options: Balance b/d, balance c/d, Bank charges, R Sterling Ltd, Olsen & Lane, Frith Ltd, Hodgetts & Co, Bert Cooper, Hetko & Sons, Barrett Ltd, K Plomer, I&E Brown, T Roberts, AMB Ltd, Ricketts & Co, D Draper, Opening balance, Overdraft fees.

(a) Check the items on the bank statement against the items in the cash book.

(b) Enter any items in the cash book as needed.

(c) Total the cash book and clearly show the balance carried down at 24 April (closing balance) and brought down at 25 April (opening balance).

97   WHOLESALE FLOORING

The bank statement and cash book for Wholesale Flooring is shown below.

Money Bags Bank PLC
52 Oak Road, Timperley, SK10 8LR

To: Wholesale Flooring   Account No: 47013799   23 June 20XX

Statement of Account

Date 20XX	Detail	Paid out £	Paid in £	Balance £	
04 June	Balance b/d			5,125	D
05 June	Cheque 104373	890		6,015	D
05 June	Cheque 104374	1,725		7,740	D
05 June	Cheque 104375	210		7,950	D
11 June	Cheque 104378	784		8,734	D
12 June	Bank Giro credit Aintree and Co		1,250	7,484	D
13 June	Cheque 104376	1,275		8,759	D
15 June	Cheque 104377	725		9,484	D
17 June	Paid in at Money Bags bank plc		550	8,934	D
20 June	Direct debit MD County council	400		9,334	D
23 June	Bank charges	160		9,494	D
23 June	Overdraft fee	90		9,584	D

D = Debit   C = Credit

Cash book

Date 20XX	Details	Bank £	Date 20XX	Cheque number	Details	Bank £
			01 June		Balance b/d	5,125
16 June	Beeston's	550	01 June	104373	Good iron	890
19 June	Airfleet exteriors	3,025	01 June	104374	Ashworth & Co	1,725
22 June	Jones's	2,775	01 June	104375	Ironfit	210
			05 June	104376	OSS Ltd	1,275
			07 June	104377	Perfect tools	725
			08 June	104378	Campden Ltd	784
			14 June	104379	Thornley & Thwaite	675
			14 June	104380	Castle & Cove	178

Details columns options: Balance b/d, Balance c/d, Bank charges, Good Iron, Beeston's, Aintree & Co, Perfect Tools, Closing balance, Ashworth & Co, Thornley & Thwaite, MD County Council, Campden Ltd, Airfleet Exteriors, Castle & Cove, OSS Ltd, Opening balance, Overdraft Fee, Ironfit, Jones's.

(a)   Check the items on the bank statement against the items in the cash book.

(b)   Enter any items in the cash book as needed.

(c)   Total the cash book and clearly show the balance carried down at 23 June (closing balance) and brought down at 24 June (opening balance).

98   MCKEOWN

The bank statement and cash book for McKeown is shown below.

Money Bags Bank PLC					
To: McKeown Ltd		Account No: 47013799		23 June 20XX	

Statement of Account

Date 20XX	Detail	Paid out £	Paid in £	Balance £	
01 June	Balance b/d			7,420	C
01 June	Bank Giro credit Pond		180	7,600	C
01 June	Cheque 110156	420		7,180	C
01 June	Interest received		85	7,265	C
11 June	Cheque 110157	430		6,835	C
12 June	Cheque 110158	520		6,315	C
13 June	Cheque 110161	750		5,565	C
15 June	Bank Giro credit Sherwood		640	6,205	C
17 June	Paid in to Money Bags bank		1,200	7,405	C
20 June	Bank Giro credit Coyne		1,630	9,035	C
23 June	Direct debit Wilmott	300		8,735	C
23 June	Interest received		35	8,770	C

D = Debit   C = Credit

Cash book

Date 20XX	Details	Bank £	Date 20XX	Cheque number	Details	Bank £
01 June	Balance b/d	7,180	07 June	110157	Williams	430
12 June	Sherwood	640	07 June	110158	Forecast	520
14 June	Cash sales	1,200	07 June	110159	Beasant	1,240
22 June	Tweedy	860	07 June	110160	Davison	1,420
23 June	Butterwood	440	07 June	110161	Mildenhall	750

(a)   Check the items on the bank statement against the items in the cash book.

(b)   Enter any items in the cash book as needed.

(c)   Total the cash book and clearly show the balance carried down at 23 June (closing balance) and brought down at 24 June (opening balance).

99   LUXURY BATHROOMS

Below is the bank statement and updated cash book for Luxury Bathrooms.

SKB Bank plc
68 London Road, Reading, RG8 4RN

To: Luxury Bathrooms   Account No: 55548921   24 April 20XX

Statement of Account

Date	Detail	Paid out	Paid in	Balance	
20XX		£	£	£	
03 April	Balance b/d			17,845	C
03 April	Cheque 120045	8,850		8,995	C
04 April	Bank Giro Ricketts & Co		465	9,460	C
04 April	Cheque 120046	2,250		7,210	C
05 April	Cheque 120047	64		7,146	C
08 April	Cheque 120048	3,256		3,890	C
14 April	Direct debit AMB Ltd	2,265		1,625	C
14 April	Direct debit D Draper	2,950		1,325	D
14 April	Cheque 120050	655		1,980	D
22 April	Paid in at SKB Bank		2,150	170	C
22 April	Bank charges	63		107	C
23 April	Overdraft fee	25		82	C

D = Debit   C = Credit

Date	Details	Bank	Date	Cheque	Details	Bank
01 April	Balance b/d	17,845	01 April	120045	R Sterling Ltd	8,850
19 April	Olsen & Lane	2,150	01 April	120046	Bert Cooper	2,250
22 April	Frith Ltd	685	01 April	120047	Hetko & Sons	64
22 April	Hodgetts & Co	282	02 April	120048	Barrett Ltd	3,256
04 April	Ricketts & Co	465	02 April	120049	K Plomer	542
			08 April	120050	I&E Brown	655
			08 April	120051	T Roberts	1,698
			14 April		AMB Ltd	2,265
			14 April		D Draper	2,950
			22 April		Bank charges	63
			23 April		Overdraft fee	25
24 April	Balance c/d	1,191				
		22,618				22,618
			25 April		Balance b/d	1,191

Complete the bank reconciliation statement as at 24 April.

Note: Do not make any entries in the shaded boxes.

Bank reconciliation statement as at 24 April 20XX.

Balance per bank statement	£
Add:	
Name:	£
Name:	£
Total to add	£
Less:	
Name:	£
Name:	£
Total to subtract	£
Balance as per cash book	£

Name options: Bank charges, , R Sterling Ltd, Olsen & Lane, Frith Ltd, Hodgetts & Co, Bert Cooper, Hetko & Sons, Barrett Ltd, K Plomer, I&E Brown, T Roberts, AMB Ltd, Ricketts & Co, D Draper, Overdraft fees.

100 WHOLESALE FLOORING

Below is the bank statement and updated cash book for Wholesale Flooring.

Money Bags Bank PLC
52 Oak Road, Timperley, SK10 8LR

To: Wholesale Flooring   Account No: 47013799   23 June 20XX
Statement of Account

Date 20XX	Detail	Paid out £	Paid in £	Balance £	
04 June	Balance b/d			5,125	D
05 June	Cheque 104373	890		6,015	D
05 June	Cheque 104374	1,725		7,740	D
05 June	Cheque 104375	210		7,950	D
11 June	Cheque 104378	784		8,734	D
12 June	Bank Giro credit Aintree and Co		1,250	7,484	D
13 June	Cheque 104376	1,275		8,759	D
15 June	Cheque 104377	725		9,484	D
17 June	Paid in at Money Bags bank plc		550	8,934	D
20 June	Direct debit MD County council	400		9,334	D
23 June	Bank charges	160		9,494	D
23 June	Overdraft fee	90		9,584	D

D = Debit   C = Credit

Date 20XX	Details	Bank £	Date 20XX	Cheque number	Details	Bank £
			01 June		Balance b/d	5,125
16 June	Beeston's	550	01 June	104373	Good Iron	890
19 June	Airfleet exteriors	3,025	01 June	104374	Ashworth & Co	1,725
22 June	Jones's	2,775	01 June	104375	Ironfit	210
12 June	Aintree & Co	1,250	05 June	104376	OSS Ltd	1,275
			07 June	104377	Perfect Tools	725
			08 June	104378	Campden Ltd	784
			14 June	104379	Thornley & Thwaite	675
			14 June	104380	Castle and Cove	178
			20 June		MD County council	400
			23 June		Bank charges	160
			23 June		Overdraft fee	90
23 June	Balance c/d	4,637	23 June			
		12,237				12,237
			24 June		Balance b/d	4,637

Complete the bank reconciliation statement as at 23 June.

Note: Do not make any entries in the shaded boxes.

Bank reconciliation statement as at 23 June 20XX

Balance per bank statement	£
Add:	
Name:	£
Name:	£
Total to add	£
Less:	
Name:	£
Name:	£
Total to subtract	£
Balance as per cash book	£

Name options: Bank charges, OSS Ltd, Beeston's, Aintree and Co, Ironfit, Campden Ltd, MD County Council, Ashworth & Co, Airfleet Exteriors, Thornley & Thwaite, Perfect Tools, Overdraft Fee, Castle & Cove, Good Iron, Jones's.

101 MCKEOWN

The bank statement and cash book for McKeown is shown below.

Money Bags Bank PLC

To: McKeown Ltd Account No: 47013799 23 June 20XX

Statement of Account

Date	Detail	Paid out	Paid in	Balance	
20XX		£	£	£	
01 June	Balance b/d			7,420	C
01 June	Bank Giro credit Pond		180	7,600	C
01 June	Cheque 110156	420		7,180	C
01 June	Interest received		85	7,265	C
11 June	Cheque 110157	430		6,835	C
12 June	Cheque 110158	520		6,315	C
13 June	Cheque 110161	750		5,565	C
15 June	Bank Giro credit Sherwood		640	6,205	C
17 June	Paid in to Money Bags bank		1,200	7,405	C
20 June	Bank Giro credit Coyne		1,630	9,035	C
23 June	Direct debit Wilmott	300		8,735	C
23 June	Interest received		35	8,770	C

D = Debit   C = Credit

Cash book

Date 20XX	Details	Bank £	Date 20XX	Cheque number	Details	Bank £
01 June	Balance b/d	7,180	07 June	110157	Williams	430
12 June	Sherwood	640	07 June	110158	Forecast	520
14 June	Cash sales	1,200	07 June	110159	Beasant	1,240
22 June	Tweedy	860	07 June	110160	Davison	1,420
23 June	Butterwood	440	07 June	110161	Mildenhall	750
01 June	Interest received	85	23 June		Wilmott	300
20 June	Coyne	1,630				
23 June	Interest received	35				

(a)   Complete the bank reconciliation statement as at **23 June.**

Note: Do not make any entries in the shaded boxes.

Bank reconciliation statement as at 23 June 20XX

Balance per bank statement	
Add:	
Name:	
Name:	
Total to add	
Less:	
Name:	
Name:	
Total to subtract	
Balance as per cash book	

(b)   Refer to the cash book in (a) and check that the bank statement has correctly been reconciled by calculating:

–   the balance carried down

–   the total of each of the bank columns after the balance carried down has been recorded.

Balance carried down £	Bank column totals £

102   MONSTER MUNCHIES

This is a summary of transactions with customers of Monster Munchies during the month of June.

(a)   Show whether each entry will be a debit or credit in the Sales ledger control account in the General ledger.

Details	Amount £	Debit ✓	Credit ✓
Balance of receivables at 1 June	48,000		
Goods sold on credit	12,415		
Receipts from credit customers	22,513		
Discount allowed	465		
Sales returns from credit customers	320		

(b) **What will be the balance brought down on 1 July on the above account?**

	✓
Dr £37,117	
Cr £37,117	
Dr £83,713	
Cr £83,713	
Dr £58,883	
Cr £58,883	

The following debit balances were in the subsidiary (sales) ledger on 1 July.

	£
XXX Ltd	21,300
Brittle Homes Ltd	5,376
Colin and Campbell	333
Bashford Incorporated	1,733
Mainstreet Homes	3,426
Shamrock Interiors	4,629

(c) **Reconcile the balances shown above with the sales ledger control account balance you have calculated in part (a).**

	£
Sales ledger control account balance as at 30 June	
Total of subsidiary (sales) ledger accounts as at 30 June	
Difference	

(d) **Which TWO of the following reasons could be explanations of why the total on a sales ledger control account may be higher than the total of balances on a sales ledger?**

	✓
Sales returns may have been omitted from the subsidiary ledger.	
Discounts allowed may have been omitted from the subsidiary ledger.	
Sales returns may have been entered in the subsidiary ledger twice.	
Discounts allowed may have been entered in the subsidiary ledger twice.	

It is important to reconcile the sales ledger control account on a regular basis.

(e) **Which of the following statements is true?**

	✓
Reconciliation of the sales ledger control account assures managers that the amount showing as owed to suppliers is correct.	
Reconciliation of the sales ledger control account assures managers that the amount showing as outstanding from customers is correct.	
Reconciliation of the sales ledger control account will show if a purchase invoice has been omitted from the purchase ledger.	
Reconciliation of the sales ledger control account will show if a purchase invoice has been omitted from the sales ledger.	

103 JACK'S BOX

This is a summary of transactions with customers of Jack's Box during the month of April.

(a) **Show whether each entry will be a debit or a credit in the Sales ledger control account in the General ledger.**

Details	Amount £	Debit ✓	Credit ✓
Balance of receivables at 1 April	60,589		
Goods sold on credit	26,869		
Payments received from credit customers	29,411		
Discount allowed	598		
Goods returned from credit customers	1,223		

(b) **What will be the balance brought down on 1 May on the above account?**

	✓
Dr £55,030	
Cr £55,030	
Dr £56,226	
Cr £56,226	
Dr £52,584	
Cr £52,584	

The following debit balances were in the subsidiary (receivables) ledger on 1 May.

	£
Olsen & Lane	19,455
Frith Ltd	625
Hodgetts & Co	412
Geevor plc	17,623
Trevaskis Farm Ltd	16,888

(c) **Reconcile the balances shown above with the sales ledger control account balance you have calculated in part (b).**

	£
Sales Ledger control account balances as at 30 April	
Total of subsidiary (sales) ledger accounts as at 30 April	
Difference	

(d) **What may have caused the difference of £1,223 you calculated in part (c)?**

	✓
Sales returns may have been omitted from the subsidiary ledger	
Discounts allowed have been omitted from the subsidiary ledger	
Sales returns have been entered into the subsidiary ledger twice	
Discounts allowed have been entered into subsidiary ledger twice	

It is important to reconcile the sales ledger control account on a regular basis.

(e) **Which of the following statements is true?**

	✓
Reconciliation of the sales ledger control account will show if a purchase invoice has been omitted from the purchases ledger.	
Reconciliation of the sales ledger control account will show if a sales invoice has been omitted from the purchases ledger.	
Reconciliation of the sales ledger control account assures managers that the amount showing due to suppliers is correct.	
Reconciliation of the sales ledger control account assures managers that the amount showing due from customers is correct.	

104 ZHANG

When Zhang came to reconcile his SLCA with his list of balances on the sales ledger, he found that they did not match. The SLCA had a balance of £65,830 and the list of balances totalled £65,090. Upon further investigation, he discovered that the following errors had been made:

1   The sales day book had been incorrectly totalled and had been overcast by £1,200.

2   A contra of £800 had been made in the SLCA, but had not been recorded in the sales ledger.

3   A credit note of £130 had been posted twice in the sales ledger.

4   A discount given of £210 had only been recorded in the sales ledger.

(a) **Update the SLCA and list of balances to make sure that the two agree.**

SLCA

Details	Amount £	Details	Amount £
Balance b/d	65,830		
		Balance c/d	
Balance b/d			

List of balances:

	£
Total	65,090
Revised total	

(b) **Show whether the following statements are true or false:**

	True ✓	False ✓
An aged trade receivables analysis is used when chasing customers for outstanding payments.		
An aged trade receivables analysis is sent to credit customers when payments are being requested.		

105 HANDYSIDE

When Handyside came to reconcile his PLCA with his list of balances on the purchases ledger, he found that they did not match. The PLCA had a balance of £25,360 and the list of balances totalled £26,000. Upon further investigation, he discovered that the following errors had been made:

1   In the list of balances, a purchase of £2,400 had been entered at the net amount.

2   Returns of £350 had not been applied to the purchases ledger.

3   An invoice for £600 plus VAT had not been posted in the general ledger yet.

4   Returns of £120 were missing from the PLCA.

5   An invoice for £340 had been entered into the purchases ledger as £430.

(a) **Update the PLCA and list of balances to make sure that the two agree.**

PLCA

Details	Amount £	Details	Amount £
		Balance b/d	25,360
Balance c/d			
		Balance b/d	

List of balances:

	£
Total	26,000
Revised total	

(b) **Show whether the following statements are true or false:**

	True ✓	False ✓
The purchases ledger control account enables a business to see how much is owed to individual suppliers		
The purchases ledger control account total should reconcile to the total of the list of supplier balances in the purchases ledger		

106   RING RING TELEPHONE

The following is an extract from Ring Ring Telephone's books of prime entry.

Totals for quarter			
Sales day-book		**Purchases day-book**	
Net:	£153,000	Net:	£81,000
VAT:	£30,600	VAT:	£16,200
Gross:	£183,600	Gross:	£97,200
Sales returns day-book		**Purchases returns day-book**	
Net:	£1,800	Net:	£5,800
VAT:	£360	VAT:	£1,160
Gross:	£2,160	Gross:	£6,960
Cash book			
Net cash sales:	£240		
VAT:	£48		
Gross cash sales:	£288		

(a)   **What will be the entries in the VAT control account to record the VAT transactions in the quarter?**

VAT control

Details	Amount £	Details	Amount £

Picklist: Cash sales, Purchases, Purchases returns, Sales, Sales returns, VAT.

The VAT return has been completed and shows an amount owing from HM Revenue and Customs of £15,248.

(b)   **Is the VAT return correct?**   Yes/No

(c)   At the end of the next period, the VAT control account has debit entries amounting to £93,800 and credit entries amounting to £54,400.

The following transactions have not yet been recorded in the VAT control account:

VAT of £400 on purchase of equipment
VAT of £900 on cash sales

What will be the balance brought down on the VAT account after the transactions above have been recorded? Also identify whether the balance will be a debit or a credit.

	£	*Debit*	*Credit*
Balance brought down			

107 PHILIP'S CABINS

The following is an extract from Philip's Cabins books of prime entry.

Totals for quarter			
Sales day-book		**Purchases day-book**	
Net:	£179,800	Net:	£100,200
VAT:	£35,960	VAT:	£20,040
Gross:	£215,760	Gross:	£120,240
Sales returns day-book		**Purchases returns day-book**	
Net:	£3,000	Net:	£5,720
VAT:	£600	VAT:	£1,144
Gross:	£3,600	Gross:	£6,864
Cash book			
Net cash sales:	£560		
VAT:	£112		
Gross cash sales:	£672		

(a)   What will be the entries in the VAT control account to record the VAT transactions in the quarter?

VAT control

Details	Amount £	Details	Amount £

Picklist: Cash sales, Purchases, Purchases returns, Sales, Sales returns, VAT.

The VAT return has been completed and shows an amount due to HM Revenue and Customs of £14,540.

(b)   **Is the VAT return correct?**   Yes/No

108 DISLEY

(a)   **Show whether each item is a debit or credit balance in the VAT control account by copying the amount into the correct column.**

	£	Debit	Credit
VAT total in the sales day book	65,420		
VAT total in the purchases day book	21,340		
VAT total in the sales returns day book	480		
VAT balance brought forward, owed to HMRC	24,910		
VAT on irrecoverable debts	830		
VAT on petty cash expenses paid	210		

The VAT return has been completed and shows an amount due to HM Revenue and Customs of £67,740.

(b)   **Is the VAT return correct?** Yes/No

(c)   At the end of the next period, the VAT control account has debit entries amounting to £42,300 and credit entries amounting to £61,250.

The following transactions have not yet been recorded in the VAT control account:

VAT total in the discounts received day book of £980

VAT of £200 on an irrecoverable debt

What will be the balance brought down on the VAT account after the transactions above have been recorded? Also identify whether the balance will be a debit or a credit.

	£	Debit	Credit
Balance brought down			

109 AWESOME LTD

You are told that the opening inventory of a single raw material in the stores is 6,000 units at £6 per unit. During the month, another 6,000 units at £10 were received and the following week 7,150 units were issued.

Task 1

Identify the valuation method described in the statements below:

Characteristic	FIFO	LIFO	AVCO
• Closing inventory is valued at £48,500.			
• The issue of inventory is valued at £57,200.			
• The issue of inventory is valued at £66,900.			

Task 2

Identify whether the statements in the table below are true or false by putting a tick in the relevant column.

	True	False
• FIFO values the issue of inventory at £47,500.		
• AVCO values the closing inventory at £38,400.		
• LIFO values the closing inventory at £29,100.		

110 AMAZING LTD

You are told that the opening inventory of a single raw material in the stores is 2,000 units at £1.50 per unit. During the month, another 5,000 units at £5 were received and the following week 6,000 units were issued.

Task 1

Identify the valuation method described in the statements below:

Characteristic	FIFO	LIFO	AVCO
• Closing inventory is valued at £1,500.			
• The issue of inventory is valued at £23,000.			
• The issue of inventory is valued at £24,000.			

Task 2

Identify whether the statements in the table below are true or false by putting a tick in the relevant column.

	True	False
• LIFO values the issue of inventory at £26,500.		
• AVCO values the closing inventory at £5,000.		
• LIFO values the closing inventory at £4,000.		

111 STONE LTD

Stone Ltd sells stone to builders. It had the following movements in one type of stone for the month of June.

DATE	RECEIPTS		ISSUES	
	Tonnes	Cost	Tonnes	Cost
June 1	500	£7,500		
June 8	350	£6,125		
June 15	275	£4,950		
June 22			650	
June 29	500	£8,750		

Complete the table below for the issue and closing inventory values, stating your answers to the nearest pound.

Method	Cost of issue on 22 June	Closing inventory at 30 June
FIFO	£	£
LIFO	£	£
AVCO	£	£

112 NATAL LTD

Natal Ltd makes and sells a wide range of clothes for babies. The following is an inventory card for Natal's most popular product for the month of December.

DATE	RECEIPTS		ISSUES	
	Units	Cost	Units	Cost
December 3	10,000	£85,000		
December 18	14,000	£112,000		
December 19	50,000	£350,000		
December 25			72,500	
December 29	5,000	£30,000		

Task 1

Complete the table below for the issue and closing inventory values. Give your answers to the nearest pound.

Method	Cost of issue on 25 Dec	Closing inventory at 29 Dec
LIFO	£	£
AVCO	£	£

Task 2

Identify the following statements as true or false by putting a tick in the relevant column of the table below:

	True	False
• FIFO would give a lower closing inventory valuation on the 29 December than LIFO and AVCO.		
• FIFO would give a lower cost of issue on the 25 December than LIFO and AVCO.		

113 GANDALF LTD

Gandalf Ltd has the following movements in a certain type of inventory into and out of its stores for the month of July.

DATE	RECEIPTS			ISSUES			BALANCE
	Units	Unit cost	Total £	Units	Unit cost	Total £	Total £
July 2	600	£1.50	£900				
July 4	500	£1.70	£850				
July 15				620			
July 19	200	£1.80	£360				
July 31				400			

Calculate the costs of the issues made on July 15 and July 31 if Gandalf plc uses a LIFO inventory valuation method.

	Valuation £
• July 15 • July 31	

114 NULAB LTD

Identify the labour payment method by putting a tick in the relevant column of the table below:

Payment method	Time-rate	Piecework	Piece-rate plus bonus
• Labour is paid based solely on the production achieved.			
• Labour is paid extra if an agreed level of output is exceeded.			
• Labour is paid according to hours worked.			

115 MANDELA LTD

Identify whether the following statements are true or false in the relevant column of the table below:

Statement	True	False
• Time rate is paid based on the production achieved.		
• Overtime is paid for hours worked over the standard hours agreed.		
• Piece rate is paid according to hours worked.		

116 PERRES LTD

Identify the hourly payment method by putting a tick in the relevant column of the table below:

Payment method	Basic rate	Overtime premium	Overtime rate
• This is the amount paid above the basic rate for hours worked in excess of the normal hours.			
• This is the total amount paid per hour for hours worked in excess of the normal hours.			
• This is the amount paid per hour for normal hours worked.			

117 TEVEZ LTD

Identify the following statements as true or false by putting a tick in the relevant column of the table below:

Statement	True	False
• Direct labour costs can be identified with the goods being made or the service being provided.		
• Indirect labour costs vary directly with the level of activity.		

118 BERDYCH LTD

Identify the whether the labour payment is usually associated with a fixed or variable cost by putting a tick in the relevant column of the table below:

Payment method	Variable	Fixed
• Labour that is paid based on a time rate basis per hour worked.		
• Labour is paid on a monthly salary basis.		
• Labour that is based on number of units produced.		

119 PIECEWORK STATEMENTS

Identify the following statements as either true or false by putting a tick in the relevant column of the table below:

Statement	True	False
• Piecework encourages employees to work harder.		
• Piecework requires accurate recording of the number of hours staff have worked.		
• Piecework encourages workers to improve the quality of the units they produce.		

120 PHOENIX LTD

Phoenix plc pays its employees £8.00 per hour and expects them to make 20 units per hour. Any excess production will be paid a bonus of £1.50 per unit.

Identify the following statements as being true or false by putting a tick in the relevant column of the table below:

Statement	True	False
An employee who works 38 hours and makes 775 units will not receive a bonus.		
An employee who works 40 hours and makes 815 units will receive total pay of £342.50.		
An employee who works 37 hours and makes 744 units will earn a bonus of £6.		

121 KAHN LTD

Kahn Ltd uses a time-rate method with bonus to pay its direct labour in one of its factories. The time-rate used is £12 per hour and a worker is expected to produce 5 units an hour, any time saved is paid at £6 per hour.

Calculate the gross wage for the week including bonus for the three workers in the table below:

Worker	Hours worked	Units produced	Basic wage	Bonus	Gross wage
A. Smith	35	175	£	£	£
J. O'Hara	35	180	£	£	£
M. Stizgt	35	185	£	£	£

122 ENTERPRISE LTD

Enterprise Ltd pays a time-rate of £12 per hour to its direct labour force for a standard 35 hour week. Any of the labour force working in excess of 35 hours is paid an overtime rate of time and a half.

Calculate the gross wage for the week for the three workers in the table below:

Worker	Hours worked	Basic wage	Overtime	Gross wage
J. Picard	37 hours	£	£	£
B. Crusher	42 hours	£	£	£
D. Troi	31 hours	£	£	£

123 SGC LTD

SGC Ltd uses a basic salary plus piecework method to pay labour in one of its factories. The basic salary is £285 per week the piece rate used is £0.75 per unit produced.

Calculate the gross wage for the week for the two workers in the table below. Enter your answer to the nearest penny.

Worker	Units produced in week	Gross wage
J. O'Neill	500 units	£
S. Carter	650 units	£

124 GOTHIC LTD

Gothic Ltd uses a time-rate method with bonus to pay its direct labour in one of its factories. The time-rate used is £17 per hour and a worker is expected to produce 8 units an hour, anything over this and the worker is paid a bonus of £5 per unit.

Calculate the gross wage for the week including bonus for the three workers in the table below:

Worker	Hours worked	Units produced	Basic wage	Bonus	Gross wage
M. Shelley	37	300	£	£	£
G. Leroux	37	312	£	£	£
E. A. Poe	37	296	£	£	£

125 AVENGERS LTD

Avengers Ltd pays a time-rate of £10 per hour to its direct labour force a standard 35 hour week. Any of the labour force working in excess of this over the four week period is paid an overtime rate of time and a quarter.

Calculate the gross wage for the **4-week** period for the three workers in the table below. Enter your answers to the nearest pound.

Worker	Hours worked	Basic wage	Overtime	Gross wage
T. Stark	138	£	£	£
B. Banner	142	£	£	£
S. Rogers	145	£	£	£

126 DRACO LTD

Draco Ltd uses a piecework method to pay labour in one of its factories. The rate used is 80p per unit produced up to the standard number of units to be produced per week of 250. For any units over that the workers will get £10 per 20 units.

Calculate the gross wage for the week for the three workers in the table below:

Worker	Units produced in week	Gross wage
P. Jones	240 units	£
D. Bannatyne	350 units	£
L. Redford	250 units	£

127 JLA PLC

JLA plc pays its employees £5 per hour and expects them to make 6 units per hour. Any time saved will be paid as a bonus at £8 per hour.

Identify the following statements as being true or false by putting a tick in the relevant column of the table below:

Statement	True	False
During a 30 hour week, an employee producing 192 units would receive a bonus of £16.		
During a 35 hour week, an employee producing 240 units would receive total pay of £215.		
During a 30 hour week, an employee producing 180 units would not receive a bonus.		

128 INJUSTICE LTD

Davidson Ltd pays a basic wage of £175/week plus £1.20 per unit produced.

Calculate the gross wage for the week for the three workers in the table below:

Worker	Units produced	Basic wage	Piece work	Gross wage
N. Wing	295	£	£	£
W. Woman	355	£	£	£
T. Flash	385	£	£	£

129 GREENWOOD LTD

Greenwood Ltd pays a basic wage of £350/week equivalent to a time-rate of £10 per hour and a standard 35 hour week. Workers are expected to produce 5 units an hour and for units produced in excess of this a bonus is paid based on £7 for every hour saved.

So, for example, if 10 additional units are produced, then this would be equivalent to two hours saved and a bonus of £14 awarded.

Calculate the gross wage for the week including bonus for the three workers in the table below:

Worker	Hours worked	Units produced	Basic wage	Bonus	Gross wage
B. Ryan	35	175	£	£	£
S. Chang	35	190	£	£	£
E. Schneider	35	210	£	£	£

130 DOOMSDAY LTD

Doomsday Ltd is costing a single product which has the following cost details:

Variable costs per unit	Per unit	Cost
Materials	45kg	£0.50/kg
Labour	2.5hrs	£16/hour

Total fixed costs

Production overhead	£75,000
Administration overhead	£110,000
Sales and distribution	£75,000

Complete the following total cost and unit cost table for a production level of 20,000 units. Overheads are absorbed on a cost per unit basis. Give your answer to the nearest penny for the unit cost and the nearest pound for total cost.

Element	Total cost for 20,000 units	Unit cost
Direct costs	£	£
Production overhead	£	£
Non production overhead	£	£
Total costs	£	£

131 OLSEN LTD

Olsen Ltd is costing a single product which has the following cost details:

Variable costs	Per unit
Materials	£12
Labour	£17

Total Fixed Costs

Production overhead   £80,000

Administration overhead   £40,000

Complete the following total cost and unit cost table for a production level of 80,000 units. Give your answer to the nearest penny for the unit cost and the nearest pound for total cost.

Element	Total cost	Unit cost
Materials	£	£
Labour	£	£
Production overheads	£	£
Administration overheads	£	£
Total	£	£

132 CORONATION LTD

Coronation Ltd is costing a single product which has the following cost details

Variable costs	Per unit	Cost
Materials	50g	£10/kg
Labour	1hr	£6/hour

Total fixed costs

Production overhead   £40,000

Administration overhead   £20,000

Sales and distribution   £25,000

Complete the following total cost and unit cost table for a production level of 5,000 units. Overheads are absorbed on a cost per unit basis. Give your answer to the nearest penny for the unit cost and the nearest pound for total cost.

Element	Total cost for 5,000 units	Unit cost
Direct costs	£	£
Production overhead	£	£
Non production overhead	£	£
Total costs	£	£

133   LUTHOR LTD

Luthor Ltd makes a single product and for a production level of 15,000 units has the following cost details:

Materials	60,000kg	at £15/kilo
Labour	37,500hrs	at £9/hour
Fixed overheads		£570,000

Complete the table below to show the unit cost at the production level of 15,000 units. Overheads are absorbed on a cost per unit basis. Give your answer to the nearest penny.

Element	Unit cost
Materials	£
Labour	£
Fixed overheads	£
Total	£

134   WILKINSON LTD

Wilkinson Ltd is looking to calculate the unit cost for one of the products it makes. It needs to calculate an overhead absorption rate to apply to each unit. The methods it is considering are a rate per machine hour, a rate per labour hour, and a rate per unit.

Total factory activity is forecast as follows:

Machine hours	10,000
Labour hours	12,500
Units	60,000
Overheads	£150,000

Task 1

Complete the table below to show the possible overhead absorption rates that Wilkinson Ltd could use. The absorption rates should be calculated to two decimal places.

	Machine hour	Labour hour	Unit
Overheads (£)			
Activity			
Absorption rate (£)			

Task 2

The following data relates to making one unit of the product:

Material	2 kilos at £5 per kilo
Labour	15 minutes at £10 per hour
Production time	10 minutes

Complete the table below (to two decimal places) to calculate the total unit cost, using the three overhead absorption rates you have calculated in task 1.

Cost	Machine hour (£)	Labour hour (£)	Unit (£)
Material			
Labour			
Direct cost			
Overheads			
Total unit cost			

135 HODGSON LTD

Hodgson Ltd is looking to calculate the unit cost for one of the products it makes. It needs to calculate an overhead absorption rate to apply to each unit. The methods it is considering are a rate per machine hour, a rate per labour hour, and a rate per unit.

Total factory activity is forecast as follows:

Machine hours	15,000
Labour hours	20,000
Units	100,000
Overheads	£250,000

Task 1

Complete the table below to show the possible overhead absorption rates that Hodgson Ltd could use. The absorption rates should be calculated to two decimal places.

	Machine hour	Labour hour	Unit
Overheads (£)			
Activity			
Absorption rate (£)			

Task 2

The following data relates to making one unit of the product:

Material	4 kilos at £6 per kilo
Labour	30 minutes at £12 per hour
Production time	20 minutes

Complete the table below (to two decimal places) to calculate the total unit cost, using the three overhead absorption rates you have calculated in task 1.

Cost	Machine hour (£)	Labour hour (£)	Unit (£)
Material			
Labour			
Direct cost			
Overheads			
Total unit cost			

136 BARNES LTD

Barnes Ltd is looking to calculate the unit cost for one of the products it makes. It needs to calculate an overhead absorption rate to apply to each unit. The methods it is considering are a rate per machine hour, a rate per labour hour, and a rate per unit.

Total factory activity is forecast as follows:

Machine hours	17,500
Labour hours	12,000
Units	40,000
Overheads	£130,000

Task 1

Complete the table below to show the possible overhead absorption rates that Barnes Ltd could use. The absorption rates should be calculated to two decimal places.

	Machine hour	Labour hour	Unit
Overheads (£)			
Activity			
Absorption rate (£)			

Task 2

The following data relates to making one unit of the product:

Material	3 kilos at £5 per kilo
Labour	20 minutes at £15 per hour
Production time	30 minutes

Complete the table below (to two decimal places) to calculate the total unit cost, using the three overhead absorption rates you have calculated in task 1.

Cost	Machine hour (£)	Labour hour (£)	Unit (£)
Material			
Labour			
Direct cost			
Overheads			
Total unit cost			

137 ANDREW LTD

Andrew Ltd is looking to calculate the unit cost for one of the products it makes. It needs to calculate an overhead absorption rate to apply to each unit. The methods it is considering are a rate per machine hour, a rate per labour hour, and a rate per unit.

Total factory activity is forecast as follows:

Machine hours	9,000
Labour hours	11,000
Units	60,000
Overheads	£145,000

Task 1

Complete the table below to show the possible overhead absorption rates that Andrew Ltd could use. The absorption rates should be calculated to two decimal places.

	Machine hour	Labour hour	Unit
Overheads (£)			
Activity			
Absorption rate (£)			

Task 2

The following data relates to making one unit of the product:

Material	1 kilo at £8 per kilo
Labour	30 minutes at £14 per hour
Production time	20 minutes

Complete the table below (to two decimal places) to calculate the total unit cost, using the three overhead absorption rates you have calculated in task 1.

Cost	Machine hour (£)	Labour hour (£)	Unit (£)
Material			
Labour			
Direct cost			
Overheads			
Total unit cost			

138   JOKER LTD

Reorder the following costs into a manufacturing account format on the right-hand side of the table below for the year ended 31 December.

	£		£
Closing inventory of work in progress	52,000		
Direct labour	140,000		
Opening inventory of raw materials	50,000		
Closing inventory of finished goods	61,000		
Closing inventory of raw materials	65,000		
Manufacturing overheads	85,000		
COST OF GOODS SOLD			
MANUFACTURING COST			
Purchases of raw materials	120,000		
Opening inventory of work in progress	48,000		
Opening inventory of finished goods	57,000		
DIRECT COST			
DIRECT MATERIALS USED			
COST OF GOODS MANUFACTURED			

Enter the correct figures for the following costs which were not provided in the table above.

	£
DIRECT MATERIALS USED	
DIRECT COST	
MANUFACTURING COST	
COST OF GOODS MANUFACTURED	
COST OF GOODS SOLD	

139   RIDDLER LTD

Reorder the following costs into a manufacturing account format on the right-hand side of the table below for the year ended 31 May. Enter the correct figures for the costs in bold that are not provided.

	£		£
DIRECT COST			
Closing inventory of raw materials	20,000		
Closing inventory of work in progress	20,000		
Opening inventory of finished goods	60,000		
Direct labour	194,000		
Closing inventory of finished goods	50,000		
Manufacturing overheads	106,000		
Purchases of raw materials	100,000		
Opening inventory of work in progress	16,000		
COST OF GOODS SOLD			
DIRECT MATERIALS USED			
Opening inventory of raw materials	14,000		
MANUFACTURING COST			
COST OF GOODS MANUFACTURED			

140   BOOKWORM LTD

Reorder the following costs into a manufacturing account format on the right side of the table below for the year ended 31 December. Enter the correct figures for the costs in bold that are not provided.

	£		£
DIRECT COST			
Direct labour	15,000		
MANUFACTURING COST			
Opening inventory of raw materials	5,000		
Closing inventory of finished goods	16,000		
Purchases of raw materials	15,000		
DIRECT MATERIALS USED			
Manufacturing overheads	25,000		
Closing inventory of raw materials	8,000		
COST OF GOODS SOLD			
COST OF GOODS MANUFACTURED			
Opening inventory of finished goods	12,000		
Opening inventory of work in progress	4,000		
Closing inventory of work in progress	6,000		

141 VARIOUS LTD

Identify the following statements as being true or false by putting a tick in the relevant column of the table below:

Statement	True	False
A variance is the difference between budgeted and actual cost		
A favourable variance occurs when actual costs are less than budgeted.		
An adverse variance occurs when actual income is less than budgeted.		
A favourable variance occurs when actual income is the same as budgeted income.		

142 JONES LTD

Identify the following statements as being true or false by putting a tick in the relevant column of the table below:

Statement	True	False
If budgeted sales are 6,000 units at £7.50 per unit and actual sales are £47,600, the sales variance is favourable		
A favourable cost variance occurs when an actual cost of £9,800 is compared to a budgeted cost of £24 per unit for a budgeted output of 400 units		
A variance arises from a comparison of budgeted costs for last year with actual costs for this year		
If actual material costs are the same as budgeted costs for materials then no variance arises		

143 LANCASTER LTD

Identify the following statements as being true or false by putting a tick in the relevant column of the table below:

Statement	True	False
If budgeted sales are 14,000 units at £3.50 per unit and actual sales are £45,200, the sales variance is favourable		
An adverse cost variance occurs when an actual cost of £68,400 is compared to a budgeted cost of £14 per unit for a budgeted output of 5,000 units		
A variance arises from a comparison of budgeted costs for this year with actual costs for this year		
If actual material costs are the same as budgeted costs for materials then the materials variance is favourable		

144 GOODE LTD

Identify the following statements as being true or false by putting a tick in the relevant column of the table below:

Statement	True	False
The variance for the Direct Material cost of Department B should be reported to the purchasing manager		
The variance for the Direct Labour cost for Department A should be reported to the sales manager		
The variance for the Direct Labour cost for Department B should be reported to the production manager of Department A		
A Direct Material cost variance that has been deemed Not Significant should not be reported		

145 BROWN LTD

Identify the following statements as being true or false by putting a tick in the relevant column of the table below:

Statement	True	False
The variance for the Direct Material cost of Department A should be reported to the purchasing manager		
The variance for the Direct Labour cost for Department A should be reported to the production manager of Department B		
The variance for sales should be reported to the sales manager		
A Direct Material cost variance that has been deemed Significant should not be reported		

146 BLUEBELL LTD

The following performance report for this month has been produced for Bluebell Ltd as summarised in the table below.

Calculate the variances in the table below and indicate whether they are adverse or favourable by putting an A or F in the relevant column and calculate the variance as a % to the nearest whole number.

Cost type	Budget £	Actual £	Variance £	Adverse/ Favourable	%
Sales	£204,555	£197,455			
Direct materials	£39,000	£42,300			
Direct labour	£75,000	£83,000			
Production overheads	£69,000	£64,800			
Administration overheads	£53,000	£58,900			

147 TRIUMPH LTD

Task 1

Identify the type of cost behaviour (fixed, variable or semi-variable) described in each statement by ticking the relevant boxes in the table below.

Statement	Fixed	Variable	Semi-variable
At 9,000 units this cost is £29,250, and at 12,000 units it is £39,000			
At 5,000 units this cost is £5.20 per unit, and at 8,000 units it is £3.25 per unit			
At 19,800 units, this cost is £64,500, and at 27,000 units it is £82,500			

Task 2

Complete the table below by inserting all costs for activity levels of 6,000 and 14,000.

	6,000 units	7,000 units	10,000 units	14,000 units
Variable cost (£)				
Fixed cost (£)				
Total cost (£)		45,000	54,000	

148 BUNGLE LTD

Bungle Ltd usually produces 9,000 units but is planning to increase production to 14,000 units during the next period.

Identify the following statements as either true or false by putting a tick in the relevant column of the table below:

Statement	True	False
Total variable costs will decrease.		
Total fixed costs will remain the same.		
The variable cost per unit will remain the same.		
The fixed cost per unit will increase.		

149 TF

Identify the following statements as either true or false by putting a tick in the relevant column of the table below:

Statement	True	False
Variable costs change directly with changes in activity.		
Fixed costs change directly with changes in activity		
Stepped costs are fixed within a set range of output.		

150 GLACIER

Glacier has a corporate commitment to improving the local environment and has implemented a number of initiatives, such as maximising the use of recyclable materials in its manufacturing processes. Additionally, Glaciers' Corporate Social Responsibility Team organised an event, a 'three-drop challenge' which required a sponsored team to abseil down the side of three local high-rise buildings.

The challenge required that the CSR Team obtained a licence from the local public authority to close a road and divert traffic whilst the event took place. The cost of the licence was estimated to be £1,500. It was also estimated that the sponsorship funds that would be raised from the event would be £25,000. The CSR team is responsible for reporting on the costs incurred and funds raised from the event. The sponsorship proceeds raised would be donated to a local charity.

The licence was obtained prior to the event taking place at a cost of £1,250. The sponsorship funds raised were £27,200. You have been asked to compare the budgeted costs and funds raised with the actual results by completing the table below.

Complete the table below by:

- Inserting the budgeted amount for each item

- Inserting the actual amount for each item

- Inserting the variance for each item

- Selecting whether each variance is adverse or favourable.

∇ Drop down list for task:

Adverse
Favourable

Event performance report				
Cost	Budget (£)	Actual (£)	Variance (£)	Adverse/ Favourable
Licence cost				∇
Funds				
Sponsorship funds raised				∇

151 BERLINE

Berline has a corporate commitment to improving the local environment, and has implemented a number of initiatives, such as setting targets to minimise wastage resulting from its production processes. Additionally, The Corporate Social Responsibility Team at Berline organised a fund-raising event, a charity football match, to which members of the public would pay an admission fee, the proceeds of which would be donated to a local charity.

Amongst other things, the event required that a sports centre be hired, and that refreshments would be available for spectators to purchase during the event. It was estimated that 1,000 spectators would attend the event and that the cost of providing refreshments would be £2 per spectator. A commemorative souvenir magazine of the event would be produced and given to each spectator at a budgeted cost £1 per spectator. The CSR team is responsible for reporting on the costs of the event.

The actual cost of providing the refreshments was £2,250 and the actual cost of producing the souvenir magazine was £950. You have been asked to compare the actual costs with the budgeted costs and to identify whether any variance calculated is significant, that is in excess of 4% of budget.

Complete the table below by:

- Inserting the budgeted amount for each item

- Inserting the actual amount for each item

- Inserting the variance for each item

- Selecting whether each variance is adverse or favourable

- Selected whether each variance is significant or not.

∇ Drop down list for task :

Adverse	Yes
Favourable	No

Event cost performance report					
Cost	Budget (£)	Actual (£)	Variance (£)	Adverse/ Favourable	Significant
Refreshments				∇	∇
Magazine				∇	∇

Section 4

PRACTICE QUESTIONS

AO4 COMMUNICATE FINANCIAL INFORMATION EFFECTIVELY

152 MRS MAY

In your role as Financial Assistant you have recently received a purchase invoice (invoice number 3576) from Maybe Ltd relating to the purchase of 10 units of product ZXY. The invoice applied a cost per unit of £63, instead of the correct cost per unit of £36.

Draft a letter to Mrs May of Maybe Ltd to request a credit note to cancel that invoice and also to request a corrected invoice so that payment can be made, ensuring that you include all relevant information.

153 BILLY

Below is a response to a customer complaint.

Please highlight five words that are spelt incorrectly, or are inappropriate:

Dear Billy,

I was very cheesed to here that you did not receive your goods in proper working order. We have very strict internal procedures, which are designed to prevent faulty goods reaching our customers. Please rest assured that we are investigating fully you're case and are striving to ensure that this does not happen again in the future.

By way of an apolojy we will be refunding you in full and offering you a 20% discount off your next purchase.

Kind regards

John Anderson

Store manager

154 MR CADBURY

Review the draft correspondence below highlighting the spelling errors and inappropriate wording used.

> Dear Mr Cadbury
>
> I enclose a copy of the invoice which your requested during are telephone conversation this morning.
>
> Please note this invoice is dated 31 June and therefor is overdue for payment.
>
> I look forward to receiving your cheque in full settlement by return of post.
>
> Yours faithfully

155 JEEPERS LTD

(a) **Indicate whether each of the following costs are direct or not by putting a tick in the relevant column of the table below:**

Cost	Yes	No
Materials used in production.		
Piecework labour costs.		
Salary of chief executive.		

Jeepers Ltd makes a single product. At a production level of 15,000 units, the company has the following costs:

Materials	37,500 kilos at £14.00 per kilo
Labour	7,500 hours at £16.00 per hour
Overheads	£570,000

(b) **Complete the table below to show the unit product cost at the production level of 15,000 units. Overheads are absorbed on a cost per unit basis. Give your answer to the nearest pound.**

Element	Unit product cost
Materials	£
Labour	£
Direct cost	£
Overheads	£
Total	£

156 GLORIA LTD

Gloria Ltd is costing a single product which has the following cost details:

Variable costs per unit

Materials	£2
Labour	£3
Royalties	£0.50

Total fixed costs

Production overhead	£80,000
Sales and distribution	£90,000

(a) **Complete the following total cost and unit cost table for a production level of 20,000 units. Give your answer to the nearest penny for the unit cost and the nearest pound for the total cost.**

Element	Unit cost	Total cost for 20,000 units
Variable production costs	£	£
Fixed production costs	£	£
Total production cost	£	£

(b) **In the box below, write notes in preparation for a meeting you will have with your manager, including:**

- **a brief introduction outlining the areas you will discuss**

- **an explanation of what a fixed production cost is, including an example of a fixed production cost**

- **an example of what a variable production cost is, including an example of a variable production cost**

- **an explanation of what happens to fixed and variable production costs if output is increased from 20,000 to 25,000 units.**

Your notes must be sufficiently detailed, clearly written and well-structured as they will be a formal record of your meeting discussion.

157 BIZARRO LTD

Bizarro Ltd makes a single product and for a production level of 17,000 units has the following cost details:

	Per unit	Cost
Materials	2.5kg	£18/kilo
Labour	1.0hrs	£9/hour
Fixed overheads		£42,500

(a) **Complete the table below to show the unit cost and total cost at the production level of 17,000 units. Overheads are absorbed on a cost per unit basis. Give your answer to the nearest penny for the unit cost and the nearest pound for total cost.**

Element	Unit cost	Total cost
Materials	£	£
Labour	£	£
Overheads	£	£
Total	£	£

(b) **In the box below, write notes in preparation for a meeting you will have with your supervisor regarding different methods of paying employees including:**

- **a brief introduction outlining the areas you will discuss**

- **an explanation of what a basic pay is, including an example of basic pay**

- **an example of what bonus pay is, including an example of bonus pay**

- **an explanation of what overtime pay is, including an example of overtime pay.**

Your notes must be sufficiently detailed, clearly written and well-structured as they will be a formal record of your meeting discussion.

158 VINNY LTD

Vinny Ltd is a commercial laundrette below are the costings for 15,000 units:

Variable costs

Materials	£75,000
Labour	£120,000

Fixed costs

Production overhead	£100,000

Complete the following total cost and unit cost table for a REVISED production level of 20,000 units. Give your answer to the nearest penny for the unit cost and the nearest pound for total cost.

Element	Unit cost	Total cost
Materials	£	£
Labour	£	£
Overheads	£	£
Total	£	£

159 DARKSEID LTD

Darkseid Ltd makes a single product and for a production level of 95,000 units has the following cost details:

Materials	47,500kg	at £7/kilo
Labour	71,250hrs	at £9/hour
Fixed overheads		£242,000

Complete the table below to show the unit cost at a REVISED production level of 100,000 units. Overheads are absorbed on a cost per unit basis. Give your answer to the nearest penny.

Element	Unit cost
Materials	£
Labour	£
Fixed overheads	£
Total	£

160 EREBOR PLC

Erebor Ltd has produced a performance report detailing budgeted and actual cost for last month.

(a) Calculate the amount of the variance for each cost type and then determine whether it is adverse or favourable (enter A or F).

Cost type	Budget £	Actual £	Variance £	Adverse or favourable (A or F)
Sales	600,500	597,800		
Direct materials	205,800	208,500		
Direct labour	155,000	154,800		
Production overheads	65,000	72,100		
Administration overheads	58,400	55,200		

(b) In the box below, write a brief report for the Warehouse Manager that explains the FIFO, AVCO and LIFO methods of inventory valuations of paying employees including:

Your report must be sufficiently detailed, clearly written and well-structured.

> **Report to the Warehouse Manager**
>
> **Methods of inventory valuation**

161   BELEGOST LTD

The following performance report for this month has been produced for Belegost Ltd as summarised in the table below. Any variance in excess of 6% of budget is deemed to be significant and should be reported to the relevant manager for review and appropriate action.

(a)   **Determine whether the variance for each figure is adverse or favourable by putting an A or F into the relevant column of the table below. Put an S in the relevant column if the variance is significant or an NS if the variance is not significant.**

	Budget £	Actual £	Adverse or Favourable (A or F)	Significant or not significant (S or NS)
Sales	205,000	207,100		
Direct materials	75,150	78,750		
Direct labour	110,556	107,950		
Production overheads	14,190	12,500		
Non-production overheads	16,190	17,880		

(b)   **In the box below, write a brief report to the Production Manager which covers the following:**

- **a brief introduction outlining the areas included in your report**

- **an explanation of what a variance is**

- **why only significant variances may be investigated by an organisation.**

Your report must be detailed, clearly written and well-structured.

> **Report to the Production Manager**
>
> **Variances and their investigation**

162 MORIA LTD

The following performance report for this month has been produced for Moria Ltd. Any variance in excess of 7% of budget is deemed to be significant.

(a) Calculate the variance as a % of the budget and enter your answer into the table below to the nearest whole percentage. Indicate whether the variance is significant or not by entering S for significant and NS for not significant.

Cost type	Budget	Variance	Variance as % of budget	Significant or Not significant
Sales	45,100	4,214		
Material	15,750	1,260		
Labour	12,915	805		
Variable overheads	5,750	315		
Fixed overheads	8,155	1,011		

(b) In the box below, write notes in preparation for a meeting with a colleague from the costing department which explains

- a brief introduction outlining the areas you will discuss

- an explanation of what the direct cost of production is

- an explanation of what the manufacturing cost of production is.

Your report must be detailed, clearly written and well-structured.

Notes for meeting with colleague
Direct cost and manufacturing cost of a product

Section 5

ANSWERS TO PRACTICE QUESTIONS

ASSESSMENT OBJECTIVE 1

LO1 UNDERSTAND THE FINANCE FUNCTION WITHIN AN ORGANISATION

1   POLICIES AND PROCEDURES

Select THREE policies and procedures from the following list which are likely to apply to the accounting function:

A   Data Protection Act

B   Health and Safety at Work

D   Authorised Signatory Procedure

2   DOCUMENTS

The accounts department of an organisation receives documents and information from other departments.

Match the department with the ONE document they would send to the accounts department:

Department	Document
Purchasing Department	(b) Copy of Purchase order
HR Department	(d) New employee forms
Payroll Department	(e) Statutory Sick pay forms

3   DEPARTMENTS

Match the following departments to **one** information type it would normally use:

Department	Information
Sales Dept	Commission payable to sales staff
Accounts Dept	Cheque book stubs
Payroll Dept	List of all new employees for the period

4   PRINCIPLES

Select THREE principles from the list below that are not a part of the Data Protection Act 1998.

- Information obtained for personal use

- Historic information that is not up to date

- Transferred to other countries without authorisation

5   DATA SECURITY

(a)   Which ONE item would be the best method to back up data from your computer?

- printing out paper copies of everything and filing them away
- make a copy on a removable storage device e.g. DVD, external hard drive
- keep a second copy of the data on your hard disk

(b)   Where should data back-ups from your computer be kept?

- in a separate locked room or off site
- in a drawer near the computer
- on the computer's hard disk

(c)   Which ONE of the following is less likely to damage or delete data?

- archiving
- a virus
- system breakdown

(d)   State three features of a secure password.

- Feature 1 – Do not share your password with others. You should not use a word or phrase of special importance to you—like a birthday or family member.
- Feature 2 – Choose a password that no one will easily guess.
- Feature 3 – Make sure your password is long and consists of letters, numbers and at least one special character

(e)   Which ONE of the following is not a physical control to protect data?

- Restricting access to an office
- Installing an alarm system
- Passwords – this is not a physical control

6   INFORMATION

(a)   **Identify the FOUR key characteristics of useful information from the list below:**

- understandable
- accurate
- legible
- complete
- timely
- credible
- fit for purpose

(b) **Identify whether each of the following statements is TRUE or FALSE.**

- Only information stated in monetary terms is useful to accountants — **False**

- Non-financial information is useful information to individuals who make decisions — **True**

7 SERVICE PROVISION

Which TWO of the following services are staff in the finance function most likely to provide to staff in the sales department?

- Conducting job interviews

- Preparing sales brochures

- Budget report analysis

- Photocopier servicing

- Marketing new products

- Payment of sales commission

8 STAKEHOLDERS

Identify which TWO of the following stakeholders a trainee in the finance function is most likely to communicate with.

- People living in houses close to the organisation's Head Office

- The local MP

- HM Revenue & Customs

- The Head teacher of the local school

- Receivables

- An AAT examiner

9 REPORTING LINES

A business employs 2 Directors, 3 Managers and 6 Assistants. Identify who each person should report to by selecting from the picklist.

Person	Should report to the following
Sales and Purchase Ledger Assistant	Accounts department manager
Administration Assistant	General manager
3 Sales Assistants	Sales manager
Payroll Assistant	Accounts department manager
Accounting Department Manager	Finance director

10 PERSON AND ROLE

Match which **one** person each role must report to:

Role	Reports to
Accounts assistant	Accounting department manager
Sales Ledger clerk	Accounting department manager
Machine operator	Factory manager

11 COMPLIANCE AND SOLVENCY

Select TWO actions that will ensure the legal compliance and two actions that will help the solvency of a business

Action	Legal Compliance	Solvency
Ensure financial statements are filed on time	✓	
Improve credit control procedures		✓
Maintain a petty cash book		
Create and maintain a cash budget		✓
Ensure the work place is a safe environment for staff and visitors	✓	

12 THE ACCOUNTING FUNCTION

The Accounting function is an essential part of the business. Select TWO actions for each of the columns. Actions should only be selected once:

Actions	Efficient running of the business	Solvency of the business	Legal Compliance
Monitor cashflow		✓	
Provide quotation to customer			
Ensure Sales Tax is paid to HMRC on time			✓
Regularly chase outstanding receivables		✓	
Ensure inventory is ordered when it falls to the minimum level	✓		
Ensure members of staff are first aid trained			✓
Regular maintenance of machinery	✓		
Produce a staff rota for tea making			

13 ISSUES

Which TWO of the following issues would you try to resolve yourself?

- The paper for the photocopier keeps running out without a new order being placed.
- Somebody in the office continues to prop the fire door open.

14 PETTY CASH

Identify the most likely effect on the organisation if you were unable to complete the petty cash reconciliation on time.

- Fraudulent activity may have taken place and go undetected

15 CONFLICT

Some issues may lead to conflict in the workplace. Indicate which issues can be resolved by you and which should be referred to your line manager.

Issue	Resolve myself	Refer to line manager
Your manager has asked you to complete a Statement of Financial position, however you do not have the accounting knowledge to do this		✓
You suspect your colleague knows your computer password	✓	
You suspect an expenses form which has been passed to you has non-business expenses on it and the form has been submitted by a manager		✓

LO2 USE PERSONAL SKILLS DEVELOPMENT IN FINANCE

16 CPD

(a) Identify TWO of the following activities that count towards an employee's continuing professional development requirements.

- Complete a course to further relevant knowledge
- Read articles online related to the trade in which the employee works

(b) Identify the strength, weakness, opportunity and threat from the information listed below.

	Strength	Weakness	Opportunity	Threat
Attend a time management course			✓	
Leaves filing to the end of the week		✓		
Excellent customer service	✓			
Insufficient staff members to cover time off for courses				✓

17 PERFORMANCE

Indicate which TWO courses would be appropriate for you to attend:

- Bookkeeping course

- Communication and presentation skills

Identify whether each of the following statements is TRUE or FALSE.

A qualified accountant does not need to attend Continued Professional Development courses – False

CPD must be undertaken for a minimum of 1 day per month – False

18 WEAKNESSES

(a) Your manager has assessed that you have the following weaknesses:

(1) Poor communications skills – Attend a 'how to communicate in an office' course

(2) Poor timekeeping – Adopt a new clock in and out system for the office

(3) Inadequate technical accounting skills – Attend a bookkeeping course

(b) Identify whether each of the following statements is TRUE or FALSE

All accountants, qualified and unqualified must complete CPD – False

CPD must be carried out on an annual basis by unqualified members – False

CPD must be carried out on an annual basis by qualified members – True

19 APPRAISAL

(a) **Identify whether each of the following statements is TRUE or FALSE.**

An employee performance appraisal is designed to focus solely upon weaknesses problems experienced by an employee during the appraisal period. – False

There is a benefit in an employee undertaking a self-appraisal exercise even if their employer operates a system of annual appraisal. – True

An appraisal is a 'backward looking process' that concentrates solely upon what has happened during the previous year. – False

An appraisal process should allow an employee the opportunity to identify and discuss aspects of their work that they have either performed very well or performed less well during the previous year. – True

An effective appraisal process should result in objectives or goals to be achieved during the following year. – True

20   SELF-DEVELOPMENT

(a)   You currently work in the financial accounting department of your organisation and have identified the need for some self-development activities.

Identify the development activity from the picklist below that will help you to meet each of your self-development needs.

Self-development need	Development activity
To improve your practical experience of using the purchase ledger management system used by your organisation	Work shadowing of an experienced colleague who deals with management of the purchase ledger
To develop a better understanding of financial accounting theory, principles and techniques	Study for a professional accountancy qualification
To improve your knowledge of the goods and services provided by your organisation	Review the product catalogue of your organisation
To improve your knowledge and understanding of how the management accounting department compiles product costings	Request a brief secondment to the management accounting department to develop knowledge and understanding of product costing
To improve your communication and presentation skills in meetings	Attend a practical course for 'effective communication skills' course.

LO3 PRODUCE WORK EFFECTIVELY

21   (a)   REGIONAL SALES

(a)   What is the total sales figure for the quarter?   **£690,000**

(b)   What percentage of the total sales was made by the North (round your answer to 2 decimal places)?   **23.19%**

(c)   What percentage of total sales was made by the Eastern and Western regions (round your answer to 2 decimal places)?   **55.07%**

(b)   WIGGINS LTD

(a)   What were the total sales for the first 3 months?   **£1,377,292**

(b)   What was the percentage increase from March to April?   **0.76%**

(c)   What will sales be in September 20X4 if they are 5% higher than August 20X4?
£495,912.90

(d)   How much higher (in £) are sales in June than March?   **£9,714**

22 BOB

From: bob@accountancyfirm.co.uk

To: ally@accountancyfirm.co.uk

Subject: AAT Exam Performance

Hello Ally,

I would like to discuss the above with you tomorrow afternoon. In particular I would like to review the performance of John Barnes with a view to finding out why he has performed poorly. I also hope we can resolve this issue by working together with John.

Regards

Bob

23 K KIPLING

From AATstudent@Kaplan.co.uk

To: kk@cakes4tea.org.uk

Subject: Meeting confirmation – Mrs Anna Howes

Good morning Mr Kipling

Following our telephone conversation I confirm the meeting which is to take place at your premises on Monday at 2.30pm.

I will bring a copy of the business plan I have prepared.

Kind regards

Anna Howes

24 JOSHUA VALENTINE

From: AATstudent@atoz.org.uk

To: jvalentine@atoz.org.uk; cjenton@atoz.org.uk; dwheeler@atoz.org.uk

Subject: Conference

Hello All,

This conference is being held at King's Hotel on Thursday at 10 am.

The conference will be held regarding the issue of recycling within organisations.

Please confirm your attendance.

Regards,

AAT Student

25   PURCHASE OF LAPTOPS

To:	j.wriggle@kplittle.co.uk
From:	b.coalie@kplittle.co.uk
Subject:	Laptops
Date:	2 October 20X8

Hi Joe,

I'm pleased to inform you that we have been able to approve your purchase request for 6 laptops. The budget has been set at £6,000 in total for all 6 laptops.

You will need to speak with the relevant sales team staff so that they are aware their laptop will be replaced in the near future.

If you have any further questions, please do not hesitate to contact me.

Kind regards,

Bernie

26   WORK SCHEDULE

Complete your to-do list for Monday in order of task completion.

(1)   Weekly planning meeting

(2)   Open and distribute post

(3)   Process sales invoices

(4)   Assist payroll manager

(5)   Frank post and take to PO

27   WORK PLANNING

Process payroll	5th
Bank reconciliation	3rd
Wages reconciliation	2nd
Overtime calculation	6th
Team meeting	1st
Cash to bank	4th

28 FEEDBACK

Select two conclusions that could be drawn from the feedback

- Most delegates found the venue difficult to find
- The course was relevant to the delegates' job role

Select two items which should be investigated

- Why was there so little feedback received
- Look for a different venue

29 SURVEY

(a) How many people were asked each question? 60

(b) In terms of work/life balance, are staff unhappy

(c) In terms of current pay/ are most people happy

(d) Do the majority of people agree that there are good promotion prospects – no

30 REPORT CONTENT

What information is usually contained within the areas of a report listed below?

	Introduction	Appendices
Information regarding what the report is based upon	✓	
Supporting calculations for figures contained within the body of the report		✓

LO4 CORPORATE SOCIAL RESPONSIBILITY, ETHICS AND SUSTAINABILITY

31 PRINCIPLES

The fundamental code of ethics set out five principles that a professional accountant is required to comply with. Two principles are objectivity and professional competence/due care. Select TWO other ethical principles from the list below.

B   Integrity

D   Confidentiality

32 COMPANY SHARES

Your father owns some shares in a company which your company audits. You have recently found out that the company is struggling. This is going to be announced publicly shortly and will have an adverse effect on the share price. Which TWO fundamental ethical principles prevent you from telling your father about this?

A   Confidentiality

B   Objectivity

Section 6

ANSWERS TO PRACTICE QUESTIONS

ASSESSMENT OBJECTIVE 2

47 HLB WHOLESALE

(a)

<table>
<tr><td colspan="6" align="center">Painting Supplies Ltd
19 Edmund St
Newcastle, NE6 5DJ

VAT Registration No. 402 2958 02</td></tr>
<tr><td colspan="3">HLB Wholesale
98 Back St
Consett
DH4 3PD</td><td colspan="3">Customer account code: HLB24

Delivery note number: 46589

Date: 1 Feb 20XX</td></tr>
<tr><td colspan="6">Invoice No: 298</td></tr>
<tr><td>Quantity</td><td>Product code</td><td>Total list price £</td><td>Net amount after discount £</td><td>VAT £</td><td>Gross £</td></tr>
<tr><td>20</td><td>SD19</td><td>300</td><td>270</td><td>54</td><td>324</td></tr>
</table>

(b)

Trade discount

48   MASHED LTD

(a)

Hickory House					
22 Nursery Road					
Keighley, BD22 7BD					

VAT Registration No. 476 1397 02

Mashed Ltd   **Customer account code:** MA87
42 Moorside Court
Ilkley   **Delivery note number:** 472
Leeds, LS29 4PR
                                                          Date: 1 Aug 20XX
Invoice No: 47

Quantity of pots	Product code	Total list price £	Net amount after discount £	VAT £	Gross £
20	P10	100	90	18	108

(b)

Bulk discount

49   SDB

Sales day-book

Date 20XX	Details	Invoice number	Total £	VAT £	Net £	Sales type 1 £	Sales type 2 £
31 Dec	Poonams	105	3,600	600	3,000		3,000
31 Dec	D. Taylor	106	7,680	1,280	6,400	6,400	
31 Dec	Smiths	107	3,840	640	3,200		3,200
	Totals		15,120	2,520	12,600	6,400	6,200

50   WILLIAM & SAMMY LTD

(a)

Sales invoice 286

(b)

£4,481.28

(c)

£4,668.00

51   PIXIE PAPERS

Has the correct product been supplied by Pixie Paper?	Y
Has the correct net price been calculated?	N see N1
Has the total invoice price been calculated correctly?	N
What would be the VAT amount charged if the invoice was correct?	£90.00
What would be the total amount charged if the invoice was correct?	£540.00

N1 – the trade discount of 10% should have been deducted so that the net price was £450.

VAT @ 20% on the net price of £450 is then calculated as £90.00.

52   FREDDIE LTD

Purchases day-book

Date 20XX	Details	Invoice number	Total £	VAT £	Net £	Product 14211 £	Product 14212 £
31 July	Box Ltd	2177	960	160	800	800	
31 July	Shrew Ltd	2175	14,400	2,400	12,000	12,000	
31 July	Novot & Co	2176	4,800	800	4,000		4,000
	Totals		20,160	3,360	16,800	12,800	4,000

53   HOLLY LTD

(a)

Purchase return 286

(b)

£928.80

(c)

£172.00

(d)

£1,032.00

What would be the total amount charged if the invoice was correct?	£192.00

54   EP MANUFACTURERS

(a)

Cheque for £1,200

(b)

Invoice 488

(c)

£4,850.00

55 STANNY LTD

(a)

	Ringo Rings	
	37 Parker Lane	
	Stoke SK1 0KE	
	REMITTANCE ADVICE	
To: Stanny Ltd		**Date:** 31 Mar 20XX

Please find attached our cheque in payment of the following amounts.

Invoice number	Credit note number	Amount
694		2,300
658		3,640
	198	650
	154	1,250
	Total amount paid	**4,040**

(b)   A remittance note is for ours and the suppliers records   T

A remittance note is sent by a supplier confirming amounts
received from them   F

56 TOYWORLD

(a)

Cheque for £500

(b)

Invoice 505

(c)

£4,000

57   GREY GARAGES

Remittance advice

To: Mulberry Motors

From: Grey Garages

Payment method: BACS   **Date of payment:** 25 July

Items outstanding			Tick if included in payment
Date 20XX	*Details*	*Amount £*	
23-Jun	Invoice 213	740	✓
06-Jul	Credit note 14	120	✓
13-Jul	Invoice 216	620	✓
19-Jul	Invoice 257	870	
Total amount paid		£1,240	

58   ERRICO

Supplier	£	Date by which the payment should be received by the supplier
Giacomo	67.51	11 June 20XX
Gaetani	39.33	9 June 20XX

59   LADY LTD

General ledger

Purchases ledger control account

	£		£
		1 Dec Balance b/d	5,103.90
		18 Dec Purchases & Vat	**903.23**

VAT account

	£		£
		1 Dec Balance b/d	526.90
18 Dec PLCA	**150.53**		

Purchases account

	£		£
1 Dec Balance b/d	22,379.52		
18 Dec PLCA	**752.70**		

Subsidiary ledger

M Brown

	£		£
		1 Dec Balance b/d	68.50
		1 Dec PDB	**300.00**

H Madden

	£		£
		1 Dec Balance b/d	286.97
		5 Dec PDB	**183.55**

L Singh

	£		£
		1 Dec Balance b/d	125.89
		7 Dec PDB	**132.60**

A Stevens

	£		£
		1 Dec Balance b/d	12.36
		10 Dec PDB	**90.00**

N Shema

	£		£
		1 Dec Balance b/d	168.70
		18 Dec PDB	**197.08**

60   SPARKY LTD

(a)   What will be the entries in the sales ledger?

Sales ledger

Account name	Amount £	Debit ✓	Credit ✓
Clarkson Ltd	1,680		✓
Kyle & Co	720		✓

(b)   What will be the entries in the general ledger?

General ledger

Account name	Amount £	Debit ✓	Credit ✓
Sales ledger control account	2,400		✓
Sales returns	2,000	✓	
VAT	400	✓	

61   LOUIS LTD

(a)   What will be the entries in the sales ledger?

Account name	Amount £	Debit ✓	Credit ✓
Sheep & Co	3,840	✓	
Cow Ltd	11,760	✓	
Chicken & Partners	6,720	✓	
Pig Ltd	14,496	✓	

(b)   What will be the entries in the general ledger?

Account name	Amount £	Debit ✓	Credit ✓
Sales ledger control	36,816	✓	
VAT	6,136		✓
Sales	30,680		✓

62   THOMAS & TILLY

(a)   What will be the entries in the purchase ledger?

Purchases ledger

Account name	Amount £	Debit ✓	Credit ✓
May Ltd	1,920	✓	
Hammond & Co	1,200	✓	

(b)   What will be the entries in the general ledger?

General ledger

Account name	Amount £	Debit ✓	Credit ✓
Purchase ledger control account	3,120	✓	
Purchase returns	2,600		✓
VAT	520		✓

63   JESSICA & CO

(a)   What will be the entries in the purchases ledger?

Purchases ledger

Account name	Amount £	Debit ✓	Credit ✓
Iona Ltd	1,680	✓	
Matilda Ltd	4,320	✓	

(b)   What will be the entries in the general ledger?

General ledger

Account name	Amount £	Debit ✓	Credit ✓
Purchases ledger control account	6,000	✓	
Purchases returns	5,000		✓
VAT	1,000		✓

64 HORSEY REACH

(a)

Account name	Amount £	Debit ✓	Credit ✓
Sales ledger control	226.80		✓
VAT	37.80	✓	
Discounts allowed	189.00	✓	

(b)

Account name	Amount £	Debit ✓	Credit ✓
Ashleigh Buildings	36.00		✓
143 WGT	54.00		✓
McDuff McGregor	43.20		✓
Cameron Travel	93.60		✓

65 BUTTERFLY BEES

(a)

Account name	Amount £	Debit ✓	Credit ✓
Discounts received	356.00		✓
VAT	71.20		✓
PLCA	427.20	✓	

(b)

Account name	Amount £	Debit ✓	Credit ✓
Bella Bumps	24.00	✓	

66 OLIVIA ROSE BRIAL SUPPLIES

(a)

Account name	Amount £	Debit ✓	Credit ✓
Discounts allowed	189.00	✓	
VAT	37.80	✓	
SLCA	226.80		✓

(b)

Account name	Amount £	Debit ✓	Credit ✓
Bridezilla	54.00		✓

67 CHUGGER LTD

(a) General ledger

Account name	Amount £	Debit ✓	Credit ✓
Stationery expense	80	✓	
Repairs	200	✓	
VAT	56	✓	

(b) Sales ledger

Account name	Amount £	Debit ✓	Credit ✓
BBG Ltd	7,200		✓
EFG Ltd	5,000		✓

(c) General ledger

Account name	Amount £	Debit ✓	Credit ✓
Sales ledger control	12,200		✓

68 ITALIAN STALLIONS LTD

(a) General ledger

Account name	Amount £	Debit ✓	Credit ✓
Office supplies	80	✓	
Repairs	160	✓	
VAT	48	✓	

(b) Sales ledger

Account name	Amount £	Debit ✓	Credit ✓
AAG Ltd	4,000		✓
HLG Ltd	3,000		✓

(c)   General ledger

Account name	Amount £	Debit ✓	Credit ✓
Sales ledger control	7,000		✓

69   FRED'S FISH

(a)   Sales ledger

Account name	Amount £	Debit ✓	Credit ✓
K and D Ltd	8,200		✓

(b)   General ledger

Account name	Amount £	Debit ✓	Credit ✓
Sales ledger control	8,200		✓

(c)   General ledger

Account name	Amount £	Debit ✓	Credit ✓
Stationery	100	✓	
VAT	20	✓	
Postage	800	✓	

70   ABC LTD

(a)   Cash-book – credit side

Details	Cash	Bank	VAT	Payables	Cash purchases	Repairs and renewals
Balance b/f						
S. Lampard	216		36		180	
S. Bobbins	264		44		220	
Penny Rhodes	530				530	
Henley's Ltd		4,925		4,925		
Epic Equipment Maintenance		480	80			400
Total	1,010	5,405	160	4,925	930	400

(b)   **Cash book – debit side**

Details	Cash	Bank	Receivables
Balance b/f	1,550	7,425	
D. Davies		851	851
E. Denholm		450	450
Total	1,550	8,726	1,301

(c)   £540 ($1,550 - $1,010)

(d)   £3,321 ($8,726 - $5,405)

(e)   Debit

71   BEDS

(a)   **Cash-book – credit side**

Details	Cash	Bank	VAT	Payables	Cash purchases	Repairs and renewals
Balance b/f						
A Blighty Ltd	708		118		590	
R Bromby	228		38		190	
Roxy Bland	230				230	
Burgess Ltd		2,400		2,400		
Fast Equipment Repairs		96	16			80
Total	1,166	2,496	172	2,400	1,010	80

(b)   **Cash book – debit side**

Details	Cash	Bank	Receivables
Balance b/f	1,175	3,825	
A Barnett		698	698
H Connelly		250	250
Total	1,175	4,773	948

(c)   £9 ($1,175 - $1,166)

(d)   £2,277 ($4,773 - $2,496)

(e)   Debit

72 HICKORY HOUSE

General ledger

Account name	Amount £	Debit ✓	Credit ✓
VAT	6.80	✓	
Postage	15.00	✓	
Motor expenses	12.40	✓	
Office expenses	21.60	✓	
Bank	90		✓

73 MESSI & CO

General ledger

Account name	Amount £	Debit ✓	Credit ✓
VAT	7.25	✓	
Postage	4.50	✓	
Motor expenses	8.00	✓	
Office expenses	28.28	✓	
Petty cash control	48.03		✓

74 YUMMY CUPCAKES

General ledger

Account name	Amount £	Debit ✓	Credit ✓
VAT	11.07	✓	
Sundry expenses	10.00	✓	
Business travel	45.37	✓	
Postage	4.00	✓	
Petty cash control	70.44		✓

75   BROOKLYN BOATS

Telephone

Date 20XX	Details	Amount £	Date 20XX	Details £	Amount £
01 Dec	Balance b/f	870	31 Dec	Balance c/d	1,220
12 Dec	Bank	350			
	Total	1,220		**Total**	1,220
1 Jan	Balance b/d	1,220			

Discounts received

Date 20XX	Details	Amount £	Date 20XX	Details £	Amount £
31 Dec	Balance c/d	600	1 Dec	Balance b/f	500
			15 Dec	Purchase Ledger control	100
	Total	600		**Total**	600
			1 Jan	Balance b/d	600

76   CRAZY CURTAINS

Electricity expense

Date 20XX	Details	Amount £	Date 20XX	Details £	Amount £
01 Jan	Bal b/f	200	31 Jan	Balance c/d	450
22 Jan	Bank	250			
	Total	450		**Total**	450
1 Feb	Balance b/d	450			

Rental income

Date 20XX	Details	Amount £	Date 20XX	Details £	Amount £
31 Jan	Balance c/d	1,000	01 Jan	Balance b/f	400
			28 Jan	Bank	600
	Total	1,000		**Total**	1,000
			1 Feb	Balance b/d	1,000

77   SMITH & SON

Account name	Amount £	Debit £	Credit £
Fixtures and fittings	8,250	8,250	
Capital	18,400		18,400
Bank overdraft	4,870		4,870
Petty cash control	350	350	
Sales ledger control (SLCA)	42,870	42,870	
Purchases ledger control (PLCA)	23,865		23,865
VAT owed to tax authorities	10,245		10,245
Inventory	9,870	9,870	
Loan from bank	22,484		22,484
Sales	180,264		180,264
Sales returns	5,420	5,420	
Purchases	129,030	129,030	
Purchases returns	2,678		2,678
Discount allowed	2,222	2,222	
Discount received	3,432		3,432
Heat and light	1,490	1,490	
Motor expenses	2,354	2,354	
Wages	42,709	42,709	
Rent and rates	10,600	10,600	
Repairs	3,020	3,020	
Hotel expenses	1,890	1,890	
Telephone	2,220	2,220	
Delivery costs	1,276	1,276	
Miscellaneous expenses	2,667	2,667	
Totals	532,476	266,238	266,238

78   EXPIALIDOCIOUS LTD

Account name	Amount £	Debit £	Credit £
Capital	25,360		25,360
Petty cash control	250	250	
Loan from bank	11,600		11,600
Sales ledger control (SLCA)	159,242	159,242	
Purchases ledger control (PLCA)	83,682		83,682
Motor vehicles	35,900	35,900	
Inventory	28,460	28,460	
Bank overdraft	10,063		10,063
VAT owing from tax authorities	15,980	15,980	
Purchases	343,014	343,014	
Purchases returns	1,515		1,515
Wages	56,150	56,150	
Motor expenses	2,950	2,950	
Interest income	400		400
Sales	532,900		532,900
Sales returns	5,760	5,760	
Stationery	1,900	1,900	
Light & heat	6,500	6,500	
Discount received	200		200
Discount allowed	2,160	2,160	
Interest paid on overdraft	550	550	
Travel	1,800	1,800	
Marketing	650	650	
Telephone	1,510	1,510	
Miscellaneous expenses	2,944	2,944	
Totals		665,720	665,720

Section 7

ANSWERS TO PRACTICE QUESTIONS

ASSESSMENT OBJECTIVE 3

79   INTREPID INTERIORS

(a)

Account name	Amount £	Debit ✓	Credit ✓
Cash at bank	7,250	✓	
Bank Loan	5,000		✓
Capital	10,625		✓
Motor vehicles	4,750	✓	
Insurances	575	✓	
Stationery	300	✓	
Sundry expenses	225	✓	
Motor expenses	135	✓	
Advertising	990	✓	
Rent and rates	1,400	✓	

(b)

Recording of a contra

80   DOWN & OUT

(i)

Account name	Amount £	Debit ✓	Credit ✓
Wages expense	9,567	✓	
Wages control	9,567		✓

(ii)

Account name	Amount £	Debit ✓	Credit ✓
HM Revenue and Customs	3,673		✓
Wages control	3,673	✓	

(iii)

Account name	Amount £	Debit ✓	Credit ✓
Bank	5,469		✓
Wages control	5,469	✓	

(iv)

Account name	Amount £	Debit ✓	Credit ✓
Trade union	425		✓
Wages control	425	✓	

Proof (not required to answer the question correctly):

Wages control

HM Revenue and Customs	3,673	Wages expense	9,567
Bank	5,469		
Trade union	425		
	———		———
	9,567		9,567
	———		———

81 RHYME TIME

(i)

Account name	Amount £	Debit ✓	Credit ✓
Wages expense	11,915	✓	
Wages control	11,915		✓

(ii)

Account name	Amount £	Debit ✓	Credit ✓
HM Revenue and Customs	5,026		✓
Wages control	5,026	✓	

(iii)

Account name	Amount £	Debit ✓	Credit ✓
Bank	5,739		✓
Wages control	5,739	✓	

(iv)

Account name	Amount £	Debit ✓	Credit ✓
Pension	1,150		✓
Wages control	1,150	✓	

Wages control

HM Revenue and Customs	5,026	Wages expense	11,915
Bank	5,739		
Pension	1,150		
	11,915		11,915

82 BEDROOM BITS

Account name	Amount £	Debit ✓	Credit ✓
Irrecoverable debts	2,000	✓	
VAT	400	✓	
Sales ledger control	2,400		✓

83 CHESTNUT

SLCA

Details	Amount £	Details	Amount £
Balance b/d	46,000	Contra	4,000
		Balance c/d	42,000
	46,000		**46,000**
Balance b/d	42,000		

PLCA

Details	Amount £	Details	Amount £
Contra	4,000	Balance b/d	31,000
Balance c/d	27,000		
	31,000		**31,000**
		Balance b/d	27,000

84 BEANZ

Account name	Amount £	Debit ✓	Credit ✓
Irrecoverable debts	4,350	✓	
VAT	870	✓	
Sales ledger control	5,220		✓

85 RENT ERROR

(i)

Account name	Amount £	Debit ✓	Credit ✓
Bank	500	✓	
Rent received	500		✓

(ii)

Account name	Amount £	Debit ✓	Credit ✓
Bank	500	✓	
Rent received	500		✓

86 GAS ERROR

Account name	Amount £	Debit ✓	Credit ✓
Gas expenses	300	✓	
Electricity expenses	300		✓

87 BUILDING ERROR

Account name	Amount £	Debit ✓	Credit ✓
Suspense	360,000	✓	
Bank	360,000		✓

88 SALES ERROR

Account name	Amount £	Debit ✓	Credit ✓
Sales	2,000	✓	
VAT	2,000		✓

89   CB INTERIORS

(i)

Account name	Amount £	Debit ✓	Credit ✓
Purchase ledger control	960	✓	

(ii)

Account name	Amount £	Debit ✓	Credit ✓
Purchase ledger control	9,600		✓

(iii)

Account name	Amount £	Debit ✓	Credit ✓
Suspense	8,640	✓	

90   ROGER DODGER

(i)

Account name	Amount £	Debit ✓	Credit ✓
VAT	1,680	✓	

(ii)

Account name	Amount £	Debit ✓	Credit ✓
VAT	1,320		✓

(iii)

Account name	Amount £	Debit ✓	Credit ✓
Suspense	360		✓

91   BUCKLEY DRAINS

(a)

Account name	Amount £	Debit ✓	Credit ✓
Suspense	10,805		✓

(b)

Account name	Amount £	Debit ✓	Credit ✓
Suspense	10,805	✓	
PLCA	10,805		✓

(c) Show one reason for maintaining the journal

	✓
To correct errors only	
To correct errors and record transactions that have not been recorded in any other book of prime entry	✓
To record transactions from every other book of prime entry.	

92 MENDONCA

(a)

Account name	Amount £	Debit ✓	Credit ✓
Suspense	1,980		✓

(b)

Account name	Amount £	Debit ✓	Credit ✓
Suspense	1,980	✓	
Wages	900	✓	
Bank	2,880		✓

93 BEASANT

(a)

Account name	Amount £	Debit ✓	Credit ✓
Suspense	15,000		✓

(b)

Account name	Amount £	Debit ✓	Credit ✓
Suspense	15,000	✓	
Sales	12,500		✓
VAT	2,500		✓

(c) **Show one reason for maintaining the journal**

	✓
To detect fraud	
To record non-regular transactions	✓
To record goods sold on credit	

94 HEARN

Journal entries

Account name	Debit £	Credit £
Rent	90	
Suspense		90
VAT	120	
Suspense		120

	Balances extracted on 30 June £	Balances at 1 July	
		Debit £	Credit £
Sales ledger control	34,560	34,560	
Purchases ledger control	21,420		21,420
VAT owing to HM Revenue and Customs	3,412		3,292
Capital	50,000		50,000
Sales	201,327		201,327
Sales returns	1,465	1,465	
Purchases	87,521	87,521	
Purchase returns	252		252
Plant and equipment	15,200	15,200	
Motor expenses	4,310	4,310	
Office expenses	10,321	10,321	
Rent and rates	21,420	21,510	
Heat and light	8,920	8,920	
Wages	53,205	53,205	
Irrecoverable debt	1,450	1,450	
Office equipment	42,030	42,030	
Bank overdraft	4201		4201
Suspense account (debit balance)	210		
Totals		280,492	280,492

95 RODMAN

Journal entries

Account name	Debit £	Credit £
Suspense	1,250	
VAT		1,250
Wages	8,600	
Suspense		8,600

	Balances extracted on 30 June £	Balances at 1 July	
		Debit £	Credit £
Sales ledger control	38,070	38,070	
Purchases ledger control	20,310		20,310
VAT owed from HM Revenue and Customs	2,510	1,260	
Capital	70,000		70,000
Sales	153,488		153,488
Sales returns	2,135	2,135	
Purchases	63,261	63,261	
Purchase returns	542		542
Plant and equipment	17,319	17,319	
Motor expenses	3,214	3,214	
Office expenses	6,421	6,421	
Rent and rates	17,414	17,414	
Heat and light	6,421	6,421	
Wages	45,532	54,132	
Irrecoverable debt	1,532	1,532	
Office equipment	35,313	35,313	
Bank overdraft	2,152		2,152
Suspense account (debit balance)	7,350		
Totals		**246,492**	**246,492**

96   LUXURY BATHROOMS

(a) – (c)

Date	Details	Bank	Date	Cheque	Details	Bank
01 April	Balance b/d	17,845	01 April	120045	R Sterling Ltd	8,850
19 April	Olsen & Lane	2,150	01 April	120046	Bert Cooper	2,250
22 April	Frith Ltd	685	01 April	120047	Hetko & Sons	64
22 April	Hodgetts & Co	282	02 April	120048	Barrett Ltd	3,256
04 April	Ricketts & Co	465	02 April	120049	K Plomer	542
			08 April	120050	I&E Brown	655
			08 April	120051	T Roberts	1,698
			14 April		AMB Ltd	2,265
			14 April		D Draper	2,950
			22 April		Bank charges	63
			23 April		Overdraft fee	25
24 April	Balance c/d	1,191				
		22,618				**22,618**
			25 April		Balance b/d	1,191

97   WHOLESALE FLOORING

(a) – (c)

Date 20XX	Details	Bank £	Date 20XX	Cheque number	Details	Bank £
			01 June		Balance b/d	5,125
16 June	Beeston's	550	01 June	104373	Good Iron	890
19 June	Airfleet exteriors	3,025	01 June	104374	Ashworth and Co	1,725
22 June	Jones's	2,775	01 June	104375	Ironfit	210
12 June	Aintree and Co	1,250	05 June	104376	OSS Ltd	1,275
			07 June	104377	Perfect Tools	725
			08 June	104378	Campden Ltd	784
			14 June	104379	Thornley and Thwaite	675
			14 June	104380	Castle and Cove	178
			20 June		MD County council	400
			23 June		Bank charges	160
23 June	Balance c/d	4,637	23 June		Overdraft fee	90
		12,237				12,237
			24 June		Balance b/d	4,637

98 MCKEOWN

(a) – (c)

Date 20XX	Details	Bank £	Date 20XX	Cheque number	Details	Bank £
01 June	Balance b/d	7,180	07 June	110157	Williams	430
12 June	Sherwood	640	07 June	110158	Forecast	520
14 June	Cash sales	1,200	07 June	110159	Beasant	1,240
22 June	Tweedy	860	07 June	110160	Davison	1,420
23 June	Butterwood	440	07 June	110161	Mildenhall	750
01 June	Interest received	85	23 June		Wilmott	300
20 June	Coyne	1,630				
23 June	Interest received	35				
			23 June		Balance c/d	7,410
		12,070				12,070
24 June	Balance b/d	7,410				

99 LUXURY BATHROOMS

Balance per bank statement	**£82**
Add:	
Name: Frith Ltd	£685
Name: Hodgetts & Co	£282
Total to add	**£967**
Less:	
Name: K Plomer	£542
Name: T Roberts	£1,698
Total to subtract	**£2,240**
Balance as per cash book	**(£1,191)**

100   WHOLESALE FLOORING

Balance per bank statement	(£9,584)
Add:	
Name: Airfleet Exteriors	£3,025
Name: Jones'	£2,775
Total to add	**£5,800**
Less:	
Name: Thornley & Thwaite	£675
Name: Castle & Cove	£178
Total to subtract	**£853**
Balance as per cash book	**(£4,637)**

101   MCKEOWN

(a)

Balance per bank statement	£8,770
Add:	
Name: Tweedy	£860
Name: Butterwood	£440
Total to add	**£1,300**
Less:	
Name: Beasant	£1,240
Name: Davison	£1,420
Total to subtract	**£2,660**
Balance as per cash book	**£7,410**

(b)

Balance carried down £	Bank column totals £
7,410	12,070

Workings: – Cash book

Date 20XX	Details	Bank £	Date 20XX	Cheque number	Details	Bank £
01 June	Balance b/d	7,180	07 June	110157	Williams	430
12 June	Sherwood	640	07 June	110158	Forecast	520
14 June	Cash sales	1,200	07 June	110159	Beasant	1,240
22 June	Tweedy	860	07 June	110160	Davison	1,420
23 June	Butterwood	440	07 June	110161	Mildenhall	750
01 June	Interest received	85	23 June		Wilmott	300
20 June	Coyne	1,630				
23 June	Interest received	35				
			23 June		Balance c/d	7,410
		12,070				12,070
24 June	Balance b/d	7,410				

102   MONSTER MUNCHIES

(a)

Details	Amount £	Debit ✓	Credit ✓
Balance of receivables at 1 June	48,000	✓	
Goods sold on credit	12,415	✓	
Receipts from credit customers	22,513		✓
Discount allowed	465		✓
Sales returns from credit customers	320		✓

(b)

Dr £37,117	✓

(c)

	£
Sales ledger control account balance as at 30 June	37,117
Total of subsidiary (sales) ledger accounts as at 30 June	36,797
Difference	320

(d)

Sales returns may have been omitted from the subsidiary ledger.	
Discounts allowed may have been omitted from the subsidiary ledger.	
Sales returns may have been entered in the subsidiary ledger twice.	✓
Discounts allowed may have been entered in the subsidiary ledger twice.	✓

(e)

Reconciliation of the sales ledger control account assures managers that the amount showing as owed to suppliers is correct.	
Reconciliation of the sales ledger control account assures managers that the amount showing as outstanding from customers is correct.	✓
Reconciliation of the sales ledger control account will show if a purchase invoice has been omitted from the purchase ledger.	
Reconciliation of the sales ledger control account will show if a purchase invoice has been omitted from the sales ledger.	

103 JACK'S BOX

(a)

Details	Amount £	Debit ✓	Credit ✓
Balance of receivables at 1 April	60,589	✓	
Goods sold on credit	26,869	✓	
Payments received from credit customers	29,411		✓
Discount allowed	598		✓
Goods returned from credit customers	1,223		✓

(b)

Dr £55,030	
Cr £55,030	
Dr £56,226	✓
Cr £56,226	
Dr £52,584	
Cr £52,584	

(c)

	£
Sales Ledger control account balances as at 30 April	56,226
Total of subsidiary (sales) ledger accounts as at 30 April	55,003
Difference	1,223

(d)

Sales returns may have been omitted from the subsidiary ledger	
Discounts allowed have been omitted from the subsidiary ledger.	
Sales returns have been entered into the subsidiary ledger twice	✓
Discounts allowed have been entered into the subsidiary ledger twice	

(e)

Reconciliation of the sales ledger control account will show if a purchase invoice has been omitted from the purchases ledger.	
Reconciliation of the sales ledger control account will show if a sales invoice has been omitted from the purchases ledger.	
Reconciliation of the sales ledger control account assures managers that the amount showing due to suppliers is correct.	
Reconciliation of the sales ledger control account assures managers that the amount showing due from customers is correct.	✓

104 ZHANG

(a)

SLCA

Details	Amount £	Details	Amount £
Balance b/d	65,830	SBD overcast	1,200
		Discount given	210
		Balance c/d	64,420
	65,830		**65,830**
Balance b/d	64,420		

List of balances:

	£
Total:	65,090
Contra missing	(800)
Credit note posted twice	130
Revised total:	64,420

(b) **Show whether the following statements are true or false:**

	True ✓	False ✓
An aged trade receivables analysis is used when chasing customers for outstanding payments.	✓	
An aged trade receivables analysis is sent to credit customers when payments are being requested.		✓

105 HANDYSIDE

(a)

PLCA

Details	Amount £	Details	Amount £
Returns	120	Balance b/d	25,360
		Missing invoice	720
Balance c/d	25,960		
	26,080		**26,080**
		Balance b/d	25,960

List of balances:

	£
Total	26,000
Net amount entered	400
Returns	(350)
Transposition error	(90)
Revised total	25,960

(b)　**Show whether the following statements are true or false:**

	True ✓	False ✓
The purchases ledger control account enables a business to see how much is owed to individual suppliers		✓
The purchases ledger control account total should reconcile to the total of the list of supplier balances in the purchases ledger	✓	

106 RING RING TELEPHONE

(a)

VAT control

Details	Amount £	Details	Amount £
Sales returns	360	Sales	30,600
Purchases	16,200	Cash sales	48
		Purchases returns	1,160
Balance c/d	15,248		
	31,808		**31,808**
		Balance b/d	15,248

(b)　No – it is £15,248 owed **to** HMRC

(c)

	£	Debit	Credit
Balance brought down	38,900	✓	

Workings:

VAT control

Details	Amount £	Details	Amount £
Debit balances	93,800	Credit balances	54,400
Purchase of equipment	400	Cash sales	900
		Balance c/d	38,900
	94,200		**94,200**
Balance b/d	38,900		

107 PHILIP'S CABINS

(a)

VAT control

Details	Amount £	Details	Amount £
Sales returns	600	Sales	35,960
Purchases	20,040	Cash sales	112
		Purchases returns	1,144
Balance c/d	16,576		
	37,216		**37,216**
		Balance b/d	16,576

(b)   No – the amount owed to HMRC is £16,576.

108 DISLEY

(a)

	£	Debit	Credit
VAT total in the sales day book	65,420		65,420
VAT total in the purchases day book	21,340	21,340	
VAT total in the sales returns day book	480	480	
VAT balance brought forward, owed to HMRC	24,910		24,910
VAT on irrecoverable debts	830	830	
VAT on petty cash expenses paid	210	210	

(b)   No – the amount owed to HMRC is £67,470.

(c)

	£	Debit	Credit
Balance brought down	19,730		✓

Workings:

VAT control

Details	Amount £	Details	Amount £
Debit balances	42,300	Credit balances	61,250
Irrecoverable debt	200	Discounts received	980
Balance c/d	19,730		
	62,230		**62,230**
		Balance b/d	19,730

109 AWESOME LTD

Task 1

Characteristic	FIFO	LIFO	AVCO
• Closing inventory is valued at £48,500.	✓		
• The issue of inventory is valued at £57,200.			✓
• The issue of inventory is valued at £66,900.		✓	

Task 2

	True	False
• FIFO values the issue of inventory at £47,500.	✓	
• AVCO values the closing inventory at £38,400.		✓
• LIFO values the closing inventory at £29,100.	✓	

110 AMAZING LTD

Task 1

Characteristic	FIFO	LIFO	AVCO
• Closing inventory is valued at £1,500.		✓	
• The issue of inventory is valued at £23,000.	✓		
• The issue of inventory is valued at £24,000.			✓

Task 2

	True	False
• LIFO values the issue of inventory at £26,500.	✓	
• AVCO values the closing inventory at £5,000.		✓
• FIFO values the closing inventory at £4,000.		✓

111 STONE LTD

Method	Cost of issue on 22 June	Closing inventory at 30 June
FIFO	£10,125 (500 × £15) + (150 × £17.50)	£17,200 (£8,750 + £4,950 + £6,125 + £7,500) – £10,125
LIFO	£11,450 (275 × £18) + (350 × £17.50) + (25 × £15)	£15,875 (£8,750 + £4,950 + £6,125 + £7,500) – £11,450
AVCO	£10,732 ((£7,500 + £6,125 + £4,950)/ (500 + 350 + 275)) × 650	£16,593 (£8,750 + £4,950 + £6,125 + £7,500) – £10,732

112 NATAL LTD

Task 1

Method	Cost of issue on 2 Dec	Closing inventory at 29 Dec
LIFO	£534,250 (50,000 × £7) + (14,000 × £8) + (8500 × £8.50)	£42,750 (£85,000 + £112,000 + £350,000 + £30,000) – £534,250
AVCO	£535,912 ((£85,000 + £112,000 + £350,000)/ (10,000 + 14,000 + 50,000)) × 72,500	£41,088 (£85,000 + £112,000 + £350,000 + £30,000) – £535,912

Task 2

	True	False
• FIFO would give a lower closing inventory valuation on the 29th December than LIFO and AVCO.	✓	
• FIFO would give a lower cost of issue on the 25th of December than LIFO and AVCO.		✓

113 GANDALF LTD

	Valuation £
• July 15	£1,030 (500 × £1.70) + (120 × £1.50)
• July 31	£660 (200 × £1.80) + (200 × £1.50)

inventory as total purchases (£4,750) less cost of issue

114 NULAB LTD

Payment method	Time-rate	Piecework	Piece-rate plus bonus
• Labour is paid based on the production achieved.		✓	
• Labour is paid extra if an agreed level of output is exceeded.			✓
• Labour is paid according to hours worked.	✓		

115 MANDELA LTD

Statement	True	False
• Time rate is paid based on the production achieved.		✓
• Overtime is paid for hours worked over the standard hours agreed.	✓	
• Piece rate is paid according to hours worked.		✓

116 PERRES LTD

Payment method	Basic rate	Overtime premium	Overtime rate
• This is the amount paid above the basic rate for hours worked in excess of the normal hours.		✓	
• This is the total amount paid per hour for hours worked in excess of the normal hours.			✓
• This is the amount paid per hour for normal hours worked.	✓		

117 TEVEZ LTD

Statement	True	False
• Direct labour costs can be identified with the goods being made or the service being provided.	✓	
• Indirect labour costs vary directly with the level of activity.		✓

118 BERDYCH LTD

Payment method	Variable	Fixed
• Labour that is paid based on a time rate basis per hour worked.	✓	
• Labour is paid on a monthly salary basis.		✓
• Labour that is based on number of units produced.	✓	

119 PIECEWORK STATEMENTS

Statement	True	False
• Piecework encourages employees to work harder.	✓	
• Piecework requires accurate recording of the number of hours staff have worked.		✓
• Piecework encourages workers to improve the quality of the units they produce.		✓

120 PHOENIX LTD

Statement	True	False
An employee who works 38 hours and makes 775 units will not receive a bonus.		✓
An employee who works 40 hours and makes 815 units will receive total pay of £342.50.	✓	
An employee who works 37 hours and makes 744 units will earn a bonus of £6.	✓	

121 KAHN LTD

Worker	Hours worked	Units produced	Basic wage	Bonus	Gross wage
A. Smith	35	175	£420	£0	£420
J. O'Hara	35	180	£420	£6	£426
M. Stizgt	35	185	£420	£12	£432

122   ENTERPRISE LTD

Worker	Hours worked	Basic wage	Overtime	Gross wage
J. Picard	37 hours	£420	£36	£456
B. Crusher	42 hours	£420	£126	£546
D. Troi	31 hours	£372	£0	£372

123   SGC LTD

Worker	Units produced in week	Gross wage
J. O'Neill	500 units	£660.00
S. Carter	650 units	£772.50

124   GOTHIC LTD

Worker	Hours worked	Units produced	Basic wage	Bonus	Gross wage
M. Shelley	37	300	£629	£20	£649
G. Leroux	37	312	£629	£80	£709
E. A. Poe	37	296	£629	£0	£629

125   AVENGERS LTD

Worker	Hours worked	Basic wage	Overtime	Gross wage
T. Stark	138	£1,380	£0	£1,380
B. Banner	142	£1,400	£25	£1,425
S. Rogers	145	£1,400	£63	£1,463

126   DRACO LTD

Worker	Units produced in week	Gross wage
P. Jones	240 units	£192
D. Bannatyne	350 units	£250
L. Redford	250 units	£200

127   JLA PLC

Statement	True	False
During a 30 hour week, an employee producing 192 units would receive a bonus of £16.	✓	
During a 35 hour week, an employee producing 240 units would receive total pay of £215.	✓	
During a 30 hour week, an employee producing 180 units would not receive a bonus.	✓	

128 INJUSTICE LTD

Worker	Units produced	Basic wage	Piece work	Gross wage
N. Wing	295	£175	£354	£529
W. Woman	355	£175	£426	£601
T. Flash	385	£175	£462	£637

129 GREENWOOD LTD

Worker	Hours worked	Units produced	Basic wage	Bonus	Gross wage
B. Ryan	35	175	£350	£0	£350
S. Chang	35	190	£350	£21	£371
E. Schneider	35	210	£350	£49	£399

130 DOOMSDAY LTD

Element	Total cost for 20,000 units	Unit cost
Direct costs	£1,250,000	£62.50
Production overhead	£75,000	£3.75
Non production overhead	£185,000	£9.25
Total costs	£1,510,000	£75.50

131 OLSEN LTD

Element	Total cost	Unit cost
Materials	£960,000	£12.00
Labour	£1,360,000	£17.00
Production overheads	£80,000	£1.00
Administration overheads	£40,000	£0.50
Total	£2,440,000	£30.50

132 CORONATION LTD

	Total cost for 5,000 units	Unit cost
Direct costs	£32,500	£6.50
Production overhead	£40,000	£8.00
Non production overhead	£45,000	£9.00
Total costs	£117,500	£23.50

133 LUTHOR LTD

Element	Unit cost
Materials	£60.00
Labour	£22.50
Fixed overheads	£38.00
Total	£120.50

134 WILKINSON LTD

Task 1

	Machine hour	Labour hour	Unit
Overheads (£)	150,000	150,000	150,000
Activity	10,000	12,500	60,000
Absorption rate (£)	15.00	12.00	2.50

Task 2

Cost	Machine hour (£)	Labour hour (£)	Unit (£)
Material	10.00	10.00	10.00
Labour	2.50	2.50	2.50
Direct cost	12.50	12.50	12.50
Overheads	2.50	3.00	2.50
Total unit cost	15.00	15.50	15.00

135 HODGSON LTD

Task 1

	Machine hour	Labour hour	Unit
Overheads (£)	250,000	250,000	250,000
Activity	15,000	20,000	100,000
Absorption rate (£)	16.67	12.50	2.50

Task 2

Cost	Machine hour (£)	Labour hour (£)	Unit (£)
Material	24.00	24.00	24.00
Labour	6.00	6.00	6.00
Direct cost	30.00	30.00	30.00
Overheads	5.56	6.25	2.50
Total unit cost	35.56	36.25	32.50

136   BARNES LTD

Task 1

	Machine hour	Labour hour	Unit
Overheads (£)	130,000	130,000	130,000
Activity	17,500	12,000	40,000
Absorption rate (£)	7.43	10.83	3.25

Task 2

Cost	Machine hour (£)	Labour hour (£)	Unit (£)
Material	15.00	15.00	15.00
Labour	5.00	5.00	5.00
Direct cost	20.00	20.00	20.00
Overheads	3.72	3.61	3.25
Total unit cost	23.72	23.61	23.25

137   ANDREW LTD

Task 1

	Machine hour	Labour hour	Unit
Overheads (£)	145,000	145,000	145,000
Activity	9,000	11,000	60,000
Absorption rate (£)	16.11	13.18	2.42

Task 2

Cost	Machine hour (£)	Labour hour (£)	Unit (£)
Material	8.00	8.00	8.00
Labour	7.00	7.00	7.00
Direct cost	15.00	15.00	15.00
Overheads	5.37	6.59	2.42
Total unit cost	20.37	21.59	17.42

138 JOKER LTD

Manufacturing account – Y/E 31 December

	£
Opening inventory of raw materials	50,000
Purchases of raw materials	120,000
Closing inventory of raw materials	65,000
DIRECT MATERIALS USED	
Direct labour	140,000
DIRECT COST	
Manufacturing overheads	85,000
MANUFACTURING COST	
Opening inventory of work in progress	48,000
Closing inventory of work in progress	52,000
COST OF GOODS MANUFACTURED	
Opening inventory of finished goods	57,000
Closing inventory of finished goods	61,000
COST OF GOODS SOLD	

	£
DIRECT MATERIALS USED	105,000
DIRECT COST	245,000
MANUFACTURING COST	330,000
COST OF GOODS MANUFACTURED	326,000
COST OF GOODS SOLD	322,000

139 RIDDLER LTD

Manufacturing account – Y/E 31 May

	£
Opening inventory of raw materials	14,000
Purchases of raw materials	100,000
Closing inventory of raw materials	20,000
DIRECT MATERIALS USED	**94,000**
Direct labour	194,000
DIRECT COST	**288,000**
Manufacturing overheads	106,000
MANUFACTURING COST	**394,000**
Opening inventory of work in progress	16,000
Closing inventory of work in progress	20,000
COST OF GOODS MANUFACTURED	**390,000**
Opening inventory of finished goods	60,000
Closing inventory of finished goods	50,000
COST OF GOODS SOLD	**400,000**

140 BOOKWORM LTD

Manufacturing account – Y/E 31 December

	£
Opening inventory of raw materials	5,000
Purchases of raw materials	15,000
Closing inventory of raw materials	8,000
DIRECT MATERIALS USED	**12,000**
Direct labour	15,000
DIRECT COST	**27,000**
Manufacturing overheads	25,000
MANUFACTURING COST	**52,000**
Opening inventory of work in progress	4,000
Closing inventory of work in progress	(6,000)
COST OF GOODS MANUFACTURED	**50,000**
Opening inventory of finished goods	12,000
Closing inventory of finished goods	(16,000)
COST OF GOODS SOLD	**46,000**

141 VARIOUS LTD

Statement	True	False
• A variance is the difference between budgeted and actual cost.	✓	
• A favourable variance occurs when actual costs are less than budgeted.	✓	
• An adverse variance occurs when actual income is less than budgeted.	✓	
• A favourable variance occurs when actual income is the same as budgeted income.		✓

142 JONES LTD

Statement	True	False
If budgeted sales are 6,000 units at £7.50 per unit and actual sales are £47,600, the sales variance is favourable	✓	
A favourable cost variance occurs when an actual cost of £9,800 is compared to a budgeted cost of £24 per unit for a budgeted output of 400 units		✓
A variance arises from a comparison of budgeted costs for last year with actual costs for this year		✓
If actual material costs are the same as budgeted costs for materials then no variance arises	✓	

143 LANCASTER LTD

Statement	True	False
If budgeted sales are 14,000 units at £3.50 per unit and actual sales are £45,200, the sales variance is favourable		✓
An adverse cost variance occurs when an actual cost of £68,400 is compared to a budgeted cost of £14 per unit for a budgeted output of 5,000 units		✓
A variance arises from a comparison of budgeted costs for this year with actual costs for this year	✓	
If actual material costs are the same as budgeted costs for materials then the materials variance is favourable		✓

144 GOODE LTD

Statement	True	False
The variance for the Direct Material cost of Department B should be reported to the purchasing manager	✓	
The variance for the Direct Labour cost for Department A should be reported to the sales manager		✓
The variance for the Direct Labour cost for Department B should be reported to the production manager of Department A		✓
A Direct Material cost variance that has been deemed Not Significant should not be reported	✓	

145 BROWN LTD

Statement	True	False
The variance for the Direct Material cost of Department A should be reported to the purchasing manager	✓	
The variance for the Direct Labour cost for Department A should be reported to the production manager of Department B		✓
The variance for sales should be reported to the sales manager	✓	
A Direct Material cost variance that has been deemed Significant should not be reported		✓

Direct labour	110,556	107,950	F	NS
Production overheads	14,190	12,500	F	S
Non-production overheads	16,190	17,880	A	S

146 BLUEBELL LTD

Cost type	Budget £	Actual £	Variance £	Adverse/ Favourable	%
Sales	£204,555	£197,455	7,100	A	3
Direct materials	£39,000	£42,300	3,300	A	8
Direct labour	£75,000	£83,000	8,000	A	11
Production overheads	£69,000	£64,800	4,200	F	6
Administration overheads	£53,000	£58,900	5,900	A	11

147 TRIUMPH LTD

Task 1

Statement	Fixed	Variable	Semi-variable
At 9,000 units this cost is £29,250, and at 12,000 units it is £39,000		✓	
At 5,000 units this cost is £5.20 per unit, and at 8,000 units it is £3.25 per unit	✓		
At 19,800 units, this cost is £64,500, and at 27,000 units it is £82,500			✓

Proof of variable and fixed costs:

£29,250 ÷ 9,000 units = £3.25, £39,000 ÷ 12,000 units = £3.25, therefore variable cost

5,000 units × £5.20 = £26,000, 8,000 units × £3.25 = £26,000, therefore fixed cost

£64,500 ÷ 19,800 units = £3.26, £82,500 ÷ 27,000 units = £3.06, therefore must be a **semi-variable** cost – it cannot be fixed (it changes as the number of units changes) and it cannot be purely variable as the cost per unit changes at different levels of activity.

Task 2

	6,000 units	7,000 units	10,000 units	14,000 units
Variable cost (£)	18,000			42,000
Fixed cost (£)	24,000			24,000
Total cost (£)	42,000	45,000	54,000	66,000

Using the hi-lo method:

For the volumes given, difference in costs = 54,000 – 45,000 = £9,000

Difference in volumes = 10,000 – 7,000 = 3,000 units

Therefore variable cost per unit = £9,000 ÷ 3,000 units = £3/unit

At 10,000 units, fixed costs = £54,000 – (10,000 × £3) = £24,000

148 BUNGLE LTD

Statement	True	False
Total variable costs will decrease.		✓
Total fixed costs will remain the same.	✓	
The variable cost per unit will remain the same.	✓	
The fixed cost per unit will increase.		✓

149 TF

Statement	True	False
Variable costs change directly with changes in activity.	✓	✓
Fixed costs change directly with changes in activity.		
Stepped costs are fixed within a set range of output.	✓	

150 GLACIER

Event performance report				
Cost	Budget (£)	Actual (£)	Variance (£)	Adverse/ Favourable
Licence cost	1,500	1,250	250	Favourable ▽
Funds				
Sponsorship funds raised	25,000	27,200	2,200	Favourable ▽

Note that the licence cost variance is favourable as the actual cost was less than the budgeted cost. The sponsorship funds raised exceeded the amount expected, and this variance is therefore a favourable variance.

151 BERLINE

Event cost performance report					
Cost	Budget (£)	Actual (£)	Variance (£)	Adverse/ Favourable	Significant
Refreshments	2,000	2,250	250	Adverse ▽	Yes ▽
Magazine	1,000	950	50	Favourable ▽	No ▽

Note that there is an adverse variance for the cost of refreshments. This is significant as the actual cost was more than 4% in excess of the budgeted cost. There is a favourable variance for the cost of producing the magazine. As this is a favourable variance, it does not need to be identified as significant. Only adverse variances of more than 4% are regarded as significant.

Section 8

ANSWERS TO PRACTICE QUESTIONS

AO4 COMMUNICATE FINANCIAL INFORMATION EFFECTIVELY

152 MRS MAY

> Dear Mrs May,
>
> Invoice 3576 – 10 units of ZXY
>
> I have recently checked the details of your invoice 3576 relating to the purchase of 10 units of product ZXY. The unit price stated on the invoice of £63 is incorrect; it should be £36.
>
> Please issue a credit note to cancel your invoice 3576 and issue a new invoice using the correct unit price of £36. When we have received the credit note and corrected invoice, I will arrange to make payment to you.
>
> Yours sincerely
>
> Financial Assistant

153 BILLY

> Dear Billy,
>
> I was very cheesed to here that you did not receive your goods in proper working order. We have very strict internal procedures, which are designed to prevent faulty goods reaching our customers. Please rest assured that we are investigating fully you're case and are striving to ensure that this does not happen again in the future.
>
> By way of an apolojy we will be refunding you in full and offering you a 20% discount on your next purchase,
>
> Kind regards
>
> John Anderson
>
> Store manager

154 MR CADBURY

Dear Mr Cadbury

I enclose a copy of the invoice which **your** requested during **are** telephone conversation this morning.

Please note this invoice is dated **31** June and **therefor** is overdue for payment.

I look forward to receiving your cheque in full settlement by return of post.

Yours **faithfully**

155 JEEPERS LTD

(a)

Cost	Yes	No
• Materials used in production.	✓	
• Piecework labour costs.	✓	
• Salary of chief executive.		✓

(b)

Element	Unit product cost
Materials	£35
Labour	£8
Direct cost	£43
Overheads	£38
Total	£81

156 GLORIA LTD

(a)

Element	Unit cost	Total cost for 20,000 units
Variable production costs	£5.50	£110,000
Fixed production costs	£4.00	£80,000
Total production cost	£9.50	£190,000

(b)

During the meeting I will explain what a fixed production cost is, and provide an example of a fixed production cost. I will also explain what a variable production cost is, and provide an example of a variable production cos. I will then explain what a semi-variable cost is, and provide an example of a semi-variable cost. Finally, I will explain what happens to variable and fixed production costs if output increases from 20,000 units to 25,000 units.

A fixed production cost is one that does not change with the level of output. An example of a fixed production cost is factory rent. Factory rent will not change, irrespective of whether output is 20,000 or 25,000 units.

A **variable production cost** is one that changes with the level of output. An example of a variable production cost is the direct labour cost. For example, it may require two hours of labour at £12 per hour to product a unit of production.

If output increased from 20,000 units to 25,000 the fixed production cost (e.g. factory rent) will not change. However, the total variable production costs (e.g. direct labour cost) will change if output increases. Using the information in the previous paragraph, the total direct labour cost will increase by (2 hours × £12.00 × 5,000 units) £120,000.

157 BIZARRO LTD

(a)

Element	Unit cost	Total cost
Materials	£45.00	£765,000
Labour	£9.00	£153,000
Overheads	£2.50	£42,500
Total	£56.50	£960,500

(b)

During the meeting I will explain what the different methods of paying employees, including providing an example of each method of pay.

Basic pay is the payment made based upon hours worked, irrespective of what the employee actually does during those hours. For example, an employee may be paid at £250 per a standard working week of 35 hours, or a fixed salary of £1,000 per month.

Bonus pay is an amount earned in addition to basic pay for achieving or exceeding a target. For example, a bonus of £5 per unit may be paid if an employee exceeds their weekly production target of 75 units per week. No bonus will be paid if the employee produced 75 or fewer units in a week.

Overtime pay is an amount earned in addition to basic pay for additional hours worked in a given time period. Overtime is often paid at a premium rate in excess of the rate of basic pay. For example, An employee may be paid at a basic rate of £15 per hour for a 35-hour working week. If they work an extra 5 hours in excess of 35 hours in a specified week, they will be paid overtime at a rate of 'time and a half' for the additional hours. They would be paid at an increased hourly rate of £22.50 for the additional five hours worked.

158 VINNY LTD

Element	Unit cost	Total cost
Materials	£5.00	£100,000
Labour	£8.00	£160,000
Overheads	£5.00	£100,000
Total	£18.00	£360,000

159 DARKSEID LTD

Element	Unit cost
Materials	£3.50
Labour	£6.75
Fixed overheads	£2.42
Total	£12.67

160 EREBOR LTD

(a)

Cost type	Budget £	Actual £	Variance £	Adverse or favourable (A or F)
Sales	600,500	597,800	2,700	A
Direct materials	205,800	208,500	2,700	A
Direct labour	155,000	154,800	200	F
Production overheads	65,000	72,100	7,100	A
Administration overheads	58,400	55,200	3,200	F

(b)

Report to the Warehouse Manager

Methods of inventory valuation

This report explains the three different methods of inventory valuation

FIFO (first in, first out)

This method of inventory valuation assumes that the first units received are the first units used or issued from stores. Therefore, the inventory valuation will be based upon the cost of the most recently received items.

AVCO (average cost)

This method bases the inventory valuation upon the average cost of units received during the accounting period. A new average cost is calculated each time prior to an issue ur usage to accommodate any recent receipts into stores.

LIFO (last in, first out)

This method of inventory valuation assumes that the most recently received units are the first units used or issued from stores. Consequently, the inventory valuation will be based upon the cost of the oldest items.

161 BELEGOST LTD

(a)

	Budget £	Actual £	Adverse or Favourable (A or F)	Significant or Not significant (S or NS)
Sales	205,000	207,100	F	NS
Direct materials	75,150	78,750	A	NS
Direct labour	110,556	107,950	F	NS
Production overheads	14,190	12,500	F	S
Non-production overheads	16,190	17,880	A	S

(b)

Report to the Production Manager

Variances and their investigation

Introduction

This report explains what a variance is. It then goes on to explain why only significant variances may be investigated by an organisation.

Variance explanation

A variance is a difference between what was expected to occur and what has actually happened. This is usually resented in monetary terms, or as a percentage of the budgeted figure. A variance may be either favourable, e.g. when actual cost is less than budgeted cost or it may be adverse e.g. when actual cost exceeds budgeted cost.

Investigation of variances

Normally, a business will investigate only significant variances. This is because significant variances are an indication of possible significant issues that were not anticipated or expected when the budget was prepared. Following investigation, appropriate action can be taken to rectify the problem.

162 MORIA LTD

(a)

Cost type	Budget	Variance	Variance as % of budget	Significant or Not significant
Sales	45,100	4,214	9	S
Material	15,750	1,260	8	S
Labour	12,915	805	6	NS
Variable overheads	5,750	315	5	NS
Fixed overheads	8,155	1,011	12	S

(b)

Notes for meeting with colleague

Direct cost and manufacturing cost of a product

During the meeting I will explain what the direct cost of a product is and what the manufacturing cost of a product is.

The direct cost of production comprises the cost of all direct raw materials used during the production period, plus the direct labour cost for the production period. This will include materials and components used in the manufacturing process to produce the finish product, along with manufacturing labour costs.

The manufacturing cost of production includes the direct cost of production plus manufacturing overheads. Manufacturing overheads include items such as heat, fuel and power costs for the factory.

Section 9

MOCK ASSESSMENT QUESTIONS

Scenario: The tasks are set in a business situation where the following conditions apply:

- You are employed as an accounts assistant in the financial accounting function at MM Manufacturing (MM).

- MM uses a manual bookkeeping system.

- Double entry takes place in the general ledger. Individual accounts of trade receivables and trade payables are kept in the sales and purchases ledgers as subsidiary accounts.

- The cash book and petty cash book should be treated as part of the double entry system unless the task instructions state otherwise.

- The VAT rate is 20%.

TASK 1.1   **(12 marks)**

Your workload for the week has been prepared by your supervisor and is listed in the table below. Your hours of work are 9am to 5pm with an hour for lunch from 12.00 to 13.00. There is a compulsory staff meeting on a Monday afternoon at 1pm, which lasts for one hour. You are required to take the minutes of this meeting.

In the event of any clash of workload activities, priority should be given to the tasks which are performed on a daily basis.

Task	Task to be completed by:		Task Duration
	Day	Time	
Complete supplier payment run.	Thursday	14.00	2 hours
Perform supplier statement reconciliations	Wednesday	17.00	2 hours
Answer customer and supplier emails	Daily	12.00	1 hour
Bank reconciliation	Friday	17.00	2 hours
Process purchase invoices	Tuesday	15.00	3 hours
Prepare banking summary	Daily	10.00	1 hour
Process sales invoices	Mon & Thurs	17.00	2 hours each
Prepare sales invoices	Thursday	16.00	2 hours
Prepare bank payments information	Wed & Fri	16.00	2 hours each

---

Your supervisor has sent you the following email:

Hi,

I have been asked to prepare a report for senior management relating to the petty cash expenditure of the business, as it seems to be increasing quite dramatically. I require you to prepare an analysis of petty cash expenditure for the previous month, which should take no longer than 1 hour to complete. My meeting is at 16.00 on Wednesday afternoon and I require this information by 14.00 on Wednesday.

Thank you

(a) **Complete a to-do list for Wednesday in order of priority. If an activity takes more than one hour, it can be done in stages as long as the task is completed by the required time. Daily tasks should be prioritised ahead of other tasks. Identify any lack of time to complete the required tasks separately.** (4 marks)

To-do List – Wednesday	
	9.00 – 10.00
	10.00 – 11.00
	11.00 – 12.00
Lunch	12.00 – 13.00
	13.00 – 14.00
	14.00 – 15.00
	15.00 – 16.00
	16.00 – 17.00
Lack of time	

(b) **Identify on which day, and which hours, you will be busiest with routine tasks. If an activity takes more than one hour, it can be done in stages as long as the task is completed by the required time. Identify any lack of time to complete the required tasks separately.** (4 marks)

To-do List	
	9.00 – 10.00
	10.00 – 11.00
	11.00 – 12.00
Lunch	12.00 – 13.00
	13.00 – 14.00
	14.00 – 15.00
	15.00 – 16.00
	16.00 – 17.00
Lack of time	

(c)   Identify what you should do in the event that you find you have too many activities planned on the 'to-do' list prepared by your supervisor.   **(1 mark)**

Course of action	Tick as appropriate
Advise your supervisor at the end of the day that you could not complete all work that was in your 'to-do' list	
Try to complete all tasks within the available time, but don't be concerned if work is left uncompleted	
Panic about not completing work and decide to work part of your lunch-hour and/or work late in the evening	
Discuss your workload at an early stage with your supervisor to prioritise tasks within the available time	
Leave it to your supervisor to find out whether or not work has been completed when expected	

You realise that you have two petty cash receipts, one for the purchase of some stationery supplies from a local business at a cost of £23.50 plus VAT, and the other for purchase of office cleaning materials at a cost of £29.34 inclusive of VAT.

(d)   **What will be the combined amounts included in your petty cash claim form to record the two transactions?**   **(2 marks)**

Net amount   £ [   ]

VAT amount   £ [   ]

Total amount   £ [   ]

After you have claimed your petty cash claim, you are advised that there is still a balance of cash amounting to £27.74.

(e)   **What will be the accounting entries required to record the amount required to restore the petty cash float to the imprest amount of £125.00?**   **(1 marks)**

Item	Debit entry	Credit entry
Cash book	£	£
Petty cash	£	£

TASK 2   **(12 marks)**

1.2

Scenario:

In response to employee feedback, MM Manufacturing has recently recruited a new Head of Corporate Communications, Louise Hardy. She has decided to introduce a monthly newsletter, to which all departments will have the opportunity to contribute. Contributions to the newsletter could be work-related or may also include news of other articles such as publication and explanation of corporate policies.

You have been asked to contribute to the first newsletter on behalf of the financial accounting department to make suggestions that may help employees in other departments to understand the work of the financial accounting department.

(a) From the list below, identify FOUR suggestions that may help employees in other departments to understand the work of the financial accounting department.

(4 marks)

Monthly Newsletter Number 1

Suggestions to help employees in other departments to understand the work of the financial accounting department.

∇ Drop down list for task 1.2 (a):

Benefits:

Produce only a printed copy of the newsletter which is made available in the staff refectory
Introduce cross-departmental teams to deal with issues and policies which affect the organisation as a whole
Introduce a system of compulsory secondment of individuals to work in other departments, irrespective of the business needs and of the skills, qualifications and experience an individual may have
Quarterly meetings with departmental representatives to explain what information the financial accounting department requires from each department, and why that information is needed
There is no need to introduce additional communication between departments
Each department should nominate a 'lead person' who would liaise and communicate with a nominated member of the financial accounting department, with both individuals feeding back comments to members of their own department as necessary
Leave it to individual employees to contact the financial accounting department if they would like information on what the financial accounting department does.
Introduce a 'buddy' system to enable an individual to shadow a member of the financial accounting department, perhaps for a day, so that they can gain a better understanding of how the work of the financial accounting department interacts with their own department

Louise has now been working at MM Manufacturing for three months and has decided that all staff should have awareness of how their work may impact upon the financial solvency of the organisation. She would like the next edition of the monthly newsletter to focus on this topic and has asked you to prepare a list of actions that the financial accounting department could introduce to improve solvency.

(b) **From the list below, identify FOUR actions to help improve solvency by dragging them into the monthly newsletter.** (4 marks)

Monthly Newsletter
Suggested ways for the financial accounting department to improve solvency

▽ Drop down list for task 1.2 (b):

Suggestions to improve solvency:

Renegotiate credit terms offered to credit customers and shorten the agreed credit period
Maintain the maximum possible level of inventory for all products so that, if an order is received, it can be fulfilled immediately
Monitor inventory levels so that goods are only manufactured when customers have ordered goods
Renegotiate credit terms with credit suppliers and shorten the agreed credit period
Identify alternative suppliers who can supply the goods and services required at a reduced price, or will offer bulk-purchase discounts
Rent or hire items of equipment which ae used only occasionally, rather than purchasing them and leaving them unused for periods of time
Purchase new items of plant and machinery now for new products that the organisation intends to commence production of in two years' time
Retain items of plant and equipment that are no longer need, rather than selling them.

The finance director, Ed Stone, wants to introduce a new accounting system into MM Manufacturing and is selecting members of a project team to implement the new system. The new system will integrate the financial accounting and management accounting systems, along with payroll and inventory management. He would like you to be a member of the team and has asked you to propose four colleagues that you feel have the attributes to work well within the project team.

To help you decide you have made some notes about each member of staff, as shown below.

Name	Experience	Brief assessment of skills and attributes
Che	Management accounts and inventory	Popular member of the department with excellent communication skills. Recognised as an 'IT geek' by colleagues who use him to resolve IT problems.
Evita	All areas of the finance function	An employee of MM Manufacturing for almost 30 years. Senior financial accountant, who has also worked as a management accountant. A good technical understanding of accounting issues, but finds IT systems problematic.
Nicola	Trainee in all areas of the finance function	A new, but inexperienced, colleague as who has recently left college. She does appear to be a confident person and is settling in well as a member of the finance team. Limited practical experience and has not yet started studying for professional accounting exams.
Leon	Financial accounting and management accounting	Good knowledge of current systems and also has a general knowledge of management and financial accounting processes. He is highly organised with good written communication skills.
Faisal	All areas of the finance function	Tends to work on his own, although he does appear to be efficient and organised. Tends not to speak or communicate during staff meetings.
Imelda	Financial accounting and Payroll	Excellent verbal communication skills and is normally focussed upon completion of work tasks and activities with positive results. She is respected by colleagues for her 'can do' attitude.
Nelson	Financial and management accounting	Basic knowledge of financial and management accounts, communicates well with close friends, does not communicate well in wider departmental activities. Has no experience of MM Manufacturing outwith his accounting work.
Benito	Inventory and payroll	Good knowledge of payroll systems and was a key member of a previous IT implementation team. He has very strong verbal communication skills and also has experience of inventory management.

(c) **Identify the FOUR members of staff that would be most effective as part of the project team.** **(4 marks)**

Che		Evita		Nicola		Leon	

Faisal		Imelda		Nelson		Benito	

TASK 1.3 **(12 marks)**

You have received the purchase invoice below from a credit supplier. The supplier has agreed to allow a 5% bulk discount off the list price of £0.80 per item.

Carter & Co

91 Mercer Street, Monkchester, MK16 8ST
VAT Registration No. 478 9245 01

Invoice No. 0369

To: MM Manufacturing   18 June 20X8
      5 Liverpool Way
      Blayton BA42 5YZ

                                                                £
1,500 ... Product CD693 @ £0.80 each   1,200.00
VAT @ 20%   240.00
                                                         _____
                                                         1440.00
                                                         _____

Terms of payment: Net monthly account

You notice that the invoice amounts are incorrect.

(a) **What should be the correct amounts of the invoice?** **(3 marks)**

Net £	VAT £	Total £

You have received another invoice from Carter & Co whose account code is CAR768. There was no bulk discount offered for this order but Carter & Co has offered a prompt payment discount. You are ready to enter this invoice into the appropriate daybook

---

Carter & Co

91 Mercer Street, Monkchester, MK16 8ST

VAT Registration No. 478 9245 01

Invoice No. 0375

To: MM Manufacturing   20 June 20X8
       5 Liverpool Way
       Blayton BA42 5YZ

                                                                          £
350 ... Product CD680 @ £0.65 each   227.50
VAT @ 20%   45.50
                                                                 _____
                                                                     273.00
                                                                 _____

Terms of payment: 4% discount for payment within 10 days of date of invoice

---

(b)   **Complete the entries in the daybook below by:**

- **selecting the correct daybook title, and**

- **making the necessary entries.**   **(7 marks)**

Title	▽

▽ Drop down list for task 1.3 (b):

Discounts allowed daybook
Discounts received daybook
Purchases daybook
Purchases returns daybook
Sales daybook
Sales returns daybook

Date 20X8	Details	Supplier account code	Invoice number	Total £	VAT £	Net £	Product CD693	Product CD680
20 June	▽	▽	0375					

▽ Drop down lists for task 1.3 (b):

Details
Carter & Co
MM Manufacturing

Supplier account code
CAR768
CD693
CD680

You must now prepare a payment to the supplier for invoice 0375 in order to take advantage of the prompt payment discount offered.

(c)   **What will be the amount paid and what is the latest date by which the supplier should receive payment?**   **(2 marks)**

Amount to be paid £	Date by which payment should be received
	▽

▽ Drop down list for task 1.3 (c):

18 June 20X8
20 June 20X8
28 June 20X8
30 June 20X8
18 July 20X8
20 July 20X8

TASK 1.4   (16 marks)

Scenario

It is now 7 July 20X8 and you are reconciling the bank statement with the cash book as at 30 June. The bank statement shows a bank overdraft of £1,959 and the cash book shows a credit bank balance of £1,449.

You have checked the bank statement against the cash book and made a note of the unmatched items, as shown below.

Unmatched items on bank statement:
• A direct debit payment to Blayton Council of £540
• A BACS receipt from Alpha Products of £620
Unmatched items in cash book
• A cheque from a credit customer, Acme Ltd, of £850
• A cheque sent to a credit supplier, Darke Supplies, of £260.

(a)   **Show the entries needed to update the cash book by:**   **(4 marks)**

- **selecting which TWO items will be entered in the cash book**

- **showing whether each item selected will be a debit or credit entry.**

Item	Enter in cash book	Debit entry	Credit entry
Blayton Council	☐	☐	☐
Alpha Products	☐	☐	☐
Acme Ltd	☐	☐	☐
Darke Supplies	☐	☐	☐

(b) **Complete the bank reconciliation statement as at 30 June 20X8.** **(6 marks)**

Bank reconciliation statement	£
Balance as per bank statement – overdraft	
Add: item to increase overdraft	
▽	
Less: item to reduce overdraft	
▽	
Balance as per cash book (CR)	

▽ Drop down list for task 4 (b):

Blayton Council
Alpha Products
Acme Ltd
Darke Supplies

Having just completed the bank reconciliation statement, you are aware that the bank overdraft is close to the agreed overdraft limit of £2,500. You estimate that payments to credit suppliers in July 20X8 are likely to be likely to be £4,500 and receipts from credit customers will be £3,600. In accordance with organisational policy the Head of Treasury Services, Joann Davis, is to be advised so that funds can be transferred from elsewhere to ensure that the bank account remains within its authorised limit. An email needs to be written, dated 7 July 20X8, to Joann Davis (jdavis@MMManufacturing.com) from accounts@MMManufacturing.com.

(c) **Write an email to Joann Davis. You should include information on the expected payments and receipts in July and request funds to be transferred from another account so that the overdraft limit is not exceeded. The email can be finished with your job title, Accounts Assistant.** **(6 marks)**

From:
To:
Subject:
Date

TASK 1.5 (12 marks)

Scenario

MM Manufacturing has developed a strong commitment to identify and introduce suitable Corporate Social Responsibility initiatives (CSR) with a particular focus upon sustainability. You have been invited to join a team that has been asked to compile a report which outlines the sustainability initiatives planned for the year ahead.

(a) Drag **TWO** appropriate statements to create the introduction to the Corporate Social Responsibility and Sustainability Report below. (2 marks)

	Statements
MM Manufacturing Corporate Social Responsibility and Sustainability Report	being a responsible business by requiring all employees to have a personal development plan which is reviewed annually
Introduction	being a responsible business by sourcing goods from suppliers who have a similar commitment to sustainability and who publish their sustainability policies and the results of applying those policies
MM Manufacturing is committed to:	being a responsible business and paying all employees at least 5% in excess of the national minimum wage
	being a responsible business and minimising the adverse impact our activities have upon sustainability and the environment
	being responsible business by buying materials from suppliers without considering the impact our suppliers may have on sustainability and the environment

(b) Drag FOUR appropriate initiatives in the local community and wider society section of the Corporate Social Responsibility and Sustainability report below. **(4 marks)**

	Initiatives:
MM Manufacturing Products Corporate Social Responsibility and Sustainability Report	Ensuring that all employees are able to pursue further education opportunities and study for appropriate professional qualifications
Our commitment to improving the local community and wider society. **Initiatives planned that will directly impact on the local community and wider society:**	Developing links with local schools and colleges to offer work experience programmes to final year students
	Purchasing staff laptops and PCs that conform to current best practice for energy conservation
	Donating surplus office equipment to a local day care centre
	Permitting employees two days leave of absence each year to use for charitable purposes, such as volunteering at a local charity or school
	Holding a company meeting every six months which require all employees to travel to a central location from numerous locations throughout the UK
	Ensuring that the organisation maximises profits by any means, so that they can pay more tax on those profits
	Choosing a local charity to sponsor and support throughout the following year

In support of its current CSR commitment, MM Manufacturing instigated a project to install more energy efficient equipment in the packing and despatch department which was completed last month.

You have been asked by your supervisor to complete a budget report for the direct costs incurred on the project. The budget report must clearly indicate whether each variance is favourable or adverse, and whether any variance calculated is significant, that is in excess of 5% of budget.

Budget costs are to be calculated as follows:

Boxes and cartons	3,500 items @ 5.25 per item
Packing paper	500 rolls at £12.50 per roll

Actual costs have already been entered into the report.

(c)   Complete the table below by:

- inserting the budget cost for boxes and packing paper

- inserting the variance for each cost

- selecting whether each variance is favourable or adverse

- selecting whether each variance is significant or not.   **(6 marks)**

Cost	Budget £	Actual £	Variance £	Favourable /Adverse	Significant
		Budget report			
Boxes etc.		19,475		∇	∇
Packaging		6,065		∇	∇

∇ Drop down lists for task 5 (c):

Favourable	Yes
Adverse	No

TASK 1.6   **(24 marks)**

Scenario

You have been seconded to the management accounting department to cover for the illness of a colleague. Your temporary supervisor has asked you to assist in an exercise dealing with cost behaviour exercise for a new product. Although total costs have been estimated for projected minimum and maximum levels of output, she would like a clearer indication of cost behaviour for all levels of output, with a segregation of fixed and variable costs.

(a)   Complete the table below by: **(12 marks)**

- inserting the variable costs for each level of output

- inserting the fixed costs for each level of output

- inserting total costs for 8,000 units and 12,500 units levels of output.

Units	3,000	8,000	12,500	15,000
Variable costs (£)				
Fixed costs (£)				
Total costs (£)	62,500			152,500

(b)   In the box below, write notes in preparation for a meeting you will have with your temporary supervisor, including: (12 marks)

- a brief introduction outlining the areas you will discuss

- an explanation of how fixed and variable costs behave as levels of output change, using your figures in (a) to illustrate your answer

- a re-calculation of the fixed costs you calculated in (a) above, assuming they increased by 5% and provide an explanation of the effect of this on total costs

- an explanation of the effect on the total cost per unit as levels of output increase if fixed costs increased by 10% whilst variable cost per unit remains unchanged.

Your notes must be sufficiently detailed, clearly written and well-structured as they will be a formal record of your meeting discussion.

TASK 1.7 (12 marks)

Scenario

You are preparing for the month end at MM Manufacturing. The following three accounts are an extract from the general ledger.

Discount allowed

Details	Amount £	Details	Amount £
Balance b/f	2,489	Journal	426

Purchases returns

Details	Amount £	Details	Amount £
Journal	1,977	Balance b/f	2,546

Office expenses

Details	Amount £	Details	Amount £
Balance b/f	1,357		
Cash	145		

(a)   What will be the entries in the trial balance? (6 marks)

Account name	Amount £	Debit	Credit
Discount allowed		☐	☐
Purchases returns		☐	☐
Office expenses		☐	☐

You have now completed and totalled the trial balance, but find it does not balance. The credit column is £378 more than the debit column so you have opened a suspense account.

(b)   Will the opening balance in the suspense account be a debit or credit entry?

(1 mark)

Debit   ☐

Credit   ☐

You have identified that the error in the trial balance arose as a result of posting the total of the sales daybook for the final week of June as £13,246 instead of £13,624 in the trade receivables control account ('TRCA'). The entry in the bank account was correct.

You have partially prepared journal entries to correct the error and clear the suspense account.

(c)   Complete each journal entry by inserting the appropriate amount in either the debit or credit column. Do NOT enter a zero in unused debit or credit column cells.

(3 marks)

Journal to remove the incorrect entry

Account name	Debit £	Credit £
TRCA		

Journal to record the correct entry

Account name	Debit £	Credit £
TRCA		

Journal to clear the suspense account

Account name	Debit £	Credit £
Suspense		

The trial balance showed an amount for the trade receivables control account travel of £110,754 before the error was identified.

(d)   What will be the entry in the trial balance following the journal entries in (c)?

(2 marks)

Account name	Amount £	Debit	Credit
TRCA		☐	☐

Section 10

MOCK ASSESSMENT ANSWERS

TASK 1.1 **(12 marks)**

(a)   Complete a to-do list for Wednesday in order of priority. If an activity takes more than one hour, it can be done in stages as long as the task is completed by the required time. Identify any lack of time to complete the required tasks separately.

(4 marks)

To-do List - Wednesday	
Prepare banking summary	9.00 – 10.00
Supplier statement reconciliations	10.00 – 11.00
Customer and supplier emails	11.00 – 12.00
Lunch	12.00 – 13.00
Petty cash analysis	13.00 – 14.00
Bank payments run information	14.00 – 15.00
Bank payments run information	15.00 – 16.00
Supplier statement reconciliations	16.00 – 17.00
Lack of time	

(b)   Identify on which day, and which hours, you will be busiest with routine tasks. If an activity takes more than one hour, it can be done in stages as long as the task is completed by the required time. Daily tasks should be prioritised ahead of other tasks. Identify any lack of time to complete the required tasks separately.   (4 marks)

To-do List Thursday	
Prepare banking summary	9.00 – 10.00
Supplier payment run (1 of 2 hours)	10.00 – 11.00
Customer and supplier emails	11.00 – 12.00
Lunch	12.00 – 13.00
Supplier payment run (1 of 2 hours)	13.00 – 14.00
Prepare sales invoices	14.00 – 15.00
Prepare sales invoices	15.00 – 16.00
Process sales invoices (1 of 2 hours)	16.00 – 17.00
Lack of time	
Process sales invoices (1 of 2 hours)	1 hour

Note that sales invoices should be prepared before they can be processed.

(c) **Identify what you should do in the event that you find you have too many activities planned on the 'to-do' list prepared by your supervisor.** **(1 mark)**

Course of action	Tick as appropriate
Advise your supervisor at the end of the day that you could not complete all work that was in your 'to-do' list	
Try to complete all tasks within the available time, but don't be concerned if work is left uncompleted	
Panic about not completing work and decide to work part of your lunch-hour and/or work late in the evening	
Discuss your workload at an early stage with your supervisor to prioritise tasks within the available time	✓
Leave it to your supervisor to find out whether or not work has been completed when expected	

(d) **What will be the combined amounts included in your petty cash claim form to record the two transactions?** **(2 marks)**

Net amount	£	47.95
VAT amount	£	9.59
Total amount	£	57.54

(e) **What will be the accounting entries required to record the amount required to restore the petty cash float to the imprest amount of £125.00?** **(1 mark)**

Item	Debit entry	Credit entry
Cash book	£	£97.26
Petty cash	£97.26	£

TASK 1.2 (12 marks)

(a) From the list below, identify FOUR suggestions that may help employees in other departments to understand the work of the financial accounting department.

(4 marks)

Monthly Newsletter Number 1

Suggestions to help employees in other departments to understand the work of the financial accounting department.

Introduce cross-departmental teams to deal with issues and policies which affect the organisation as a whole

Quarterly meetings with departmental representatives to explain what information the financial accounting department requires from each department, and why that information is needed

Each department should nominate a 'lead person' who would liaise and communicate with a nominated member of the financial accounting department, with both individuals feeding back comments to members of their own department as necessary

Introduce a 'buddy' system to enable an individual to shadow a member of the financial accounting department, perhaps for a day, so that they can gain a better understanding of how the work of the financial accounting department interacts with their own department

---

(b) From the list below, identify FOUR actions to help improve solvency by dragging them into the monthly newsletter. (4 marks)

Monthly Newsletter

Suggested ways for the financial accounting department to improve solvency

Renegotiate credit terms offered to credit customers and shorten the agreed credit period

Monitor inventory levels so that goods are only manufactured when customers have ordered goods

Identify alternative suppliers who can supply the goods and services required at a reduced price, or will offer bulk-purchase discounts

Rent or hire items of equipment which ae used only occasionally, rather than purchasing them and leaving them unused for periods of time

---

(c) Identify the FOUR members of staff that would be most effective as part of the project team. (4 marks)

Che	✓	Evita		Nicola		Leon	✓
Faisal		Imelda	✓	Nelson		Benito	✓

TASK 1.3 (12 marks)

(a) What should be the correct amounts of the invoice? (3 marks)

Net £	VAT £	Total £
1,140.00	228.00	1,368.00

(b) Complete the entries in the daybook below by:

- selecting the correct daybook title, and
- making the necessary entries. (7 marks)

Title	Purchases daybook ▽

Date 20X8	Details	Supplier account code	Invoice number	Total £	VAT £	Net £	Product CD693	Product CD680
20 June	Carter & Co ▽	CAR768 ▽	0375	273.00	45.50	227.50		227.50

(c) What will be the amount paid and what is the latest date by which the supplier should receive payment? (2 marks)

Amount to be paid £	Date by which payment should be received
262.08	30 June 20X8 ▽

TASK 1.4 (16 marks)

(a) Show the entries needed to update the cash book by: (4 marks)

- selecting which TWO items will be entered in the cash book
- showing whether each item selected will be a debit or credit entry.

Item	Enter in cash book		Debit entry	Credit entry
Blayton Council	✓			✓
Alpha Products	✓		✓	
Acme Ltd				
Darke Supplies				

(b) Complete the bank reconciliation statement as at 30 June 20X8. **(6 marks)**

Bank reconciliation statement	£
Balance as per bank statement – overdraft	1,959
Add: item to increase overdraft	
Darke Supplies ∇	260
Less: item to reduce overdraft	
Acme Ltd ∇	850
Balance as per cash book (CR)	1,369

(c) Write an email to Joann Davis. You should include information on the expected payments and receipts in July and request funds to be transferred from another account so that the overdraft limit is not exceeded. The mail can be finished with your job title, Accounts Assistant. **(6 marks)**

From:	accounts@MMManufacturing.com
To:	jdavis@MMManufacturing.com
Subject:	Bank account balance
Date	7 July 20X8

Hi Joanne

Following completion of June's bank reconciliation statement, I can advise you that I expect payments of £4,500 and receipts of £3,600 by the end of this month. On that basis I would suggest that some funds should be transferred to the bank account to ensure that the account stays within the authorised limit.

If you require further information, please contact me.

Kind regards

Accounts Clerk

TASK 1.5 **(12 marks)**

(a) Drag TWO appropriate statements to create the introduction to the Corporate Social Responsibility and Sustainability Report below. **(2 marks)**

MM Manufacturing **Corporate Social Responsibility and Sustainability Report**
Introduction
MM Manufacturing is committed to:
being a responsible business by sourcing goods from suppliers who have a similar commitment to sustainability and who publish their sustainability policies and the results of applying those policies
being a responsible business and minimising the adverse impact our activities have upon sustainability and the environment

(b) Drag FOUR appropriate initiatives in the local community and wider society section of the Corporate Social Responsibility and Sustainability report below. **(4 marks)**

MM Manufacturing Products **Corporate Social Responsibility and Sustainability Report**
Our commitment to improving the local community and wider society.
Initiatives planned that will directly impact on the local community and wider society:
Developing links with local schools and colleges to offer work experience programmes to final year students
Donating surplus office equipment to a local day care centre
Permitting employees two days leave of absence each year to use for charitable purposes, such as volunteering at a local charity or school
Choosing a local charity to sponsor and support throughout the following year

(c) Complete the table below by:

- inserting the budget cost for boxes and packing paper

- inserting the variance for each cost

- selecting whether each variance is favourable or adverse

- selecting whether each variance is significant or not. **(6 marks)**

	Budget report				
Cost	**Budget £**	**Actual £**	**Variance £**	**Favourable /Adverse**	**Significant**
Boxes etc.	18,375	19,475	1,100	Adverse ▽	Yes ▽
Packaging	6,250	6,065	185	Favourable ▽	No ▽

TASK 1.6 **(24 marks)**

(a) Complete the table below by: **(12 marks)**

- inserting the variable costs for each level of output

- inserting the fixed costs for each level of output

- inserting total costs for 8,000 units and 12,500 units levels of output.

Units	3,000	8,000	12,500	15,000
Variable costs (£)	22,500	60,000	93,750	112,500
Fixed costs (£)	40,000	40,000	40,000	40,000
Total costs (£)	62,500	100,000	133,750	152,500

Proof of split of total cost:

Total cost at 15,000 units = £152,500 and total cost at 3,000 units = £62,500
Difference in total cost = variable costs = £90,000 spread over 12, 000 units
Variable cost per unit = £90,000/12,000 = £7.50.
For 15,000 units, if total cost is £152,500, and total variable cost is calculated as £112,500 (15,000 × £7.50), then fixed costs must be £40,000.

(b) **In the box below, write notes in preparation for a meeting you will have with your temporary supervisor, including:** **(12 marks)**

- **a brief introduction outlining the areas you will discuss**

- **an explanation of how fixed and variable costs behave as levels of output change, using your figures in (a) to illustrate your answer**

- **a re-calculation of the fixed costs you calculated in (a) above, assuming they increased by 5% and provide an explanation of the effect of this on total costs**

- **an explanation of the effect on the total cost per unit as levels of output increase if fixed costs increased by 10% whilst variable cost per unit remains unchanged.**

Your notes must be sufficiently detailed, clearly written and well-structured as they will be a formal record of your meeting discussion.

During the meeting I will discuss the behaviour of fixed costs and variable costs at different levels of output. I will also discuss the impact of an increase in fixed costs upon total costs. In conclusion, I will explain the effect of a 10% increase in fixed costs on the total cost per unit as levels of output increase.

Fixed costs do not change as the level of output changes. Using the cost information for the new product, fixed costs were calculated to be £40,000 and they do not change. The variable cost was calculated as £7.50 per unit for the new product. As output increases, the total variable costs will increase by £7.50 per unit.

If fixed costs increase by 5%, they will increase from £40,000 to £42,000, and this will remain unchanged, irrespective of the level of output. The total cost of production will therefore consist of fixed costs of £42,000 plus a variable cost of £7.50 per unit. As the level of output increases, total costs will increase, but the total cost per unit will fall as the fixed costs will be spread over an increased number of units produced.

If fixed costs increase by 10% from the original calculation, then fixed costs will be £44,000. As before, they will remain unchanged if the level of output changes. Total cost will therefore increase by £4,000 for each level of output, and will consequently increase the total cost per unit. Note that the increase in total cost per unit will be smaller as the level of output increases. This is because fixed costs will be spread over a greater number of units produced.

TASK 1.7 (12 marks)

(a) What will be the entries in the trial balance? (6 marks)

Account name	Amount £	Debit	Credit
Discount allowed	2,063	✓	☐
Purchases returns	569	☐	✓
Office expenses	1,502	✓	☐

(b) Will the opening balance in the suspense account be a debit or credit entry? (1 mark)

Debit ✓

Credit ☐

(c) Complete each journal entry by inserting the appropriate amount in either the debit or credit column. Do NOT enter a zero in unused debit or credit column cells. (3 marks)

Journal to remove the incorrect entry

Account name	Debit £	Credit £
TRCA		13,246

Journal to record the correct entry

Account name	Debit £	Credit £
TRCA	13,624	

Journal to clear the suspense account

Account name	Debit £	Credit £
Suspense		378

(d) What will be the entry in the trial balance following the journal entries in (c)? (2 marks)

Account name	Amount £	Debit	Credit
TRCA	111,132	✓	☐

AAT AQ2016

SAMPLE ASSESSMENT 2

FOUNDATION SYNOPTIC ASSESSMENT

Time allowed: 2 hours

Scenario: The tasks are set in a business situation where the following conditions apply:

- You are employed as an accounts assistant in the finance function at SCM Products.

- The finance function includes the financial and management accounting teams.

- SCM Products uses a manual bookkeeping system.

- Double entry takes place in the general ledger. Individual accounts of trade receivables and trade payables are kept in the sales and purchases ledgers as subsidiary accounts.

- The cash book and petty cash book should be treated as part of the double entry system unless the task instructions state otherwise.

- The VAT rate is 20%.

TASK 1   (12 marks)

Each week you work Monday to Friday from 09.00 until 16.00, and you are required to take lunch between 12.00 and 13.00. Each finance period is four weeks in duration so you plan your work in a four-week cycle.

The work schedules below show the days when routine tasks must be completed and the amount of time each task takes to complete. It is very important that you complete the management accounts tasks by the end of the identified day and the financial accounts tasks by the day and time indicated.

Monthly work schedules – management accounts					
	Monday	**Tuesday**	**Wednesday**	**Thursday**	**Friday**
Week 1	Material cost report (1 hour)		Material cost report (1hour)	Budget report (1 hour)	Product cost analysis (1 hour)
Week 2	Labour cost report (2 hours)			Budget report (1 hour)	Product cost analysis (2 hours)
Week 3		Labour cost report (1 hour)	Process invoices (1 hour)		
Week 4	Data gathering (1 hour)	Labour cost report (1 hour)		Variance analysis (1 hour)	Cost coding (2 hours)

Weekly work schedule – financial accounts			
Task	**Task to be completed each week by:**		**Task duration**
	Day	**Time**	
Reconcile statements	Friday	13.00	1 hour
Contact customers	Tuesday	13.00	2 hours
Post cheques	Every day	11.00	1 hour
Contact suppliers	Monday	11.00	1 hour
Departmental report	Wednesday	12.00	1 hour
Departmental charges	Thursday	12.00·	2 hours

You are planning your work at the start of the day on Friday of week 4. You are required to attend a one-hour departmental meeting at 14.00 and you have also been asked to complete a non-routine petty cash book task by 10.00. Both of these tasks are already included on your to-do list.

1.1

(a) **Complete your to-do list for today, Friday of week 4. Refer to the management and financial accounts schedules and drag the tasks to be completed into the to-do list below.** **(5 marks)**

Note: You should drag a task into the to-do list more than once if the task takes more than one hour to complete.

Tasks:

Budget report	Lunch
Contact customers	Material cost report
Contact suppliers	Post cheques
Cost coding	Process invoices
Data gathering	Product cost analysis
Departmental charges	Reconcile statements
Departmental report	Variance analysis
Labour cost report	

Friday, week 4 to-do list	Time
Petty cash book	09.00 – 10.00
	10.00 – 11.00
	11.00 – 12.00
	12.00 – 13.00
	13.00 – 14.00
Departmental meeting	14.00 – 15.00
	15.00 – 16.00

(b) **Identify the week in which you are least busy with tasks from the management and financial accounts schedules.** **(1 mark)**

▽ Drop down list for task 1.1 (b):

Week number
Week 1
Week 2
Week 3
Week 4

The petty cash task in your to-do list requires you to begin by entering a petty cash payment of £31.62 including VAT into the petty cash book.

(c) **What will be the amounts entered in the petty cash book to record this transaction?** **(3 marks)**

Net amount   £ ☐

VAT amount   £ ☐

Total amount   £ ☐

You must now balance the petty cash book. The petty cash book shows a debit total of £150.00 and a credit total of £98.67.

(d) **What will be the amount of the balance carried down?** **(1 mark)**

£ ☐

(e) **What will be the entry in the petty cash book to record the cash withdrawn from the bank to restore the imprest level of £150?** **(2 marks)**

Amount £	Debit	Credit
	☐	☐

TASK 2 (12 marks)

1.2

Scenario:

SCM Products has recruited a new Head of Finance, Rajesh Kumar, who wants to improve performance within the finance function. He has decided to introduce a system of weekly bulletins, prepared by finance staff, highlighting key aspects of their work.

You have been asked to contribute to the first week's bulletin and have decided to focus on the importance of finance staff establishing good business relationships.

(a) From the list below, identify **FOUR** benefits of finance staff at SCM Products establishing good business relationships by dragging them into the weekly bulletin.

(4 marks)

Weekly Bulletin Number 1
What are the benefits of finance staff establishing good working relationships?

∇ Drop down list for task 1.2 (a):

Benefits:

To build trust which may result in better sharing of information
To develop customer confidence which may result in them remaining solvent
To create improved communication channels which may improve efficiency
To build a better reputation which may lead to suppliers offering less credit
To develop respect which may assist in resolving disputes
To create communications that are fit for purpose and always understood
To build loyalty from customers which may lead to improved sales
To develop supplier confidence and ensure they maintain confidentiality

Rajesh has now been working at SCM Products for two months and has decided finance staff should be more aware of how their activities impact on solvency. He wants this week's bulletin to focus on this topic and has asked you to prepare a list of actions to help improve solvency.

(b) **From the list below, identify FOUR actions to help improve solvency by dragging them into the weekly bulletin.** **(4 marks)**

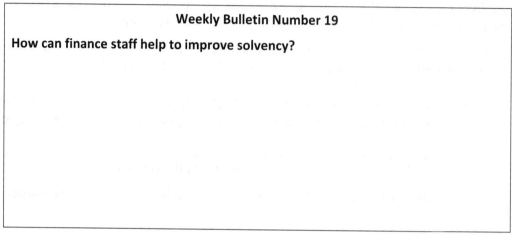

Weekly Bulletin Number 19

How can finance staff help to improve solvency?

∇ Drop down list for task 1.2 (b):

Benefits:

Extend the payment terms of all credit customers
Monitor bank balances and invest surplus funds
Monitor production output to ensure as many goods as possible are made
Negotiate low interest rates on amounts borrowed
Obtain credit where possible for all expenditure
Offer bulk discounts to maximise profit
Pay credit suppliers as late as possible without incurring penalties
Purchase a new vehicle for use by employees

Rajesh now wants to set up a project team of five staff to implement a new computer-based accounting system at SCM Products. He has said you will be part of the team and asked you to suggest four other members of staff that you feel have the attributes to work well within the project team.

To help you decide you have made some notes about each member of staff, as shown below.

Name	Experience	Brief assessment of skills and attributes
Bital	All areas of the finance function	Senior accountant, very knowledgeable, works primarily on his own, does not communicate well, finds IT systems challenging.
Zhe	Management accounts and cashiers	Popular member of the department, strong communication skills, good knowledge of the current IT system.
Borak	Financial accounts and Payroll	Valuable team member, great motivator, very focused on team objectives, strong verbal communication skills, popular with all staff.
Abdul	All areas of the finance function	Extremely quiet, works well on his own, completes tasks to a high standard, fails to appreciate wider team goals.
Jessica	Cashiers	Good knowledge of cashier procedures and general knowledge of finance systems, highly organised with good written communication skills.
Emily	Financial and management accounts	Basic knowledge of financial and management accounts, communicates well with close friends, does not communicate well in wider departmental activities.
Foday	Payroll	Good knowledge of payroll systems, key member of a previous IT implementation team, very strong verbal communication skills.
Simon	Trainee in all areas of the finance function	A new member of the team, first job since leaving school, limited knowledge of the finance department, lacks confidence, reluctant to communicate with colleagues.

(c)   **Identify the FOUR members of staff that would be most effective as part of the project team.**   **(4 marks)**

Bilal [   ]   Borak [   ]   Jessica [   ]   Foday [   ]

Zhe [   ]   Abdul [   ]   Emily [   ]   Simon [   ]

TASK 3 (12 marks)

You have received the invoice below from a credit supplier. The supplier has agreed to allow a 10% bulk discount off the list price of £0.75 per item.

Dawson Ltd

11 Hove Street, Grangeton, GX11 4HB

VAT Registration No. 398 4673 00

Invoice No. D1672

To: SCM Products   15 May 20XX
      14 London Road
      Parton, PA21 7NL

                                                                           £
1,200 ... Product D92 @ £0.75 each   900.00
VAT @ 20%   180.00
                                                                  _____
                                                                    1,080.00
                                                                  _____

Terms of payment: Net monthly account

You notice that the invoice amounts are incorrect.

(a)   What should be the correct amounts of the invoice?   (3 marks)

Net £	VAT £	Total £

You have received another invoice from the same supplier whose account code is DAW322. There was no bulk discount offered for this order but the supplier has offered a prompt payment discount. You are ready to enter this invoice into the appropriate daybook

---

Dawson Ltd

11 Hove Street, Grangeton, GX11 4HB

VAT Registration No. 398 4673 00

Invoice No. D1676

To: SCM Products   17 May 20XX
      14 London Road
      Parton, PA21 7NL

                                                                           £
250 ... Product D87 @ £0.62 each   155.00
VAT @ 20%   31.00
                                                                  _____
                                                                     186.00
                                                                  _____

Terms of payment: 3% discount for payment within 10 days of date of invoice

---

(b) Complete the entries in the daybook below by:

- selecting the correct daybook title, and

- making the necessary entries.   **(7 marks)**

Title	▽

▽ Drop down list for task 1.3 (b):

Discounts allowed daybook
Discounts received daybook
Purchases daybook
Purchases returns daybook
Sales daybook
Sales returns daybook

Date 20XX	Details	Supplier account code	Invoice number	Total £	VAT £	Net £	Product D87	Product D92
17 May	▽	▽	D1676					

▽ Drop down list for task 1.3 (b):

Details

Dawson Ltd
SCM Products

Supplier account code

DAW32
D1672
D1676

You must now prepare a payment to the supplier for invoice D1676 in order to take advantage of the prompt payment discount offered.

(c) What will be the amount paid and what is the latest date by which the supplier should receive payment?   **(2 marks)**

Amount to be paid £	Date by which payment should be received
	▽

▽ Drop down list for task 1.3 (c):

15 May 20XX
17 May 20XX
25 May 20XX
27 May 20XX
31 May 20XX
30 June 20XX

TASK 4 (16 marks)

Scenario

You have received the bank statement for June and are checking it against the cash book.

Bank statement

Date 20XX	Details	Paid out £	Paid in £	Balance £
01 Jun	Balance b/f			791 C
04 Jun	Counter credit		1,573	2,365 C
07 Jun	Cheque 015263	605		1,759 C
16 Jun	Cheque 015265	1,428		331 C
20 Jun	Cheque 015249	387		56 D
24 Jun	Cheque 015267	211		267 D
27 Jun	Counter credit		1,195	928 C
28 Jun	Cheque 015266	509		419 C
D = Debit C = Credit				

Cash book

Date 20XX	Details	Bank £	Date 20XX	Cheque number	Details	Bank £
01 Jun	Balance b/f	404	03 Jun	015263	Amy Cox	605
04 Jun	QP Ltd	1,573	05 Jun	015264	Hal James	753
20 Jun	Koyt plc	844	10 Jun	015265	Parton Painters	1,428
27 Jun	Freya Rose	1,195	18 Jun	015266	Sal Ltd	509
			20 Jun	015267	Tay Traders	211

(a) **Identify which item has caused the difference in the opening balances.** (1 mark)

Reason	
An unpresented cheque for £387	☐
An outstanding lodgement for £387	☐
An unpresented cheque for £1,195	☐
An outstanding lodgement for £1,195	☐

Having identified that there are no additional transactions to be recorded in the cash book you are now ready to total and balance the cash book.

(b) **What will be the cash book balance carried down?** **(2 marks)**

Amount £	Debit	Credit
	☐	☐

(c) **What will be the total of each of the cash book debit and credit columns after you have recorded the balance carried down that you calculated in (b)?** **(1 mark)**

Amount £

Your next task is to check that the cash book balance reconciles with the bank statement.

(d) **Complete the bank reconciliation statement at 30 June.** **(6 marks)**

Bank reconciliation statement	£
Balance as per bank statement	
Add:	
▽	
Less	
▽	
Balance as per cash book	

▽ Drop down list for task 4 (b):

Amy Cox
Cheque 015249
Counter credit
Freya Rose
Hal James
Koyt plc
Parton Painters
QP Ltd
Sal Ltd
Tay Traders

You mow need to deal with the note below which you have received from your line manager, Orla Green.

Note

We have overpaid an invoice for £1,248 from a credit supplier. Further information is below. Supplier: Parton Painters Invoice number 612, dated 12 May 20XX Payment cheque for £1,428 sent to the supplier on 10 June 20XX   Please send an email from yourself, an accounts assistant, to Janice Frost at Parton Painters. You should explain the situation, specify the amount of the overpayment, and request a cheque to correct the error.   Thanks Orla

(e) **Prepare an appropriate business email to Parton Painters, making sure that you include all relevant information.** **(6 marks)**

To: jfrost@partonpainters.co.uk From: accounts@scmproducts.co.uk Subject --

TASK 5 (12 marks)

Scenario

SCM Products is committed to improving its Corporate Social Responsibility (CSR) activities. You are part of a team that has been asked to assist in the preparation of an annual report detailing the CSR and sustainability initiatives planned

(a) Drag TWO appropriate statements to create the introduction to the Corporate Social Responsibility and Sustainability Report below. (2 marks)

	Statements
SCM Products **Corporate Social Responsibility and Sustainability Report**	being a responsible business and maximising the environmental impact of our activities
Introduction	buying goods in a manner that drives positive change within our industry
SCM Products is committed to:	being a responsible business and maximising our suppliers' profits
	being a responsible business by enabling the personal growth and fulfilment of our staff`
	buying materials at the lowest possible cost irrespective of the environmental impact of the materials

(b) Drag FOUR appropriate initiatives in the local community and wider society section of the Corporate Social Responsibility and Sustainability report below. (4 marks)

	Initiatives:
SCM Products **Corporate Social Responsibility and Sustainability Report**	Embedding a culture of CPD (Continuing Professional Development) and training into the workforce.
Our commitment to improving the local community and wider society. **Initiatives planned that will directly impact on the local community and wider society:**	Embedding a culture of commitment to volunteering within SCM Products.
	Ensuring the organisation uses the most energy efficiency delivery vehicles.
	Investing in projects to capture renewable energy sources.
	Facilitating employees' contributions to a charity of their choice.
	Providing interest free loans to all staff who wish to purchase a motor car.
	Providing opportunities for staff to work on raising funds to rebuild a day care centre near to the main offices.
	Providing opportunities for the unemployed to gain work experience.

In support of SCM Products' CSR commitment, a project to install more energy efficient equipment in the production plant was completed last month.

Your manager has asked you to complete a budget report for the direct costs spent on the project. The budget report must clearly indicate any variance that is significant, that is in excess of 10% of budget.

Budget costs are to be calculated as follows:

Materials   1,600 kilos @ £6.50 per kilo

Labour   500 hours at £12.50 per hour

Actual costs have already been entered into the report.

(c)   Complete the table below by:

- **inserting the budget cost for material and labour cost**

- **inserting the variance for each cost**

- **selecting whether each variance is significant or not.**   **(6 marks)**

Budget report				
Cost	Budget £	Actual £	Variance £	Significant
Material		11,645		▽
Labour		7,295		▽

▽ Drop down list for task 5 (c):

Yes
No

TASK 6 (24 marks)

Scenario

Your manager has asked you to assist in a cost behaviour exercise for a new product. Although total costs have been estimated for projected minimum and maximum levels of output, she wants a clearer indication of cost behaviour for all levels of output, with a segregation of fixed and variable costs.

(a) **Complete the table below by:** (12 marks)

- inserting the variable costs for each level of output

- inserting the fixed costs for each level of output

- inserting total costs for 5,000 units and 7,500 units levels of output.

Units	3,000	5,000	7,500	11,000
Variable costs (£)				
Fixed costs (£)				
Total costs (£)	41,000			105,000

(b) **In the box below, write notes in preparation for a meeting you will have with your manager, including:** (12 marks)

- a brief introduction outlining the areas you will discuss

- an explanation of how fixed and variable costs behave as levels of output change, using your figures in (a) to illustrate your answer

- a re-calculation of the fixed costs you calculated in (a) above, assuming they increased by 5% and provide an explanation of the effect of this on total costs

- an explanation of the effect on the total cost per unit as levels of output increase if fixed costs increased by 5% whilst variable cost per unit remains unchanged.

Your notes must be sufficiently detailed, clearly written and well-structured as they will be a formal record of your meeting discussion.

TASK 7 (12 marks)

Scenario

You are preparing for the month end at SCM Products These are three accounts in the general ledger.

Drawings

Details	Amount £	Details	Amount £
Balance b/f	1,190	Journal	125
Bank	250		

Bank interest received

Details	Amount £	Details	Amount £
		Balance b/f	342
		Bank	161

Office expenses

Details	Amount £	Details	Amount £
Balance b/f	3,462		
Cash	72		

(a)   What will be the entries in the trial balance?   (6 marks)

Account name	Amount £	Debit	Credit
Drawings		☐	☐
Bank interest received		☐	☐
Office expenses		☐	☐

You have now completed and totalled the trial balance, but find it does not balance. The credit column is £270 more than the debit column so you have opened a suspense account.

(b)   Will the opening balance in the suspense account be a debit or credit entry?

(1 mark)

Debit   ☐

Credit   ☐

You have identified that the error in the trial balance has arisen from a bank payment of £636 for a rail fare being recorded in the travel account as £366. The entry in the bank account was correct.

You have partially prepared journal entries to correct the error and clear the suspense account.

(c) **Complete each journal entry by inserting the appropriate amount in either the debit or credit column. Do NOT enter a zero in unused debit or credit column cells.**

(3 marks)

Journal to remove the incorrect entry

Account name	Debit £	Credit £
Travel		

Journal to record the correct entry

Account name	Debit £	Credit £
Travel		

Journal to clear the suspense account

Account name	Debit £	Credit £
Suspense		

The trial balance showed an amount for travel of £1,589, before you discovered the error.

(d) **What will be the entry in the trial balance following the journal entries in (c)?**

(2 marks)

Account name	Amount £	Debit	Credit
Travel		☐	☐

AAT AQ2016

SAMPLE ASSESSMENT 2

FOUNDATION SYNOPTIC ASSESSMENT

Answers

TASK 1

1.1

(a)   Complete your to-do list for today, Friday of week 4. Refer to the management and financial accounts schedules and drag the tasks to be completed into the to-do list below.   **(5 marks)**

Note: You should drag a task into the to-do list more than once if the task takes more than one hour to complete.

Friday, week 4 to-do list	Time
Petty cash book	09.00 – 10.00
Post cheques	10.00 – 11.00
Reconcile statements	11.00 – 12.00
Lunch	12.00 – 13.00
Cost coding	13.00 – 14.00
Departmental meeting	14.00 – 15.00
Cost coding	15.00 – 16.00

(b)   Identify the week in which you are least busy with tasks from the management and financial accounts schedules.

Week number
Week 3   ∇

(c)   What will be the amounts entered in the petty cash book to record this transaction?

Net amount	£	26.35
VAT amount	£	5.27
Total amount	£	31.62

(d)   What will be the amount of the balance carried down?

£ | 51.33 |

(e)   What will be the entry in the petty cash book to record the cash withdrawn from the bank to restore the imprest level of £150?

Amount £	Debit	Credit
98.67	✓	

TASK 2

(a)   From the list below, identify FOUR benefits of finance staff at SCM Products establishing good business relationships by dragging them into the weekly bulletin.

Weekly Bulletin Number 1
What are the benefits of finance staff establishing good working relationships?
To build trust which may result in better sharing of information
To create improved communication channels which may improve efficiency
To develop respect which may assist in resolving disputes
To build loyalty from customers which may lead to increased sales

(b)   From the list below, identify FOUR actions to help improve solvency by dragging them into the weekly bulletin.

Weekly Bulletin Number 19
How can finance staff help to improve solvency?
Monitor bank balances and invest surplus funds
Negotiate low interest rates on amounts borrowed
Obtain credit where possible for all expenditure
Pay credit suppliers as late as possible without incurring penalties

(c)   Identify the FOUR members of staff that would be most effective as part of the project team.

Bilal		Borak	✓	Jessica	✓	Foday	✓
Zhe	✓	Abdul		Emily		Simon	

TASK 3

(a)   What should be the correct amounts of the invoice?

Net £	VAT £	Total £
810	162	972

(b)   Complete the entries in the daybook below by:

- selecting the correct daybook title, and

- making the necessary entries.

Title	Purchases daybook ∇

Date 20XX	Details	Supplier account code	Invoice number	Total £	VAT £	Net £	Product D87	Product D92
17 May	Dawson Ltd ∇	DAW32 ∇	D1676	186	31	155	155	

(c)   What will be the amount paid and what is the latest date by which the supplier should receive payment.

Amount to be paid £	Date by which payment should be received
180.42	27 May 20XX ▽

TASK 4

(a)   Identify which item has caused the difference in the opening balances.

Reason	
An unpresented cheque for £387	✓
An outstanding lodgement for £387	
An unpresented cheque for £1,195	
An outstanding lodgement for £1,195	

(b)   What will be the cash book balance carried down?

Amount £	Debit	Credit
510		✓

(c)   What will be the total of each of the cash book debit and credit columns after you have recorded the balance carried down that you calculated in (b)?

Amount £
4,016

(d)   Complete the bank reconciliation statement at 30 June.

Bank reconciliation statement		£
Balance as per bank statement		419
Add:		
Koyt plc	▽	844
Less		
Hal James	▽	753
Balance as per cash book		510

(e) **Prepare an appropriate business email to Parton Painters, making sure that you include all relevant information.**

> To: jfrost@partonpainters.co.uk
>
> From: accounts@scmproducts.co.uk
>
> Subject Incorrect payment
>
> ---
>
> Hello Janice
>
> On 10 June 20XX we sent you a cheque for £1,428 in payment of your invoice 612 dated 12 May 20XX.
>
> We have now realised that the amount of the cheque was incorrect, it should have been £1,248 which is the amount of your invoice.
>
> As a result, we have overpaid by £180 so we would appreciate it if you could send us a cheque for the amount of the overpayment.
>
> Kind regards
>
> Accounts Assistant

TASK 5

(a) **Drag TWO appropriate statements to create the introduction to the Corporate Social Responsibility and Sustainability Report below.**

SCM Products Corporate Social Responsibility and Sustainability Report
Introduction
SCM Products is committed to:
buying goods in a manner that drives positive change within our industry
being a responsible business by enabling the personal growth and fulfilment of our staff`

(b) **Drag FOUR appropriate initiatives in the local community and wider society section of the Corporate Social Responsibility and Sustainability report below.**

SCM Products Corporate Social Responsibility and Sustainability Report
Our commitment to improving the local community and wider society. **Initiatives planned that will directly impact on the local community and wider society:**
Embedding a culture of commitment to volunteering within SCM Products.
Facilitating employees' contributions to a charity of their choice.
Providing opportunities for staff to work on raising funds to rebuild a day care centre near to the main offices.
Providing opportunities for the unemployed to gain work experience.

(c)   Complete the table below by:

- inserting the budget cost for material and labour cost

- inserting the variance for each cost

- selecting whether each variance is significant or not.

Budget report				
Cost	Budget £	Actual £	Variance £	Significant
Material	10400	11,645	1245	Yes ▽
Labour	6250	7,295	1045	Yes ▽

TASK 6

(a)   Complete the table below by:

- inserting the variable costs for each level of output

- inserting the fixed costs for each level of output

- inserting total costs for 5,000 units and 7,500 units levels of output.

Units	3,000	5,000	7,500	11,000
Variable costs (£)	24000	40000	60000	88000
Fixed costs (£)	17000	17000	17000	17000
Total costs (£)	41000	57000	77000	105000

(b)   In the box below, write notes in preparation for a meeting you will have with your manager, including:

- a brief introduction outlining the areas you will discuss

- an explanation of how fixed and variable costs behave as levels of output change, using your figures in (a) to illustrate your answer

- a re-calculation of the fixed costs you calculated in (a) above, assuming they increased by 5% and provide an explanation of the effect of this on total costs

- an explanation of the effect on the total cost per unit as levels of output increase if fixed costs increased by 5% whilst variable cost per unit remains unchanged.

Your notes must be sufficiently detailed, clearly written and well structured as they will be a formal record of your meeting discussion.

> During the meeting I will discuss the behaviours of fixed and variable costs as levels of output change, a re-calculation of fixed costs assuming a 5% increase in costs and the effect this will have on total costs. Finally I will explain the effect of a 5% increase in fixed costs on the total cost per unit as levels of output increase.
>
> As the name suggests fixed costs remain constant irrespective of the levels of output. For example when 3000 units are produced the fixed costs were the same as when 11000 units were produced. Variable costs change dependent upon the levels of output. As the level of output increases then the variable costs also increase proportionately dependent upon the level of output.
>
> Fixed costs will increase by £850 to £17,850. As fixed costs have increased by £850, total costs will increase by the same amount.
>
> The unit costs will also increase as levels of output increase although the increase per unit will reduce as output increases. This is because the increase is spread out over more units.

TASK 7

(a) **What will be the entries in the trial balance?**

Account name	Amount £	Debit	Credit
Drawings	1,315	✓	☐
Bank interest received	503	☐	✓
Office expenses	3,534	✓	☐

(b) **Will the opening balance in the suspense account be a debit or credit entry?**

Debit ✓

Credit ☐

(c) Complete each journal entry by inserting the appropriate amount in either the debit or credit column. Do NOT enter a zero in unused debit or credit column cells.

Journal to remove the incorrect entry

Account name	Debit £	Credit £
Travel		366

Journal to record the correct entry

Account name	Debit £	Credit £
Travel	636	

Journal to clear the suspense account

Account name	Debit £	Credit £
Suspense		270

(d) What will be the entry in the trial balance following the journal entries in (c)?

Account name	Amount £	Debit	Credit
Travel	1859	✓	☐

Kaplan Publishing are constantly finding new ways to make a difference to your studies a̶ ̶o̶u̶r̶ exciting online resources really do offer ̶s̶o̶m̶e̶t̶h̶i̶ng different to students looking for exa̶m̶ ̶s̶u̶c̶c̶ess.

This book comes with free MyKapla̶n̶ ̶o̶n̶l̶in̶e̶ resources so that you can study anytime, anywhere. **This free online resource is not sold separately and is included in the price of the book.**

Having purchased this book, you have access to the following online study materials:

CONTENT	AAT	
	Text	Kit
Electronic version of the book	✓	✓
Progress tests with instant answers	✓	
Mock assessments online	✓	✓
Material updates	✓	✓

How to access your online resources

Kaplan Financial students will already have a MyKaplan account and these extra resources will be available to you online. You do not need to register again, as this process was completed when you enrolled. If you are having problems accessing online materials, please ask your course administrator.

If you are not studying with Kaplan and did not purchase your book via a Kaplan website, to unlock your extra online resources please go to www.mykaplan.co.uk/addabook (even if you have set up an account and registered books previously). You will then need to enter the ISBN number (on the title page and back cover) and the unique pass key number contained in the scratch panel below to gain access. You will also be required to enter additional information during this process to set up or confirm your account details.

If you purchased through Kaplan Flexible Learning or via the Kaplan Publishing website you will automatically receive an e-mail invitation to MyKaplan. Please register your details using this email to gain access to your content. If you do not receive the e-mail or book content, please contact Kaplan Publishing.

Your Code and Information

This code can only be used once for the registration of one book online. This registration and your online content will expire when the final sittings for the examinations covered by this book have taken place. Please allow one hour from the time you submit your book details for us to process your request.

Please scratch the film to access your MyKaplan code.

Please be aware that this code is case-sensitive and you will need to include the dashes within the passcode, but not when entering the ISBN. For further technical support, please visit www.MyKaplan.co.uk

BOOKKEEPING TRANSACTIONS

STUDY TEXT

Qualifications and Credit Framework

AQ2016

This Study Text supports study for the following AAT qualifications:

AAT Foundation Certificate in Accounting – Level 2

AAT Foundation Diploma in Accounting and Business – Level 2

AAT Foundation Certificate in Bookkeeping – Level 2

AAT Foundation Award in Accounting Software – Level 2

AAT Level 2 Award in Accounting Skills to Run Your Business

AAT Foundation Certificate in Accounting at SCQF Level 5

British Library Cataloguing-in-Publication Data

A catalogue record for this book is available from the British Library.

Published by
Kaplan Publishing UK
Unit 2, The Business Centre
Molly Millars Lane
Wokingham
Berkshire
RG41 2QZ

ISBN: 978-1-78740-506-6

The text in this material and any others made available by any Kaplan Group company does not amount to advice on a particular matter and should not be taken as such. No reliance should be placed on the content as the basis for any investment or other decision or in connection with any advice given to third parties. Please consult your appropriate professional adviser as necessary. Kaplan Publishing Limited and all other Kaplan group companies expressly disclaim all liability to any person in respect of any losses or other claims, whether direct, indirect, incidental, consequential or otherwise arising in relation to the use of such materials.

CONTENTS

KAPLAN PUBLISHING

INTRODUCTION

HOW TO USE THESE MATERIALS

These Kaplan Publishing learning materials have been carefully designed to make your learning experience as easy as possible and to give you the best chance of success in your AAT assessments.

They contain a number of features to help you in the study process.

The sections on the Unit Guide, the Assessment and Study Skills should be read before you commence your studies.

They are designed to familiarise you with the nature and content of the assessment and to give you tips on how best to approach your studies.

STUDY TEXT

This study text has been specially prepared for the revised AAT qualification introduced in September 2016.

It is written in a practical and interactive style:

- key terms and concepts are clearly defined

- all topics are illustrated with practical examples with clearly worked solutions based on sample tasks provided by the AAT in the new examining style

- frequent activities throughout the chapters ensure that what you have learnt is regularly reinforced

- 'pitfalls' and 'examination tips' help you avoid commonly made mistakes and help you focus on what is required to perform well in your examination

- 'Test your understanding' activities are included within each chapter to apply your learning and develop your understanding.

ICONS

The chapters include the following icons throughout.

They are designed to assist you in your studies by identifying key definitions and the points at which you can test yourself on the knowledge gained.

 Definition

These sections explain important areas of Knowledge which must be understood and reproduced in an assessment.

 Example

The illustrative examples can be used to help develop an understanding of topics before attempting the activity exercises.

 Test your understanding

These are exercises which give the opportunity to assess your understanding of all the assessment areas.

Quality and accuracy are of the utmost importance to us so if you spot an error in any of our products, please send an email to mykaplanreporting@kaplan.com with full details.

Our Quality Co-ordinator will work with our technical team to verify the error and take action to ensure it is corrected in future editions.

KAPLAN PUBLISHING

Progression

There are two elements of progression that we can measure: first how quickly students move through individual topics within a subject; and second how quickly they move from one course to the next. We know that there is an optimum for both, but it can vary from subject to subject and from student to student. However, using data and our experience of student performance over many years, we can make some generalisations.

A fixed period of study set out at the start of a course with key milestones is important. This can be within a subject, for example 'I will finish this topic by 30 June', or for overall achievement, such as 'I want to be qualified by the end of next year'.

Your qualification is cumulative, as earlier papers provide a foundation for your subsequent studies, so do not allow there to be too big a gap between one subject and another.

We know that exams encourage techniques that lead to some degree of short term retention, the result being that you will simply forget much of what you have already learned unless it is refreshed (look up Ebbinghaus Forgetting Curve for more details on this). This makes it more difficult as you move from one subject to another: not only will you have to learn the new subject, you will also have to relearn all the underpinning knowledge as well. This is very inefficient and slows down your overall progression which makes it more likely you may not succeed at all.

In addition, delaying your studies slows your path to qualification which can have negative impacts on your career, postponing the opportunity to apply for higher level positions and therefore higher pay.

You can use the following diagram showing the whole structure of your qualification to help you keep track of your progress.

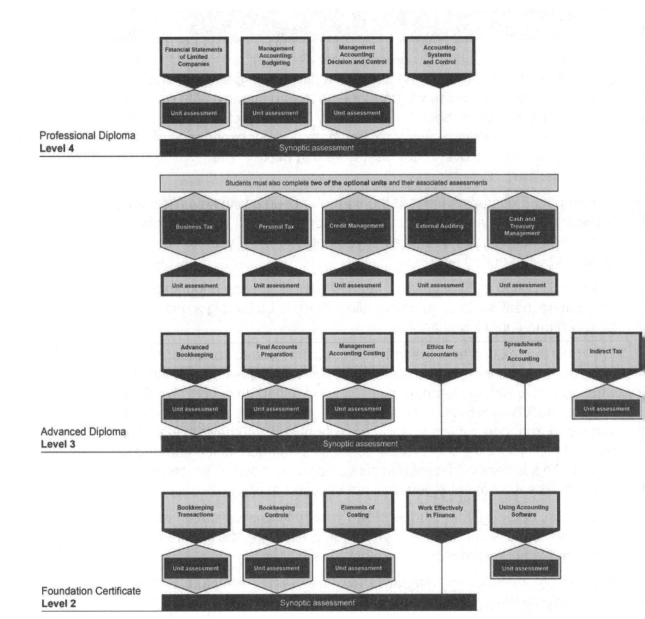

UNIT GUIDE

Introduction

Bookkeeping Transactions introduces students to the double-entry bookkeeping system and the associated documents and processes. Students will reach the stage of extracting an initial trial balance, before any adjustments are made. This unit provides students with the skills necessary to operate a manual double-entry bookkeeping system and provides a strong foundation for progression to more advanced manual and computerised activities.

On completion of this unit, students will be able to check the accuracy of invoices, credit notes, remittance advices, statements of account and petty cash vouchers. They will know how to use these documents to make entries in sales and purchases daybooks, sales and purchases returns daybooks, and discounts allowed and received daybooks using account codes, as well as how to transfer those totals to the sales, purchases and general ledgers.

The UK government department responsible for collecting taxes (HMRC) offers more than one method of accounting treatment when prompt payment discount (PPD) is allowed and received. However, students at Foundation level are only required to use credit notes to adjust for PPD. Using this approach, credit notes are recorded in separate daybooks, a discounts allowed daybook and/or a discounts received daybook, removing the need for discount columns in the cash book. There is no requirement at this level for learners to understand how to account for PPD by any other method.

The cash book and petty cash book are also covered in this unit, including making entries into both and transferring totals to the ledgers. Students will make appropriate checks on the accuracy of supplier invoices and credit notes, reconcile supplier statements with the purchases ledger account and calculate payments due to suppliers. They will also calculate sales invoice and credit note amounts and check receipts from customers.

This unit refers to value added tax or VAT. This is an indirect tax operating in the UK but this type of tax may also operate and be known by another name in other countries.

Bookkeeping Transactions is a mandatory unit in this qualification.

Learning outcomes

On completion of this unit the learner will be able to:

- understand financial transactions within a bookkeeping system

- process customer transactions

- process supplier transactions

- process receipts and payments

- process transactions through the ledgers to the trial balance

Scope of content

To perform this unit effectively you will need to know and understand the following:

Chapter

1   Understand financial transactions within a bookkeeping system

1.1   Indicate the purpose of business documents   1,8

Students need to know:

- the purpose of business documents: petty cash voucher, invoice, credit note (including for PPD), remittance advice, statement of account.

1.2   Distinguish between prompt payment, trade and bulk discounts   1, 5, 6, 8

Students need to know:

- the difference between discounts offered: prompt payment, trade and bulk

- how discounts are shown on invoices: prompt payment, trade and bulk

- how to use credit notes to adjust for PPD and how PPD is recorded once taken: discounts allowed or discounts received daybook, sales or purchases ledger account, general ledger discounts allowed or received account as income or expenditure, sales or purchases ledger control account, value added tax (VAT) account.

Chapter

1.3 Demonstrate an understanding of a coding system   1

Students need to know:

- the different types of code: customer account, supplier account, product

- where to use codes: sales, sales returns and discounts allowed daybooks and purchases, purchase returns and discounts received daybooks, sales and purchases ledgers

- how to create codes: alphabetical, numerical, alphanumerical.

1.4 Demonstrate an understanding of the process of recording financial transactions   2, 3, 4, 5, 6, 7, 8,

Students need to know:

- the role of the books of prime entry: sales and sales returns daybooks, purchases and purchases returns daybooks, discounts allowed and discounts received daybooks

- the role of the cash book and petty cash book: as a book of prime entry only, as a book of prime entry and as part of the double-entry bookkeeping system

- the ledgers: sales, purchases and general

- the accounting equation: calculation of assets, liabilities and capital, dual effect of transactions

- the classification of items: assets and liabilities

- the classification of income and expenditure: capital income, capital expenditure, revenue income, revenue expenditure

- the purpose of the trial balance.

Chapter

2   Process customer transactions

2.1   Calculate invoice and credit note amounts   1

Students need to know:

- the documents to be used: quotations, discount policy, customer order, delivery note, price list.

Students need to be able to:

- calculate invoice amounts: item price, net, VAT and total amounts, trade and bulk discounts

- calculate credit note amounts: item price, net, VAT and total amounts, trade, bulk and prompt payment discounts.

2.2   Enter sales invoices and credit notes into books of prime entry   2, 5

Students need to know:

- the books of prime entry: sales, sales returns and discounts allowed daybooks

- the columns within books of prime entry: customer name, customer account code, total, VAT, net, analysis (including product codes).

Students need to be able to:

- calculate VAT amounts from net and total figures

- calculate total and net amounts from the VAT figure

- make entries in books of prime entry

- total columns in books of prime entry.

KAPLAN PUBLISHING

Chapter

2.3 **Check the accuracy of receipts from customers**   1, 5, 8

Students need to know:

- the records and documents to use: sales ledger account, sales invoice, sales credit note, remittance advice, discount policy.

Students need to be able to:

- identify discrepancies: under- or over-payment, incorrect discount taken, incorrect amounts

- calculate amounts due from customers, including PPD.

3 **Process supplier transactions**

3.1 **Check the accuracy of supplier invoices and credit notes**   1, 6, 8

Students need to know:

- the documents to use: quotations including discounts, purchase orders, goods received notes, delivery notes, goods returned notes.

Students need to be able to:

- identify discrepancies that may be found: non-delivery of goods, incorrect type or quantity of goods, incorrect calculations, incorrect discounts (trade, bulk and prompt payment), date and terms of payment.

Chapter

3.2 **Enter supplier invoices and credit notes into books of prime entry**

2, 6

Students need to know:

- the books of prime entry: purchases, purchases returns and discounts received daybooks

- the columns within books of prime entry: supplier name, supplier account code, total, VAT, net, analysis (including product code).

Students need to be able to:

- calculate VAT amounts from net and total figures

- calculate total and net amounts from the VAT figure

- make entries in books of prime entry

- total columns in books of prime entry.

3.3 **Prepare payments to suppliers**

6, 8

Students need to know:

- the records and documents to use: purchases ledger account, invoices and credit notes (including discounts and VAT), statement of account

- the information to take into account: agreed payment terms.

Students need to be able to:

- identify discrepancies between the supplier's statement of account and the purchases ledger account: timing differences, wrong amounts, missing transactions, duplicated transactions

- calculate payments due to suppliers, including PPD.

Chapter

4 Process receipts and payments

4.1 Enter receipts and payments into a two column analysed cash book

2, 8

Students need to know:

- the format of the cash book: date, details, cash, bank, analysis columns (including VAT)

- the documents to use: direct debit/standing order schedule, remittance advice (including BACS), paying in slip, cheque stub, cash receipt, receipts and payments listing.

Students need to be able to:

- calculate VAT amounts from net and total figures

- make entries in the cash book.

4.2 Enter receipts and payments into an analysed petty cash book

2, 8

Students need to know:

- the format of the petty cash book: date, details, amount, analysis columns (including VAT)

- the documents to use: cash receipt, petty cash voucher.

Students need to be able to:

- calculate VAT amounts from net and total figures

- make entries in the petty cash book, including reimbursement, using the imprest and non-imprest systems.

4.3 Total and balance the cash book and petty cash book

8

Students need to be able to:

- present totals and balances: column totals, balance carried down, balance brought down, debit balance, credit balance, date and details.

Chapter

5 **Process transactions through the ledgers to the trial balance**

5.1	**Transfer data from the books of prime entry to the ledgers**	5, 6, 7, 8

Students need to know:

- the books of prime entry: sales and sales returns daybooks, purchases and purchases returns daybooks, discounts allowed and discounts received daybooks, cash book, petty cash book

- the ledgers: sales, purchases, general

- that the sales and purchases ledger control accounts are part of the double-entry system.

Student need to be able to:

- transfer data from books of prime entry to the relevant accounts in the ledgers.

5.2	**Total and balance ledger accounts**	4

Student need to be able to:

- total and balance ledger accounts: balance carried down, balance brought down, debit balance, credit balance.

5.3	**Extract an initial trial balance**	4

Students need to know:

- to use the general ledger to extract balances

- the column to use in the trial balance: debit, credit.

Students need to be able to:

- transfer balances to the initial trial balance

- total and balance the initial trial balance.

Delivering this unit

Unit name	Content links	Suggested order of delivery
Bookkeeping Controls	Bookkeeping Transactions is the first of two bookkeeping units at Foundation level. With Bookkeeping Controls, it is the foundation for financial accounting at Advanced level.	It is recommended that Bookkeeping Transactions is delivered either before or at the same time as Bookkeeping Controls.
Elements of Costing	The use of codes in this unit links with Elements of Costing.	Elements of Costing might be delivered before, at the same time as or after Bookkeeping Controls.
Using Accounting Software	Bookkeeping Transactions gives students underlying knowledge that may support their study of Using Accounting Software.	It is recommended that Bookkeeping Transactions is delivered either before or at the same time as Using Accounting Software.

THE ASSESSMENT

Test specification for this unit assessment

Assessment type	Marking type	Duration of exam
Computer based assessment	Computer marked	1 hour and 30 minutes

The assessment for this unit consists of 10 compulsory, independent, tasks.

The competency level for AAT assessment is 70%.

Learning outcomes		Weighting
1	Understand financial transactions within a bookkeeping system	10%
2	Process customer transactions	10%
3	Process supplier transactions	15%
4	Process receipts and payments	25%
5	Process transactions through the ledgers to the trial balance	40%
Total		100%

KAPLAN PUBLISHING

UNIT LINK TO SYNOPTIC ASSESSMENT

AAT AQ16 introduced a Synoptic Assessment, which students must complete if they are to achieve the appropriate qualification upon completion of a qualification. In the case of the Foundation Certificate in Accounting, students must pass all of the mandatory assessments and the Synoptic Assessment to achieve the qualification.

As a Synoptic Assessment is attempted following completion of individual units, it draws upon knowledge and understanding from those units. It may be appropriate for students to retain their study materials for individual units until they have successfully completed the Synoptic Assessment for that qualification.

With specific reference to this unit, the following learning objectives are also relevant to the Foundation Certificate in Accounting Synoptic Assessment

LO1 Understand financial transactions within a bookkeeping system

LO2 Process customer transactions

LO3 Process supplier transactions

LO4 Process receipts and payments

LO5 Process transactions through the ledgers to the trial balance.

STUDY SKILLS

Preparing to study

Devise a study plan

Determine which times of the week you will study.

Split these times into sessions of at least one hour for study of new material. Any shorter periods could be used for revision or practice.

Put the times you plan to study onto a study plan for the weeks from now until the assessment and set yourself targets for each period of study – in your sessions make sure you cover the whole course, activities and the associated Test your understanding activities.

If you are studying more than one unit at a time, try to vary your subjects as this can help to keep you interested and see subjects as part of wider knowledge.

When working through your course, compare your progress with your plan and, if necessary, re-plan your work (perhaps including extra sessions) or, if you are ahead, do some extra revision/practice questions.

Effective studying

Active reading

You are not expected to learn the text by rote, rather, you must understand what you are reading and be able to use it to pass the assessment and develop good practice.

A good technique is to use SQ3Rs – Survey, Question, Read, Recall, Review:

1   **Survey the chapter**

    Look at the headings and read the introduction, knowledge, skills and content, so as to get an overview of what the chapter deals with.

2   **Question**

    Whilst undertaking the survey ask yourself the questions you hope the chapter will answer for you.

3   Read

Read through the chapter thoroughly working through the activities and, at the end, making sure that you can meet the learning objectives highlighted on the first page.

4   Recall

At the end of each section and at the end of the chapter, try to recall the main ideas of the section/chapter without referring to the text. This is best done after short break of a couple of minutes after the reading stage.

5   Review

Check that your recall notes are correct.

You may also find it helpful to re-read the chapter to try and see the topic(s) it deals with as a whole.

Note taking

Taking notes is a useful way of learning, but do not simply copy out the text.

The notes must:

- be in your own words
- be concise
- cover the key points
- be well organised
- be modified as you study further chapters in this text or in related ones.

Trying to summarise a chapter without referring to the text can be a useful way of determining which areas you know and which you don't.

Three ways of taking notes:

1   Summarise the key points of a chapter

2   Make linear notes

A list of headings, subdivided with sub-headings, listing the key points.

If you use linear notes, you can use different colours to highlight key points and keep topic areas together.

Use plenty of space to make your notes easy to use.

3   Try a diagrammatic form

The most common of which is a mind map.

To make a mind map, put the main heading in the centre of the paper and put a circle around it.

Draw lines radiating from this to the main sub-headings which again have circles around them.

Continue the process from the sub-headings to sub-sub-headings.

Annotating the text

You may find it useful to underline or highlight key points in your study text – but do be selective.

You may also wish to make notes in the margins.

Revision phase

Kaplan has produced material specifically designed for your final examination preparation for this unit.

These include pocket revision notes and an exam kit that includes a bank of revision questions specifically in the style of the new syllabus.

Further guidance on how to approach the final stage of your studies is given in these materials.

Further reading

In addition to this text, you should also read the 'Accounting Technician' magazine every month to keep abreast of any guidance from the examiners.

Business documents

Introduction

The purpose of accounting is to record and classify business transactions. There are many transactions that a business may undertake; credit sales, credit purchases, cash sales, cash purchases, other expenses either paid from the bank or by cash, paying cash into the bank, withdrawing cash from the bank and owner's drawings.

Various documents may be used when dealing with business transactions. This chapter reviews the flow of a transaction through the accounting system paying particular attention to the business documents involved.

The name of a transaction or document will depend on whether we are looking at it from the point of view of the seller or the purchaser. Thus an invoice may be called a 'sales invoice' for the seller but a 'purchase invoice' for the purchaser, it is the same invoice. Similarly, the seller makes a 'sale' and the purchaser makes a 'purchase', it is the same transaction.

ASSESSMENT CRITERIA	CONTENTS
Indicate the purpose of business documents (1.1)	1 Business transactions
	2 The accounting system
Distinguish between prompt payment, trade and bulk discounts (1.2)	3 Business documents for a credit transaction
	4 Quotation
Demonstrate an understanding of a coding system (1.3)	5 Purchase order
	6 Sales order
Calculate invoice and credit note amounts (2.1)	7 Delivery note and goods received note
	8 Invoice
Check the accuracy of receipts from customers (2.3)	9 Operation of VAT
	10 Discounts
Check the accuracy of supplier invoices and credit notes (3.1)	11 Preparing an invoice
	12 Credit note
	13 Coding

1 Business transactions

1.1 Introduction

Businesses may undertake many different financial transactions every day; credit sales, credit purchases, cash sales, cash purchases, other expenses either paid from the bank or by cash, paying cash into the bank, withdrawing cash from the bank and owner's drawings. These transactions are recorded on different business documents and are entered into an accounting system.

The Bookkeeping Transactions unit introduces the double-entry bookkeeping system and associated documents and processes.

1.2 Sales, purchases and expenses

Sales of goods or services and payment for purchases and expenses can be made on a cash or credit basis. Cash sales and purchases are relatively straightforward but credit sales and purchases require more accounting knowledge. Dependent upon whether we are the seller or the buyer dictates whether we view the transaction as a sale or purchase. The details of all aspects covered here will be dealt with in greater depth in later chapters.

1.3 Cash sales and purchases

A cash sale or purchase will normally be made in a retail environment. A customer will enter the shop, choose the goods they wish to buy then pay for them at the till or counter. The seller will tell the customer the price of the goods and the customer then offers payment for them, in the form of notes and coins. Alternatively, the customer may offer to pay for the goods by debit or credit card.

Finally, when the customer has paid for the goods, a receipt of some sort will be given to the customer. This may be printed automatically by the till or may be a handwritten receipt. The transaction is now complete.

1.4 Credit sales and purchases

The procedure for a sale or purchase on credit can be a bit more involved. The sale or purchase process will normally be initiated by a seller receiving an order from a customer. The purchase order from the customer may be in writing, over the telephone, by email, by fax or via a website. When your business receives the order, the first decision to be made is whether or not to allow the customer credit for this sale i.e. the period of time they can take before paying the invoice.

1.5 Offering credit

Selling goods on credit always involves an element of risk. The goods are taken away or delivered to the customer now with the promise of payment in the future. Therefore your business must be confident that the payment will be received. The decision process as to whether or not to make the sale on credit will be different depending upon whether this is a sale to an existing credit customer or a new customer.

1.6 Existing customers

If an existing credit customer wishes to make a further purchase on credit, it would be normal practice to carry out some basic checks. When the customer was originally accepted as a credit customer, a credit limit will have been set which should not be exceeded. Checks should be made to ensure that the new sale, when added to the amount currently owing, does not take the customer over their credit limit.

It would also be sensible to check that there have been no problems recently with receiving payment from this customer. If the checks are satisfactory then the credit sale can go ahead.

1.7 New customer

If a new customer asks for credit from your business then it would be normal practice to ask the customer to supply some trade references – names of other businesses that they trade with on credit that can vouch for their creditworthiness. Your business may also wish to check the customer's creditworthiness through an agency, or by asking for references from the customer's bank.

If the references and checks are satisfactory then a credit limit will be set for this customer and the sale can go ahead.

2 The accounting system

2.1 Introduction

A business may enter into a large number of transactions on a daily basis. It is quite clear that keeping track of all these transactions can be a detailed process.

To ensure that a business does keep track of all sales earned, purchases and expenses incurred, the transactions are recorded in an accounting system.

2.2   Overview of the accounting system

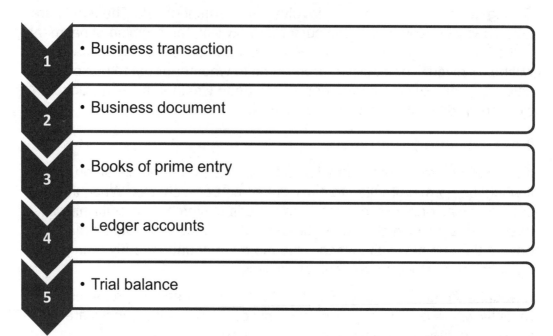

(1)   Initially a **business transaction** will take place; a credit sale, a credit purchase, a cash sale, a cash purchase, another expense either paid from the bank or by cash, cash paid into the bank, withdrawal of cash from the bank and owner's drawings.

(2)   A **business document** will be produced e.g. an invoice.

(3)   The transaction and details from the business document will be entered into the **books of prime entry**. A book of prime entry is where a transaction is first recorded. There are several books of prime entry which may also be referred to as 'day books'. These are reviewed in chapter 2 of this text.

(4)   The transactions that have been recorded in the books of prime entry are transferred into **ledger accounts** on a regular basis. Ledger accounts are used as part of the double entry accounting system. Double entry bookkeeping is introduced in chapter 3.

(5)   A **trial balance** is a list of all of the ledger accounts in the accounting system and is used as a control to check that transactions have been recorded correctly in the double entry system prior to the preparation of the financial statements. The trial balance is studied as part of ledger accounting in chapter 4.

3 Business documents for a credit transaction

3.1 Overview

The main document flows for a credit transaction are illustrated below. The various documents are described in the sections that follow.

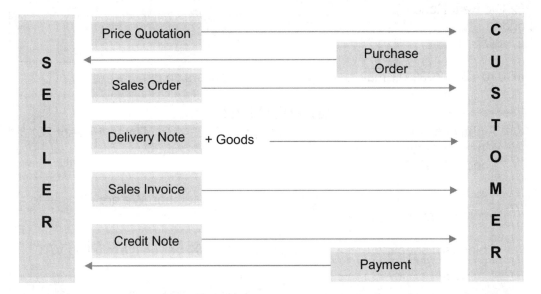

4 Quotation

4.1 Price enquiry

The first stage of the process for a credit sale may be the receipt of a price enquiry from a customer.

The price enquiry may be a formal written document, an email enquiry or a telephone call. When responding to a price enquiry it is important that you make sure that the price you quote is the correct one as if it is incorrect you may find that you are contracted to sell the goods at that price under contract law.

4.2 Price quotation

It is common practice to quote prices on a website if there is a standard price list from which there are no variations. However, some businesses will be prepared to offer certain customers goods at different prices or offer a discount. Therefore it is often the case that a price quotation is sent out to a customer showing the price at which the goods that they want can be bought.

Different types of discounts given or offered to customers will be considered in section 10 of this chapter.

A typical price quotation is shown:

City Woods Suppliers

192 Old Kent Road
London
SE1 8QT
← *Name, address and contact details of business quoting price*

Tel: 020 7248 7009 – Email: sales@citywoodssuppliers.co.uk

QUOTATION

TO: Alpha Limited
      Mountjoy Street ← *Name and address of customer*
      London W12 6RS

Date: 14 Sept 20X3
Today's date

Thank you for your telephone enquiry of 10 September. We are pleased to quote the following price:

Chipboard sheeting 6' × 4' Code CB0351 £23.00 per unit, excluding VAT

Details of goods

J Kramer ← *Authorisation signature*
Sales Manager

Price being quoted

The price quotation is an important document as this is the price that your organisation is now contracted to sell the goods at. Therefore it is important that it is authorised by an appropriate person in the organisation.

5   Purchase order

5.1   The purchase order

🔍 Definition – Purchase order

A buyer generated document that authorises a purchase transaction.

If the customer is happy with the price quotation that they have received from a business then they will place a firm order with the business. The order may be by telephone, email, fax or it may be in writing. Whichever method is used for the purchase order, it is important to check all of the details carefully.

- Does the price agree to what was quoted to the customer?

- Are the delivery terms acceptable?

- Are any discounts applicable?

A typical purchase order follows. Note that the purchase order has been authorised by an appropriate person in the customer's organisation.

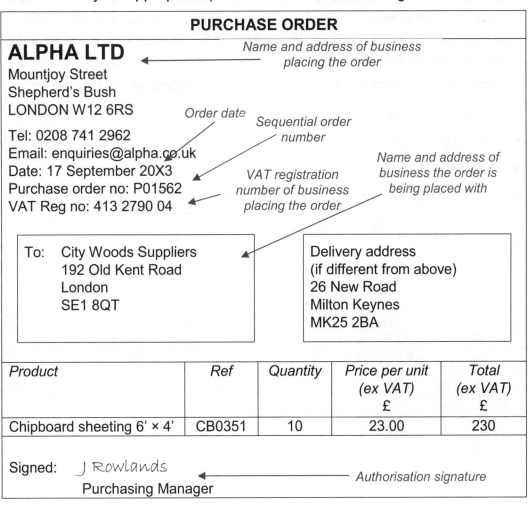

6 Sales order

6.1 Confirming sales orders

 Definition – Sales order

A seller generated document that authorises a sale to a customer, issued after the receipt of a purchase order.

To avoid misunderstandings, a supplier will normally confirm a customer's order by completing a **sales order**, even if the customer has already sent a written purchase order.

A **sales order** confirms the terms on which goods will be sold including:

- quantity/type of goods or service
- date of supply
- delivery address
- price and payment terms including any discounts given or offered.

City Woods Suppliers

192 Old Kent Road
London
SE1 8QT

*Name and address
of business making
the sale*

*Delivery address
and date*

Tel: 020 7248 7009 – Email: sales@citywoodssuppliers.co.uk
SALES ORDER

To:

Alpha Limited
Mountjoy St
London W12 6RS

*Name and
address of
customer*

Delivery:

26 New Road
Milton Keynes
MK25 2BA

Delivery date:

25 September 20X3

*Sales order
number*

Date: 20 September 20X3

Sales order number: 41161

We confirm the following order to be delivered as above.
Please note our credit terms are strictly 30 days net.

Code	Quantity	Description	Unit price (excl VAT)	Discount
CB0351	10	Chipboard sheeting 6' × 4'	£23.00	NIL

Details of goods

Price of goods

Authorised: *P. Anders*

*Authorisation
signature*

Date: 20 September 20X3

7 Delivery note and goods received note

7.1 Introduction

When negotiations over the price and terms of the credit sale have been completed, then the goods will be delivered.

7.2 Delivery notes

 Definition – Delivery note

A document accompanying goods despatched to a customer explaining what the delivery contains.

Delivery notes should have **sequential numbers** that are either pre-printed for a manual system or computer generated in a computer system, and should be used in order. Spoiled or scrapped delivery notes should be cancelled and retained.

There will normally be three parts to a delivery note:

Part one   – This is kept by the **customer** in order to compare to the purchase order and then to the sales invoice.

Part two   – This is signed and returned to the **supplier** of the goods as evidence that the goods have been received by the customer in good condition.

Part three – This is signed and kept by the **delivery organisation** such as a courier, as evidence that they have delivered the goods and that the customer has received them.

City Woods Suppliers
192 Old Kent Road
London
SE1 8QT

Tel: 020 7248 7009 – Email: sales@citywoodssuppliers.co.uk   DN 005673

DELIVERY NOTE

To:	**Delivery:**	**Delivery date:**
Alpha Limited	26 New Road	25 September 20X3
Mountjoy St	Milton Keynes	
London W12 6RS	MK25 2BA	
Date: 25 September 20X3		**Sales order number:** 41161

We confirm the following order to be delivered as above.

Product	Code	Quantity
Chipboard 6' × 4'	CB0351	10

Received in good condition: *A Patel*

7.3   Goods received notes

 Definition – Goods received note

A goods received note is an internal document completed by the purchaser that records the details of goods received and contains similar information to a delivery note.

The goods received note is often compared to the purchase order as part of a payment authorisation process. The information that a goods received note contains includes:

- supplier name

- quantity/type of goods or service

- the associated purchase order reference and delivery note number

- the name and reference of the carrier for delivery (if different from the supplier).

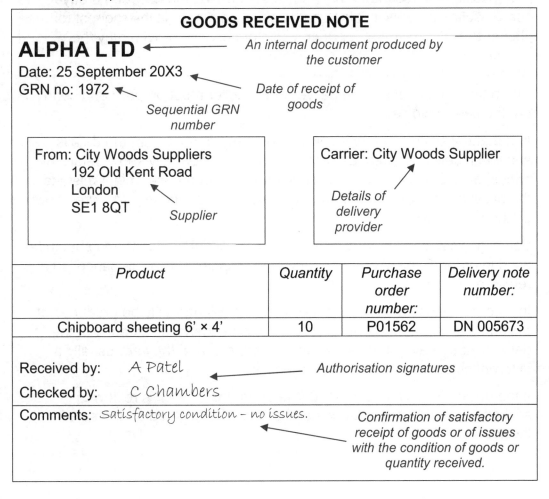

8 Invoice

8.1 The sales invoice

 Definition – Sales invoice

An invoice is a document that itemises a transaction between a buyer and a seller. A sales invoice can be simply defined as the request for the buyer to make payment for goods sold or services provided by the seller.

When the goods have been delivered the seller must prepare and send out the sales invoice.

In a manual system, sales invoices must be prepared from the details shown on delivery notes. Delivery notes do not normally show details of prices, discounts or VAT. (This is because the purchaser might mistake the delivery note for a sales invoice.) Price, discounts and VAT are shown on the sales invoice.

Sales invoices should have pre-printed sequential numbers and should be used in order. Spoiled or scrapped sales invoices should be cancelled and retained.

In a computerised system, the sales invoice will normally be produced at the same time as the delivery note and will be identical except that the delivery note may not have details of price, etc, and they are usually a different colour to distinguish them easily.

If the business is VAT registered (the operation of VAT is reviewed in section 9) the VAT registration number must be detailed on the sales invoice.

City Woods Suppliers

192 Old Kent Road
London
SE1 8QT

Tel: 020 7248 7009
Email: sales@citywoodssuppliers.co.uk

Invoice no: 1005673
Tax point: 25 September 20X3
VAT reg no: 618 2201 63
Delivery note: DN005673
Account no: AL6215

SALES INVOICE

To:

Alpha Limited
Mountjoy St
London W12 6RS

Delivery:

26 New Road
Milton Keynes
MK25 2BA

Delivery date:

25 September 20X3

Date: 25 September 20X3

Sales order number: 41161

We confirm the following order to be delivered as above.

Product	Code	Quantity	Price per unit £	Total £
Chipboard 6' × 4'	CB0351	10	23.00	230.00
			VAT (20%)	46.00
			Total	276.00

8.2 Pricing goods and services

Unit prices for goods or services are kept in master files which must be updated regularly. If a price quotation has been sent to a customer then this must be used to determine the price to use on the invoice.

Prices will normally be quoted exclusive of value added tax (VAT), as this is the true selling price to the business. We will now review the operation of VAT.

9 Operation of VAT

9.1 Introduction

 Definition – VAT (sales tax)

VAT (sales tax) is a consumption tax added to a product's selling price. It represents a tax on the 'value added' to the product at each stage of a production or supply process.

 Definitions – Output and input tax

VAT is charged on the **taxable supply of goods and services** in the United Kingdom by a **taxable person** in the course of a business carried on by him.

Output tax is the tax charged on the sale of goods and services

Input tax is the tax paid on the purchase of goods and services

Sales tax (VAT) is a tax levied on **consumer** expenditure. However the procedure is that it is collected at each stage in the production and distribution chain. Most businesses (being **taxable persons** as defined later) avoid having to treat VAT as an expense as they may deduct the VAT they have paid on their purchases **(input tax)** from the VAT they charge to customers on their sales **(output tax)** and pay only the net output tax to the tax authorities (HM Revenue and Customs).

9.2 How VAT works

Let us examine a simple illustration. We will assume a standard rate of 20%, and follow one article, a wooden table, through the production and distribution chain.

- A private individual cuts down a tree and sells it to a timber mill for £10. **Tax effect** – none. The individual is not a 'taxable person' in this case.

- The timber mill saws the log into planks and sells the timber to a furniture manufacturer for £100 + VAT.

Tax effect – Being a taxable person, the mill is obliged to charge its customers VAT at 20% on the selling price (output tax).There is no VAT paid on the purchase cost (input tax) available for offset.

Cash effect – The mill collected £120 from the customer (or has a receivable for this sum). Of this, £20 will be paid to HMRC and therefore only £100 would be recognised as sales.

- The manufacturer makes a table from the wood, and sells this to a retailer for £400 + VAT.

Tax effect – The manufacturer is obliged to charge VAT at 20% on the selling price (i.e. £80), but in this instance would be allowed to reduce this amount by setting off the input tax of £20 charged on the purchase of wood from the mill.

Cash effect – Tax of £60 is paid to the tax authorities (HM Revenue and Customs) (output less input tax = £80 - £20). £400 is recognised as sales and £100 as purchases in the accounts of the manufacturer.

- The retailer sells the table to a private customer for £1,000 plus VAT of £200. **Tax effect** – The retailer charges £200 of VAT to the customer but against this output tax may be set off the input tax of £80 charged on the purchase from the manufacturer.

Cash effect – £120 (£200 – £80) is paid to HMRC. Purchases would be shown in the books at £400 and sales at £1,000.

- **The private customer** – VAT is a tax levied on consumer expenditure and the chain ends here. The customer is not a taxable person, and cannot recover the tax paid.

You will note that everybody else has passed the sales tax on and, though the customer has paid his £200 to the retailer, HMRC has received its tax by contributions from each link in the chain, as shown below:

	£
Timber mill	20.00
Manufacturer	60.00
Retailer	120.00
	200.00

9.3   Taxable supply of goods and services

Taxable supply is the supply of all items except those which are **exempt.** Examples of exempt items are as follows:

- certain land and buildings, where sold, leased or hired
- insurance
- Post Office postal services
- Admission charges to museums, art galleries etc.
- betting, gaming and lotteries.

Input tax cannot be reclaimed where the trader's supplies are all exempt.

9.4   Rates of VAT

In the UK, there are three rates of VAT on taxable supplies. Some items are 'zero-rated' (similar to exempt except that input tax can be reclaimed), there is a special rate of 5% for domestic fuel and power, and all other items are rated at the standard rate of 20%. Examples of 'zero-rated' supplies include:

- water and most types of food stuffs (i.e. not hot food and not eating in as service is also provided which is taxable)
- books and newspapers
- drugs and medicines
- children's clothing and footwear.

9.5   Non-deductible VAT

VAT on some items is non-deductible. This means that VAT on any purchases of these items can never be deducted from the amount of tax payable to HMRC. The business has to bear the VAT as an expense.

Non-deductible items include:

- motor cars
- business entertaining.

For our purposes you will normally be dealing with taxable supplies at the standard rate of 20%.

9.6 Taxable person

A taxable person is any individual, partnership, company, etc who intends to make taxable supplies and is liable to register.

A person is liable to register if the value of his taxable supplies exceeds a specified amount in a 12-month period. Most companies and partnerships and many sole traders are liable to register.

9.7 VAT exclusive amounts

 Definition – Net of VAT

A net amount excludes VAT.

If you are given the net price of goods, the price excluding VAT, then the amount of VAT is 20/100 of this price.

Note: VAT is always rounded down to the nearest penny.

 Example 1

A sale is made for £360.48 plus VAT. What is the amount of VAT to be charged on this sale?

Solution

VAT = £360.48 × 20/100 = £72.09

Remember to round down to the nearest penny.

An alternative way of calculating this would to be to multiply the net amount of £360.48 by 20%:

VAT = £360.48 × 20% = £72.09

9.8 VAT inclusive amounts

 Definition – Gross of VAT

A gross amount includes VAT.

If a price is given that already includes the VAT then calculating the VAT requires an understanding of the price structure:

	%
Selling price incl. VAT (gross)	120
VAT	20
	____
Selling price excl. VAT (net)	100
	____

 Example 2

Goods have a selling price of £3,000 inclusive of VAT. What is the VAT on the goods and the net price of these goods?

Solution

	£
Net price (£3,000 × 100/120)	2,500
VAT (£3,000 × 20/120)	500
	____
Gross price (selling price)	3,000
	____

Test your understanding 1

What is the amount of VAT on each of the following transactions?

(i)   £100 net of VAT

(ii) £250 net of VAT

(iii) £480 including VAT (gross)

(iv) £600 including VAT (gross)

Test your understanding 2

Dora Ltd ordered some goods from Swipey Ltd, the purchase order and the sales invoice are provided below. You should review these documents and identify any discrepancies.

PURCHASE ORDER

Dora Ltd
Leek Lane
Northwich
Cheshire CW7 5HU
Tel: 01565 734 879
Email: enquiries@doraltd.co.uk

Date: 15 April 20X5
Purchase order no: P0987
VAT Reg no: 414 7985 05

To:	Swipey Ltd, Keats Lane, Knutsford, Cheshire, WA16 7HT		**Delivery address** As above	
Product	Code	Quantity	Price per unit (ex VAT) £	Total (ex VAT) £
Cream leather chairs	CL101	20	98.00	1,960.00

Signed: *Lee-Anne Rogers*
Purchasing Manager

Swipey Ltd

Keats Lane
Knutsford
Cheshire
WA16 7HT

Tel: 01565 879 852
Email: swipey@swipeyltd.co.uk

Invoice number:	15963
Invoice date:	20 April 20X5
VAT reg no:	687 2241 87
Delivery note:	DN00154
Account no:	DORA1

SALES INVOICE

To:	Delivery:	Delivery date:
Dora Ltd	Leek Lane	20 April 20X5
Leek Lane	Northwich	
Northwich	Cheshire	
Cheshire	CW7 5HU	
CW7 5HU		

Date: 20 April 20X5   **Sales order number:** 1569

We confirm the following order to be delivered as above.

Product	Code	Quantity	Price per unit £	Total £
Cream leather chairs	CL100	20	100.00	2,000.00
			VAT	400.00
			Total	2,400.00

10 Discounts

10.1 Introduction

A discount is a reduction to the price of the sales of goods or services. There are different types of discounts that may be given or offered for different reasons.

Trade discount

Bulk discount

Prompt payment discount

10.2 Trade discounts

 Definition – Trade discount

A trade discount is a definite amount that is deducted from the list price of the goods for the supplies to some customers, with the intention of encouraging and rewarding customer loyalty.

A trade discount will appear on the invoice. It will be deducted from the list price of the goods before VAT is calculated.

The calculation of the trade discount on the face of the invoice should be checked and it should be agreed that the correct percentage of trade discount has been deducted.

10.3   Bulk discounts

 Definition – Bulk discount

A bulk discount is similar to a trade discount in that it is deducted from the list price of the goods and disclosed on the invoice. However, a bulk discount is given by a supplier for sales orders above a certain quantity.

A bulk discount must be checked to the agreement between customer and supplier, to ensure that the correct discount has been deducted. The deduction of a bulk discount will appear on the invoice, deducted from the list price before VAT is calculated.

10.4   Prompt payment discount

 Definition – Prompt payment discount

Prompt payment discounts (also known as settlement or cash discounts) are offered to customers in order to encourage early payment of invoices.

The details of the prompt payment discount will normally be shown at the bottom of the sales invoice and it is up to the customer to decide whether to pay the invoice early enough to benefit from the prompt payment discount or whether to delay payment and ignore the prompt payment discount. No deduction will occur for a prompt payment discount on the invoice, it will just be offered to the customer.

The agreement between the customer and supplier should be checked to confirm that the correct percentage of prompt payment discount according to the terms has been offered.

A trade discount or a bulk discount is a definite reduction in price from the list price whereas a prompt payment discount is only a reduction in price if the organisation decides to take advantage of it by making early payment.

10.5 VAT calculations and discounts

VAT is calculated after trade and bulk discounts have been deducted from the original list price.

Prompt payment discounts are only offered on an invoice so it does not impact the VAT calculation at the point of the invoice preparation.

If the customer goes on to take advantage of a prompt payment discount offered, the VAT amount is adjusted – this is looked at in more detail in chapter 5 of this text.

11 Preparing an invoice

11.1 Preparing a sales invoice

In order to prepare the sales invoice the customer master file must be found. This will show the details of any discounts given or offered to this customer.

 Example 3

Preparing a sales invoice

Thelma Goody is the sales invoicing clerk for a VAT registered clothing wholesaler. Thelma prepares the sales invoices to be sent to the customer from the price list and a copy of the delivery note sent up to her by the sales department.

Today she has received the following delivery note from the sales department.

Delivery note: 2685

To: K Clothing Ltd
9 Port Street
MANCHESTER
M1 5EX

A B Fashions Ltd
3 Park Road
Parkway
Bristol
BR6 6SJ
Tel: 01272 695221
Fax: 01272 695222

Delivery date: 20 August 20X6

Quantity	Code	DESCRIPTION	Colour
90	SSB 330	Shawls (babies)	Assorted
30	CJA 991	Cashmere jumpers (adult)	Cream
30	GGC 442	Gloves (children)	Assorted

Received by: ....

Signature: .... Date: ....

Code	Description	Colour	Unit price £	VAT rate
SSG 001	Skirt (girls)	Black	13.50	Zero
SSW 002	Skirt (women)	Navy	15.90	Standard
TTW 037	Trousers (women)	Black	21.00	Standard
TTW 038	Trousers (women)	Navy	15.60	Standard
TTW 039	Trousers (women)	Red	15.60	Standard
SSB 330	Shawl (babies)	Assorted	11.50	Zero
SSB 331	Shawl (babies)	White	11.50	Zero
CJA 991	Cashmere jumper (adult)	Cream	65.00	Standard
CJA 992	Cashmere jumper (adult)	Pink	65.00	Standard
CJA 993	Cashmere jumper (adult)	Blue	65.00	Standard
CJA 994	Cashmere jumper (adult)	Camel	65.00	Standard
HHB 665	Hat (babies)	White	3.50	Zero
HHB 666	Hat (babies)	Blue	3.50	Zero
GGC 442	Gloves (children)	Assorted	6.20	Zero
GGC 443	Gloves (children)	White	6.50	Zero
GGC 444	Gloves (children)	Black	6.50	Zero

The customer master file identifies that K Clothing Ltd's account number is KC 0055 and that a trade discount of 10% is given to this customer.

Thelma must now prepare the sales invoice. Today's date is 22 August 20X6. The last invoice number used was 95123.

Solution

SALES INVOICE

Invoice to:
K Clothing Ltd
9 Port Street
MANCHESTER
M1 5EX

A B Fashions Ltd
3 Park Road
Parkway
Bristol
BR6 6SJ
Tel: 01272 695221
Fax: 01272 695222

Deliver to:

As above

Invoice no:	95124
Invoice date:	22 August 20X6
VAT reg no:	488 7922 26
Delivery note no:	2685
Account no:	KC 0055

Code	Description	Quantity	VAT rate %	Unit price £	Amount excl of VAT £
SSB 330	Shawls (babies) assorted	90	0	11.50	1,035.00
CJA 991	Cashmere jumper (adult) cream	30	20	65.00	1,950.00
GGC 442	Gloves (children) assorted	30	0	6.20	186.00
					3,171.00
Trade discount 10%					(317.10)
					2,853.90
VAT					351.00
Total amount payable					3,204.90

Step 1   Enter today's date on the invoice and the invoice number which should be the next number after the last sales invoice number used.

Step 2   Enter the customer details – name, address and account number.

Step 3	Refer now to the delivery note copy and enter the delivery note number and the quantities, codes and descriptions of the goods.
Step 4	Refer to the price list and enter the unit prices of the goods and the rate of VAT (note that the VAT rate for children's clothes is zero).
Step 5	Now for the calculations – firstly multiply the number of each item by the unit price to find the VAT exclusive price – then total these total prices – finally calculate the trade discount as 10% of this total, £3,171 × 10% = £317.10 and deduct it.
Step 6	Calculate the VAT – in this case there is only standard rate VAT on the cashmere jumpers but you must remember to deduct the trade discount (£1,950 – £195) before calculating the VAT amount £1,755 × 20% = £351 – add the VAT to the invoice total after deducting the trade discount.

 Test your understanding 3

You are an accounts assistant for Smith Fashions. You are required to prepare a sales invoice to be sent to a customer, Bella Boutique. You have been provided with the delivery note and an extract of Smith Fashions' price list.

Delivery note: 165

To: Bella Boutique
10 Main Street
Prestwick
South Ayrshire
KA9 4BB

Smith Fashions

4 Booth Road
Newton Mearns
G2 1PW
Tel: 0141 333 989
Email: admin@smithfashions.co.uk

Delivery date: 20 September 20X6

Quantity	Code	DESCRIPTION	Colour
20	SAZT01	Aztec embellished mini skirt	Assorted
20	TLIV02	Live, Laugh, Love slogan top	Grey
20	TMES03	Mesh stripe top	Black

Received by: ....

Signature: .... Date: ....

Extract of price list:

Code	Description	Colour	Unit price £	VAT rate
SAZT01	Aztec embellished mini skirt	Assorted	25.00	Standard
TLIV02	Live, Laugh, Love slogan top	Grey	12.50	Standard
TMES03	Mesh stripe top	Black	20.00	Standard

The customer file shows that Bella Boutique's account number is BB01 and that a trade discount of 10% is offered to this customer.

You must now prepare the sales invoice. Today's date is 22 September 20X6. The last invoice number was 1586.

SALES INVOICE

Invoice to:
Bella Boutique
10 Main Street
Prestwick
South Ayrshire
KA9 4BB

Smith Fashions
4 Booth Road
Newton Mearns
G2 1PW
Tel: 0141 333 989
Email: admin@smithfashions.co.uk

Deliver to:

As above

Invoice no:
Tax point: 22 September 20X6
VAT reg no: 488 7922 26
Delivery note no:
Account no:

Code	Description	Quantity	VAT rate %	Unit price £	Total £

Net amount of goods	
Trade discount @ 10%	
Net amount of goods after discount	
VAT	
Total amount payable	

11.2   The purchase invoice

 Definition – Purchase invoice

An invoice is a document that itemises a transaction between a buyer and a seller. We now consider the situation from the customer perspective, what we previously regarded as a sales invoice, to the customer it is a purchase invoice.

When the customer receives their purchase invoice from the seller, a number of checks need to be made before it can be passed for payment.

11.3   Order and receipt of goods

The purchase invoice received must be agreed to the purchase order, the delivery note and goods received note. This is to ensure that not only is this an invoice for goods that were ordered but also for goods that were received. In particular check the description and the quantity of the goods per the invoice against the purchase order and delivery note.

For example, suppose that the purchase order for goods shows that 100 packs were ordered and the delivery note shows that 100 packs were received. If when the invoice arrives it is for 120 packs then the supplier should be politely informed of the error and a credit note requested to rectify the discrepancy.

11.4   Calculations

All of the calculations on the invoice should also be checked to ensure that they are correct. This will include the following:

- all pricing calculations
- any trade discount or bulk discount calculations
- the VAT calculations
- the total addition of the invoice.

11.5 Other terms found on invoices

You may also find other terms and conditions shown on invoices or other documents. Here are some of the more common:

E & OE – Errors and omissions excepted. The seller is claiming the right to correct any genuine errors on the invoice (e.g. prices) at a later date.

Carriage paid – The invoice value includes delivery of the goods to the customer's premises.

Ex works – Prices quoted do not include delivery to the customer's premises. The customer must organise and pay for the delivery of the goods.

Cash on delivery – The customer is expected to pay for the goods when they are delivered.

12 Credit note

12.1 Introduction

Definition – Credit note

Document issued by a supplier to a customer cancelling part or all of a sales invoice.

Businesses normally issue credit notes for any of the following reasons:

- when a customer has returned faulty or damaged goods
- when a customer has returned undamaged goods by agreement with the supplier for a refund
- to make a refund for short deliveries
- to settle a dispute with a customer
- to adjust an account after taking advantage of a prompt payment discount.

A credit note is the reversal of all or part of the earlier invoice value.

Credit notes are issued as documentary evidence that goods have been returned and that all or part of a previous sales invoice is cancelled. Therefore a business must keep strict control over the credit notes it raises and issues.

12.2 Return of goods

When a customer returns goods for any of the reasons mentioned previously, the return of goods will often be accompanied by a goods returned note.

 Definition – Goods returned note

Document sent to the supplier by the customer detailing the goods returned and reason(s) for the return being made.

The contents of a goods returned note are similar to a goods received note but with the added detail of why a return is being made.

When a supplier receives returned goods they must be inspected, counted and recorded on receipt. They would normally be recorded on a returns inwards note.

From the perspective of a customer who is returning goods and consequently receives a credit note exactly the same checks should be made on credit notes as on invoices. The reason for the credit note and the amount that has been credited should be checked, along with all of the calculations and the VAT.

12.3 Authorising credit notes

All credit notes must be authorised by a supervisor prior to being issued to the customer.

Some credit notes may be issued without a returns inwards note. For example, an error may have been made in pricing on an invoice but the customer is satisfied with the goods and does not need to return them.

These credit notes must be issued only after written authorisation has been received from a supervisor or manager and must be reviewed and approved before being sent to the customer or recorded.

12.4 Preparing credit notes

A credit note is effectively the reverse of an invoice and therefore will tend to include all the details that would normally appear on a sales invoice.

Using the example of Alpha Limited from earlier in the chapter, if Alpha Limited returned two of the chipboard panels, the credit note would be as follows.

City Woods Suppliers

192 Old Kent Road
London
SE1 8QT

Name and address of issuer of credit note

Sequential credit note number

Tel: 020 7248 7009
Email: sales@citywoodssuppliers.co.uk

VAT registration number of supplier

Returns inwards note reference

Credit note no: CN 02542
Tax point: 30 September 20X3
VAT reg no: 618 2201 63
Return inwards note no: 01531
Invoice no: 1005673
Account no: AL 6215

Date of credit note

CREDIT NOTE

Credit to:

Alpha Limited
Mountjoy St
London W12 6RS

Name and address of customer

Customer's account code

Date: 30 September 20X3

Description	Code	Quantity	VAT rate %	Unit price £	Amount exclusive of VAT £
Chipboard 6' × 4'	CB0351	2	20	23.00	46.00
				Goods returned total	46.00
					46.00
VAT				VAT charged	9.20
				Total amount of credit	55.20

Rate of VAT on goods returned

13 Coding

13.1 Introduction

 Definition – Code

A **code** is a system of numbers, letters and symbols designed to be applied to a classified set of items, to give a brief, accurate reference, which helps entry to the accounting records, collation and analysis.

Coding is used within an organisation to provide an efficient and accurate way of referencing customers, suppliers, products and other accounts within the accounting system.

Codes are used in accounting records and the accounting system; within day books, sales and purchases ledgers and other business documents.

 Definitions

Ledger code is a unique reference given to different types of income, expenses, assets and liabilities. It may also be referred to as a general ledger (GL) or nominal code.

Customer account code is a unique reference given to each individual customer of an organisation.

Supplier account code is a unique reference given to each individual supplier of an organisation.

Product code is a unique reference given to each type of product of an organisation.

A code can be an alphabetical, numerical or alphanumeric identification system.

 Definitions

Alphabetical codes consist of letters. If ordering alphabetically the order is a system whereby characters are placed in order of their position in the conventional ordering of an alphabet.

Numerical codes consist of numbers. If ordering numerically it can be ascending or descending.

Alphanumerical codes are a combination of alphabetic and numeric characters.

Customer files will normally be filed alphabetically by name or perhaps alphanumerically if part of the name is used within the code combined with a number allocation. Sales invoices tend to be filed in sequential order based upon invoice number.

Invoices should be coded to show:

- product group/type for analysis of sales/purchases

- customer/supplier account number.

There are several different systems of coding which can be used by a business.

13.2 Sequence codes

Allocate a number, or a letter, to items in a simple list.

For example:

Code	Name
01	ADAMS, Joan
02	AITKEN, James
03	ALCOCK, Freda
04	BROWN, Joe

13.3 Block codes

These allocate bands of numbers to particular categories.

For example, consider a furniture manufacturer who produces several types of tables, chairs and entertainment units. He could assign a code to each particular brand as follows:

Product type	Block code
Tables	01 – 19
Chairs	20 – 29
Entertainment units	30 – 39

13.4 Significant digit codes

These are a particular type of group classification code where individual digits and letters are used to represent features of the coded item. The example given is one used to describe different kinds of vehicle tyres sold by a garage.

Code	Item
TT67015B	Tube Tyre 670 × 15 Blackwall
LT67015W	Tubeless Tyre 670 × 15 Whitewall

13.5   Faceted codes

Faceted codes are another type of group classification code by which the digits of the code are divided into facets of several digits and each facet represents some attribute of the item being coded. These codes are similar to significant digit codes but are purely numerical.

Example: Faceted code for types of carpet.

Facet 1	=	type of weave (1 digit)	1	=	Cord
			2	=	Twist
			3	=	Short tufted, etc
Facet 2	=	material (1 digit)	1	=	All wool
			2	=	80% wool, 20% nylon
			3	=	50% wool, 50% nylon, etc
Facet 3	=	pattern (2 digits)	01	=	Self colour (plain)
			02	=	Self colour (embossed)
			03	=	Fig leaf, etc
Facet 4	=	colour (2 digits)	01	=	Off white
			02	=	Bright yellow
			03	=	Scarlet, etc

A typical code would be 2/2/03/02 representing a twist carpet in 80% wool, 20% nylon, pattern fig leaf and colour bright yellow.

Note that a two-digit facet allows up to 100 different codings (00 to 99).

13.6   Decimal codes (or hierarchical codes)

These are yet another form of a group classification code. The most obvious example of a decimal code is the Universal Decimal Code (UDC) devised by Dewey and widely used for the classification of books in libraries. UDC divides all human knowledge into more and more detailed categories as shown.

Code	Item
3	Social science
37	Education
372	Elementary
372.2	Kindergarten
372.21	Methods
372.215	Songs and games

Whatever the coding system used it is important for accounting purposes that the invoices and credit notes are coded according to type of sales and the particular customer.

You may be expected to code items such as sales invoices or credit notes according to a coding system that is given to you in an assessment.

Test your understanding 4

Is the cheque number used in a cheque book an example of a sequential code or a hierarchical code?

Test your understanding 5

ABC Ltd uses codes within the accounting system. An extract from the general ledger coding list is given below:

General ledger account	Code number
Equipment	10
Receivables	20
Electricity	30
Purchases	40
Sales	50

Required:

(a) Why are the general ledger codes numbered in steps of 10, rather than 1,2,3,4?

(b) Give 3 examples of the use of code numbers in an accounting system, other than general ledger accounts codes.

(c) Are the following statements true or false?

	TRUE/ FALSE
General ledger codes help when barcoding an item of inventory	
General ledger codes help when filing a financial document	
General ledger codes help trace relevant accounts quickly and easily	
General ledger codes help find the total amount owing to a supplier	

Test your understanding 6

Nethan Builders code all purchase invoices and credit notes with a supplier code and a general ledger code. Extracts of the codes used are as follows:

Supplier	Supplier account code
Haddow Bros	HAD29
AJ Broom & Company Ltd	AJB14
Jenson Ltd	JEN32
JM Bond & Co	JMB33

Item	General ledger code
Softwood	GL110
Hardwood	GL112
Sand	GL130
Steel	GL140
Brick	GL145

Required:

For each of the invoices and credit note shown below select the appropriate supplier account code and general ledger code to be used to code them.

SALES INVOICE
Haddow Bros

Invoice to:
Nethan Builders
Brecon House
Stamford Road
Manchester
M16 4PL

The White House, Standing Way, Manchester
M13 6FH
Tel: 0161 560 3140
Fax: 0161 560 5140

Deliver to:
As above

Invoice no:	033912
Tax point:	22 April 20X1
VAT reg no:	460 3559 71
Purchase order no::	7166

Code	Description	Quantity	VAT rate %	Unit price £	Amount excl of VAT £
PLY8FE1	Plywood Hardwood 2440 × 1220 mm	12 sheets	20	17.80	213.60
					213.60
VAT at 20%					42.72
Total amount payable					256.32
Deduct discount of 2% if paid within 10 days					

SALES INVOICE

Jenson Ltd
30 Longfield Park, Kingsway, M45 2TP

Invoice to:
Nethan Builders
Brecon House
Stamford Road
Manchester
M16 4PL

Invoice no:	47792
Tax point:	22 April 20X1
VAT reg no:	641 3229 45
Purchase order no::	7162

Deliver to:
As above

Code	Description	Quantity	VAT rate %	Unit price £	Amount excl of VAT £
PL432115	Steel rods 32 × 115 mm	14	20	30.25	423.50
PL432140	Steel rods 32 × 138 mm	8	20	33.15	265.20
					688.70
Trade discount 15%					103.30
					585.40
VAT at 20%					117.08
Total amount payable					702.48

Deduct discount of 3% if paid within 14 days

SALES INVOICE

A J Broom & Company Limited
59 Parkway, Manchester, M2 6EG
Tel: 0161 560 3392
Fax: 0161 560 5322

Invoice to:
Nethan Builders
Brecon House
Stamford Road
Manchester
M16 4PL

Invoice no:	046123
Tax point:	22 April 20X1
VAT reg no:	661 2359 07
Purchase order no:	7164

Deliver to:
As above

Code	Description	Quantity	VAT rate %	Unit price £	Amount excl of VAT £
DGS472	SDG Softwood	9.6 m	20	8.44	81.02
CIBF653	BIC Softwood	7	20	12.30	86.10
					167.12
Trade discount 10%					16.71
					150.41
VAT at 20%					30.08
Total amount payable					180.49

CREDIT NOTE
J M Bond & Co

Credit note to:
Nethan Builders
Brecon House
Stamford Road
Manchester
M16 4PL

North Park Industrial Estate, Manchester, M12 4TU
Tel: 0161 561 3214
Fax: 0161 561 3060

Credit note no: 06192
Tax point: 22 April 20X1
VAT no: 461 4367 91
Invoice no: 331624

Code	Description	Quantity	VAT rate %	Unit price £	Amount excl of VAT £
DGSS4163	Structural softwood untreated	6m	20	6.85	41.10
					41.10
Trade discount 20%					8.22
					32.88
VAT at 20%					6.57
Total amount of credit					39.45

14 Summary

In this chapter we have concentrated on the purpose and flow of a range of business documents. Before preparing an invoice it is necessary to ensure that this is for a valid sale by checking the order and delivery details. It is important that we understand the need to check business documents that are received and sent to ensure they agree to supporting documents, the calculations are correct in accordance with discounts and the treatment of VAT.

Test your understanding answers

 Test your understanding 1

(i)	£100.00 × 20/100	=	£20.00
(ii)	£250.00 × 20/100	=	£50.00
(iii)	£480.00 × 20/120	=	£80.00
(iv)	£600.00 × 20/120	=	£100.00

 Test your understanding 2

Discrepancies:

(1) incorrect product code

(2) incorrect price per unit (per chair)

Test your understanding 3

SALES INVOICE

Invoice to:
Bella Boutique
10 Main Street
Prestwick
South Ayrshire
KA9 4BB

Smith Fashions
4 Booth Road
Newton Mearns
G2 1PW
Tel: 0141 333 989
Email: admin@smithfashions.co.uk

Deliver to:

As above

Invoice no: **1587**
Tax point: 22 September 20X6
VAT reg no: 488 7922 26
Delivery note no: **165**
Account no: **BB01**

Code	Description	Quantity	VAT rate	Unit price	Total
			%	£	£
SAZT01	Aztec embellished mini skirt	20	20	25.00	500.00
TLIV02	Live, Laugh, Love slogan top	20	20	12.50	250.00
TMES03	Mesh stripe top	20	20	20.00	400.00
Net amount of goods					1,150.00
Trade discount @ 10%					(115.00)
Net amount of goods after discount					1,035.00
VAT					207.00
Total amount payable					1,242.00

 Test your understanding 4

A sequential code (the numbers run in sequential order).

Test your understanding 5

(a) To allow for expansion of the number of accounts in the general (main) ledger

(b) Any three from:

- Customer account codes
- Supplier account codes
- Product codes
- Inventory codes
- VAT codes
- Department codes

(c)

	TRUE/ FALSE
General ledger codes help when barcoding an item of inventory	FALSE
General ledger codes help when filing a financial document	FALSE
General ledger codes help trace relevant accounts quickly and easily	TRUE
General ledger codes help find the total amount owing to a supplier	FALSE

Test your understanding 6

Invoice from:	Supplier account code	General ledger code
Haddow Bros	HAD29	GL112
Jenson Ltd	JEN32	GL140
AJ Broom & Company Ltd	AJB14	GL110
JM Bond & Co	JMB33	GL110

Books of prime entry

2

Introduction

In a typical business there will be a great number of transactions to be recorded on a daily basis. Transactions include credit sales and purchases, cash sales, purchases, expenses and other day-to-day transactions.

These transactions are initially recorded from their source document into the books of prime entry. Books of prime entry may also be referred to as 'day books'.

This chapter introduces the day books which will be used throughout the text.

ASSESSMENT CRITERIA	CONTENTS
Demonstrate an understanding of the process of recording financial transactions (1.4)	1 Books of prime entry
	2 The sales day book
Enter sales invoices and credit notes into books of prime entry (2.2)	3 The sales returns day book
	4 The purchases day book
Enter supplier invoices and credit notes into books of prime entry (3.2)	5 The purchases returns day book
Enter receipts and payments into a two column analysed cash book (4.1)	6 The cash book
	7 The discounts allowed day book
Enter receipts and payments into an analysed petty cash book (4.2)	8 The discounts received day book
	9 The petty cash book

1 Books of prime entry

1.1 Introduction

In a typical business there will be a great number of transactions to be recorded. If we were to record each transaction individually, the accounts would get cluttered.

In order to simplify the process (and exercise greater control) we divide the recording of the transactions into parts.

(a) The first part is entering the transaction into the appropriate book of prime entry (day book).

(b) The second part is recording the totals from the day books into the general ledger which contains many different ledger accounts. This is introduced in chapters 3 & 4.

(c) The third part is to ensure transactions are recorded in the subsidiary ledger which may also be referred to as a memorandum ledger. Recording transactions within subsidiary ledgers is reviewed in chapters 5, 6 & 7.

A book of prime entry is the place where the transaction (which is detailed on a business document) is first recorded in the books of the business. Whilst reviewing the day books take note of the use of codes throughout. There are several day books which will be reviewed in this chapter:

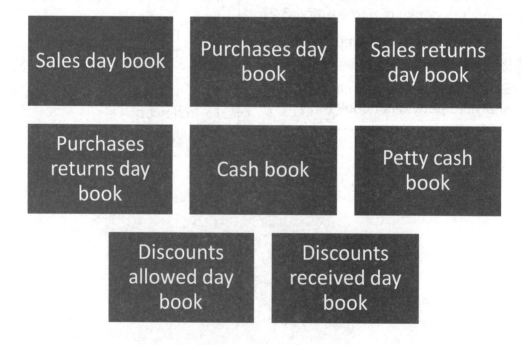

2 The sales day book

2.1 The sales day book (SDB)

In a typical business there will be numerous sales transactions to be recorded. Credit sales are recorded in the sales day book. We will review how cash sales are recorded when we study the cash book.

 Definition – Sales day book

The sales day book is a list of the sales invoices that are to be processed for a given period (e.g. a week).

In its simplest form, the SDB will comprise just the names of the customers and the amount of the invoices issued in a particular week.

The SDB is a list, the totals of which are used to perform the accounting entry. Double entry bookkeeping is introduced in chapters 3 & 4.

An example of a SDB is shown below:

Week 1			
Customer	Total £	VAT £	Net £
X	1,200	200	1,000
Y	2,400	400	2,000
Z	3,600	600	3,000
Total	7,200	1,200	6,000

2.2 The analysed sales day book

The sales day book usually includes analysis columns showing how the total value of each customer's invoice is made up.

SALES DAY BOOK								
Date	Customer	Reference	Invoice number	Total £	VAT £	Product 1 £	Product 2 £	Product 3 £
			TOTALS					

(a) The date column contains the date of the transaction

(b) The customer column contains the name of the customer

(c) The reference column may contain the code number of the customer's account

(d) The invoice number is the number of the invoice issued for this sale.

(e) The total column is the total value including VAT of the goods sold as shown on the invoice:

- after deducting any trade or bulk discounts that may have been given.

Example 1

An invoice to customer A is made up as follows:

	£
Sale of 50 units at £2 per unit	100.00
Less: 20% trade discount	(20.00)
	80.00
VAT (£80 × 20%)	16.00
Total invoice value	96.00

The £96 would be entered in the 'total' column.

(f) The VAT column – this column is the value of the VAT on the invoice – in this case (example 1) £16.00.

(g) Product 1, 2, etc. columns – these are columns that analyse the net sales value (i.e. the VAT exclusive amounts) into groupings that are of interest or use to the business. The columns may be categorised by product codes.

In this introductory section we shall not complicate things by considering more than one type of product so that there will only be one column for sales.

In this case (example 1) the entry in the sales column would be £80, the net amount after the deduction of the trade discount.

(h) The total boxes – at the end of a period (say a week or a month) the sales day book is totalled and the total values of each column are included in the total boxes. It is these totals which are used for the accounting entry.

The sales day book would look as follows for example 1:

SALES DAY BOOK								
Date	Customer	Reference	Invoice number	Total £	VAT £	Product 1 £	Product 2 £	Product 3 £
	A			96	16	80		
			TOTALS	96	16	80		

2.3 Casting and cross casting

Casting is the way we refer to adding a vertical column of figures and cross-casting is the way we refer to adding a horizontal row of figures.

It is worth very briefly doing a simple example of this just to show how a valuable check of the accuracy of your additions is provided by these two operations.

Example 2

The following table of numbers is similar to the contents of accounting records such as the 'sales day book' or the 'analysed cash book' which you will come across as part of your Bookkeeping Transactions studies.

This table might represent the sales of products A to E in three geographical areas.

You should calculate the totals yourself before looking at the solution.

	A	B	C	D	E	Total
UK	221,863	17,327	14,172	189,221	5,863	
USA	17,155	14,327	8,962	27,625	73,127	
Africa	18,627	33,563	62,815	1,003	57,100	
Total						

Solution

	A	B	C	D	E	Total
UK	221,863	17,327	14,172	189,221	5,863	**448,446**
USA	17,155	14,327	8,962	27,625	73,127	**141,196**
Africa	18,627	33,563	62,815	1,003	57,100	**173,108**
Total	**257,645**	**65,217**	**85,949**	**217,849**	**136,090**	**762,750**

3 The sales returns day book

3.1 The sales returns day book (SRDB)

 Definition – Sales returns day book

The sales returns day book is a list of the credit notes that are to be processed for a given period (e.g. a week).

Sales returns are in practice entered in a 'sales returns day book'. This is similar to the sales day book, and the columns are used in the same way. The only difference is that instead of having a column for the invoice number, there is a column for the 'credit note number'. This is because when the goods are returned to the business it will issue a credit note to the customer.

KAPLAN PUBLISHING

SALES RETURNS DAY BOOK						
Date	Customer	Reference	Credit note number	Total £	VAT £	Sales returns £

3.2 Sales returns in sales day book

In some businesses the level of sales returns are fairly low and therefore it does not justify keeping a separate sales returns day book. In these cases any credit notes that are issued for sales returns are recorded as negative amounts in the sales day book.

 Test your understanding 1

You work in the accounts department of D F Engineering and one of your tasks is to write up the day books. In your organisation there is no separate sales returns day book and therefore any credit notes are entered as negative amounts in the sales day book.

Given below are the details of the sales invoices and credit notes that have been issued this week. D F Engineering does not offer any discounts. The business is registered for VAT and all sales are for standard rated goods (at 20%).

Invoices sent out:

		Code	£	Invoice number
20X1				
1 May	Fraser & Co	SL14	128.68 plus VAT	03466
	Letterhead Ltd	SL03	257.90 plus VAT	03467
2 May	Jeliteen Traders	SL15	96.58 plus VAT	03468
3 May	Harper Bros	SL22	268.15 plus VAT	03469
	Juniper Ltd	SL17	105.38 plus VAT	03470
4 May	H G Frank	SL30	294.67 plus VAT	03471
5 May	Keller Assocs	SL07	110.58 plus VAT	03472

Credit notes sent out:

		Code	£	Credit note number
20X1				
2 May	Garner & Co	SL12	68.70 plus VAT	0746
4 May	Hill Traders	SL26	117.68 plus VAT	0747

Required:

Write up the sales day book given for the week ending 5 May 20X1 and total all of the columns.

Date	Invoice no	Customer name	Code	Total £	VAT £	Net £

4 The purchases day book

4.1 The purchases day book (PDB)

As seen earlier in the chapter, credit sales are recorded in the 'sales day book'. In the case of credit purchases, we have the 'purchases day book'.

Definition – Purchases day book

The purchases day book is a list of the purchases invoices that are to be processed for a given period (e.g. a week).

In its simplest form, the purchases day book will comprise just the names of the suppliers and the amount of the invoices received in the week.

The PDB is a list, the totals of which are used to perform the accounting entry. Double entry bookkeeping is studied later in this text.

A purchases day book will look something like this:

Week 1			
Supplier	Total £	VAT £	Net £
A	3,600	600	3,000
B	2,400	400	2,000
C	1,200	200	1,000
Total	7,200	1,200	6,000

4.2 The analysed purchases day book

The purchases day book usually includes 'analysis columns' showing how the total value of each supplier's invoice is made up.

PURCHASES DAY BOOK								
Date	Supplier	Reference	Invoice number	Total £	VAT £	Product 1 £	Product 2 £	Product 3 £
			TOTALS					

(a) The date column contains the date of the transaction.

(b) The supplier column contains the name of the supplier.

(c) The reference column may contain the code number of the supplier's account.

(d) The invoice number is the number of the invoice from the supplier.

(e) The total column is the value of the goods purchased including VAT:

   • after deducting any trade/bulk discount that may have been given.

(f) The VAT column – this column is the value of the VAT on the invoice.

(g) Product 1, 2, etc. columns – these are columns that analyse the net purchases value (i.e. the VAT exclusive amounts) into groupings that are of interest or use to the business. The columns may be categorised by product codes.

(h) The total boxes – at the end of a period (say a week or a month) the purchases day book is totalled and the total values of each column are included in the total boxes. It is these totals which are used for the accounting entry.

5 The purchases returns day book

5.1 The purchases returns day book (PRDB)

 Definition – Purchases returns day book

The purchases returns day book is a list of the credit notes that have been received from suppliers for a given period (e.g. a week).

Purchases returns are in practice entered in a 'purchases returns day book'. This is similar to the purchases day book, and the columns are used in the same way. The only difference is that instead of having a column for the invoice number, there is a column for the 'credit note number'.

PURCHASES RETURNS DAY BOOK						
Date	Supplier	Reference	Credit note number	Total £	VAT £	Purchases returns £

5.2 Purchases returns in purchases day book

In some businesses the level of purchases returns are fairly low and therefore it does not justify keeping a separate purchases returns day book. In these cases any credit notes that are received for purchases returns are recorded as negative amounts in the purchases day book. If this is the case then you will be told that this is the policy of the business. Care should be taken, however, when adding up the columns in the purchases day book as any credit notes must be deducted rather than added.

Test your understanding 2

Stevens Ltd operates an analysed purchases day book, analysing purchases by the geographical area from which the purchases are made. The areas concerned are:

Zone 1   London region

Zone 2   Scotland region

Zone 3   Other UK

The company is registered for VAT.

Today's date is 14 September 20X2. The company has received the following invoices from suppliers in the post today:

Supplier	Region	Amount net of VAT £	VAT £
Bradley Ltd	London	210.00	42.00
Hannah Ltd	Wales	470.20	94.04
Spearritt Ltd	London	402.00	80.40
Lee Ltd	Scotland	1,076.00	215.20
O'Meara Ltd	Northern Ireland	317.60	63.52
Cattermole Ltd	Scotland	62.44	12.48
Barrett Ltd	London	107.80	21.56

Required:

Write up the purchases day book given and total all of the columns.

Date	Supplier	Total £	VAT £	Zone 1 £	Zone 2 £	Zone 3 £

6 The cash book

6.1 The cash book (CB)

 Definition – Cash book

A cash book is a record of cash receipts and payments that can form part of the double entry bookkeeping system as well as being a book of prime entry.

There are various forms of cash book, a 'two-column' and a 'three-column' cash book. Bookkeeping Transactions requires you to be able to post transactions into a two-column analysed cash book. You may hear about a three-column cash book – this is not within the Bookkeeping Transactions assessment criteria.

The difference between a two-column cash book and a three-column cash book is that a three-column cash book incorporates discount columns. As part of Bookkeeping Transactions you deal with discounts in their own day books – the discounts allowed and discounts received day books, which are introduced later in this chapter.

6.2 Two column cash book

A proforma two column cash book is shown below.

CASH BOOK							
Date	Narrative	Cash £	Bank £	Date	Narrative	Cash £	Bank £

Notes:

(a) The left hand side of the cash book records money received.

(b) The right hand side of the cash book records money paid out.

(c) The date column contains the date of the transaction.

(d)   The narrative column describes the transactions – typically the name of the customer who is paying or supplier who is receiving money. It would also contain the sales ledger or purchase ledger code of the credit customer (receivable) or credit supplier (payable).

(e)   The cash column on the left hand side (debit side) represents cash received, whereas the cash column on the right hand side (credit side) represents cash paid.

(f)   The bank column on the left hand side (debit side) represents money received (by cheque or other bank payment) whereas the bank column on the right hand side (credit side) represents money paid (by cheque or other bank payment).

A business may operate a bank current account as a means to settle business transactions. Receipts may be made automatically, in the form of a cheque or cash may be deposited into the current account. Payments may be made by drawing a cheque against the current account or by an automated payment.

To be able to record these bank specific transactions, a separate column must be introduced to the cash book to account for them. This is what leads to the use of a two-column cash book; a column for cash transactions and a column for transactions made through the bank current account. Each column represents a separate account, cash account and bank account, each with its own double entry as will be shown later in the text.

The cash book may be split into two separate books – the cash receipts book and the cash payments book. In addition to being aware of the use of separate cash receipts and cash payments books, you should also be aware that a cash book may have additional columns for the purpose of analysing the receipts and payments.

6.3   The analysed cash receipts book

 Definition – Analysed cash book

An analysed cash book is a cash book with additional columns for analysing principal sources and payments for cash into types of income and expense.

A proforma analysed cash receipts book is shown below.

CASH RECEIPTS BOOK							
Date	Narrative	Reference	Cash £	Bank £	VAT £	Receivables £	Cash sales £
Totals							

Notes:

(a) The date column contains the date of the transaction.

(b) The narrative column describes the transactions – typically the name of the customer who is paying.

(c) The reference column contains any other information that may be helpful e.g. 'cash', 'cheque', 'BACS' or perhaps the customer's reference code.

(d) The cash receipts book may have a 'total' column which contains the total cash received (including VAT) – whether it is received through the bank, cheque or cash or it may have separate 'cash' and 'bank' columns to show the method of money received. A cash receipt would be recorded in the cash column whereas a cheque or other form of bank receipt would be recorded in the bank column.

(e) The VAT column contains the VAT on the transaction but not if the VAT has already been entered in the sales day book. When recording a receipt from a receivable, VAT was already considered in the sales day book. There is no requirement to analyse out the VAT from the receivable receipt – it has already been dealt with.

(f) The receivables column contains any cash received that has been received from a receivable (credit customer) in payment of an amount owed by the receivable.

(g) The cash sales will be the VAT exclusive amount otherwise known as the 'net' amount. A VAT registered business only recognises the net amount of the sale as income. The VAT collected is owed to HMRC.

Note: you may be told the total receipt of cash sales made – you should ensure you analyse this out to calculate the net and VAT amounts in order to enter these amounts into the correct columns.

Test your understanding 3

You work in the accounts department of Solid Ltd. Given below is the cheque listing for the company showing all the cheques received from receivables in the week ended 14 February 20X8. You have also been told that there were cash sales totalling £480 including VAT, which is charged at 20% on all sales.

Cheques received:

Customer name	Customer code	Cheque amount £
D Asher	ASH01	74.62
L Maffiah	MAF03	193.75
G Mann	MAN04	107.64
A Burrell	BUR07	422.91
M Morgan	MOR09	60.36
D Skatt	SKA02	150.00

Required:

Write up the cash receipts book given for the week ended 14 February 20X8 and total all of the columns.

Date	Customer name	Code	Total £	VAT £	Receivables £	Cash sales £
TOTALS						

6.4 The analysed cash payments book

A proforma analysed cash payments book is shown below

CASH PAYMENTS BOOK								
Date	Narrative	Reference	Cash £	Bank £	VAT £	Payables £	Cash purchases £	Admin £
Totals								

Notes:

(a)   The date column contains the date of the transaction.

(b)   The narrative column describes the transactions. The reference column may include a reference to the source of the information or the code of a supplier being paid.

(c)   The cash payments book may have a 'total' column which contains the total cash paid – whether it is paid through the bank, cheque or cash, or it may have separate 'cash' and 'bank' columns to show the method of money paid. A cash payment would be recorded in the cash column whereas a payment made by cheque or another form of payment via the bank would be recorded in the bank column.

(d)   The VAT column contains the VAT on the transaction but not if the VAT has already been entered in the purchases day book.

(e)   The payables column contains any cash paid that has been paid to a payable (credit supplier) in payment of an amount owed to the payable.

(f)   The cash purchases column contains cash paid for purchases that are not bought on credit. This would be the VAT exclusive amount (net). The VAT element would be accounted for in the VAT column.

(g)   We saw with the analysed cash receipts book that nearly all receipts come from receivables or cash sales. In the case of payments, there is a broader range of suppliers who are paid through the cash book – rent and rates, telephone, electricity, marketing, etc. The business will have a separate column for the categories of expense that it wishes to analyse.

Test your understanding 4

You are the accounts assistant at Brown Ltd, a small company which is not registered for VAT. Listed below are payments to credit suppliers on 31 May 20X2.

Supplier	Payment £	Supplier code
B Able	723.78	ABL02
Mann Ltd	556.98	MAN01
Sykes & Sons	689.00	SYK04
Dickens Ltd	879.95	DIC01
Barber & Co	364.84	BAR01
Ward & Ward	287.66	WAR02

Required:

You are required to enter the payments into the cash payments book and total all columns for the week ended 31 May.

Date	Supplier	Supplier code	Total £	VAT £	Payables £	Other £
TOTALS						

7 The discounts allowed day book

7.1 The discounts allowed day book

 Definition – Discounts allowed day book

The discounts allowed day book is used to record the discounts that have not been deducted at the point of the invoice being recorded in the sales day book but instead were offered on a conditional basis i.e. prompt payment discounts allowed to credit customers.

The purpose of the discounts allowed day book is to record the credit notes that must be issued due to the customer taking advantage of a prompt payment discount that has been offered. The credit note deals with the reduction to the original goods value (net amount) and also the reduction in the VAT. The total (gross amount) is then deducted from the receivable's (credit customer's) balance.

The discounts allowed day book is a list, the totals of which are used to perform the accounting entry. Double entry bookkeeping is studied later in this text.

DISCOUNTS ALLOWED DAY BOOK					
Date	Narrative	Reference	Total £	VAT £	Net £
Totals					

Notes:

(a)   The date column contains the date of the transaction.

(b)   The narrative column provides details of the customer's name. The reference column may include a reference to the source of the information (the credit note) or the customer code the transaction relates to.

(c)   The total column contains the total discount that has been allowed to the credit customer (including any VAT).

(d)   The VAT column contains the VAT element of the transaction.

(e)   The net column contains the amount of the discount excluding the VAT element.

The discounts allowed day book and associated accounting entries are studied in chapter 5.

8 The discounts received day book

8.1 The discounts received day book

 Definition – Discounts received day book

The discounts received day book is used to record the discounts that have not been deducted at the point of the invoice being recorded in the purchases day book but instead were offered on a conditional basis i.e. prompt payment discounts received from credit suppliers.

The purpose of the discounts received day book is to record the credit notes that have been received due to the business taking advantage of a prompt payment discount that was offered. The credit note deals with the reduction to the original goods value (net amount) and also the reduction in the VAT. The total (gross amount) is then deducted from the payable's (credit supplier's) balance.

The discounts received day book is a list, the totals of which are used to perform the accounting entry. Double entry bookkeeping is studied later in this text.

DISCOUNTS RECEIVED DAY BOOK					
Date	Narrative	Reference	Total £	VAT £	Net £
Totals					

Notes:

(a) The date column contains the date of the transaction.

(b) The narrative column provides details of the supplier's name. The reference column may include a reference to the source of the information (the credit note) or the code of the supplier the transaction relates to.

(c) The total column contains the total discount that has been received from the supplier (including any VAT).

(d) The VAT column contains the VAT element of the transaction.

(e) The net column contains the amount of the discount excluding the VAT element.

The discounts received day book and associated accounting entries are studied in chapter 6.

9 The petty cash book

9.1 The petty cash book

 Definition – Petty cash

Petty cash is the small amount of cash that most businesses hold in order to make small cash payments.

 Definition – Petty cash book

A petty cash book is one in which all petty or small payments made through the petty cash fund are recorded systematically.

9.2 Layout of the petty cash book

A typical petty cash book is set out below. This is a typical petty cash book that is in the format of a ledger. A petty cash book that also forms part of the double entry bookkeeping system is studied in chapter 8.

Receipts			Payments								
Date	Narrative	Total	Date	Narrative	Voucher no	Total	Postage	Cleaning	Tea & Coffee	Sundry	VAT
		£				£	£	£	£	£	£
1 Nov	Bal b/f	35.50									
1 Nov	Cheque 394	114.50	1 Nov	ASDA	58	23.50			23.50		
			2 Nov	Post Office Ltd	59	29.50	29.50				
			2 Nov	Cleaning materials	60	15.07		12.56			2.51
			3 Nov	Postage	61	16.19	16.19				
			3 Nov	ASDA	62	10.57		8.81			1.76
			4 Nov	Newspapers	63	18.90				18.90	
			5 Nov	ASDA	64	12.10				10.09	2.01

9.3 Receipts side of the petty cash book

The receipts side (left hand side) of the petty cash book, only requires one column, as the only receipt into the petty cash box is the regular receipt into the petty cash box of cash withdrawn from the bank account.

Referring to the example of a typical petty cash book (above), we can see that the balance brought forward (representing the opening balance) was £35.50. The petty cash float has then been restored up to £150 by paying in an additional £114.50.

9.4 Payments side of the petty cash book

Payments out of the petty cash float will be for a variety of different types of expense and an analysis column is required for each type of expense in the same way as the cash payments book is analysed. The example above has analysed the expenses into postage, cleaning, tea & coffee and sundry expenses.

Note that a column is also required for VAT, as if a petty cash expense includes VAT this must also be separately analysed. In addition, it is important to remember that any VAT included in a petty cash expense must be shown separately on the petty cash voucher.

Any VAT shown on the petty cash voucher must be analysed into the VAT column and the net amount shown in the appropriate expense analysis column.

10 Summary

This session has introduced the different books of original entry (day books) that invoices, credit notes, discounts, receipts and payments are recorded in. It is from these day books that we then go on to post the transactions into the general and subsidiary ledgers. We will now study how to do this by introducing 'double entry bookkeeping' in chapters 3 and 4.

Test your understanding answers

Test your understanding 1

Sales day book

Date	Invoice no	Customer name	Code	Total £	VAT £	Net £
20X1						
1/5	03466	Fraser & Co	SL14	154.41	25.73	128.68
	03467	Letterhead Ltd	SL03	309.48	51.58	257.90
2/5	03468	Jeliteen Traders	SL15	115.89	19.31	96.58
	CN0746	Garner & Co	SL12	(82.44)	(13.74)	(68.70)
3/5	03469	Harper Bros	SL22	321.78	53.63	268.15
	03470	Juniper Ltd	SL17	126.45	21.07	105.38
4/5	03471	H G Frank	SL30	353.60	58.93	294.67
	CN0747	Hill Traders	SL26	(141.21)	(23.53)	(117.68)
5/5	03472	Keller Assocs	SL07	132.69	22.11	110.58
				1,290.65	215.09	1,075.56

Test your understanding 2

Date	Supplier	Total	VAT £	Zone 1 £	Zone 2 £	Zone 3 £
20X2						
14/9	Bradley Ltd	252.00	42.00	210.00		
	Hannah Ltd	564.24	94.04			470.20
	Spearritt Ltd	482.40	80.40	402.00		
	Lee Ltd	1,291.20	215.20		1,076.00	
	O'Meara Ltd	381.12	63.52			317.60
	Cattermole Ltd	74.92	12.48		62.44	
	Barrett Ltd	129.36	21.56	107.80		
		3,175.24	529.20	719.80	1,138.44	787.80

Test your understanding 3

Date	Customer name	Code	Total £	VAT £	Receivables £	Cash sales £
14/2/X8	D Asher	ASH01	74.62		74.62	
14/2/X8	L Maffiah	MAF03	193.75		193.75	
14/2/X8	G Mann	MAN04	107.64		107.64	
14/2/X8	A Burrell	BUR07	422.91		422.91	
14/2/X8	M Morgan	MOR09	60.36		60.36	
14/2/X8	D Skatt	SKA02	150.00		150.00	
14/2/X8	Cash sales		480.00	80.00		400.00
TOTALS			**1,489.28**	**80.00**	**1,009.28**	**400.00**

Test your understanding 4

Date	Supplier	Supplier code	Total £	VAT £	Payables £	Other £
31/5/X2	B Able	ABL02	723.78		723.78	
31/5/X2	Mann Ltd	MAN01	556.98		556.98	
31/5/X2	Sykes & Sons	SYK04	689.00		689.00	
31/5/X2	Dickens Ltd	DIC01	879.95		879.95	
31/5/X2	Barber & Co	BAR01	364.84		364.84	
31/5/X2	Ward & Ward	WAR02	287.66		287.66	
TOTALS			**3,502.21**		**3,502.21**	

Double entry bookkeeping – introduction

Introduction

We have reviewed the background to business transactions, looking at the different business documents we may encounter and how we record information from these source documents into the day books (books of prime entry).

This chapter introduces the different business organisations that we may encounter. We then study the basic concepts and rules of bookkeeping. In particular:

- the dual effect principle
- the separate entity principle, and
- the accounting equation.

Together these will show how the assets of a business will always equal its liabilities and pave the way for studying ledger accounting in the next chapter.

ASSESSMENT CRITERIA	CONTENTS
Demonstrate an understanding of the process of recording financial transactions (1.4)	1 Business organisations 2 Types of accounting 3 Basic principles of accounting 4 The accounting equation: examples

1 Business organisations

1.1 Introduction

A business is an organisation that regularly enters into different transactions. There are three types of business organisations that you should have awareness of:

1.2 Sole traders

 Definition – Sole trader

Organisations that are owned and operated by one person.

They tend to be small as they are constrained by the limited financial resources of their owner. Preparing final accounts for sole traders is assessed in the Advanced Diploma level's Final Accounts Preparation unit.

1.3 Partnerships

Definition – Partnership

These are organisations owned by two or more persons working in common with a view to making a profit.

The greater number of owners compared with a sole trader increases the availability of finance and this is often the reason for forming this structure. Producing accounts for partnerships is assessed in the Advanced Diploma level's Final Accounts Preparation unit.

1.4 Companies

Definition – Company

These are organisations recognised in law as 'persons' in their own right. A company may own assets and incur liabilities in its own name. The accounting of these organisations must meet certain minimum obligations imposed by legislation, for example, via company law and other regulations.

Drafting financial statements for a limited company is assessed in the Professional Diploma level's Financial Statements of Limited Companies unit.

2 Types of accounting

2.1 Management accounting and financial accounting

Depending on what purposes the statements are being produced for, the accounts can be referred to as being either **management accounts** or **financial accounts**.

Definition – Management accounts

These are usually prepared on a monthly basis to present timely financial and statistical information to business managers. This aids managers to run the business more effectively by making day-to-day and short-term decisions.

Definition – Financial accounts

These are prepared annually, mainly for the benefit of people outside the management of the business, such as the owners of the business (for example, shareholders who have appointed directors to run the business on their behalf), HM Revenue and Customs, banks, customers, suppliers and the government.

In Bookkeeping Transactions, we focus on financial accounting principles, though the majority of concepts we encounter also apply to management accounting.

2.2 The two main financial statements

The objective of financial accounting is to provide financial information about a business. This information is given in a set of financial statements (or accounts), which consists of two principal statements:

- The **statement of profit or loss.** This is a summary of the business's transactions (income and expense) for a given period.

- The **statement of financial position.** This is a statement of the assets and liabilities of the business at a given date. This date is the end of the period covered by the statement of profit or loss.

These financial statements are the final product of the accounting system of a business and it is useful to be aware of where all of the double entry bookkeeping that you will study in this chapter is leading. However, you do not need to know anything about the format or rules governing the preparation of the financial statements for this unit.

2.3 Statement of profit or loss – definitions

The following definitions will be used throughout your studies.

🔍 Definitions

- **Sales revenue** is income generated from the trading activities of the business.

- **Cost of sales** is the cost of buying or producing the goods for resale.

- **Gross profit** is the profit remaining, after the cost of sales have been deducted from sales revenue.

- **Sundry income** – other types of income that aren't generated by the primary trading activities of the business.

- **Expenses** are the day to day running costs of the business.

- **Net profit or loss** – the profit or loss remaining after expenses have been deducted.

2.4 Statement of financial position – definitions

The following definitions will be used throughout your studies.

> **Q Definitions**
>
> - An **asset** is something owned or controlled by a business, available for use in the business.
>
> - **Non-current asset** – an asset which is to be used for the long term in the business and not resold as part of the trading activities, for example the purchase of a delivery van.
>
> - **Current asset** – a short-term asset of the business which is to be used in the business in the near future i.e. cash or something that will soon be converted into cash.
>
> - A **receivable** is an example of a current asset. A receivable is someone who owes the business money i.e. a credit customer.
>
> - **Non-current liability** – an amount owed by the business and due to be paid in the longer term (after 12 months).
>
> - A **liability** is an amount owed by the business, i.e. an obligation to pay money at some future date.
>
> - A **payable** is an example of a liability. A payable is someone the business owes money to i.e. a credit supplier.
>
> - **Capital** is the amount which the owner has invested in the business; this is owed back to the owner and is therefore a special liability of the business.
>
> - **Drawings** are amounts withdrawn by the owner for their own personal use: drawings may be of cash or items of inventory.

KAPLAN PUBLISHING

A typical statement of profit or loss is shown below.

Statement of profit or loss for the year-ended 31 December 20X2

	£	£
Sales revenue		X
Less: Cost of sales		
Inventory on 1 January (opening inventory)	X	
Add: Purchases of goods	X	
	X	
Less: Inventory on 31 December (closing inventory)	(X)	
		(X)
Gross profit		X
Sundry income:		
Discounts received	X	
Commission received	X	
Rent received	X	
		X
		X
Less: Expenses:		
Rent	X	
Rates	X	
Lighting and heating	X	
Telephone	X	
Postage	X	
Insurance	X	
Stationery	X	
Payroll expenses	X	
Accountancy fees	X	
Bank charges and interest	X	
Irrecoverable debts	X	
Delivery costs	X	
Van running expenses	X	
Selling expenses	X	
Discounts allowed	X	
		(X)
Profit/(loss) for the year		X/(X)

An example of a typical sole trader's statement of financial position is given below:

Statement of financial position as at 31 December 20X2

	Cost £	Depreciation £	CA £
Non-current assets			
Freehold factory	X	X	X
Machinery	X	X	X
Motor vehicles	X	X	X
	X	X	X
Current assets			
Inventories		X	
Trade receivables		X	
Cash at bank		X	
Cash in hand		X	
		X	
Current liabilities			
Trade payables		(X)	
Net current assets			X
Total assets less current liabilities			X
Non-current liabilities			
Loan			(X)
Net assets			X
Capital at 1 January			X
Net profit for the year			X
			X
Less: Drawings			(X)
Proprietor's funds			X

2.5 The difference between 'cash' and 'bank'

A possible confusion in terminology is caused by the apparent interchangeable use of the words 'cash' and 'bank'.

The normal use of the words suggests that a bank account operates by paying money out of the account with a cheque and paying either cash or cheques into the account. In practice you cannot pay 'cash' out of a bank account.

However, accounting terminology does not stick to this distinction, and the terms cash and bank are for the most part, interchangeable. Thus the bank account is often referred to as the 'cash book'. Similarly we will often refer to someone 'taking cash out of the bank' or we will say things like 'John bought a car for £5,000 cash', whereas in reality John would have paid for the car using a cheque.

For the early part of your studies all movements of cash/cheques shall be made through the bank account and references to 'cash' or 'cheques' effectively mean the same thing.

2.6 Capital and revenue

You must also be able to define capital expenditure, revenue expenditure, capital income and revenue income.

 Definitions

- **Capital expenditure** is the purchase of, or improvement of, non-current assets.

- **Revenue expenditure** is the day to day running costs of the business.

- **Capital income** is income from the sale of capital assets of the business.

- **Revenue income** is income generated from the sale of goods or services.

3 Basic principles of accounting

3.1 Introduction

Double entry bookkeeping is based upon three basic principles:

- the dual effect principle
- the separate entity principle
- the accounting equation.

3.2 The dual effect principle

This states that every transaction has two financial effects.

(a) If, for example, you spend £2,000 on a car and pay for it by a cheque, you will have £2,000 less money in the bank, but you will also have acquired an asset worth £2,000.

(b) Again, if you owe a payable £100 and send him a cheque for that amount, you will owe £100 less than before, but you will have £100 less money in the bank.

3.3 The separate entity principle

This states that the owner of a business is, for accounting purposes, a completely separate entity from the business itself. Therefore the money that the owner pays into the business as initial capital has to be accounted for as an amount that the business owes back to the owner. In just the same way, any money that the owner takes out of the business, known as 'drawings', is treated as a reduction of the initial capital that is owed back to the owner.

The dual effect principle works here as well. If the owner of the business pays £5,000 into his business, one effect is that the business has £5,000 more cash and the second effect is that the business has a £5,000 liability (called 'capital').

Note that we look at this from the **point of view of the business**, not from the owner's point of view. This is because when studying bookkeeping we are only interested in the business – we are not considering the owner's personal finances.

3.4   The accounting equation

At its simplest, the accounting equation simply says that:

Assets = Liabilities

If we treat the owner's capital as a special form of liability then the accounting equation is:

Assets = Liabilities + Capital

Or, rearranging:

Assets – Liabilities = Capital

Profit will increase the proprietor's capital and drawings will reduce it, so that we can write the equation as:

Assets – Liabilities = Capital + Profit – Drawings

 Test your understanding 1

(a)   State whether each of the following are classified as an asset or a liability:

(i)   Funds in the business bank account

(ii)   A payable

(iii)   Inventory of goods for resale

(iv)   A computer used in the accounts department

(v)   A receivable

(vi)   A salesman's car

(vii)   An overdrawn balance on the business bank account.

(b)   Name 3 different parties who would be interested in financial statements.

(c)   Name the 3 basic principles of double entry bookkeeping and briefly describe each.

---

4 The accounting equation: examples

 ## Example 1

John starts his business on 1 July and pays £2,000 into his business bank account.

(a) What is the dual effect of this transaction?

(b) What is the accounting equation after this transaction?

Solution

(a) **The dual effect**

The business bank account has increased by £2,000 (an asset). The business capital has increased by £2,000 (a liability).

(b) **The accounting equation**

Assets – Liabilities   = Capital

£2,000 – £0   = £2,000

 ## Example 2

Percy started business on 1 January by paying £20,000 into a business bank account. He then spent £500 on a second-hand van by cheque, £1,000 on purchases of inventory for cash, took £500 cash for his own use and bought goods on credit costing £400.

What are the two effects of each of these transactions?

What would the accounting equation look like after each of these transactions?

Solution

(a) **Percy pays £20,000 into a business bank account**

The bank balance increases from zero to £20,000 (an asset) and the business now has capital of £20,000 (a liability). Capital is the amount that is owed back to the owner of the business, Percy.

Accounting equation:

Assets – Liabilities = Capital

£20,000 – £0   = £20,000

(b) **Percy buys a second-hand van for £500 by cheque**

The bank balance decreases by £500 (a reduction of assets) but the business has acquired a new £500 asset, the van.

The van is a specific type of asset known as a non-current asset as it is for long-term use in the business rather than an asset that is likely to be sold in the trading activities of the business.

The assets of the business are now:

	£
Van	500
Bank (20,000 – 500)	19,500
	———
	20,000
	———

The liabilities and capital are unchanged.

Accounting equation:

Assets – Liabilities = Capital

£20,000 – £0   = £20,000

(c) **Percy spends £1,000 on purchases of goods for cash**

The bank balance goes down by £1,000 but the business has another asset, inventory of £1,000.

Inventory is a short-term asset as it is due to be sold to customers in the near future and is known as a current asset.

The assets of the business are now:

	£
Van	500
Inventory	1,000
Bank (19,500 – 1,000)	18,500
	———
	20,000
	———

Accounting equation:

Assets – Liabilities = Capital

£20,000 – £0   = £20,000

(d) **Percy took £500 of cash out of the business**

The bank balance has decreased by £500 and capital has also decreased as the owner has taken money out of the business – this is known as drawings.

Remember that the owner is a completely separate entity from the business itself and if he takes money out of the business in the form of drawings then this means that the business owes him less.

The assets of the business are now:

	£
Van	500
Inventory	1,000
Bank (18,500 – 500)	18,000
	19,500

The capital of the business is now £(20,000 – 500) = £19,500.

Accounting equation:

Assets – Liabilities = Capital

£19,500 – £0 = £19,500

(e) **Purchased goods on credit for £400**

The asset of inventory increases by £400 and the business now has a liability of £400, the amount that is owed to the credit supplier. A liability is an amount that is owed by the business.

The assets of the business are now:

	£
Van	500
Inventory (1,000 + 400)	1,400
Bank	18,000
	19,900

The liability of the business is £400. The capital is unchanged.

Accounting equation:

Assets – Liabilities = Capital

£19,900 – £400 = £19,500

General notes:

1 Each and every transaction that a business undertakes has two effects. The accounting equation reflects the two effects of each transaction and the accounting equation should always balance.

2 The owner is a completely separate entity from the business, any money the owner puts into the business is known as capital and any amounts taken out by the owner are known as drawings.

Test your understanding 2

Required:

Show the two effects of each of these transactions and what the accounting equation would look like after each of these transactions.

1   **Introduce capital**

Example 1

You win £10,000 and use it to create a retail business (called TLC) selling hearts and roses. What is the effect?

Answer 1

Dual effect

The business has cash of	£10,000	(asset)
The business owes you	£10,000	(capital)

TLC's position is:

Assets	*Capital*
£	£

(In this first example, we recorded the dual effect for you just to get you started. In later examples you will need to enter the dual effect yourself, as well as TLC's position after the transaction.)

2   **Buy inventory with cash**

Example 2

TLC buys 500 chocolate hearts. The cost of each heart is £5. What is the effect?

Answer 2

Dual effect

TLC's position is:

Assets	*Capital*
£	£

3 Buy inventory on credit

In reality a business will not always pay for its purchases with cash but is more likely to buy items on credit. When goods are bought on credit, a liability of the business called a **payable** is generated.

Example 3

TLC buys inventory of 200 red roses on credit. Each red rose costs £10. What is the effect?

Answer 3

Dual effect

TLC's position is:

Net assets	Capital
£	£

4 Buy a delivery van

The delivery van is bought for ongoing use within the business rather than for resale. Such assets are known as **non-current assets**.

Example 4

TLC buys a delivery van for £1,000 cash. What is the effect?

Answer 4

Dual effect

TLC's position is:

Net assets	Capital
£	£

KAPLAN PUBLISHING

5 Sell inventory for profit

Example 5

TLC sells 200 red roses for £15 cash each. What is the effect?

Answer 5

Dual effect

TLC's position is:

Net assets	Capital
£	£

6 Sell inventory (on credit) for profit

It is equally likely that a business will sell goods on credit. When goods are sold on credit, an asset of the business called a **receivable** is generated.

Example 6

TLC sells 400 chocolate hearts to Valentino for £12.50 each on credit. What is the effect?

Answer 6

Dual effect

TLC's position is:

Net assets	Capital
£	£

7 Pay expenses

Example 7

In reality, TLC will have been incurring expenses from its commencement. TLC received and paid a gas bill for £500. What is the effect?

Answer 7

Dual effect

TLC's position is:

Net assets £	Capital £

8 Take out a loan

In order to fund your future expansion plans for TLC, you persuade your Aunt to lend TLC £2,000.

Example 8

TLC is lent £2,000 cash by your Aunt. She expects to be repaid in two years' time. What is the effect?

Answer 8

Dual effect

TLC's position is:

Net assets £	Capital £

9 Payment to payables for purchases

Example 9

TLC pays cash of £1,500 towards the £2,000 owed to the supplier. What is the effect?

Answer 9

Dual effect

TLC's position is:

Net assets	Capital
£	£

10 Receive cash from receivables

Example 10

TLC's receivable sends a cheque for £3,000. What is the effect?

Answer 10

Dual effect

TLC's position is:

Net assets	Capital
£	£

11 Drawings

Example 11

You withdraw £750 from the business. Such a withdrawal is merely a repayment of the capital you introduced. Your withdrawal is called **drawings**. What is the effect?

Answer 11

Dual effect

TLC's position is:

Net assets	Capital
£	£

Test your understanding 3

Bertie Wooster started a business as an antique dealer on 1 July 20X9.

Required:

Show the accounting equation which results from each of the following transactions made during Bertie's first two weeks of trading.

(a)   Started the business with £5,000 in cash as opening capital.

(b)   Bought an Edwardian desk for £500 cash.

(c)   Bought five art deco table lamps for £200 each, on credit from Roderick Spode.

(d)   Sold the desk for £750 cash.

(e)   Sold four of the table lamps for £300 each on credit to his Uncle Tom.

(f)   Paid rent of £250 cash.

(g)   Drew £100 in cash out of the business for living expenses.

(h)   Earned £50 for writing a magazine article, but had not yet been paid for it.

(i)   Paid Roderick Spode £500 on account.

(j)   Received £1,200 from Uncle Tom in full settlement of the amount due.

(k)   Bought a van for use in the business for £4,000 cash.

(l)   Received a telephone bill for £150 but did not pay it yet.

Note: Each transaction follows on from the one before.

5   Summary

You must understand the basic definitions covered in this chapter. You must also understand the principles of dual effect and separate entity. The accounting equation underlies the whole of bookkeeping and it is imperative that you fully understand these foundations which will be built on further. Re-work the examples in this chapter if necessary.

Test your understanding answers

 Test your understanding 1

(a) (i) Asset

(ii) Liability

(iii) Asset

(iv) Asset

(v) Asset

(vi) Asset

(vii) Liability

(b) Any 3 from the choice of:

- Shareholders (investors)
- Potential investors
- HMRC
- Banks
- Customers
- Suppliers
- Employees (of the business)
- Government

(c) 1 Dual effect – each transaction has two financial effects.

2 Separate entity – the owner of the business and the business are seen as two separate entities. All transactions are recorded in the point of view of the business.

3 Accounting equation –
Assets – Liabilities = Capital + Profit – Drawings

Test your understanding 2

Answer 1

	Assets £		Capital £
Cash	10,000	Capital introduced	10,000

Answer 2

Dual effect

Increase inv.	£2,500	(↑ asset)
Decrease cash	£2,500	(↓ asset)

	Assets £		Capital £
Inventory	2,500	Capital introduced	10,000
Cash	7,500		
	10,000		10,000

Answer 3

Dual effect

Increase inv.	£2,000	(↑ asset)
Increase payable	£2,000	(↑ liability)

	Net assets £		Capital £
Inventory	4,500	Capital introduced	10,000
Cash	7,500		
	12,000		
Less: Payables	(2,000)		
	10,000		10,000

KAPLAN PUBLISHING

Answer 4

Dual effect

Increase NCA	£1,000	(↑ asset)
Decrease cash	£1,000	(↓ asset)

	Net assets £		Capital £
Non-current asset	1,000	Capital introduced	10,000
Inventory	4,500		
Cash	6,500		
	———		
	12,000		
Less: Payables	(2,000)		
	———		———
	10,000		10,000
	———		———

Answer 5

Dual effect

Increase cash	£3,000	(↑ asset)
Decrease inv.	£2,000	(↓ asset)
Increase profit	£1,000	(↑ profit)

	Net assets £		Capital £
Non-current asset	1,000	Capital introduced	10,000
Inventory	2,500	Profit	1,000
Cash	9,500		
	———		
	13,000		
Less: Payables	(2,000)		
	———		———
	11,000		11,000
	———		———

Answer 6

Dual effect

Inc. receivables	£5,000	(↑ asset)
Dec. inventory	£2,000	(↓. asset)
Increase profit	£3,000	(↑ profit)

	Net assets £			Capital £
Non-current asset	1,000		Capital introduced	10,000
Inventory	500		Profit	4,000
Receivables	5,000			
Cash	9,500			
	16,000			
Less: Payables	(2,000)			
	14,000			14,000

Answer 7

Dual effect

Decrease cash	£500	(↓ asset)
Decrease profit	£500	(↓ profit)

	Net assets £			Capital £
Non-current asset	1,000		Capital introduced	10,000
Inventory	500		Profit	3,500
Receivables	5,000			
Cash	9,000			
	15,500			
Less: Payables	(2,000)			
	13,500			13,500

Answer 8

Dual effect

Increase cash	£2,000	(↑ asset)
Increase loan	£2,000	(↑ liability)

	Net assets £		Capital £
Non-current asset	1,000	Capital introduced	10,000
Inventory	500	Profit	3,500
Receivables	5,000		
Cash	11,000		
	———		
	17,500		
Less: Payables	(2,000)		
Loan	(2,000)		
	———		———
	13,500		13,500
	———		———

The loan will be shown separately from payables for purchases, which are known as trade payables.

Answer 9

Dual effect

Decrease cash	£1,500	(↓ asset)
Decrease payables	£1,500	(↓ liability)

	Net assets £		Capital £
Non-current asset	1,000	Capital introduced	10,000
Inventory	500	Profit	3,500
Receivables	5,000		
Cash	9,500		
	———		
	16,000		
Less: Payables	(500)		
Loan	(2,000)		
	———		———
	13,500		13,500
	———		———

Answer 10

Dual effect

Dec. receivables	£3,000	(↓ asset)
Increase cash	£3,000	(↑ asset)

Net assets	£		Capital	£
Non-current asset	1,000		Capital introduced	10,000
Inventory	500		Profit	3,500
Receivables	2,000			
Cash	12,500			
	_____			
	16,000			
Less: Payables	(500)			
Loan	(2,000)			
	_____			_____
	13,500			13,500
	_____			_____

Answer 11

Dual effect

Decrease cash	£750	(↓ asset)
Increase drawings	£750	(↓ capital)

Net assets	£		Capital	£
Non-current asset	1,000		Capital	10,000
Inventory	500		Profit	3,500
Receivables	2,000			
Cash	11,750			
	_____			_____
	15,250			13,500
Less: Payables	(500)		Less: Drawings	(750)
Loan	(2,000)			
	_____			_____
	12,750			12,750
	_____			_____

We do not simply deduct drawings from profit as we want to show separately the profit or loss for the period before any drawings were made.

Test your understanding 3

(a) Opening capital

		£		£
Assets	Cash	5,000	Capital	5,000

(b) Cash purchase

		£		£
Assets	Inventory	500	Capital	5,000
	Cash (5,000 – 500)	4,500		
		5,000		5,000

(c) Credit purchase

		£		£
Assets	Inventory (500+(5×200))	1,500	Capital	5,000
	Cash	4,500		
		6,000		
Liabilities	Payables	(1,000)		
		5,000		5,000

(d) Cash sale

		£		£
Assets	Inventory (1,500 – 500)	1,000	Capital	5,000
	Cash (4,500 + 750)	5,250	Profit (750 – 500)	250
		6,250		
Liabilities	Payables	(1,000)		
		5,250		5,250

(e) Credit sale

		£		£
Assets	Inventory (1,000 – 800)	200	Capital	5,000
	Receivables	1,200	Profit (250 + 1,200 – 800)	650
	Cash	5,250		
		6,650		
Liabilities	Payables	(1,000)		
		5,650		5,650

(f) **Paid rent**

		£		£
Assets	Inventory	200	Capital	5,000
	Receivables	1,200	Profit (650 – 250)	400
	Cash (5,250 – 250)	5,000		
		6,400		
Liabilities	Payables	(1,000)		
		5,400		5,400

(g) **Drawings**

		£		£
Assets	Inventory	200	Capital	5,000
	Receivables	1,200	Profit	400
	Cash (5,000 – 100)	4,900		
		6,300	Drawings	(100)
Liabilities	Payables	(1,000)		
		5,300		5,300

(h) **Sundry income**

		£		£
Assets	Inventory	200	Capital	5,000
	Receivables(1,200+50)	1,250	Profit (400 + 50)	450
	Cash	4,900		
		6,350	Drawings	(100)
Liabilities	Payables	(1,000)		
		5,350		5,350

(i) **Payment to payable**

		£		£
Assets	Inventory	200	Capital	5,000
	Receivables	1,250	Profit	450
	Cash (4,900 – 500)	4,400		
		5,850	Drawings	(100)
Liabilities	Payables(1,000–500)	(500)		
		5,350		5,350

(j) **Receipt from receivable**

		£		£
Assets	Inventory	200	Capital	5,000
	Receivables(1,250–1,200)	50	Profit	450
	Cash (4,400 + 1,200)	5,600		
		5,850	Drawings	(100)
Liabilities	Payables	(500)		
		5,350		5,350

(k) **Purchase of van**

		£		£
Assets	Van	4,000	Capital	5,000
	Inventory	200	Profit	450
	Receivables	50		5,450
	Cash (5,600 – 4,000)	1,600	Drawings	(100)
		5,850		
Liabilities	Payables	(500)		
		5,350		5,350

(l) **Telephone bill**

		£		£
Assets	Van	4,000	Capital	5,000
	Inventory	200	Profit (450 – 150)	300
	Receivables	50		5,300
	Cash	1,600	Drawings	(100)
		5,850		
Liabilities Payables (500 + 150)		(650)		
		5,200		5,200

Ledger accounting

Introduction

In the first two chapters of this text we looked at different business documents and how these documents are entered into the books of prime entry. In the third chapter we reviewed the basic concepts and principles underlying double entry bookkeeping.

Before we review how details from the books of prime entry are entered into the accounting system we shall introduce how to record basic transactions in a 'ledger account' as part of the 'general ledger'. We will review the procedure for balancing a ledger account and how those balances are brought together to prepare the trial balance.

ASSESSMENT CRITERIA	CONTENTS
Demonstrate an understanding of the process of recording financial transactions (1.4)	1 Ledger accounting
	2 Worked example
	3 Additional example
	4 Credit purchases
Total and balance ledger accounts (5.2)	5 Credit sales
	6 Balancing a ledger account
Extract an initial trial balance (5.3)	7 The trial balance

1 Ledger accounting

1.1 Introduction

The accounting equation introduced in Chapter 3 has limitations. Although we are able to calculate a profit figure, we are unable to determine which part of the profit are sales and which part are expenses. To be able to make this determination, we will now account for the movement in sales and purchases, rather than simply the movement of inventory.

Another limitation of the accounting equation is that in practice it would be far too time consuming to write up the accounting equation each time that the business undertakes a transaction. Instead the two effects of each transaction are recorded in ledger accounts.

1.2 The ledger account

A typical ledger account is shown below:

Title of account							
DEBIT				**CREDIT**			
Date	Details	Folio	Amount £	Date	Details	Folio	Amount £

The important point to note is that it has two sides. The left hand side is known as the **debit** side **(Dr)** and the right hand side is known as the **credit** side **(Cr).**

- The date column contains the date of the transaction.

- The details column (can also be referred to as the narrative column) usually contains the title of the other account that holds the second part of the dual effect. It may also have a brief description of the nature of the entry (e.g. 'rent 1.1.X3 to 31.3.X3').

- The folio column contains a reference to the source of the information, for example, 'sales day book p17' or 'payroll month 6'. You may not always see the folio column being used within a ledger account.

- The amount column simply contains the monetary value of the transaction.

- The title of the account is a name that reflects the nature of the transaction ('van account', 'bank account', 'electricity account', etc).

The importance of completing the ledger account correctly, in terms of the presentation, should not be underestimated. Vital marks can be gained in the exam by ensuring all details, including the date and narrative are completed accurately.

1.3 Simplified account

The ledger account in 1.2 is very detailed and in much of this book we use a simpler form of the account. Part of the reason for this is that it is easier to 'see' the entries being made if there is less detail in the accounts. Thus, we sometimes do without the date or folio to keep things clear and simple.

For example, we will often use accounts which look like this:

Bank account			
	£		£
		Van	500

Van account			
	£		£
Bank	500		

1.4 The golden rule for making entries in the ledger accounts

The golden rule for making entries in ledger accounts is:

Every debit entry must have an equal and opposite credit entry.

This reflects the dual effect of each transaction and ensures the accounting equation always balances.

It is also why we refer to the process as 'double entry bookkeeping'.

1.5 Which accounts to debit and credit?

The mnemonic 'DEAD/CLIC' is a good way to help determine if an entry should be made on the debit side or on the credit side of a ledger account.

Ledger account	
Debits increase:	**Credits increase:**
Expenses	Liabilities
Assets	Income
Drawings	Capital

We need to appreciate the effect a debit or a credit entry will have.

Ledger account	
A **debit entry** represents:	A **credit entry** represents:
• An increase in the value of an asset	• A decrease in the value of an asset
• A decrease in the value of a liability	• An increase in the value of a liability
• An increase to an item of expenditure	• An increase to an item of income (revenue)
• A decrease to an item of income	• A decrease to an item of expense

1.6 What goes on the debit or credit side?

Example (part 1)

If John pays £2,000 into his business bank account as capital, we need to ask a number of questions to determine the double entry required.

(a) **Which** accounts are affected?

(b) What **type** of accounts are they i.e. asset/liability/income/expense?

(c) Is the transaction **increasing or decreasing** the account?

So let's consider these questions for John's investment of capital into his business.

(a)　The accounts that are affected are the bank account and the capital account.

(b)　The bank account is an asset whereas the capital is a special kind of liability.

(c)　As we have paid money into the bank account, the asset is increasing – therefore a debit entry is required.

As John (the owner) has invested £2,000 into the business, the business owes him this amount back. This is an increase to a liability – therefore a credit entry is required.

To summarise:

Debit　　　Bank account

Credit　　　Capital account

Bank account			
	£		£
Capital	2,000		

Capital account			
	£		£
		Bank	2,000

Example (part 2)

If John's business now pays £1,000 out of the bank to buy a van, considering the questions again:

(a)　The accounts that are affected are the bank account and the van account.

(b)　The bank account is an asset and the van account is also an asset (a non-current asset).

(c)   As we have paid money out of the bank account, the asset is decreasing – therefore a credit entry is required.

The business has acquired a van, which is a non-current asset, this is an increase to an asset – therefore a debit entry is required.

To summarise:

Debit   Van account

Credit   Bank account

	Bank account		
	£		£
Capital	2,000	Van	1,000

	Capital account		
	£		£
		Bank	2,000

	Van account		
	£		£
Bank	1,000		

2   Worked example

2.1   Introducing capital into the business – explanation

The owner of a business starts the business by paying money into the business bank account. This is the capital of the business. The business will need this money to 'get going'. It may need to pay rent, buy inventory for sale or pay wages to its staff before it has actually generated money itself through making sales.

Example 1

Frankie starts a business and pays £5,000 into the business bank account. What is the double entry for this transaction?

Solution

- £5,000 has been paid into the bank account.

  It represents an asset of the business.

  This is therefore a debit in the bank account.

- The business has a liability because it owes Frankie (the owner) £5,000.

  This liability will be a credit in the capital account.

Bank		Capital	
Capital £5,000			Bank £5,000

2.2 Purchasing goods for resale

A business buys goods for resale to customers – that is how most businesses (e.g. shops) make their money. These goods (known as 'inventory') are assets which the business owns (until the inventory is sold). Buying inventory is referred to as making a 'purchase' which is a type of expense.

 Example 2

Frankie buys £300 of chocolate bars for resale. He pays with a cheque to his supplier.

What is the double entry for this transaction?

Solution

- The business has paid £300 out of its bank account.

  Therefore, the £300 will be credited to the bank account.

- Buying the chocolate bars (inventory) is known as making a purchase (a type of expense).

  This expense will be debited to the purchases account.

Purchases		Bank	
Bank £300			Purchases £300

2.3 Paying office rent

A business will typically rent premises in order to carry out its operations. It will pay rent to the landlord of the premises. Rent is an expense of the business.

 Example 3

Frankie pays £1,000 per quarter for the rent of his offices. He pays with a cheque to the landlord.

What is the double entry for this transaction?

Solution

- The business has paid £1,000 out of its bank account.

  Therefore, the £1,000 will be credited to the bank account.

- The rent is an expense.

  This expense will be debited to the rent account.

Rent			Bank		
Bank	£1,000			Rent	£1,000

2.4 Buying stationery

A business will buy stationery in order to be able to operate. The items of stationery (pens, paper, etc) are not for resale to customers but they tend to be used quickly after they are purchased. Therefore, stationery tends to be classified as an expense of the business, as opposed to an asset.

Example 4

Frankie pays £200 for items of stationery. He pays with a cheque to the supplier.

What is the double entry for this transaction?

Solution

- The business has paid £200 out of its bank account.

  Therefore, the £200 will be credited to the bank account.

- The stationery is an expense.

  This expense will be debited to the stationery account.

Stationery		Bank	
Bank £200			Stationery £200

2.5   Buying a computer

A business will buy computers in order to streamline its operations. These computers are not bought with a view to re-sale and are to be used in the business for the long term. They are therefore a non-current asset of the business.

 Example 5

Frankie pays £900 to purchase a computer. He pays with a cheque to the supplier.

What is the double entry for this transaction?

Solution

- Once again start with the bank account.

  The business has paid £900 out of its bank account.

  Therefore, the £900 will be credited to the bank account.

- The computer is a non-current asset.

  The £900 will be debited to the non-current asset computer account.

Computer		Bank	
Bank £900			Computer £900

2.6 Receiving income from sales of goods

A business will sell the goods it has purchased for re-sale. This is income for the business and is referred to as 'sales'. You may also hear the terms 'revenue' or 'sales revenue'.

 Example 6

Frankie sells goods for £1,500. The customer pays cash.

What is the double entry for this transaction?

Solution

- Once again start with the bank account.

  The business has received £1,500 into its bank account.

  Therefore, the £1,500 will be debited to the bank account.

- The cash received is income.

  This income will be credited to the sales account.

Sales				Bank	
	Bank	£1,500	Sales	£1,500	

2.7 Receiving income for services provided

A business may provide services to its customers, e.g.it may provide consultancy advice. This is income for the business and will usually be referred to as 'sales'.

 Example 7

Frankie provides consultancy services to a client who pays £2,000 in cash. What is the double entry for this transaction?

Solution

- Once again start with the bank account.

  The business has received £2,000 into its bank account.

  Therefore, the £2,000 will be debited to the bank account.

- The cash received is income.

  This income will be credited to the sales account.

Sales				Bank	
	Bank	£2,000	Sales	£2,000	

3 Additional example

Example 8

Percy started business on 1 January and made the following transactions.

1 Paid £20,000 into a business bank account.

2 Spent £500 on a second-hand van.

3 Paid £1,000 on purchases of inventory.

4 Took £50 cash for his own personal use.

5 On 5 January bought goods for cash costing £500.

6 Made sales for cash of £2,000.

7 On 15 January paid £200 of rent.

Task 1

Show how the debit and credit entries for each transaction are determined.

Task 2

Enter the transactions into the relevant ledger accounts.

Solution

Task 1

(1) *Capital invested*

Percy has paid £20,000 into the bank account – therefore the bank account is debited.

Debit (Dr)   Bank   £20,000

The business now owes the owner £20,000. Capital is the amount owed by the business to its owner – this is a liability, therefore a credit entry is required in the capital account.

Credit (Cr)   Capital   £20,000

(2) *Purchase of van*

The business has paid £500 out of the bank account – therefore a credit entry in the bank account.

Cr   Bank   £500

The business now has a van costing £500 – this is an asset therefore a debit entry in the van account. This is a non-current asset of the business.

Dr   Van   £500

(3) *Purchase of inventory for cash*

The business has paid out £1,000 out of the bank account – therefore a credit to the bank account.

Cr   Bank   £1,000

The business has made purchases of inventory costing £1,000 – this is an item of expenditure therefore a debit entry in the purchases account. Note that the debit entry is to a purchases account not an inventory account. The inventory account is a different account altogether and inventory movements will be considered later.

Dr   Purchases   £1,000

(4) *Drawings*

The business has paid £50 out of the bank account – therefore credit the bank account.

Cr   Bank   £50

The proprietor has made drawings of £50 – this is a reduction of capital and therefore a debit entry to the drawings account.

Dr   Drawings   £50

Drawings should not be directly debited to the capital account. A separate drawings account should be used.

(5) *Purchase of goods for cash*

The business has paid out £500 – therefore credit the bank account.

Cr   Bank   £500

The business has made purchases of inventory costing £500 – an expense therefore debit the purchases account.

Dr   Purchases   £500

(6) *Sale for cash*

The business has paid £2,000 into the bank account – therefore a debit to the bank account.

Dr   Bank   £2,000

The business has made sales of £2,000 – this is income therefore a credit to the sales account.

Cr   Sales   £2,000

(7) *Payment of rent*

The business now paid £200 out of the bank account – therefore a credit to the bank account.

Cr   Bank   £200

The business has incurred an expense of rent – as an expense item the rent account must be debited.

Dr   Rent   £200

Task 2

Bank

Date			£	Date			£
1 Jan	Capital	(1)	20,000	1 Jan	Van	(2)	500
5 Jan	Sales	(6)	2,000		Purchases	(3)	1,000
					Drawings	(4)	50
				5 Jan	Purchases	(5)	500
				15 Jan	Rent	(7)	200

Capital

Date			£	Date			£
				1 Jan	Bank	(1)	20,000

Van

Date			£	Date			£
1 Jan	Bank	(2)	500				

Purchases

Date			£	Date			£
1 Jan	Bank	(3)	1,000				
5 Jan	Bank	(5)	500				

Drawings

Date			£	Date			£
1 Jan	Bank	(4)	50				

Sales

Date			£	Date			£
				5 Jan	Bank	(6)	2,000

Rent

Date			£	Date			£
15 Jan	Bank	(7)	200				

📝 Test your understanding 1

Write up the following cash transactions in the ledger accounts.

Transaction	Details
1	Set up the business by introducing £150,000 in cash.
2	Purchase property costing £140,000. Pay in cash.
3	Purchase goods costing £5,000. Pay in cash.
4	Sell goods for £7,000. All cash sales.
5	Purchase goods costing £8,000. Pay in cash.
6	Pay a sundry expense of £100, by cheque.
7	Sell goods for £15,000. All cash sales.
8	Pay wages of £2,000 to an employee.
9	Pay postage costs of £100, by cheque.

4 Credit purchases

 Definition – Cash purchase

A cash purchase occurs when goods are bought (or a service received) and the customer pays immediately using cash, cheques or credit cards. A receipt is issued for the amount of cash paid.

 Definition – Credit purchase

A credit purchase occurs when goods are bought (or a service received) and the customer does not have to pay immediately but can pay after a specified number of days. An invoice is then issued to request that payment is made.

 Example 9

We have already seen the double entry for a cash purchase and we shall now contrast this with the double entry for a credit purchase by means of an illustration.

John buys goods from Sam for £2,000.

(a) Record the double entry in John's books if John pays for the goods immediately with a cheque.

(b) Record the double entry in John's books if John buys the goods on credit and pays some time later.

Solution

(a) **Cash purchase**

The double entry is simply to:

Credit the bank account with £2,000 because £2,000 has been paid out.

Debit the purchases account with £2,000 because goods have been purchased with £2,000.

Bank

	£		£
		Purchases	2,000

Purchases

	£		£
Bank	2,000		

(b) **Credit purchase**

We have to record two transactions separately:

(i) *At the time the purchase is made*

At the time the purchase is made we debit £2,000 to the purchases account because a purchase has been made, but we do not make any entry in the bank account yet, because at that point, no cash has been paid. The other effect is that John has a liability, he owes £2,000 to the supplier, Sam, who we can refer to as a payable.

The double entry is:

Debit the purchases account with £2,000 because expenses have increased by £2,000.

Credit payables account with £2,000 (this is a liability of the business).

Purchases

	£		£
Payables	2,000		

Payables

	£		£
		Purchases	2,000

(ii) *When John pays the £2,000*

The double entry now will be:

Credit the bank account with £2,000 because £2,000 has been paid out.

Debit the payable account because John has paid and the payable has been reduced by £2,000.

Payables

	£		£
Bank	2,000	Purchases	2,000

Purchases

	£		£
Payables	2,000		

Bank

	£		£
		Payables	2,000

4.1 Summary

The net effect of the above credit purchase is that the payable has a nil balance because John has paid, and we are left with a debit in the purchases account and a credit in the cash book. This is exactly as for a cash purchase – we just had to go through the intermediate step of the payables account to get there.

5 Credit sales

Definition – Cash sale

A cash sale occurs when goods are sold (or a service provided) and the customer pays immediately with cash, cheque or credit card. A receipt is issued for the amount of cash received.

Definition – Credit sale

A credit sale occurs when goods are sold (or a service provided) and the customer does not have to pay immediately but can pay after a specified number of days. An invoice is issued to request that the balance owed is then paid.

Example 10

We have already seen the double entry for a cash sale and we shall now contrast this with the double entry for a credit sale by means of an illustration.

George sells goods to Harry for £1,000.

(a) Record the double entry in George's books if Harry pays for the goods immediately with a cheque.

(b) Record the double entry in George's books if Harry buys the goods on credit and pays some time later.

Solution

(a) **Cash sale**

The double entry is simply to:

Debit the bank account with £1,000 because £1,000 has been paid in.

Credit the sales account with £1,000 because income has increased by £1,000.

Bank

	£		£
Sales	1,000		

Sales

	£		£
		Bank	1,000

(b) **Credit sale**

The double entry will be made at two separate times.

(i) *At the time the sale is made*

At the time the sale is made we credit £1,000 to the sales account because a sale has been made, but we cannot make any entry in the bank account at the time of the sale because no cash is received. However, the dual effect principle means that there must be another effect to this transaction, and in this case it is that the business has acquired a receivable.

The double entry is:

Debit receivables account with £1,000 (this is an asset of the business).

Credit the sales account with £1,000 because income has increased by £1,000.

Receivables

	£		£
Sales	1,000		

Sales

	£		£
		Receivables	1,000

(ii) *When Harry pays the £1,000*

The double entry now will be:

Debit the bank account with £1,000 because £1,000 has been paid in.

Credit the receivables account because Harry has paid and the receivable has been reduced by £1,000.

Receivables

	£		£
Sales	1,000	Bank	1,000

Sales

	£		£
		Receivables	1,000

Bank

	£		£
Receivables	1,000		

5.1 Summary

The net effect of the above credit sale is that the receivable has a nil balance because Harry has paid and we are left with a credit in the sales account and a debit in the cash book. This is exactly as for a cash sale – we just had to go through the intermediate step of the receivable account to get there.

 Test your understanding 2

We shall now revisit TLC from Chapter 3 and record the transactions with debits and credits to ledger accounts.

Date	Detail
1.1.X5	TLC commenced business with £10,000 cash introduced by you, the proprietor
2.1.X5	TLC bought inventory of 500 chocolate hearts for £2,500 cash
3.1.X5	TLC bought inventory of 200 red roses on credit for £2,000
4.1.X5	TLC bought a delivery van for £1,000 cash
5.1.X5	TLC sold all the red roses for £3,000 cash
6.1.X5	TLC sold 400 chocolate hearts for £5,000 on credit
7.1.X5	TLC paid a gas bill for £500 cash
8.1.X5	TLC took out a loan of £2,000
9.1.X5	TLC paid £1,500 cash to trade payables
10.1.X5	TLC received £3,000 cash from receivables
11.1.X5	The proprietor withdrew £750 cash

Required:

Record these transactions in the relevant ledger accounts. Make your entries in the ledger accounts below.

Cash

£		£

Capital

	£		£

Purchases

	£		£

Payables

	£		£

Delivery van

	£		£

Sales

	£		£

Receivables

£	£

Gas

£	£

Loan

£	£

Drawings

£	£

Test your understanding 3

Z, the owner of a consultancy firm, has the following transactions:

(a)   Pays £4,000 into the bank as capital.

(b)   Buys a computer for £1,000.

(c)   Pays rent of £400.

(d)   Earns £800 for consultancy services.

Write up the ledger accounts for the above.

 Test your understanding 4

B makes the following cash transactions:

(a)   Pays £4,000 into the bank as capital.

(b)   Buys goods for £700.

(c)   Buys champagne to entertain the staff for £300.

(d)   Purchases three computers for £3,000.

(e)   Sells goods for £1,500 cash.

(f)   Draws £500 cash.

(g)   Purchases goods for £1,200 cash.

(h)   Pays telephone bill of £600.

(i)   Receives telephone bill rebate of £200.

(j)   Buys stationery for £157.

Write up the ledger accounts for the above.

 Test your understanding 5

A sells books to B for £1,000 on credit.

A also sells books to C for £90 credit.

B pays £500 and C pays £90.

Write up these transactions in the sales ledger accounts of A, using individual receivable accounts for each customer.

6 Balancing a ledger account

6.1 Procedure for balancing a ledger account

Step 1	Total both the debit and the credit side of the ledger account and make a note of each total.
Step 2	Insert the higher of the two totals as the total on both sides of the ledger account leaving a line beneath the final entry on each side of the account.
Step 3	On the side with the smaller total insert the figure needed to make this column add up to the total. Call this figure the balance carried down (or 'Bal c/d' as an abbreviation).
Step 4	On the opposite side of the ledger account, below the total insert this same figure and call it the balance brought down (or 'Bal b/d' as an abbreviation).

6.2 Step by step example

Example 11

The bank account of a business has the following entries:

Bank

	£		£
Capital	1,000	Purchases	200
Sales	300	Drawings	100
Sales	400	Rent	400
Capital	500	Stationery	300
Sales	800	Purchases	400

Calculate the balance on the account and bring the balance down as a single amount.

Solution

Step 1 Total both sides of the account and make a note of the totals. (Note that these totals that are asterisked below would not normally be written into the ledger account itself. They are only shown here to explain the process more clearly.)

Bank

	£		£
Capital	1,000	Purchases	200
Sales	300	Drawings	100
Sales	400	Rent	400
Capital	500	Stationery	300
Sales	800	Purchases	400
	———		———
*Sub-total debits**	*3,000*	*Sub-total credits**	*1,400*

Step 2   Insert the higher total as the total of both sides.

Bank

	£		£
Capital	1,000	Purchases	200
Sales	300	Drawings	100
Sales	400	Rent	400
Capital	500	Stationery	300
Sales	800	Purchases	400
	———		———
*Sub-total debits**	*3,000*	*Sub-total credits**	*1,400*
	———		———
Total	3,000	Total	3,000
	———		———

Step 3 Insert a balancing figure on the side of the account with the lower sub-total. This is referred to as the 'balance carried down' or 'bal c/d' for short.

Bank

	£		£
Capital	1,000	Purchases	200
Sales	300	Drawings	100
Sales	400	Rent	400
Capital	500	Stationery	300
Sales	800	Purchases	400
Sub-total debits*	3,000	Sub-total credits*	1,400
		Bal c/d	1,600
Total	3,000	Total	3,000

Step 4 Insert the balance carried down figure beneath the total on the other side of the account. This is referred to as 'bal b/d' for short.

Bank

	£		£
Capital	1,000	Purchases	200
Sales	300	Drawings	100
Sales	400	Rent	400
Capital	500	Stationery	300
Sales	800	Purchases	400
Sub-total debits*	3,000	Sub-total credits*	1,400
		Bal c/d	1,600
Total	3,000	Total	3,000
Bal b/d	1,600		

The closing balance carried down at the end of the period is also the opening balance brought down at the start of the next period. This opening balance remains in the account as the starting position and any further transactions are then added into the account. In this case the balance brought down is a debit balance as there is money in the bank account making it an asset.

Example 12

Consider again the ledger accounts from the earlier example Percy in this chapter which are reproduced below and balance them.

Bank

Date			£	Date			£
1 Jan	Capital	(1)	20,000	1 Jan	Van	(2)	500
5 Jan	Sales	(6)	2,000		Purchases	(3)	1,000
					Drawings	(4)	50
				5 Jan	Purchases	(5)	500
				15 Jan	Rent	(7)	200

Capital

Date			£	Date			£
				1 Jan	Bank	(1)	20,000

Van

Date			£	Date			£
1 Jan	Bank	(2)	500				

Purchases

Date			£	Date			£
1 Jan	Bank	(3)	1,000				
5 Jan	Bank	(5)	500				

Drawings

Date			£	Date			£
1 Jan	Bank	(4)	50				

Sales

Date			£	Date			£
				5 Jan	Bank	(6)	2,000

Rent

Date			£	Date			£
15 Jan	Bank	(7)	200				

Solution

(a) The bank account

Bank

Date		£	Date		£
1 Jan	Capital	20,000	1 Jan	Van	500
5 Jan	Sales	2,000		Purchases	1,000
				Drawings	50
			5 Jan	Purchases	500
			15 Jan	Rent	200

Step 1 Total both the debit and the credit side of the ledger account and make a note of each total – debit side £22,000, credit side £2,250.

Step 2 Insert the higher of the two totals, £22,000, as the total on both sides of the ledger account leaving a line beneath the final entry on each side of the account.

Bank

Date		£	Date		£
1 Jan	Capital	20,000	1 Jan	Van	500
5 Jan	Sales	2,000		Purchases	1,000
				Drawings	50
			5 Jan	Purchases	500
			15 Jan	Rent	200
		———			———
		22,000			22,000
		———			———

Step 3 On the side with the smaller total insert the figure needed to make this column add up to the total. Call this figure the balance carried down (or Bal c/d as an abbreviation).

Step 4 On the opposite side of the ledger account, below the total insert this same figure and call it the balance brought down (or Bal b/d as an abbreviation).

Bank

Date		£	Date		£
1 Jan	Capital	20,000	1 Jan	Van	500
5 Jan	Sales	2,000		Purchases	1,000
				Drawings	50
			5 Jan	Purchases	500
			15 Jan	Rent	200
			31 Jan	Balance c/d	19,750
		_____			_____
		22,000			22,000
		_____			_____
1 Feb	Balance b/d	19,750			

This shows that the business has £19,750 left in the bank account at the end of January and therefore also on the first day of February. As the balance that is brought down to start the next period is on the debit side of the account this is known as a debit balance and indicates that this is an asset – money in the bank account.

(b) **Capital**

Capital

Date		£	Date		£
			1 Jan	Bank	20,000

As there is only one entry in this account there is no need to balance the account. The entry is on the credit side and is known as a credit balance. A credit balance is a liability of the business and this account shows that the business owes the owner £20,000 of capital.

(c) **Van**

Van

Date		£	Date		£
1 Jan	Bank	500			

Again, there is no need to balance this account as there is only one entry. This is a debit balance as it is an asset – the non-current asset, the van, which cost £500.

(d) Purchases

Purchases

Date		£	Date		£
1 Jan	Bank	1,000			
5 Jan	Bank	500	31 Jan	Balance c/d	1,500
		1,500			1,500
1 Feb	Balance b/d	1,500			

This now shows that during the month £1,500 of purchases was made. This is a debit balance as purchases are an expense of the business.

(e) Drawings

Drawings

Date		£	Date	£
1 Jan	Bank	50		

This is a debit balance as drawings are a reduction of the capital owed to the owner which is a credit balance.

(f) Sales

Sales

Date	£	Date		£
		5 Jan	Bank	2,000

There is no need to balance the account as there is only one entry – a £2,000 credit balance representing income.

(g) Rent

Rent

Date		£	Date	£
15 Jan	Bank	200		

As there is only one entry there is no need to balance the account. This is a debit balance indicating that there has been an expense of £200 of rent incurred during the month.

Test your understanding 6

Given below is a bank account ledger account for the month of March. You are required to 'balance off' the ledger account.

Bank

Date		£	Date		£
1 Mar	Capital	12,000	3 Mar	Purchases	3,000
7 Mar	Sales	5,000	15 Mar	Non-current asset	2,400
19 Mar	Sales	2,000	20 Mar	Purchases	5,300
22 Mar	Sales	3,000	24 Mar	Rent	1,000
			28 Mar	Drawings	2,000

 Test your understanding 7

The following bank account has been written up for the month of May 20X9. There was no opening balance.

Bank

	£		£
Capital	10,000	Computer	1,000
Sales	2,000	Telephone	567
Sales	3,000	Rent	1,500
Sales	2,000	Rates	125
		Stationery	247
		Petrol	49
		Purchases	2,500
		Drawings	500
		Petrol	42

Bring down the balance on the account.

Test your understanding 8

The following bank account has been written up during May 20X9. There was no brought forward balance.

Bank

	£		£
Capital	5,000	Purchases	850
Sales	1,000	Fixtures	560
Sales	876	Van	1,500
Rent rebate	560	Rent	1,300
Sales	1,370	Rates	360
		Telephone	220
		Stationery	120
		Petrol	48
		Car repairs	167

Bring down the balance on the account.

 Test your understanding 9

The following bank account has been written up during June 20X9.

Bank

	£		£
Balance b/f	23,700	Drawings	4,000
Sales	2,300	Rent	570
Sales	1,700	Purchases	6,000
Receivables	4,700	Rates	500
		Salaries	3,600
		Car expenses	460
		Petrol	49
		Petrol	38
		Electricity	210
		Stationery	89

Bring down the balance on the account.

7 The trial balance

7.1 Introduction

> **Definition – Trial balance**
>
> The trial balance is a list showing the balance brought down on each ledger account. It is a check point to ensure that every debit has an equal and opposite credit entry and therefore the totals of the trial balance columns should balance. However, it does not confirm that the account you have debited or credited is correct.

7.2 Format of the trial balance

An example of a simple trial balance is given below:

	Debit £	Credit £
Sales		5,000
Opening inventory	100	
Purchases	3,000	
Rent	200	
Car	3,000	
Receivables	100	
Payables		1,400
	6,400	6,400

The trial balance is produced immediately after the double entry has been completed and balances extracted on the accounts.

The first column will detail the name of the ledger account and the balance will be noted in either the debit or credit column depending on the side it has been brought down on.

If the double entry has been completed correctly, the total of the debits will equal the total of the credits. Drafting a trial balance is a way of ensuring that double entries have been correctly completed.

Example 13

The following are the balances on the accounts of Ernest at 31 December 20X8.

	£
Sales	47,140
Purchases	26,500
Receivables	7,640
Payables	4,320
General expenses	9,430
Loan	5,000
Plant and machinery at cost	7,300
Motor van at cost	2,650
Drawings	7,500
Rent and rates	6,450
Insurance	1,560
Bank overdraft	2,570
Capital	10,000

Required:

Prepare Ernest's trial balance as at 31 December 20X8.

Solution

Step 1   Set up a blank trial balance

Step 2   Work down the list of balances one by one using what you have learned so far about debits and credits. Assets and expenses are debit balances and liabilities and income are credit balances.

The mnemonic DEAD CLIC may help.

Debit:	**Credit:**
Expenses	Liabilities
Assets	Income
Drawings	Capital

Trial balance at 31 December 20X8

	Dr £	Cr £
Sales		47,140
Purchases	26,500	
Receivables	7,640	
Payables		4,320
General expenses	9,430	
Loan		5,000
Plant and machinery at cost	7,300	
Motor van at cost	2,650	
Drawings	7,500	
Rent and rates	6,450	
Insurance	1,560	
Bank overdraft		2,570
Capital		10,000
	69,030	69,030

Take care with drawings. These are a reduction of the capital owed back to the owner therefore as a reduction of a liability they must be a debit balance.

The bank overdraft is an amount owed to the bank therefore it must be a credit balance.

 Test your understanding 10

Continuing with the example of Percy, complete the trial balance.

Test your understanding 11

The following are the balances on the accounts of XYZ at 31 August 20X9:

	£
Sales	41,770
Purchases	34,680
Receivables	6,790
Payables	5,650
General expenses	12,760
Loan	10,000
Plant and machinery at cost	5,000
Motor van at cost	6,000
Drawings	2,000
Rent and rates	6,700
Insurance	4,000
Bank overdraft	510
Capital	20,000

Prepare XYZ's trial balance as at 31 August 20X9.

 Test your understanding 12

Tony makes the following transactions during the month of July 20X9:

(a) Purchases good on credit for £1,000.

(b) Pays cash for rent of £500.

(c) Makes sales on credit for £1,500.

(d) Buys a computer for £900 cash.

(e) Pays cash for wages of £1,000.

(f) Receives cash from a credit customer of £400.

(g) Pays £300 cash to a credit supplier.

(h) Pays £200 cash for a telephone bill.

(i) Receives £50 cash refund for overcharge on telephone bill.

(j) Makes cash purchases of £400.

(k) Makes cash sales of £2,000.

Write up the ledger accounts for these transactions, balance the accounts off and extract Tony's Trial Balance at 31 July 20X9.

8 Summary

In this chapter we have studied cash and credit transactions. It is important to always start with the bank account and remember that cash received is a debit in the bank account and cash paid out is a credit in the bank account. If you get that right then the rest really does fall into place.

You should also be aware of the definitions of assets, expenses and income and the normal entries that you would make in the accounts for these.

Balancing an account is a very important technique which you must be able to master. You must understand how to bring the balance down onto the correct side and what that balance represents.

Test your understanding answers

Test your understanding 1

The figures in brackets are used here to indicate the transaction number in the test your understanding. They can be used to match the debit entry for the transaction with the corresponding credit entry.

Capital

	£		£
		Cash at bank (1)	150,000

Property

	£		£
Cash at bank (2)	140,000		

Purchases

	£		£
Cash at bank (3)	5,000		
Cash at bank (5)	8,000		

Sales

	£		£
		Cash at bank (4)	7,000
		Cash at bank (7)	15,000

Sundry expenses

	£		£
Cash at bank (6)	100		

Wages expense

	£		£
Cash at bank (8)	2,000		

Postage

	£		£
Cash at bank (9)	100		

Cash at bank

	£		£
Capital (1)	150,000	Property (2)	140,000
Sales (4)	7,000	Purchases (3)	5,000
Sales (7)	15,000	Purchases (5)	8,000
		Sundry expenses (6)	100
		Wages payable (8)	2,000
		Postage (9)	100

Test your understanding 2

Cash

Date	Narrative	£	Date	Narrative	£
1.1.X5	Capital	10,000	2.1.X5	Purchases	2,500
5.1.X5	Sales	3,000	4.1.X5	Delivery van	1,000
8.1.X5	Loan	2,000	7.1.X5	Gas	500
10.1.X5	Receivables	3,000	9.1.X5	Payables	1,500
			11.1.X5	Drawings	750

Capital

Date	Narrative	£	Date	Narrative	£
			1.1.X5	Cash	10,000

Purchases

Date	Narrative	£	Date	Narrative	£
2.1.X5	Cash	2,500			
3.1.X5	Payables	2,000			

Payables

Date	Narrative	£	Date	Narrative	£
9.1.X5	Cash	1,500	3.1.X5	Purchases	2,000

Delivery van

Date	Narrative	£	Date	Narrative	£
4.1.X5	Cash	1,000			

Sales

Date	Narrative	£	Date	Narrative	£
			5.1.X5	Cash	3,000
			6.1.X5	Receivables	5,000

Receivables

Date	Narrative	£	Date	Narrative	£
6.1.X5	Sales	5,000	10.1.X5	Cash	3,000

Gas

Date	Narrative	£	Date	Narrative	£
7.1.X5	Cash	500			

Loan

Date	Narrative	£	Date	Narrative	£
			8.1.X5	Cash	2,000

Drawings

Date	Narrative	£	Date	Narrative	£
11.1.X5	Cash	750			

Test your understanding 3

Bank

		£			£
(a)	Capital	4,000	(b)	Computer	1,000
(d)	Sales	800	(c)	Rent	400

Capital

		£			£
			(a)	Bank	4,000

Rent

		£		£
(c)	Bank	400		

Sales

		£			£
			(d)	Bank	800

Computers

		£		£
(b)	Bank	1,000		

Test your understanding 4

Capital

		£			£
			(a)	Bank	4,000

Purchases

		£			£
(b)	Bank	700			
(g)	Bank	1,200			

Entertainment

		£			£
(c)	Bank	300			

Computers

		£			£
(d)	Bank	3,000			

Sales

		£			£
			(e)	Bank	1,500

Drawings

		£			£
(f)	Bank	500			

Telephone

		£			£
(h)	Bank	600	(i)	Bank	200

Stationery

		£			£
(j)	Bank	157			

Bank

		£				£
(a)	Capital	4,000	(b)	Purchases	700
(e)	Sales	1,500	(c)	Entertainment	300
(i)	Telephone	200	(d)	Computers	3,000
			(f)	Drawings	500
			(g)	Purchases	1,200
			(h)	Telephone	600
			(j)	Stationery	157

Test your understanding 5

Sales

	£		£
		B	1,000
		C	90

Receivable B

	£		£
Sales	1,000	Bank	500

Receivable C

	£		£
Sales	90	Bank	90

Bank

	£		£
Receivable B	500		
Receivable C	90		

Test your understanding 6

Bank

Date		£	Date		£
1 Mar	Capital	12,000	3 Mar	Purchases	3,000
7 Mar	Sales	5,000	15 Mar	Non-current asset	2,400
19 Mar	Sales	2,000	20 Mar	Purchases	5,300
22 Mar	Sales	3,000	24 Mar	Rent	1,000
			28 Mar	Drawings	2,000
			31 Mar	Balance c/d	8,300
		22,000			22,000
1 Apr	Balance b/d	8,300			

Test your understanding 7

Bank

	£		£
Capital	10,000	Computer	1,000
Sales	2,000	Telephone	567
Sales	3,000	Rent	1,500
Sales	2,000	Rates	125
		Stationery	247
		Petrol	49
		Purchases	2,500
		Drawings	500
		Petrol	42
Sub-total	17,000	Sub-total	6,530
		Balance c/d	10,470
	17,000		17,000
Balance b/d	10,470		

Test your understanding 8

Bank

	£		£
Capital	5,000	Purchases	850
Sales	1,000	Fixtures	560
Sales	876	Van	1,500
Rent rebate	560	Rent	1,300
Sales	1,370	Rates	360
		Telephone	220
		Stationery	120
		Petrol	48
		Car repairs	167
Sub-total	8,806	Sub-total	5,125
		Balance c/d	3,681
	8,806		8,806
Balance b/d	3,681		

Test your understanding 9

Bank

	£		£
Balance b/d	23,700	Drawings	4,000
Sales	2,300	Rent	570
Sales	1,700	Purchases	6,000
Receivables	4,700	Rates	500
		Salaries	3,600
		Car expenses	460
		Petrol	49
		Petrol	38
		Electricity	210
		Stationery	89
Sub-total	32,400	Sub-total	15,516
		Balance c/d	16,884
	32,400		32,400
Balance b/d	16,884		

Test your understanding 10

Trial balance

	Dr £	Cr £
Bank	19,750	
Capital		20,000
Van	500	
Purchases	1,500	
Drawings	50	
Sales		2,000
Rent	200	
	22,000	22,000

Test your understanding 11

Trial balance at 31 August 20X9

	Dr £	Cr £
Sales		41,770
Purchases	34,680	
Receivables	6,790	
Payables		5,650
General expenses	12,760	
Loan		10,000
Plant and machinery at cost	5,000	
Motor van at cost	6,000	
Drawings	2,000	
Rent and rates	6,700	
Insurance	4,000	
Bank overdraft		510
Capital		20,000
	77,930	77,930

Test your understanding 12

Purchases

		£			£
(a)	Payables	1,000			
(j)	Bank	400	Balance c/d		1,400
		1,400			1,400
	Balance b/d	1,400			

Payables

		£			£
(g)	Bank	300	(a)	Purchases	1,000
	Balance c/d	700			
		1,000			1,000
				Balance b/d	700

Rent

		£		£
(b)	Bank	500	Balance c/d	500
		500		500
	Balance b/d	500		

Sales

	£			£
		(c)	Receivables	1,500
Balance c/d	3,500	(k)	Bank	2,000
	3,500			3,500
			Balance b/d	3,500

Receivables

	£		£
(c) Sales	1,500	(f) Bank	400
		Balance c/d	1,100
	1,500		1,500
Balance b/d	1,100		

Computers

	£		£
(d) Bank	900	Balance c/d	900
	900		900
Balance b/d	900		

Wages

	£		£
(e) Bank	1,000	Balance c/d	1,000
	1,000		1,000
Balance b/d	1,000		

Telephone

	£		£
(h) Bank	200	(i) Bank	50
		Balance c/d	150
	200		200
Balance b/d	150		

Bank

		£			£
(f)	Receivables	400	(b) Rent		500
(i)	Telephone	50	(d) Computer		900
(k)	Sales	2,000	(e) Wages		1,000
			(g) Payables		300
			(h) Telephone		200
			(j) Purchases		400
Balance c/d		850			
		———			———
		3,300			3,300
		———			———
			Balance b/d		850

Trial balance as at 31 July 20X9:

	Dr £	Cr £
Purchases	1,400	
Payables		700
Rent	500	
Sales		3,500
Receivables	1,100	
Computers	900	
Wages	1,000	
Telephone	150	
Bank overdraft		850
	———	———
	5,050	5,050
	———	———

KAPLAN PUBLISHING

Accounting for credit sales, VAT and discounts

5

Introduction

In this chapter we will consider, in more detail, the accounting for credit sales considering the effects of discounts and VAT as well as reviewing the accounting for receipts from receivables.

ASSESSMENT CRITERIA	CONTENTS
Distinguish between prompt payment, trade and bulk discounts (1.2)	1 Recording credit sales
	2 Discounts
Demonstrate an understanding of the process of recording financial transactions (1.4)	3 VAT and discounts
	4 Accounting for receipts from receivables and prompt payment discounts
Enter sales invoices and credit notes into books of prime entry (2.2)	
Check the accuracy of receipts from customers (2.3)	
Transfer data from the books of prime entry to the ledgers (5.1)	

1 Recording credit sales

1.1 The sales day book

In chapter 2 we were introduced to the sales day book (SDB) which is where a credit sale is primarily recorded. The sales day book details the names and references in relation to the customer we have sold goods to or provided a service to on credit. It also contains a breakdown of the transaction value – the net, VAT and gross (total) amounts (as detailed on the invoice).

The SDB is not part of the double entry; it is not part of the ledger accounts. The totals from the sales day book are used to perform the double entry to enter into the general ledger on a timely basis.

1.2 Accounting for credit sales and VAT

When recording a credit sale, the financial effects of the transaction include; the recognition of a receivable, the income generated from the sale and the amount of VAT that has been charged and is liable to be paid to HM Revenue & Customs.

The sales day book has been reproduced below along with summaries of the accounting entries required.

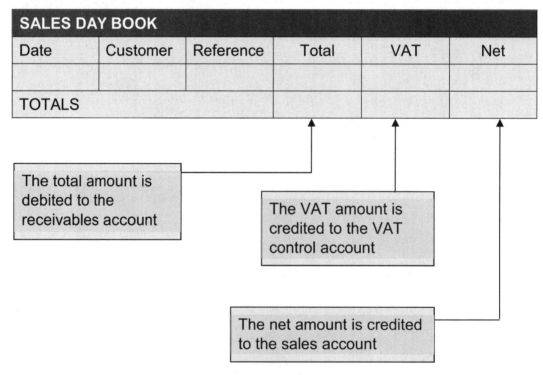

SALES DAY BOOK					
Date	Customer	Reference	Total	VAT	Net
TOTALS					

The total amount is debited to the receivables account

The VAT amount is credited to the VAT control account

The net amount is credited to the sales account

1.3 Summary of entries

In summary, the accounting entries for a credit sale with VAT are:

Debit	Receivables account with the gross amount
Credit	Sales account with the net amount
Credit	VAT control account with the VAT amount

The total amount is debited to the receivables account. This is recognising the asset of a credit customer owing us (the business) the gross amount of the transaction, including VAT.

The net amount is credited to the sales account. This is recognising an increase to income. It is only the net amount that is credited to the sales account as the VAT charged on the transaction is merely collected by the business on behalf of HM Revenue & Customs.

The VAT amount is credited to the VAT control account in recognition that this amount is owed to HMRC – this is a liability.

2 Discounts

2.1 Introduction

We have already been introduced to different types of discounts in an earlier chapter but we shall revise them here. There are three main types of discount that a business might offer to its credit customers; a bulk discount, a trade discount and a prompt payment discount.

2.2 Bulk discounts

A bulk discount is a percentage of the list price of the goods being sold that is deducted when purchasing large quantities.

A bulk discount is a definite amount deducted from the list price total of the invoice. The amounts recorded in the sales day book will be after a bulk discount has been deducted.

2.3 Trade discounts

A trade discount is a percentage of the list price of the goods being sold that is deducted for certain customers. This discount may be offered for frequent and valued customers, encouraging loyalty.

A trade discount is a definite amount deducted from the list price total of the invoice. The amounts recorded in the sales day book will be after the trade discount has been deducted.

2.4 Prompt payment discounts

A prompt payment discount (which may also be referred to as a cash or settlement discount) is offered to customers if they settle the invoice within a certain time period. It is up to the customer to decide whether or not to pay within the required timescale and therefore take advantage of the prompt payment discount.

The discount is expressed as a percentage of the invoice total but is not deducted from the invoice total as it is not certain when the invoice is sent out whether or not it will be taken advantage of. Instead the details of the prompt payment discount being offered will be noted at the bottom of the invoice.

A prompt payment discount can be offered but it is up to the customer whether or not to take advantage of it. The amounts recorded in the sales day book will be before any deductions of prompt payment discounts, as at that point we do not know if the discount will be taken advantage of or not.

3 VAT and discounts

3.1 Calculating VAT

A business makes no profit out of any VAT charged on its sales. Instead this amount is paid over to HM Revenue and Customs.

 Test your understanding 1

Calculate the VAT on the following sales:

(a) A sale for £140.00 net of VAT

(b) A sale for £560.00 net of VAT

(c) A sale for £720.00 inclusive of VAT

(d) A sale for £960.00 inclusive of VAT

3.2 Bulk and trade discounts

At the time of generating and recording an invoice it is known if a bulk or trade discount has been given. There are no later conditions to be met.

VAT is calculated on the net amount of the transaction after the deduction of these discounts.

Example 1

L sells £1,000 of goods net of VAT (at 20%) to M on credit. There is an agreed 10% trade discount with M. Enter these transactions in the ledger accounts.

Solution

Step 1 Calculate the discount and VAT on the sale.

	£
Original list price of goods	1,000.00
Less: 10% trade discount	(100.00)
Net invoice value	900.00
VAT (20% x £900)	180.00
Total (gross) invoice value	1,080.00

Step 2 Enter the invoice amounts into the ledger accounts.

Receivables

	£		£
Sales and VAT	1,080.00		

Sales

	£		£
		Receivables	900.00

VAT

	£		£
		Receivables	180.00

3.3 Prompt payment discounts

Prompt payment VAT legislation was amended (Revenue and Customs Brief 49 (2014)) and the changes took effect from 1 April 2015. The AAT made these changes examinable for Bookkeeping Transactions from September 2016.

Although a customer may be offered a prompt payment discount no reflection of this discount is shown within the accounting records until the customer does take advantage of this, if they choose to do so. When initially raising an invoice, VAT should be charged on the full price of the goods or services (although this would be after deducting trade or bulk discounts).

If the customer takes advantage of the prompt payment discount the VAT would be adjusted to reflect the discount taken. This adjustment could be by way of a credit note – the chosen method for the Bookkeeping Transactions assessment criteria. The credit note to reflect this prompt payment discount is entered into the discounts allowed day book. This is considered in more detail in section 4.

 Example 2

Leo, a trader, sells goods for £500 (exclusive of VAT at 20%). He offers a 10% discount if payment is made within 7 days.

The amounts shown as due on the invoice will be:

Sales price	£500
VAT	£100
Amount due	£600

The invoice will state that a prompt payment discount of £60 can be deducted from the amount due, if payment is made within 7 days. If the trader takes the discount the supplier must then issue a credit note for £60 i.e. £50 + VAT of £10. This credit note will be recorded in the discounts allowed day book.

Test your understanding 2

Calculate the VAT **paid** on the following sales:

(a) A sale for £280.00 net of VAT where a prompt payment discount of 2% is offered but not taken advantage of.

(b) A sale for £480.00 net of VAT where a prompt payment discount of 3% is offered but not taken advantage of.

(c) A sale for £800.00 net of VAT where a prompt payment discount of 5% is offered and is taken advantage of.

(d) A sale of £650.00 net of VAT where a prompt payment discount of 4% is offered and is taken advantage of.

 4 **Accounting for receipts from receivables and prompt payment discounts**

4.1 Accounting for receipts from receivables

When a receivable makes a payment for an amount owed the double entry is:

Debit	Bank account
Credit	Receivable account

The debit to the bank account is recognising the increase in our funds – we have received money from the receivable.

The credit entry to the receivable account is to reduce the receivable balance now that the receivable has made a payment to reduce what they owed the business.

When initially recording a receipt from a receivable, the amounts will be recorded into the cash receipts book. Recording receipts from receivables into the cash receipts book was reviewed in chapter 2.

4.2 Checking the accuracy of receipts from customers

Prior to making the accounting entries for the receipt from a receivable, it should be established whether the amount being received from the customer is correct.

Discrepancies causing under or over payment may occur. Such discrepancies may be due to the incorrect application and calculation of discounts so errors need to be identified. Checks should be made by agreeing the receipt to supporting documentation, re-performing calculations and agreeing discounts to a discount policy.

There are numerous reasons why a credit customer may make the incorrect payment including it being a genuine mistake or perhaps there being a dispute over the invoices due. In the event of a genuine mistake the seller should contact the customer to explain the issue and request for the issue to be rectified. If there is a dispute the seller should contact the customer attempting to resolve the issue.

4.3   Accounting for prompt payment discounts

If a receivable takes advantage of a prompt payment discount, the receivable will pay less than what has been recorded within the accounting records. The adjustment required impacts the receivable account, the VAT account and a discounts allowed account.

When accounting for a discount allowed to a credit customer, we do not revise the original sales value, instead we recognise an expense for this discount.

When initially recording a discount allowed to a customer, due to the customer taking advantage of a prompt payment discount, the amounts will be recorded into the discounts allowed day book.

The discounts allowed day book has been reproduced along with a summary of the accounting entries required.

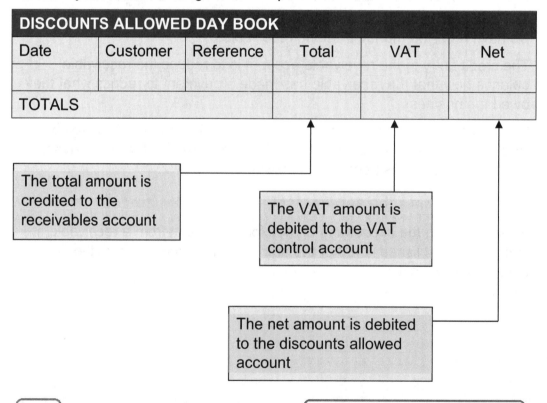

DISCOUNTS ALLOWED DAY BOOK					
Date	Customer	Reference	Total	VAT	Net
TOTALS					

The total amount is credited to the receivables account

The VAT amount is debited to the VAT control account

The net amount is debited to the discounts allowed account

To summarise, the accounting entries for a prompt payment discount are:

Debit	Discounts allowed account with the net amount
Debit	VAT account with the VAT amount
Credit	Receivable account with the gross amount

The gross amount is credited to the receivables account. This is recognising the reduction to the receivable of the discount and associated VAT charge.

The net amount is debited to the discounts allowed account. This is recognising an expense of allowing a discount. Note that this is for the VAT exclusive amount.

The VAT amount based on the discount allowed is debited to the VAT account in recognition that this amount is no longer owed to HMRC as there has been a reduction to the original price due to the customer taking advantage of a prompt payment discount.

The example that follows shows the procedures of calculating invoice amounts and amounts due from receivables as well as how to account for these transactions.

 Example 3

Enzo sells goods for £200 net of VAT (at 20%) to Emilia on credit. Enzo offers Emilia a 2% prompt payment discount if Emilia pays within 10 days. Emilia does pay within the required time and takes the prompt payment discount.

Required:

(a) Calculate the invoice value.

(b) Record the required entries for the credit sale to Emilia in the sales day book and the relevant accounts in the general ledger of Enzo.

(c) Calculate the amount paid by Emilia (taking the prompt payment discount).

(d) Record the receipt by Enzo of Emilia's payment in the cash receipts book, the prompt payment discount in the discounts allowed day book and make the required entries into the ledger accounts in the general ledger of Enzo.

Solution

(a) Calculate the invoice value.

	£
Sales value net of VAT	200.00
VAT = 200 × 20%	40.00
Invoice value	240.00

(b) Record the required entries for the credit sale to Emilia in the sales day book and the relevant accounts in the general ledger of Enzo.

SALES DAY BOOK

Customer	Total £	VAT £	Net £
Emilia	240.00	40.00	200.00

Receivables

	£		£
Sales and VAT	240.00		

Sales

	£		£
		Receivables	200.00

VAT

	£		£
		Receivables	40.00

(c) Calculate the amount paid by Emilia (taking the prompt payment discount).

	£
Sales value net of VAT	200.00
Less: prompt payment discount	
= 2% × 200	(4.00)
VAT (196 × 20%)	39.20
Amount paid by Emilia	235.20

(d) Record the receipt by Enzo of Emilia's payment in the cash receipts book, the prompt payment discount allowed in the discounts allowed day book and make the required entries into the ledger accounts in the general ledger of Enzo.

CASH RECEIPTS BOOK

Narrative	Total £	VAT £	Receivables £	Cash sales £
Emilia	235.20		235.20	

DISCOUNTS ALLOWED DAY BOOK

Narrative	Total	VAT	Net
Emilia	4.80	0.80	4.00

Because Emilia takes the prompt payment discount, she pays Enzo £4.80 less than the invoice value – this is made up by the £4 reduction to the net price of the goods (2% of £200) and a £0.80 reduction to the VAT charge (the VAT should be 20% based on the discounted amount of £196).

In order to clear the receivables account we have to credit that account with the £4.80, debit a discount allowed account with £4 and debit the VAT account with £0.80.

The discount allowed of £4 is an expense of the business as we have allowed our customer to pay less than the invoice value in order for us to have the benefit of receiving the money earlier.

The £0.80 debit to VAT is reducing down the original VAT calculated on the sale as the price of the goods has now decreased because of the discount given to the customer.

Receivables

	£		£
Sales and VAT	240.00	Bank	235.20
		Discount allowed	4.80

Sales

	£		£
		Receivables	200.00

VAT

	£		£
Receivables	0.80	Receivables	40.00

Discount allowed

	£		£
Receivables	4.00		

Bank

	£		£
Receivables	235.20		

Now that we have reviewed accounting for receipts from receivables and prompt payment discounts, work through the following examples to practise the double entries involved.

Example 4

C sells £2,000 of goods net of VAT (at 20%) to Z on credit. He offers Z a 5% prompt payment discount if Z pays within 5 days. Z does not pay his account within 5 days and so does not take the prompt payment discount. Z pays after 10 days. Enter these transactions in the accounts.

Solution

Step 1   Calculate the VAT on the sale.

	£
Sales value net of VAT	2,000.00
VAT = 2,000 × 20%	400.00
Invoice value	2,400.00

At the point of raising the invoice it is not known whether the prompt payment discount will be taken or not. The discount offer would be stated at the bottom of the invoice but the sales value would not be adjusted on the invoice.

Step 2   Enter the invoice in the accounts.

Receivables

	£		£
Sales and VAT	2,400.00		

Sales

	£		£
		Receivables	2,000.00

VAT

	£		£
		Receivables	400.00

Step 3   Enter the payment by Z in the accounts.

Receivables

	£		£
Sales and VAT	2,400.00	Bank	2,400.00

Sales

	£		£
		Receivables	2,000.00

VAT

	£		£
		Receivables	400.00

Bank

	£		£
Receivables	2,400.00		

As Z does not take advantage of the prompt payment discount, there is no entry for the prompt payment discount at all in the accounts.

Example 5

Two months later C sells another £2,000 of goods net of VAT (at 20%) to Z on credit. He offers Z a 5% prompt payment discount if Z pays within 5 days. This time Z does pay his account within 5 days and takes the prompt payment discount. Enter these transactions in the accounts.

Solution

Step 1 Calculate the VAT on the sale.

Note: This is exactly the same as the previous example.

	£
Sales value net of VAT	2,000.00
VAT = 2,000 × 20%	400.00
Invoice value	2,400.00

Step 2 Enter the invoice in the accounts.

Note: This is exactly the same as the previous example because the value of the invoice is exactly the same.

Receivables

	£		£
Sales and VAT	2,400.00		

Sales

	£		£
		Receivables	2,000.00

VAT

	£		£
		Receivables	400.00

Step 3   Calculate the amount paid by Z.

Note: The amount paid by Z will be different from the previous example because Z does take the 5% prompt payment discount offered.

	£
Sales value net of VAT	2,000.00
Less: prompt payment discount	
= 5% × 2,000	(100.00)
VAT (1,900 × 20%)	380.00
Amount paid by Z	2,280.00

Step 4   Enter this amount in the accounts.

Receivables

	£		£
Sales and VAT	2,400.00	Bank	2,280.00

Bank

	£		£
Receivables	2,280.00		

Because Z takes the prompt payment discount, he pays C £120 less than the invoice value – this is made up by the £100 reduction to the net price of the goods (5% of £2,000) and a £20 reduction to the VAT charge (the VAT should be 20% based on the discounted amount of £1,900).

In order to clear the receivables account we have to credit that account with the £120, debit a discount allowed account with £100 and debit the VAT account with £20.

The discount allowed of £100 is an expense of the business as we have allowed our customer to pay less than the invoice value in order for us to have the benefit of receiving the money earlier.

The £20 debit to VAT is reducing down the original VAT calculated on the sale as the price of the goods has now decreased because of the discount given to the customer.

Sales			
	£		£
		Receivables	2,000.00

VAT			
	£		£
Receivables	20.00	Receivables	400.00

Receivables			
	£		£
Sales and VAT	2,400.00	Bank	2,280.00
		Discount allowed	100.00
		VAT	20.00

Discount allowed			
	£		£
Receivables	100.00		

Bank			
	£		£
Receivables	2,280.00		

 Test your understanding 3

A sells £600 of goods to B – VAT is still to be added. A offers B a prompt payment discount of 3%.

(a) What will the accounting entries be to record the initial sale if:

    (i) B does not take the prompt payment discount.

    (ii) B does take the prompt payment discount.

(b) Calculate the amount that B will pay A if:

    (i) B does not take the prompt payment discount.

    (ii) B does take the prompt payment discount.

(c) What are the accounting entries for recording the payment received from B if the prompt payment discount has been taken?

5 Summary

We have covered some fairly tricky areas in this chapter and it is very important that you really do understand them.

The calculations of VAT (sales tax) are fairly straightforward but do make sure you can calculate the VAT element of a sale when you are given the sales value gross of VAT.

Quite tricky is the adjustment needed when a customer takes advantage of a prompt payment discount. You have to ensure the discounted price of the goods is accounted for as well as the reduction to the VAT amount.

It is necessary for you to be able to check the accuracy of receipts from customers, identifying any discrepancies that may have occurred.

Test your understanding answers

Test your understanding 1

(a)	VAT =	£140.00 × 20%	=	£28.00
(b)	VAT =	£560.00 × 20%	=	£112.00
(c)	VAT =	£720.00 × $\frac{20}{120}$	=	£120.00
(d)	VAT =	£960.00 × $\frac{20}{120}$	=	£160.00

Test your understanding 2

(a) VAT =   £280 × 20% = £56.00

(b) VAT =   £480 × 20% = £96.00

(c) VAT =   £(800 − (5% × 800)) × 20% = £152.00

(d) VAT =   £(650 − (4% × 650)) × 20% = £124.80

Although a prompt payment discount was offered in (a) and (b) the discount was not taken advantage of so the VAT paid is not discounted.

In (c) and (d) the prompt payment discounts offered were taken advantage of and so the VAT paid would be calculated based on the discounted sales price.

Test your understanding 3

(a) What will the accounting entries be to record the initial sale if:

(i) B does not take the prompt payment discount.

(ii) B does take the prompt payment discount.

The invoice value and the accounting entries required will be the same regardless of whether B takes the prompt payment discount or not.

Invoice value:

	£
Net price	600.00
VAT £600 × 20%	120.00
	———
Invoice value	720.00
	———

Accounting entries:

Debit receivables	£720.00
Credit sales	£600.00
Credit VAT	£120.00

(b) Calculate the amount that B will pay A if:

(i) **B does not take the prompt payment discount:**

Amount paid by B: £720.00

(ii) **B does take the prompt payment discount:**

If B does take the prompt payment discount the original invoice value will be the same as seen in part (a). However the payment if the discount is taken is calculated as follows:

	£
Net price	600.00
Less: prompt payment discount	
(£600 × 3%)	(18.00)
Revised sales price	582.00
VAT (£582 × 20%)	116.40
	———
Amount paid by B:	698.40
	———

The net amount of the discount is £18.00, with a reduction to VAT of £3.60 and therefore a total deduction to the amount owed by the receivable of £21.60.

(c) What are the accounting entries for recording the payment received from B if the prompt payment discount has been taken?

Accounting entries:

For the bank receipt:

Debit bank	£698.40
Credit receivables	£698.40

For the discount allowed:

Debit discounts allowed	£18.00
Debit VAT	£3.60
Credit receivables	£21.60

Accounting for credit purchases, VAT and discounts

Introduction

In this chapter we move on from considering the accounting entries for sales and look here at the equivalent accounting entries for purchases.

ASSESSMENT CRITERIA

Distinguish between prompt payment, trade and bulk discounts (1.2)

Demonstrate an understanding of the process of recording financial transactions (1.4)

Check the accuracy of supplier invoices and credit notes (3.1)

Enter supplier invoices and credit notes into books of prime entry (3.2)

Prepare payments to suppliers (3.3)

Transfer data from the books of prime entry to the ledgers (5.1)

CONTENTS

1 Recording credit purchases
2 VAT and discounts
3 Accounting for payments to suppliers and prompt payment discounts

1 Recording credit purchases

1.1 The purchases day book

In an early chapter we were introduced to the purchases day book which is where a credit purchase is primarily recorded. The purchases day book (PDB) details the names and references in relation to the supplier we have bought goods from or received a service from on credit. It also contains a breakdown of the transaction value – the net, VAT and gross (total) amounts (as detailed on the invoice).

The PDB is not part of the double entry; it is not part of the ledger accounts. The totals from the purchases day book are used to perform the double entry to enter into the general ledger on a timely basis.

1.2 Accounting for credit purchases and VAT

When recording a credit purchase, the financial effects of the transaction include; the recognition of a payable, expense from a purchase and an amount of VAT that has been paid but which we can use to offset against a VAT liability to HM Revenue & Customs.

The purchases day book has been reproduced below along with summaries of the accounting entries required.

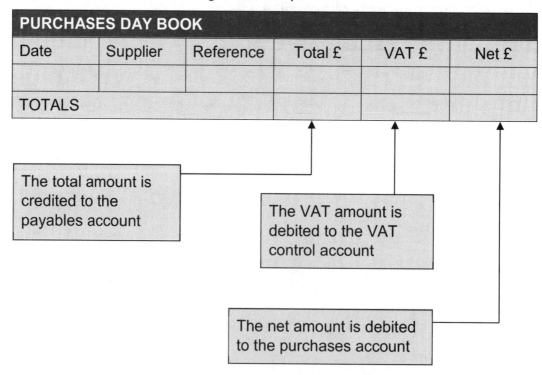

PURCHASES DAY BOOK					
Date	Supplier	Reference	Total £	VAT £	Net £
TOTALS					

The total amount is credited to the payables account

The VAT amount is debited to the VAT control account

The net amount is debited to the purchases account

1.3 Summary of entries

In summary the accounting entries for a credit purchase with VAT are:

Debit	Purchases account with the net amount
Debit	VAT account with the VAT
Credit	Payables account with the gross amount

Purchases have been debited with the net amount as the VAT is not a cost to the business. Instead the VAT is an amount that can be offset against the amount of VAT due to HMRC and therefore the VAT is a debit entry in the VAT account.

The payables account is credited with the gross amount as this is the amount that must be paid to the supplier.

Work through the following example to practise the double entry for credit purchases.

Example 1

B sells goods on credit to Y for £500 plus VAT at 20%. Y pays B the full amount due. Record these transactions in the accounts of Y.

Solution

Step 1   Calculate the VAT on the purchase and enter the transaction in the payables, purchases and VAT accounts.

Calculation of VAT

	£
Net value of sale	500.00
VAT at 20%	100.00
Gross value of purchase	600.00

Payables

	£		£
		Purchases and VAT	600.00

Purchases

	£		£
Payables	500.00		

VAT

	£		£
Payables	100.00		

Step 2   Enter £600.00 paid by Y in the payables & the bank account.

Payables

	£		£
Bank	600.00	Purchases and VAT	600.00

Purchases

	£		£
Payables	500.00		

VAT

	£		£
Payables	100.00		

Bank

	£		£
		Payables	600.00

2   VAT and discounts

2.1   Introduction

We studied discounts and VAT (sales tax) when studying sales in chapter 5. The calculation of VAT and discounts are **exactly** the same when considering purchases. Remember that it is the seller who offers the discounts and it is the seller who charges the VAT, the fact that we are now studying purchases does not change the calculations.

The purchaser will receive a 'sales invoice' from the seller. This will have details of discounts and VAT exactly as we saw before when studying sales. The purchaser will call this a 'purchase invoice' and enter it in the books accordingly as we shall see.

We shall not therefore go through all the details of VAT and discounts but will simply revise this with a short example.

Example 2

Carl buys £1,000 of goods from Susan on credit. Susan sends a sales invoice with the goods offering a 5% prompt payment discount if Carl pays within 7 days. Carl does pay within 7 days.

Calculate:

(a)   the VAT

(b)   the total value of the invoice, and

(c)   the amount that Carl will pay.

Solution

(a)   VAT = £1,000 × 20% = £200

   Note: although the discount is offered at the point of the invoice being generated it does not impact the calculation of VAT or the net goods value until the prompt payment discount is taken advantage of.

(b)   **Total value of invoice**

	£
Goods	1,000.00
VAT	200.00
Invoice value	1,200.00

(c)   **Amount Carl will pay**

	£
Goods	1,000.00
Less prompt payment discount (5% × 1,000)	(50.00)
Revised goods amount	950.00
VAT (950 × 20%)	190.00
Amount Carl will pay	1,140.00

Test your understanding 1

Calculate the VAT for the following:

(a)   X purchases £400 goods from Y net of VAT at 20%.

(b)   X purchases £650 goods from Y net of VAT at 20%.

(c)   X purchases £528 goods from Y including VAT at 20%.

(d)   X purchases £120 goods from Y including VAT at 20%.

 Test your understanding 2

Calculate the VAT **paid** on the following:

(a)   X purchases £850 goods from Y and takes the 3% prompt payment discount offered.

(b)   X purchases £600 goods from Y and takes the 5% prompt payment discount offered.

(c)   X purchases £325 goods from Y and does not take the 2% prompt payment discount offered.

(d)   X purchases £57 goods from Y and does not take the 4% prompt payment discount offered.

3 Accounting for payments to suppliers and prompt payment discounts

3.1   Accounting for payments to payables

When we make a payment for an amount owed to a payable the double entry is:

Debit	Payable account
Credit	Bank account

The credit to the bank account is recognising the decrease in bank funds – we have paid money to the payable.

The debit entry to the payable account is to reduce the payable balance now that we have made the payment, the liability is reduced.

When initially recording a payment to a payable, the amounts will be recorded into the cash payments book. Recording payments to payables into the cash payments book was reviewed in chapter 2.

3.2 Preparing payments to suppliers

Prior to making the accounting entries for a payment to a payable, checks should be performed on the invoice received to identify any discrepancies. The details of quantities and amounts should be agreed to the purchase order, the delivery note and the goods received note to ensure correct billing.

3.3 Accounting for prompt payment discounts

If a business takes advantage of a prompt payment discount, the business will pay a lower amount to the payable than the amount that is recorded as the payable balance in the accounting records. The adjustment required for this discount received impacts the payable account; the VAT account and a discounts received account.

When accounting for a discount received from a credit supplier, we do not revise the original purchase value; instead we recognise this discount as a form of income.

When initially recording a prompt payment discount received from a supplier, the amounts will be recorded into a discounts received day book.

The discounts received day book has been reproduced along with the summaries of the accounting entries required.

DISCOUNTS RECEIVED DAY BOOK					
Date	Supplier	Reference	Total £	VAT £	Net £
TOTALS					

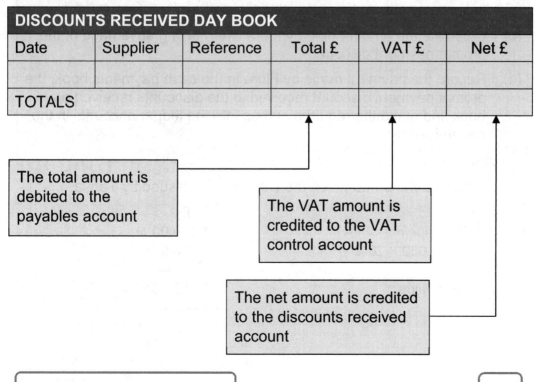

The total amount is debited to the payables account

The VAT amount is credited to the VAT control account

The net amount is credited to the discounts received account

To summarise, the accounting entries for a prompt payment discount received are:

Debit	Payables with the gross amount
Credit	VAT account with the VAT amount
Credit	Discounts received account with the net amount

The gross amount is debited to the payables account. This is recognising the reduction to the payable of the discount and associated VAT charge.

The net amount is credited to the discounts received account. This is recognising a form of income from receiving a discount. Note this is for the VAT exclusive amount.

The VAT amount based on the discount received is credited to the VAT account in recognition that the VAT on the purchase that was originally debited has now decreased.

 Example 3

Tanya sells goods for £1,050 net of VAT at 20% to Flora on credit. Flora is offered a 5% prompt payment discount if payment is made within 5 working days. Flora does pay within the required time and takes advantage of the prompt payment discount that was offered by Tanya.

Required:

(a) Calculate the amounts on the sales invoice issued by Tanya.

(b) Record the required entries for the credit purchase in Flora's accounting records – the purchases day book and the relevant ledger accounts in the general ledger.

(c) Calculate the amount paid by Flora when taking advantage of the prompt payment discount.

(d) Record the payment made by Flora in the cash payments book, the prompt payment discount received in the discounts received day book and make the required entries into the ledger accounts in the general ledger.

Solution

(a) Calculate the amounts on the sales invoice issued by Tanya.

	£
Sales value net of VAT	1,050.00
VAT = 1,050 × 20%	210.00
Invoice value	1,260.00

(b) Record the required entries for the credit purchase in Flora's accounting records – the purchases day book and the relevant accounts in the general ledger.

PURCHASES DAY BOOK

Supplier	Total £	VAT £	Net £
Tanya	1,260.00	210.00	1,050.00

Purchases

	£		£
Payables	1,050.00		

VAT

	£		£
Payables	210.00		

Payables

	£		£
		Purchases & VAT	1,260.00

(c) Calculate the amount paid by Flora when taking advantage of the prompt payment discount.

	£
Purchases value net of VAT	1,050.00
Less: prompt payment discount	
= 5% × 1,050	(52.50)
VAT (997.50 × 20%)	199.50
	————
Amount paid by Flora	1,197.00
	————

(d) Record the payment made by Flora in the cash payments book, the prompt payment discount received in the discounts received day book and make the required entries into the ledger accounts in the general ledger.

CASH PAYMENTS BOOK

Narrative	Total £	VAT £	Payables £	Other £
Tanya	1,197.00		1,197.00	

DISCOUNTS RECEIVED DAY BOOK

Narrative	Total £	VAT £	Net £
Tanya	63.00	10.50	52.50

As Flora takes the prompt payment discount, she pays Tanya £63 less than the invoice value – this is made up by the £52.50 reduction to the net price of the goods (5% of £1,050) and a £10.50 reduction to the VAT charge (the VAT should be 20% based on the discounted amount of £997.50).

In order to clear the balance on the payables account we have to debit that account with £63, credit a discounts received account with £52.50 and credit the VAT account with £10.50.

The discount received of £52.50 is treated as an income of the business. The £10.50 credit to VAT is reducing down the original VAT calculated on the purchase price, which has now reduced due to taking advantage of the prompt payment discount.

	Purchases			
	£			£
Payables	1,050.00			

	VAT			
	£			£
Payables	210.00	Payables		10.50

Payables

	£		£
Bank	1,197.00	Purchases and VAT	1,260.00
Discounts received and VAT	63.00		

Discounts received

	£		£
		Payables	52.50

Bank

	£		£
		Payables	1,197.00

 Example 4

B sells £1,000 of goods to Y net of VAT on credit. He gives Y a deduction of 20% trade discount from the £1,000 net value. Y pays his account in full. Enter these amounts in the accounts of Y.

Solution

Step 1   Calculate the value of the sale net of discount and the VAT at 20% thereon.

	£
Sales value	1,000
Less: 20% discount	(200)
Net value	800
VAT at 20%	160
Total invoice value	960

Step 2   Enter the invoice in the payables, purchases and VAT accounts.

Payables

	£		£
		Purchases and VAT	960

Purchases

	£		£
Payables	800		

VAT

	£		£
Payables	160		

Note: Note that the trade discount does not feature at all in the accounts. The invoice value is expressed after deduction of the trade discount and it is this invoiced amount that is entered in the purchases day book and relevant ledger accounts.

Step 3   Enter the cash paid by Y.

Payables

	£		£
Bank	960	Purchases and VAT	960

Purchases

	£		£
Payables	800		

VAT

	£		£
Payables	160		

Bank

	£		£
		Payables	960

Example 5

C sells £2,000 of goods net of VAT to Z on credit. He offers Z a 5% prompt payment discount if Z pays within 7 days. Z pays his account within 7 days and takes the prompt payment discount. Enter these transactions in the accounts of Z.

Solution

Step 1 Calculate the VAT on the purchase.

	£
Invoice value net of VAT	2,000.00
VAT = 20% × 2,000	400.00
Invoice value	2,400.00

Step 2 Enter the invoice in the accounts of Z.

Payables

	£		£
		Purchases and VAT	2,400.00

Purchases

	£		£
Payables	2,000.00		

VAT

	£		£
Payables	400.00		

Step 3 Calculate the amount paid by Z.

	£
Invoice value net of VAT	2,000.00
Less: prompt payment discount = 5% × 2,000	(100.00)
VAT (1,900 × 20%)	380.00
Amount paid by Z	2,280.00

Step 4   Enter this amount in the accounts.

Payables

	£		£
Bank	2,280.00	Purchases and VAT	2,400.00

As Z takes the prompt payment discount, he pays C £120 less than the invoice value – this is made up by the £100 reduction to the net price of the goods (5% of £2,000) and a £20 reduction to the VAT charge (the VAT should be 20% based on the discounted amount of £1,900).

In order to clear the balance on the payables account we have to debit that account with £120, credit a discounts received account with £100 and credit the VAT account with £20.

The discount received of £100 is treated as an income of the business. The £20 credit to VAT is reducing down the original VAT calculated on the purchase price, which has now reduced due to taking advantage of the prompt payment discount.

Payables

	£		£
Bank	2,280.00	Purchases and VAT	2,400.00
Discounts received and VAT	120.00		

Purchases

	£		£
Payables	2,000.00		

VAT

	£		£
Payables	400.00	Payables	20.00

Bank

	£		£
		Payables	2,280.00

Discount received

	£		£
		Payables	100.00

Test your understanding 3

Z buys £600 of goods net of VAT at 20% from A and takes the 3% prompt payment discount offered.

Post these transactions in the ledger accounts of Z.

Purchases

	£		£

Payables

	£		£

Bank

	£		£

VAT

	£		£

Discounts received

	£		£

3.4 Checking the accuracy of supplier invoices

We have considered the calculations that are required when dealing with invoices reviewing the impact of VAT and discounts. We should apply this knowledge when checking the accuracy of supplier invoices. This is studied in more detail in chapter 8.

4 Summary

The topics covered in this chapter will have been familiar to you as you have already studied the similar topics for sales.

Make sure you understand the accounting entries required when a business takes advantage of a prompt payment discount offered by a credit supplier.

Test your understanding answers

 Test your understanding 1

(a) VAT = £400 × 20% = £80.00

(b) VAT = £650 × 20% = £130.00

(c) VAT = £528 × $\frac{20}{120}$ = £88.00

(d) VAT = £120 × $\frac{20}{120}$ = £20.00

 Test your understanding 2

(a) VAT = £(850 – (3% × 850)) × 20% = £164.90

(b) VAT = £(600 – (5% × 600)) × 20% = £114.00

(c) VAT = £325 × 20% = £65.00

(d) VAT = £57 × 20% = £11.40

 Test your understanding 3

Calculate the invoice value and amount paid by Z.

	£
Net price	600.00
VAT £600 × 20%	120.00
Invoice value	720.00
Less: Discount 3% × 720	(21.60)
Amount paid	698.40

The discount can be broken down as follows:

	£
Discount on net amount £600 × 3%	18.00
Discount on VAT amount £120 × 3%	3.60
Total discount received	21.60

Purchases

	£		£
Payables	600.00		

Payables

	£		£
Bank	698.40	Purchases and VAT	720.00
Discounts received and VAT	21.60		
	720.00		720.00

Bank

	£		£
		Payables	698.40

VAT

	£		£
Payables	120.00	Payables	3.60

Discounts received

	£		£
		Payables	18.00

Control accounts and subsidiary ledgers

7

Introduction

We have already seen how different transactions including credit sales and credit purchases are recorded into the books of prime entry. In this chapter we introduce the control accounts which form part of the general ledger and the individual memorandum accounts which are maintained for receivables and payables in the subsidiary sales and purchases ledgers.

ASSESSMENT CRITERIA
Demonstrate an understanding of the process of recording financial transactions (1.4)
Transfer data from the books of prime entry to the ledgers (5.1)

CONTENTS
1   The accounting system
2   The general and subsidiary ledgers
3   Credit sales
4   Sales returns
5   Credit purchases
6   Purchases returns

1 The accounting system

1.1 Introduction

In order to simplify the process of recording transactions and exercise greater control, we divide the recording of the transactions into three parts.

(1) The first part is the **books of prime entry**.

(2) The second part is transferring the amounts from the books of prime entry into the **ledger accounts** within the **general ledger** where the double entry takes place.

(3) The third part is the **subsidiary (memorandum) ledgers** – individual receivable and payable accounts known as the '**sales ledger**' and the '**purchases ledger**'.

Invoices, credit notes, receipts and payments will form the basis of accounting entries in all parts.

2 The general and subsidiary ledgers

2.1 The general ledger

 Definition – General ledger

A general ledger contains all the ledger accounts for recording transactions occurring within an entity.

Note: The AAT's preferred term is 'general ledger' but the general ledger may also be referred to as the 'main' or 'nominal' ledger.

The general ledger is the place where the double entry takes place in the appropriate ledger accounts. The general ledger contains all the accounts you have become familiar with so far, for example:

Capital

Drawings

Van

Rent

Electricity

Purchases

Sales

Bank

etc.

Two of these typical accounts are the receivables and payables accounts.

When credit sales are posted to the receivables account and credit purchases are posted to the payables account we can balance it off and see how much in total is owed to us by our customers and owed by us to our suppliers. However, we cannot see how much each individual customer owes us and how much we owe each individual supplier.

We need another set of ledger accounts, a subsidiary ledger, which records the individual amounts owed by the receivables and to the payables, as well as having the main receivables and payables account with the totals in it, in the general ledger.

The receivables account in the general ledger will now be referred to as the **sales ledger control account**.

 Definition – Sales ledger control account

The sales ledger control account contains the total value of all the invoices and credit notes issued to and cash receipts from credit customers for a given period.

The payables account in the general ledger will now be referred to as the **purchases ledger control account**.

 Definition – Purchases ledger control account

The purchases ledger control account contains the total value of all the invoices and credit notes received from and cash payments made to credit suppliers for a given period.

2.2 The subsidiary ledgers

 Definition – Subsidiary ledger

A subsidiary ledger provides details behind the entries in the general ledger. Subsidiary ledgers are maintained for individual receivables and payables.

Subsidiary ledgers (which can also be known as memorandum ledgers) do not form part of the double entry system i.e. no corresponding debit and credit entries are required.

 Definition – Subsidiary sales ledger

A subsidiary sales ledger is more commonly referred to as the 'sales ledger'. It is a set of accounts for individual receivables.

 Definition – Subsidiary purchases ledger

A subsidiary purchases ledger is more commonly referred to as the 'purchases ledger'. It is a set of accounts for individual payables.

As well as information about our receivables in total we have to keep track of each individual receivable. How much has been invoiced? What payments have been received? How much is owed to us?

We do this in the sales ledger. The sales ledger contains a separate ledger account for each individual receivable.

As we require information about individual receivables, the same applies to individual payables. How much have we been invoiced? What have we paid? How much do we owe?

We do this in the purchases ledger. The purchases ledger contains a separate ledger account for each individual payable.

3 Credit sales

We have now looked at the three elements of a typical accounting system. We must now see how it all fits together.

We will first consider three credit sales invoices.

Customer	Amount
A	£1,500
B	£2,000
C	£2,500

Step 1

Each invoice is recorded in the sales day book and in the personal account of each receivable in the sales ledger. The entry required for each invoice is a debit in each individual receivable account to indicate that this is the amount that each one owes us.

Step 2

At the end of the period the sales day book is totalled and the total is entered into the sales ledger control account (SLCA) in the general ledger.

The full double entry is as we saw in a previous chapter (ignoring VAT at the moment):

Debit	Sales ledger control account (receivables)
Credit	Sales

Step 3

Now consider the following cheques being received in payment of these debts.

Customer	Amount
A	£1,000
B	£2,000

Each receipt is recorded in the cash book and in the personal account of each receivable in the sales ledger. The entry for cash received in the individual accounts is a credit entry to indicate that they no longer owe us these amounts – reducing the asset we originally recognised.

Step 4

At the end of the period the cash book is totalled and the total is entered into the sales ledger control account (total receivables account) in the general ledger.

The full double entry is:

Debit	Cash account (money in)
Credit	Sales ledger control account (receivables)

This is illustrated on the next page.

Summary

1 The invoices are entered into the SDB and the cheques are entered into the cash book.

2 The totals from the SDB and the cash book are posted to the SLCA.

3 The individual invoices and cash receipts from receivables are posted to the subsidiary sales ledger.

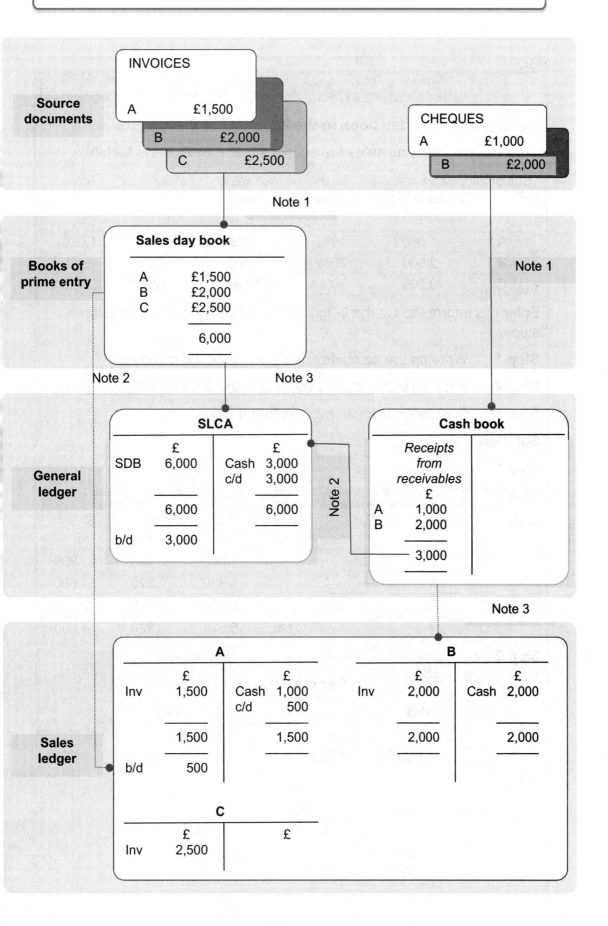

Example 1

Posting the sales day book to the accounts in the ledgers

Consider the following sales transactions made by Roberts Metals.

Customer	Sales value (ex VAT)	Trade discount	Net sales value	VAT	Total
	£	£	£	£	£
A	1,000	10%	900	180	1,080
B	2,000	20%	1,600	320	1,920
C	3,000	30%	2,100	420	2,520

Enter this information in the ledger accounts using the following three steps.

Step 1 Write up the sales day book, and total the columns.

Step 2 Post the totals to the accounts in the general ledger.

Step 3 Post the individual invoices to the sales ledger.

Solution

Step 1

SALES DAY BOOK						
Date	Customer	Ref.	Invoice number	Total £	VAT £	Sales £
	A			1,080	180	900
	B			1,920	320	1,600
	C			2,520	420	2,100
			TOTALS	5,520	920	4,600

Step 2

General ledger

Sales					VAT			
£		£			£		£	
	SLCA	4,600				SLCA	920	

SLCA			
£		£	
Sales & VAT	5,520		

Step 3

Sales ledger

A			B	
£	£		£	£
SDB 1,080		SDB	1,920	

C	
£	£
SDB 2,520	

Note to solution

(a) The totals of the SDB are entered in the general ledger.

(b) The individual invoices (total value including VAT) are entered in the individual receivables accounts in the sales ledger. This is the amount that the receivable will pay.

(c) Note that there are no entries for trade discounts either in the SDB or in the ledger accounts.

Test your understanding 1

An analysed sales day book has the following totals for a week.

Date	Invoice no	Customer name	Code	Total	VAT	Europe	Asia	America
				£	£	£	£	£
23/04/X0		Total		65,340	10,890	21,250	15,400	17,800

How would the totals be posted to the general ledger accounts?

Test your understanding 2

You work in the accounts department of Keyboard Supplies, a supplier of a wide range of electronic keyboards to a variety of music shops on credit. Given below are three sales invoices that you have just sent out to customers and these are to be written up into the sales day book given below.

Sales of four different types of keyboard are made and the sales are analysed into each of these four types and coded as follows:

Atol keyboards	01
Bento keyboards	02
Garland keyboards	03
Zanni keyboards	04

Required:

(a) Write up the analysed sales day book and total each of the columns.

INVOICE

Keyboard Supplies

Invoice to:
BZS Music
42 Westhill
Nutford TN11 3PQ

Trench Park Estate
Fieldham
Sussex TN21 4AF
Tel: 01829 654545
Fax: 01829 654646

Deliver to:
As above

Invoice no:	06116
Tax point:	18 April 20X1
VAT reg no:	466 1128 30
Purchase order no:	77121

Code	Description	Quantity	VAT rate %	Unit price £	Amount excl of VAT £
B4012	Bento Keyboard	3	20	180.00	540.00
Z2060	Zanni Keyboard	6	20	164.00	984.00
					1,524.00
Trade discount 20%					304.80
					1,219.20
VAT					243.84
Total amount payable					1,463.04

Prompt payment discount of 3% if paid within 10 days, net 30 days

---

INVOICE
Keyboard Supplies

Invoice to:
M T Retail
Fraser House
Perley TN7 8QT

Trench Park Estate
Fieldham
Sussex TN21 4AF
Tel: 01829 654545
Fax: 01829 654646

Deliver to:
As above

Invoice no:		06117	
Tax point:		18 April 20X1	
VAT reg :		466 1128 30	
Purchase order no:		PO4648	

Code	Description	Quantity	VAT rate %	Unit price £	Amount excl of VAT £
A6060	Atol Keyboard	1	20	210.00	210.00
Z4080	Zanni Keyboard	1	20	325.00	325.00
					535.00
VAT					107.00
Total amount payable					642.00

Net 30 days

INVOICE
Keyboard Supplies

Invoice to:
Hammer & Co
1 Acre Street
Nutford TN11 6HA

Trench Park Estate
Fieldham
Sussex TN21 4AF
Tel: 01829 654545
Fax: 01829 654646

Deliver to:
As above

Invoice no:		06118	
Tax point:		18 April 20X1	
VAT reg :		466 1128 30	
Purchase order no:		7486	

Code	Description	Quantity	VAT rate %	Unit price £	Amount excl of VAT £
G4326	Garland Keyboard	3	20	98.00	294.00
B2040	Bento Keyboard	5	20	115.00	575.00
					869.00
VAT					173.80
Total amount payable					1,042.80

Prompt payment discount of 3% if paid within 10 days, net 30 days

Sales day book									
Date	Invoice no	Customer name	Code	Total £	VAT £	01 £	02 £	03 £	04 £

(b) Complete the required accounting entries from the SDB in part (a) to the accounts within the general ledger.

Account	Amount £	Debit/credit
SLCA		
VAT		
Sales – 01		
Sales – 02		
Sales – 03		
Sales – 04		

Test your understanding 3

Graham Haddow runs a buildings maintenance and decorating business and sends out invoices for the work that he has done. He analyses his sales between the maintenance work and decorating work. You are given three sales invoices that he sent out last week.

Required:

(a) Enter the sales invoice details into the analysed sales day book given and total all of the columns.

INVOICE

Graham Haddow

Invoice to:
Portman & Co
Portman House
Tonbridge TN1 4LL

59 East Street
Medford
MF6 7TL
Tel: 0122 280496

Invoice no:	07891
Tax point:	1 May 20X1
VAT reg :	431 7992 06
Your reference:	P2

	Amount excl of VAT £
Repair of window	66.00
Clearing of guttering	73.00
	139.00
VAT	27.80
Total amount payable	166.80

Prompt payment discount of 2% if paid within 14 days, net 30 days

---

INVOICE

Graham Haddow

Invoice to:
Stanton Associates
323 Main Road
Tonbridge TN1 6EL

59 East Street
Medford
MF6 7TL
Tel: 0122 280496

Invoice no:	07892
Tax point:	3 May 20X1
VAT reg :	431 7992 06
Your reference:	S3

	Amount excl of VAT £
Decoration of meeting room	1,100.00
VAT	220.00
Total amount payable	1,320.00

Prompt payment discount of 2% if paid within 14 days, net 30 days

INVOICE

Graham Haddow

Invoice to:
Boreham Bros
40/54 Hill Drive
Medford MF2 8AT

59 East Street
Medford
MF6 7TL
Tel: 0122 280496

Invoice no:	07893
Tax point:	5 May 20X1
VAT reg :	431 7992 06
Your reference:	B7

	Amount excl of VAT £
Repair of door frames	106.00
Re-decorating of door frames	130.00
	236.00
VAT	47.20
Total amount payable	283.20

Sales day book							
Date	Invoice no	Customer name	Code	Total £	VAT £	Maintenance £	Decorating £

(b)   Complete the required accounting entries from the SDB in part (a) to the accounts within the general ledger.

Account	Amount £	Debit/credit
SLCA		
VAT		
Sales – Maintenance		
Sales – Decorating		

4   Sales returns

4.1   Introduction

When customers return goods, the accounting system has to record the fact that goods have been returned. If the goods were returned following a cash sale then cash would be repaid to the customer. If goods were returned following a credit sale then the SLCA in the general ledger and the customer's individual account in the sales ledger will need to be credited with the value of the goods returned.

Example 2

Returns following a cash sale

X sells £500 of goods to A for cash plus £100 VAT

X subsequently agrees that A can return £200 worth of goods (excluding the VAT)

Record these transactions in the ledger accounts.

Solution

Step 1

First of all we need to set up a new account called the 'sales returns account' in the general ledger. This will be used in addition to the sales account and cash book with which you are familiar.

Step 2

Enter the cash sale in the accounts.

Debit bank account for cash received   £600
Credit sales with net amount   £500
Credit VAT account with VAT   £100

Bank account

	£		£
Sales & VAT	600		

Sales

	£		£
		Bank	500

Sales returns

	£		£

VAT

	£		£
		Bank	100

Step 3

X will repay A £200 plus VAT of (£200 × 20%) = £40. We therefore need to enter the sales return, the cash and the VAT in the accounts.

Debit sales returns account	£200
Debit VAT account £200 × 20%	£40
Credit bank account with cash paid out	£240

Bank

	£		£
Sales & VAT	600	Sales returns & VAT	240

Sales

	£		£
		Bank	500

Sales returns

	£		£
Bank	200		

VAT

	£		£
Bank	40	Bank	100

4.2 Sales returns for credit sales – no VAT

When a credit customer returns goods, he does not receive cash for the return. Instead the seller will issue a credit note to record the fact that goods have been returned. This credit note is sent to the customer and is entered in the seller's books.

Example 3

X sells goods on credit to A for £500. A returns goods worth £200. X sends a credit note for £200 to A. Enter these transactions in the general ledger of X's books. There is no VAT.

Solution

Step 1

Record the invoice issued for the credit sale for £500:

Debit the SLCA in the general ledger with £500.

Credit the sales account in the general ledger with £500.

SLCA

	£		£
Sales	500		

Sales

	£		£
		SLCA	500

Step 2

Record the credit note for £200. The return is debited to a 'sales returns account' to reflect the reduction in sales. The SLCA is credited to show that the receivable has been reduced.

SLCA

	£		£
Sales	500	Sales returns	200

Sales

	£			£
		SLCA		500

Sales returns

	£			£
SLCA	200			

4.3 Sales returns with VAT

When a return is made and we include VAT, the VAT has to be accounted for both on the invoice when the sale is made, and on the credit note when the goods are returned. This VAT has to be entered in the books.

Example 4

X sells goods on credit to B for £1,000 + VAT at 20%.

B returns goods worth £400 + VAT at 20%.

Enter these transactions in the general ledger of X's books.

Solution

Step 1

Enter the invoice in the usual way, including the VAT.

SLCA

	£			£
Sales & VAT	1,200			

Sales

	£			£
		SLCA		1,000

VAT

	£		£
		SLCA	200

Step 2

Enter the credit note. The VAT on the return will be £400 × 20% = £80.

SLCA

	£		£
Sales & VAT	1,200	Sales returns & VAT	480

Sales

	£		£
		SLCA	1,000

VAT

	£		£
SLCA	80	SLCA	200

Sales returns

	£		£
SLCA	400		

The books will reflect the position after the return. The balance on the SLCA is £720. This is made up as:

	£
Sale	1,000
Sale return	(400)
	———
	600
VAT 600 × 20%	120
	———
	720
	———

Example 5

A and B are credit customers of Ellis Electricals. The balances on their accounts in the sales ledger are £1,200 and £2,400 (VAT inclusive amounts) because both A and B made earlier purchases which have not yet been paid.

A returns goods which cost £600 excluding VAT. B returns goods which cost £400 excluding VAT. VAT is at 20%.

Enter the above returns in the sales returns day book and in the general and sales ledgers of Ellis Electricals.

Solution

Step 1

Enter the original sales invoices in the general ledger.

SLCA

	£		£
Sales & VAT	3,600		

Sales

	£		£
		SLCA	3,000

VAT

	£		£
		SLCA	600

Step 2

Write up the sales returns day book.

SALES RETURNS DAY BOOK						
Date	Customer	Ref.	Credit note number	Total £	VAT £	Sales returns £
	A			720	120	600
	B			480	80	400
				1,200	200	1,000

Step 3

Enter the SRDB totals in the general ledger accounts.

SLCA

	£		£
Sales & VAT	3,600	Sales returns & VAT	1,200

Sales

	£		£
		SLCA	3,000

VAT

	£		£
SLCA	200	SLCA	600

Sales returns

	£		£
SLCA	1,000		

Step 4

Enter the individual amounts in the sales ledger.

A

	£		£
SDB	1,200	SRDB	720

B

	£		£
SDB	2,400	SRDB	480

Test your understanding 4

Given below are the totals of an analysed sales returns day book for a week.

Date	Customer name	Credit note no	Code	Total	VAT	Europe	Asia	America
				£	£	£	£	£
23/04/X0				3,360	560	1,458	650	692

Post these totals to the general ledger accounts.

5 Credit purchases

5.1 Introduction

When we studied accounting for sales earlier, we dealt with the three parts of the accounting records as they affected sales.

In the case of purchases, the parts are exactly the same except that instead of a 'sales day book' we have the 'purchases day book', and instead of the sales ledger we have the purchases ledger. The third part, namely the general ledger contains the account for the total payables, the purchases ledger control account (PLCA). Remember that, as for sales, the double entry goes through the general ledger, and the purchases ledger is just a memorandum ledger that holds the details of the individual payable's accounts (it is sometimes called the subsidiary (purchases) ledger).

Below we will illustrate how these parts fit together with a diagram.

5.2 Fitting it all together

Consider these three credit purchases invoices.

Supplier	Amount
X	£4,000
Y	£5,000
Z	£6,000

Step 1

Each invoice is recorded in the purchases day book by the purchaser.

Step 2

At the end of the period the purchases day book is totalled and the total is entered into the purchases ledger control account in the general ledger.

The full double entry is as we saw in a previous chapter (ignoring VAT at the moment):

Debit	Purchases
Credit	Purchases ledger control account (payables)

The individual entries are recorded in the individual payable accounts in the purchases ledger.

Now consider these cheques being paid to the payables.

Supplier	Amount
X	£2,000
Y	£3,000

Step 3

Each payment is recorded in the cash book.

Step 4

At the end of the period the cash book is totalled and the total is entered into the purchases ledger control account in the general ledger. The individual entries are recorded in the individual payable accounts in the purchases ledger.

This is illustrated on the next page.

Summary

1   The invoices are entered into the PDB and the cheques are entered into the cash book.

2   The totals from the cash book and PDB are posted to the PLCA.

3   The individual invoices and cash paid are posted to the purchases ledger.

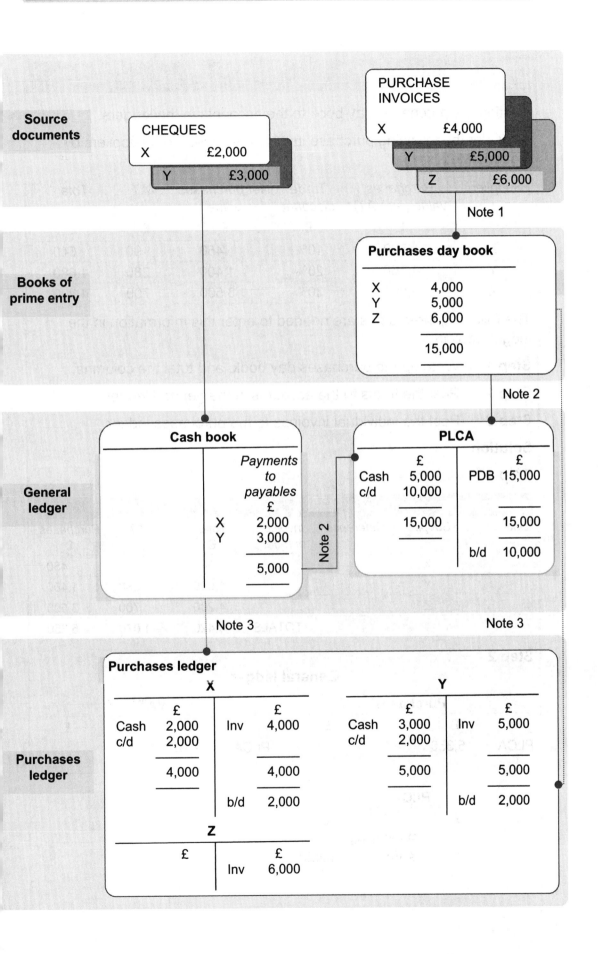

Example 6

Posting the purchases day book to the accounts in the ledgers.

Consider the following purchase invoices received from suppliers by Roberts Metals.

Supplier	Purchases value (ex VAT)	Trade discount	Net purchases value	VAT	Total
	£	£	£	£	£
X	500	10%	450	90	540
Y	1,750	20%	1,400	280	1,680
Z	5,000	30%	3,500	700	4,200

The following three steps are needed to enter this information in the ledger accounts.

Step 1 Write up the purchases day book, and total the columns.

Step 2 Post the totals to the accounts in the general ledger.

Step 3 Post the individual invoices to the purchases ledger.

Solution

Step 1

PURCHASES DAY BOOK

Date	Supplier	Reference	Invoice number	Total £	VAT £	Purchases £
	X			540	90	450
	Y			1,680	280	1,400
	Z			4,200	700	3,500
			TOTALS	6,420	1,070	5,350

Step 2

General ledger

Purchases

	£		£
PLCA	5,350		

VAT

	£		£
PLCA	1,070		

PLCA

	£		£
		Purchases & VAT	6,420

Step 3

Purchases ledger

X

£		£	
		PDB	540

Y

£		£	
		PDB	1,680

Z

£		£	
		PDB	4,200

Note to solution

(a) The totals of the PDB are entered in the general ledger.

(b) The individual invoices (total value including VAT) are entered in the individual payable accounts in the purchases ledger. This is the amount that will be paid to the payable.

(c) Note that there are no entries for trade discounts either in the PDB or in the ledger accounts.

Test your understanding 5

Date	Invoice no	Supplier	Code	Total	VAT	Dept 1	Dept 2	Dept 3
				£	£	£	£	£
		Total		90,000	15,000	20,000	15,000	40,000

How would the totals be posted to the general ledger accounts?

Test your understanding 6

Curtain Decor is a business that makes curtains and blinds to order. Its purchases are analysed between fabric purchases, header tape purchases and others. A separate purchases returns day book is not kept so any credit notes received are recorded as negative amounts in the purchases day book. The business only has five credit suppliers and they are as follows:

Mainstream Fabrics	PL01
C R Thorne	PL02
Fabric Supplies Ltd	PL03
Lillian Fisher	PL04
Headstream & Co	PL05

(a) Today's date is 12 April 20X1 and given below are three invoices and a credit note. These are to be entered into the analysed purchases day book and each column is to be totalled.

INVOICE

Invoice to:
Curtain Décor
Field House
Warren Lane
Hawkhurst TN23 1AT

Fabric Supplies Ltd
12/14 Tike Road
Wadfield
TN11 4ZP
Tel: 01882 467111
Fax: 01882 467112

Deliver to:

As above

Invoice no:	06783
Tax point:	7 April 20X1
VAT reg:	532 6741 09

Code	Description	Quantity	VAT rate %	Unit price £	Amount excl of VAT £
B116-14	Header Tape 14cm	30 m	20	4.62	138.60
P480-G	Fabric – Green	56 m	20	14.25	798.00
					936.60

VAT	187.32
Total amount payable	1,123.92

Prompt payment discount of 2% if paid within 10 days

INVOICE

Lillian Fisher

Invoice to:
Curtain Décor
Field House
Warren Lane
Hawkhurst TN23 1AT

61 Park Crescent
Hawkhurst
TN23 8GF
Tel: 01868 463501
Fax: 01868 463502

Deliver to:

As above

Invoice no:		0328
Tax point:		7 April 20X1
VAT reg:		469 7153 20

Code	Description	Quantity	VAT rate %	Unit price £	Amount excl of VAT £
TB06	Tie Back Cord – Yellow	10 m	20	6.55	65.50
TB09	Tie Back Cord – Green	4 m	20	6.55	26.20
					91.70
VAT					18.34
Total amount payable					110.04

CREDIT NOTE

Headstream & Co

Credit note to:
Curtain Décor
Field House
Warren Lane
Hawkhurst TN23 1AT

140 Myrtle Place
Fenham
TN16 4SJ
Tel: 01842 303136
Fax: 01842 303137

Credit note no:		CN0477
Tax point:		7 April 20X1
VAT reg:		663 4892 77

Code	Description	Quantity	VAT rate %	Unit price £	Amount excl of VAT £
HT479	Header Tape 22 cm	2 m	20	8.30	16.60
CCF614Y	CC Fabric – Yellow	4 m	20	12.85	51.40
					68.00
VAT					13.60
Total credit					81.60

INVOICE

Mainstream Fabrics

Invoice to:
Curtain Décor
Field House
Warren Lane
Hawkhurst TN23 1AT

Tree Tops House
Farm Road
Tonbridge
TN2 4XT
Tel: 01883 214121
Fax: 01883 214122

Deliver to:

As above

Invoice no:	07359
Tax point:	8 April 20X1
VAT reg:	379 4612 04

Code	Description	Quantity	VAT rate %	Unit price £	Amount excl of VAT £
DG4167F	Design Guild Fabric – Fuchsia	23 m	20	13.60	312.80
					312.80
Trade discount 10%					31.28
					281.52
VAT					56.30
Total amount payable					337.82

Prompt payment discount of 1½% if paid within 14 days

Purchases day book°								
Date	Invoice no	Code	Supplier	Total	VAT	Fabric	Header tape	Other

(b) Complete the required accounting entries from the PDB in part (a) to the accounts within the general ledger.

Account	Amount £	Debit/credit
PLCA		
VAT		
Purchases – fabric		
Purchases – Header tape		
Purchases – Other		

Test your understanding 7

Kingdon Builders analyse their purchases into wood, bricks and cement, and small consumables such as nails and screws. You are given three purchase invoices, recently received, to enter into the purchases day book given.

An extract from the purchase ledger coding manual is given:

Supplier	Purchase ledger code
JR Ryan & Co	PL08
HT Todd plc	PL13
Magnum Supplies	PL16

Today's date is 3 May 20X1.

(a) Enter the invoices into the analysed purchases day book and total each of the columns.

INVOICE

Magnum Supplies

Invoice to:
Kingdon Builders
Brecon House
Stamford Road
Manchester
M16 4PL

140/150 Park Estate
Manchester
M20 6EG
Tel: 0161 561 3202
Fax: 0161 561 3200

Deliver to:

As above

Invoice no:	077401
Tax point:	1 May 20X1
VAT reg:	611 4337 90

Code	Description	Quantity	VAT rate %	Unit price £	Amount excl of VAT £
BH47732	House Bricks – Red	400	20	1.24	496.00
					496.00
Trade discount 15%					74.40
					421.60
VAT					84.32
Total amount payable					505.92

Prompt payment discount of 2% if paid within 10 days

INVOICE

Invoice to:
Kingdon Builders
Brecon House
Stamford Road
Manchester
M16 4PL

J.R. Ryan & Co
59 Parkway
Manchester
M2 6EG
Tel: 0161 560 3392
Fax: 0161 560 5322

Deliver to:

As above

Invoice no: 046193
Tax point: 1 May 20X1
VAT reg: 661 2359 07

Code	Description	Quantity	VAT rate %	Unit price £	Amount excl of VAT £
DGT 472	SDGS Softwood 47 × 225 mm	11.2 m	20	8.44	94.53
NBD021	Oval Wire Nails	7 boxes	20	2.50	17.50
					112.03
Trade discount 10%					11.20
					100.83
VAT					20.16
Total amount payable					120.99

INVOICE

HT Todd plc
30 Longfield Park
Kingsway
M45 2TP
Tel: 0161 511 4666
Fax: 0161 511 4777

Invoice to:
Kingdon Builders
Brecon House
Stamford Road
Manchester
M16 4PL

Deliver to:

As above

Invoice no:	47823
Tax point:	1 May 20X1
VAT reg:	641 3229 45
Purchase order no:	7211

Code	Description	Quantity	VAT rate %	Unit price £	Amount excl of VAT £
PLY8FU	Plywood Hardboard	16 sheets	20	17.80	284.80
BU611	Ventilator Block	10	20	8.60	86.00
					370.80

VAT	74.16
Total amount payable	444.96

Prompt payment discount of 3% if paid within 14 days

Purchases day book								
Date	Invoice no	Code	Supplier	Total	VAT	Wood	Bricks/ Cement	Consum- ables

(b) Complete the required accounting entries from the PDB in part (a) to the accounts within the general ledger.

Account	Amount £	Debit/credit
PLCA		
VAT		
Purchases – Wood		
Purchases – Bricks/cement		
Purchases – Consumables		

6 Purchases returns

6.1 Introduction

When a business buys and then returns goods to a supplier, the accounting system has to record the fact that goods have been returned. If the goods were returned following a cash purchase then cash would be repaid by the supplier to the customer who had bought the goods. If goods were returned following a credit purchase then the PLCA in the general ledger will need to be debited and the individual supplier's account in the purchases ledger will need to be debited with the value of the goods returned (we shall see the other entries required below).

 Example 7

Returns following a cash purchase

Y buys £1,000 plus £200 VAT of goods from B for cash.

B subsequently agrees that Y can return £500 worth of goods (excluding VAT at 20%).

Record these transactions in the ledger accounts of Y.

Solution

Step 1

First of all we need to set up a new account called the 'purchases returns account' in the general ledger.

Step 2

Enter the cash purchases in the accounts of Y.

Credit cash book for cash paid	£1,200.00
Debit purchases with expense	£1,000.00
Debit VAT account with VAT	£200.00

Bank

	£		£
		Purchases and VAT	1,200

Purchases

	£		£
Bank	1,000		

Purchases returns

	£		£

VAT

	£		£
Bank	200		

Step 3

B will repay Y £500 plus VAT of £100. We therefore need to enter the purchases returns, the cash and the VAT in the accounts.

Bank

	£		£
Purchases returns and VAT	600	Purchases and VAT	1,200

Purchases

	£		£
Bank	1,000		

Purchases returns

	£		£
		Bank	500

VAT

	£		£
Bank	200	Bank	100

6.2 Purchases returns for credit purchases with VAT

When a credit customer returns goods, he does not receive cash for the return; the seller will issue a credit note to record the fact that goods have been returned. This credit note is sent to the customer and is entered in the customer's books.

When a return is made for goods that incur VAT, we include VAT; the VAT was accounted for on the invoice when the purchase was made, and now has to be accounted for on the credit note when the goods are returned. This VAT has to be entered in the books.

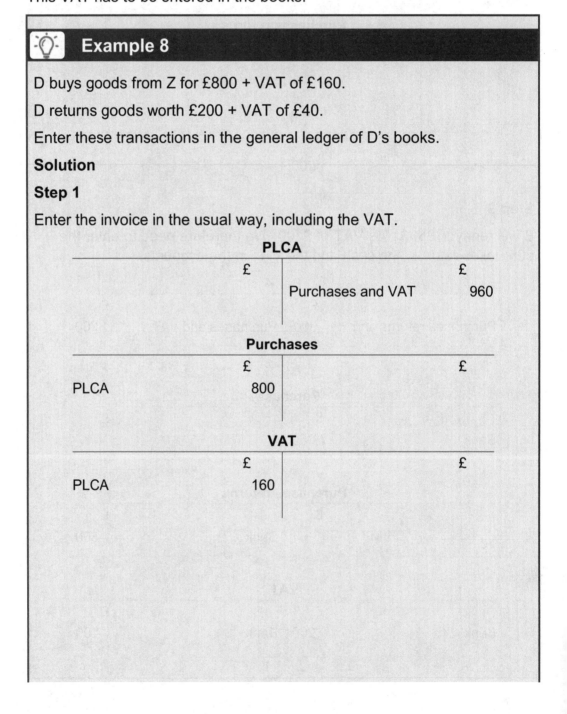

Example 8

D buys goods from Z for £800 + VAT of £160.

D returns goods worth £200 + VAT of £40.

Enter these transactions in the general ledger of D's books.

Solution

Step 1

Enter the invoice in the usual way, including the VAT.

PLCA

	£		£
		Purchases and VAT	960

Purchases

	£		£
PLCA	800		

VAT

	£		£
PLCA	160		

Step 2

Enter the credit note. The VAT on the return is £40. This gives a total credit note of £240.

PLCA

	£		£
Purchases returns and VAT	240	Purchases and VAT	960

Purchases

	£		£
PLCA	800		

VAT

	£		£
PLCA	160	PLCA	40

Purchases returns

	£		£
		PLCA	200

The books will reflect the position after the return. The balance on the PLCA is £720. This is made up as:

	£
Purchase	800
Purchase return	(200)
	600
VAT 600 × 20%	120
	720

Example 9

John bought goods for £750 + VAT from X and £1,000 + VAT from Y.

John returns goods which cost £200 excluding VAT to X, and goods which cost £400 excluding VAT to Y. VAT is at 20%.

Enter the purchases and returns in the general and purchases ledger of John, using a purchases returns day book.

Solution

Step 1

Enter the original purchases invoices in the general ledger.

PLCA

£		£
	Purchases and VAT	2,100

Purchases

	£		£
PLCA	1,750		

VAT

	£		£
PLCA	350		

Step 2

Write up the purchases returns day book.

PURCHASES RETURNS DAY BOOK						
Date	Supplier	Reference	Credit note number	Total £	VAT £	Purchases returns £
	X			240	40	200
	Y			480	80	400
				720	120	600

Step 3

Enter the PRDB totals in the general ledger accounts.

PLCA

	£		£
Purchases returns and VAT	720	Purchases and VAT	2,100

Purchases

	£		£
PLCA	1,750		

VAT

	£		£
PLCA	350	PLCA	120

Purchases returns

	£		£
		PLCA	600

Step 4

Enter the individual amounts in the purchases ledger. The amounts will be debited to the individual payable accounts as the return is reducing the amount that is owed to the payable.

X

	£		£
PRDB	240	PDB	900

Y

	£		£
PRDB	480	PDB	1,200

Test your understanding 8

Given below are the totals of an analysed purchases returns day book for a week.

Date	Supplier	Credit note no	Code	Total	VAT	Dept 1	Dept 2	Dept 3
				£	£	£	£	£
23/04/X0				9,600	1,600	1,000	2,000	5,000

Post these totals to the general ledger accounts.

7 Summary

In this chapter we have reviewed how transactions are recorded.

Initially a transaction is recorded in the relevant book of prime entry (day book).

The double entry takes place in the general ledger, with the total of the gross sales being recorded in a sales ledger control account (SLCA) which we have previously called receivables. The total of the gross purchases is recorded in a purchases ledger control account (PLCA) which we have previously called payables.

Subsidiary sales ledgers contain individual entries for individual receivables whereas the subsidiary purchases ledgers contain individual entries for individual payables.

It is in the Foundation Certificate level's Bookkeeping Controls unit that control accounts are studied in more detail. The reconciliation of the sales and purchases ledger control accounts to the individual ledgers will be reviewed including identifying and explaining discrepancies upon performing a reconciliation.

Test your understanding answers

Test your understanding 1

The required double entry is as follows:

Debit	Sales ledger control account	£65,340
Credit	VAT	£10,890
	Europe sales	£21,250
	Asia sales	£15,400
	America sales	£17,800

Note carefully that it is the net amount that is credited to each sales account and the gross amount (including VAT) that is debited to the sales ledger control account. The VAT total is credited to the VAT account.

The ledger entries would appear as follows:

Sales ledger control account

	£		£
SDB	65,340		

VAT

	£		£
		SDB	10,890

Europe sales

	£		£
		SDB	21,250

Asia sales

	£		£
		SDB	15,400

America sales

	£		£
		SDB	17,800

Test your understanding 2

(a)

Sales day book									
Date	Invoice no	Customer name	Code	Total £	VAT £	01 £	02 £	03 £	04 £
18/4/X1	06116	B Z S Music		1,463.04	243.84		432.00		787.20
18/4/X1	06117	M T Retail		642.00	107.00	210.00			325.00
18/4/X1	06118	Harmer & Co		1,042.80	173.80		575.00	294.00	
				3,147.84	524.64	210.00	1,007.00	294.00	1,112.20

Note that when a trade discount has been deducted on the invoice in total it must be deducted from each type of sale when entering the figures in the analysed sales day book.

(b)

Account	Amount £	Debit/credit
SLCA	3,147.84	Debit
VAT	524.64	Credit
Sales – 01	210.00	Credit
Sales – 02	1,007.00	Credit
Sales – 03	294.00	Credit
Sales – 04	1,112.20	Credit

Test your understanding 3

(a)

Sales day book							
Date	Invoice no	Customer name	Code	Total £	VAT £	Maintenance £	Decorating £
01/5/X1	07891	Portman & Co	P2	166.80	27.80	139.00	
03/5/X1	07892	Stanton Assocs	S3	1,320.00	220.00		1,100.00
05/5/X1	07893	Boreham Bros	B7	283.20	47.20	106.00	130.00
				1,770.00	295.00	245.00	1,230.00

(b)

Account	Amount £	Debit/credit
SLCA	1,770.00	Debit
VAT	295.00	Credit
Sales – Maintenance	245.00	Credit
Sales – Decorating	1,230.00	Credit

Test your understanding 4

Sales returns – Europe account

	£		£
SLCA	1,458		

Sales returns – Asia account

	£		£
SLCA	650		

Sales returns – America account

	£		£
SLCA	692		

VAT account

	£		£
SLCA	560		

Sales ledger control account

	£		£
		Sales returns & VAT	3,360

Note carefully that it is the net amount that is debited to each returns account and the gross amount to the sales ledger control account. The difference, the VAT, is debited to the VAT account.

Test your understanding 5

The required double entry is as follows:

Debit	VAT	£15,000
	Department 1 purchases	£20,000
	Department 2 purchases	£15,000
	Department 3 purchases	£40,000
Credit	Purchases ledger control account	£90,000

Note carefully that it is the net amount that is debited to each purchases account and the gross amount (including VAT) that is credited to the purchases ledger control account. The VAT total is debited to the VAT account.

The ledger entries would appear as follows:

Purchases ledger control account

	£		£
		Purchases & VAT	90,000

VAT

	£		£
PLCA	15,000		

Department 1 purchases

	£		£
PLCA	20,000		

Department 2 purchases

	£		£
PLCA	15,000		

Department 3 purchases

	£		£
PLCA	40,000		

 Test your understanding 6

(a)

Date	Invoice no	Code	Supplier	Total	VAT	Fabric	Header tape	Other
07/4/X1	06783	PL03	Fabric Supplies Ltd	1,123.92	187.32	798.00	138.60	
07/4/X1	0328	PL04	Lillian Fisher	110.04	18.34			91.70
07/4/X1	CN0477	PL05	Headstream & Co	(81.60)	(13.60)	(51.40)	(16.60)	
08/4/X1	07359	PL01	Mainstream Fabrics	337.82	56.30	281.52		
				1,490.18	248.36	1,028.12	122.00	91.70

Table title: **Purchases day book**

(b)

Account	Amount £	Debit/credit
PLCA	1,490.18	Credit
VAT	248.36	Debit
Purchases – fabric	1,028.12	Debit
Purchases – Header tape	122.00	Debit
Purchases – Other	91.70	Debit

Test your understanding 7

(a)

Purchases day book								
Date	Invoice no	Code	Supplier	Total	VAT	Wood	Bricks/ Cement	Consum -ables
1/5/X1	077401	PL16	Magnum Supplies	505.92	84.32		421.60	
1/5/X1	046193	PL08	JR Ryan & Co	120.99	20.16	85.08		15.75
1/5/X1	47823	PL13	HT Todd plc	444.96	74.16	284.80	86.00	
				1,071.87	178.64	369.88	507.60	15.75

(b)

Account	Amount £	Debit/credit
PLCA	1,071.87	Credit
VAT	178.64	Debit
Purchases – Wood	369.88	Debit
Purchases – Bricks/cement	507.60	Debit
Purchases – Consumables	15.75	Debit

✎ Test your understanding 8

Purchases returns – Department 1 account

	£			£
			PLCA	1,000

Purchases returns – Department 2 account

	£			£
			PLCA	2,000

Purchases returns – Department 3 account

	£			£
			PLCA	5,000

VAT account

	£			£
			PLCA	1,600

Purchases ledger control account

	£		£
Purchases returns & VAT	9,600		

Note carefully that it is the net amount that is credited to each returns account and the gross amount to the purchases ledger control account. The difference, the VAT, is credited to the VAT account.

Payments and receipts

Introduction

We will now consider the procedures and requirements of making and recording payments and receipts which includes maintaining the cash book and petty cash records.

ASSESSMENT CRITERIA	CONTENTS
Indicate the purpose of business documents (1.1)	1 Statements of accounts
Distinguish between prompt payment, trade and bulk discounts (1.2)	2 Receiving and making payments
Demonstrate an understanding of the process of recording financial transactions (1.4)	3 Remittances 4 Recording cash receipts and cash payments
Check the accuracy of receipts from customers (2.3)	5 The cash book as part of the general ledger
Check the accuracy of supplier invoices and credit notes (3.1)	6 Petty cash
Prepare payments to suppliers (3.3)	
Enter receipts and payments into a two column analysed cash book (4.1)	
Enter receipts and payments into an analysed petty cash book (4.2)	
Total and balance the cash book and petty cash book (4.3)	
Transfer data from the books of prime entry to the ledgers (5.1)	

1 Statements of accounts

1.1 Introduction

When sales to a customer are on a credit basis, it is important that there are procedures in place to ensure the monies outstanding are received promptly.

In practice most customers do not settle their debt after receiving every invoice, as customers can purchase from their suppliers numerous times within a month. Therefore, payment will tend to be made when a statement has been sent by the supplier. The statement will detail all the invoices, credit notes and any payments that have occurred within the month. The information contained on the statement will come from the individual receivable's account within the subsidiary sales ledger.

When these statements are sent out and then received by the customer, the customer should compare them to the account they hold for the supplier in their subsidiary purchases ledger.

Once the statement has been reconciled against the customer's own accounting records, the customer will then pay the amount due.

 Definition – Receivable (customer) statement

A statement that shows all the invoices and credit notes that have been sent to a particular credit customer for that month, together with any amounts outstanding from previous months. The statement also details any payments received from credit customers.

 Definition – Payable (supplier) statement

A statement that shows all the invoices and credit notes that have been received from a particular credit supplier for that month, together with any amounts outstanding from previous months. The statement also details any payments sent to the credit supplier.

1.2 Preparing a receivables' statement

A receivables' statement will normally be prepared from the information in the receivables' individual account in the sales ledger. Different businesses will use different formats but the basics that must be shown are all invoices, credit notes, payments received and discounts for the period together with a running total of the balance. An example is shown in section 1.3.

1.3 Procedure for preparing a statement of account

When preparing a statement for a credit customer, it is important that all details are correct therefore a logical and accurate approach is required.

Step 1
- Find the customer's account in the filing system of the sales ledger.

Step 2
- Work through the account by date order listing each transaction in turn on the statement – invoices as debits and credit notes, payments and discounts as credits.

Step 3
- Return to the start of the statement and calculate the balance at each transaction date to appear in the balance column.

Example 1

Given below are the sales ledger accounts for two of Nick Brookes' customers. We will start by balancing each account to show the total amount due by each customer. Note: the accounts provide details of the invoice and credit note numbers as well as bank receipts and discounts allowed.

		Mayer Ltd				SL01
		£				£
03/04	INV001	189.60	10/04	CN001		50.40
14/04	INV005	211.20	18/04	Bank		136.30
21/04	INV007	259.20				
26/04	INV009	196.80	Balance c/d			670.10
		────				────
		856.80				856.80
		────				────
Balance b/d		670.10				

		Penken Bros				SL04
		£				£
10/04	INV004	162.00	17/04	CN002		40.80
24/04	INV008	171.60	21/04	Bank		115.11
28/04	INV011	141.60	21/04	Discount allowed		3.03
				Balance c/d		316.26
		────				────
		475.20				475.20
		────				────
Balance b/d		316.26				

We can now use this information to prepare statements for these two customers as at the end of April 20X2.

Solution

To: Mayer Ltd	NICK BROOKES 225 School Lane Weymouth Dorset WE36 5NR Tel: 0149 29381 Fax: 0149 29382 Date: 30/04/X2

STATEMENT

Date	Transaction	Debit £	Credit £	Balance £
03/04	INV001	189.60		189.60
10/04	CN001		50.40	139.20
14/04	INV005	211.20		350.40
18/04	Payment		136.30	214.10
21/04	INV007	259.20		473.30
26/04	INV009	196.80		670.10

May we remind you that our credit terms are 30 days
With prompt payment discount of 3% for payment within 14 days

To: Penken Bros	NICK BROOKES 225 School Lane Weymouth Dorset WE36 5NR Tel: 0149 29381 Fax: 0149 29382 Date: 30/04/X2

STATEMENT

Date	Transaction	Debit £	Credit £	Balance £
10/04	INV004	162.00		162.00
17/04	CN002		40.80	121.20
21/04	Payment		115.11	
21/04	Discount		3.03	3.06
24/04	INV008	171.60		174.66
28/04	INV011	141.60		316.26

May we remind you that our credit terms are 30 days
With prompt payment discount of 3% for payment within 14 days

These are documents that are being sent to customers; therefore it is extremely important they are completely accurate. Always check the figures and additions.

Test your understanding 1

You are to prepare a statement to be sent out to one customer, Jack Johnson, for the month of May 20X6. At the start of May this customer did not owe your business, Thames Traders, any money. The sales ledger account for Jack for the month of May is given below.

Jack Johnson

Date		£	Date		£
03 May	Invoice 1848	38.79	08 May	Credit note 446	12.40
07 May	Invoice 1863	50.70	15 May	Cash receipt	77.09
10 May	Invoice 1870	80.52	24 May	Credit note 458	16.50
18 May	Invoice 1881	42.40			
23 May	Invoice 1892	61.20			
30 May	Invoice 1904	27.65			

You are required to prepare a statement for Jack on the blank statement given below.

Thames Traders

To: Date:

STATEMENT

Date	Transaction	Debit £	Credit £	Balance £

May we remind you that our credit terms are 30 days

1.4 Checking suppliers' statements

We will now consider the perspective of the business receiving a supplier statement. Before any payments are made it is important to check the supplier's statement is correct. Each invoice and credit note should be checked either to the original documentation or to the supplier's account in the purchases ledger.

Differences between the balances on the supplier statement and the individual supplier's account may occur due to omissions, incorrect amounts being recorded, duplicated transactions or timing differences such as a payment being sent to a supplier but not being received at the time the statement was prepared.

When the accuracy of the statement has been ascertained then it must be determined exactly which invoices from the statement are to be paid.

Example 2

Given below is a statement from a supplier together with that supplier's account from the purchases ledger.

To: Scott Brothers 34 Festival Way Oldham OL2 3BD	Nemo Limited Date: 31 August 20X3

STATEMENT

Date	Transaction	Total £	Current £	30+ £	60+ £
12 May 20X3	Invoice 2569	92.35			92.35
13 June 20X3	CN 2659	(23.60)			(23.60)
09 July 20X3	Invoice 2701	102.69		102.69	
18 July 20X3	Invoice 2753	133.81		133.81	
02 Aug 20X3	Invoice 2889	56.50	56.50		
10 Aug 20X3	Invoice 2901	230.20	230.20		
28 Aug 20X3	Invoice 3114	243.24	243.24		
	TOTALS	835.19	529.94	236.50	68.75

May we remind you our credit terms are 30 days

	Nemo Ltd	
	£	£
13 June CN 2659	23.60	12 May Invoice 2569	92.35
		09 July Invoice 2701	102.69
		18 July Invoice 2753	133.81
		02 Aug Invoice 2889	56.50
		10 Aug Invoice 2901	203.20
		28 Aug Invoice 3114	243.24

To check that the supplier's statement is correct prior to paying any amounts, the statement should be carefully checked to the supplier's account in the purchases ledger.

Solution

Invoice number 2901 is in the purchases ledger at a total of £203.20 whereas it appears on the supplier's statement as £230.20.

The purchase invoice itself should be accessed from the filing system to determine whether the amount is £203.20 or £230.20. If the supplier's statement is incorrect then a polite telephone call should be made or an email or letter sent to the supplier, Nemo Ltd, explaining the problem.

1.5   Which invoices to pay

Once the supplier's statement has been checked for accuracy then it has to be decided which invoices shall be paid. Most organisations will have a policy regarding the payment of supplier's invoices or, alternatively, a fairly senior figure in the business will decide each month which invoices are to be paid.

 Example 3

Using the supplier's statement shown above suppose that payment has been authorised for all amounts that have been outstanding for 30 days or more. What amount should the cheque be made out for?

Solution

	£
60+ days total	68.75
30+ days total	236.50
	────
Cheque amount	305.25
	────

2 Receiving and making payments

2.1 Introduction

Different types of business will receive money from their customers and pay money to their suppliers in different forms.

 Definitions

Cash

Money in coins or notes.

Credit card

A plastic card that is issued by a bank allowing the holder to purchase goods or services on credit.

Debit card

A plastic card that is issued by a bank allowing the holder to transfer money electronically from their bank account when making a purchase of goods or services.

Cheque

An order to a bank written on a specially printed form that states a sum to be paid from the drawer's (account holder's) account.

BACS

BACS (Bankers' Automated Clearing Services) is an electronic system to make payments directly from one bank account to another. They're mainly used for direct debits and direct credits. Transfers usually take three working days.

Faster Payment

Faster Payments Service (FPS) is an electronic system which makes payments directly from one bank account to another. Transfers typically take a few seconds.

Standing order

An instruction to a bank by an account holder to make regular fixed payments to a particular person or organisation.

Direct debit

An instruction to a bank by an account holder authorising the organisation the account holder wants to pay, to collect varying amounts from the account. Advanced notice of the amounts and dates of collection must be given.

3 Remittances

3.1 Introduction

When a customer makes a payment for a credit sale, they will also send a remittance advice to detail the invoices that are being paid.

 Definition – Remittance advice

A remittance advice is a blank document that the customer completes when making a payment to the supplier. It shows the total payment being made and which invoices (less credit notes) the payment is paying off.

3.2 Remittance lists

All cash received should be listed on a remittance list by the supplier. The list should give details of:

- the customer
- the invoice numbers to which the payment relates (if known)
- the amount paid, and
- any discount allowed (see later in this chapter).

The list should be totalled and signed.

3.3 Using remittance advices

When a business issues an invoice to a customer, the invoice will often have a detachable slip. This slip, which is to be returned by the customer when making a payment, is the remittance advice identifying what the payment is for.

A remittance advice is used to either advise of a payment being made directly to the seller's bank account or to accompany a cheque. This makes it much easier for the business receiving the payment to know which outstanding invoices (less credit notes) are actually being paid. An example of a remittance advice follows on the next page.

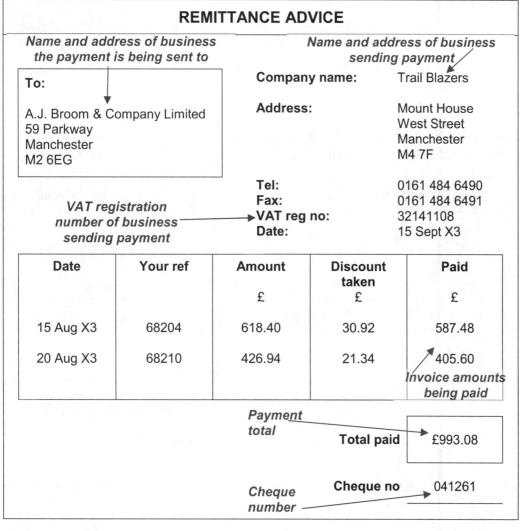

REMITTANCE ADVICE

Name and address of business the payment is being sent to

To:

A.J. Broom & Company Limited
59 Parkway
Manchester
M2 6EG

VAT registration number of business sending payment

Name and address of business sending payment

Company name:	Trail Blazers
Address:	Mount House West Street Manchester M4 7F
Tel:	0161 484 6490
Fax:	0161 484 6491
VAT reg no:	32141108
Date:	15 Sept X3

Date	Your ref	Amount £	Discount taken £	Paid £
15 Aug X3	68204	618.40	30.92	587.48
20 Aug X3	68210	426.94	21.34	405.60

Invoice amounts being paid

Payment total

Total paid	£993.08

Cheque number

Cheque no	041261

When receiving payments from customers it is vital to ensure the correct amounts are paid. When agreeing receipts you should check:

- Does the payment amount agree to the invoice and remittance advice?
- If a cheque payment is received, can it be banked i.e. is it valid?
- Does the amount paid agree with what is shown as owed?
- Is the customer eligible (within the required timescale) to take any prompt payment discount offered?
- Has the customer calculated the discount percentage correctly?

 Test your understanding 2

A remittance advice is a document sent by a supplier to a customer to advise the customer that goods ordered have been sent off to the customer. True/False

Example 4

This morning the following cheques and supporting remittance advices were received in the post by your organisation, A. J. Broom & Company Ltd.

You are required to check the remittance advice and cheque amounts to the invoices given to ensure that the correct amount has been received.

WESTERN BANK
21 High Street
Bristol
BS1 4TZ

20 – 16 – 80

14 Sept 20 X3

Pay   A.J. Broom & Company Ltd   or order

Two Thousand and nine pounds   £2,009.04

And 4 pence

Account Payee

P Smithson
PATRICK CARPENTERS

046178   20–16–80   41643121

CENTRAL BANK
52 Warwick Road
Birmingham
B13 4XT

40 – 18 – 30

15 Sept 20 X3

Pay   A.J. Broom & Company Ltd   or order

One thousand three hundred and   £1,306.16

Six pounds and 16 pence

Account Payee

J P Roberts
ROBERTS CONSTRUCTION

020106   40–18–30   31164992

REMITTANCE ADVICE

To:	Company name:	Patrick Carpenters
	Address:	Simba Industrial Est.
A.J. Broom & Company Limited		Leeds
59 Parkway		
Manchester	Tel:	0714 304 2990
M2 6EG	Fax:	0714 304 2963
	VAT reg:	318 4861 27
	Date:	14 Sept 20X3

Date	Your ref	Amount	Discount taken	Paid
		£	£	£
23 Aug	68229	1,649.04	–	1,649.04
23 Aug	3217	(360.00)	–	(360.00)
4 Sept	68237	720.00	–	720.00
			Total paid	£ 2,009.04
			Cheque no	046178

REMITTANCE ADVICE

To:	Company name:	Roberts Construction
	Address:	Chillian Park
A.J. Broom & Company Limited		Oldham
59 Parkway		
Manchester	Tel:	0201 632 497
M2 6EG	Fax:	0201 632 498
	VAT reg:	331 4986 91
	Date:	15 Sept 20X3

Date	Your ref	Amount	Discount taken	Paid
		£	£	£
23 Aug	68230	1,306.16	–	1,306.16
			Total paid	£ 1,306.16
			Cheque no	020106

Invoice 68229

A.J. Broom & Company Limited

59 Parkway	
Manchester	
M2 6EG	
Tel: 0161 560 3392	
Fax: 0161 560 5322	
Tax Point:	23 August 20X3
VAT reg:	452 4585 48

**Patrick Carpenters
Samba Industrial Estate
Leeds**

Code	Supply	Description	Quantity	VAT rate %	Unit price £	Amount excl of VAT £
336 BTB	Sale	Roof tiles – black	10	20	123.00	1,230.00
667 LL5	Sale	Softwood plank – 20 cm	14	20	10.30	144.20
						1,374.20
VAT						274.84
Total amount payable						**1,649.04**

Invoice 68237

A.J. Broom & Company Limited

59 Parkway	
Manchester	
M2 6EG	
Tel: 0161 560 3392	
Fax: 0161 560 5322	
Tax Point:	4 September 20X3
VAT reg :	452 4585 48

**Patrick Carpenters
Samba Industrial Estate
Leeds**

Code	Supply	Description	Quantity	VAT rate %	Unit price £	Amount excl of VAT £
630 CC4	Sale	Oak veneer in Panels	3	20	200.00	600.00
VAT						120.00
Total amount payable						**720.00**

Credit note 3217

A.J. Broom & Company Limited

59 Parkway

Manchester

M2 6EG

Tel: 0161 560 3392

Fax: 0161 560 5322

Patrick Carpenters
Samba Industrial Estate
Leeds

		Tax Point:	23 August 20X3
		VAT reg:	452 4585 48

Code	Supply	Description	Quantity	VAT rate %	Unit price £	Amount excl of VAT £
950 BB3	Return	Cotswold bricks	1	20	300.00	300.00
VAT						60.00
Total amount credited						**360.00**

Invoice 68230

A.J. Broom & Company Limited

59 Parkway

Manchester

M2 6EG

Tel: 0161 560 3392

Fax: 0161 560 5322

Roberts Construction
Chillian Park
Oldham

		Tax Point:	23 August 20X3
		VAT reg no:	452 4585 48

Code	Supply	Description	Quantity	VAT rate %	Unit price £	Amount excl of VAT £
160 TT7	Sale	Insulation	5	20	95.50	477.50
632 BS4	Sale	Brick tiles	20	20	33.25	665.00
						1,142.50
Trade discount 4%						45.70
						1,096.80
VAT						219.36
Total amount payable						**1,316.16**

Solution

From Patrick Carpenters

	£
Invoice number 68229	1,649.04
Invoice number 68237	720.00
Credit note 3217	(360.00)
	————
	2,009.04
	————

This agrees with the cheque.

From Roberts Construction

Invoice number 68230	£1,316.16

This does not agree with the cheque as the cheque is made out for £1,306.16 This discrepancy should be brought to the attention of the manager responsible for credit control at Roberts Construction and a polite letter should be written to the customer explaining an error has been made. Request can be made for payment but if this is a regular customer then the additional amount may simply be added to the next cheque that Roberts Construction sends.

3.4 Payments received with no accompanying remittance advice

If a payment from a customer is received with no remittance advice or other confirmation of which invoices are being paid then it will be necessary to examine the details of this customer's transactions in the sales ledger.

The individual account for this receivable must be extracted from the subsidiary ledger in an attempt to match the payment received to invoices and credit notes.

Example 5

A payment has been received into the business bank account from A J Holland, a credit customer, for £878.00 but no remittance advice has been sent to advise which transactions the payment relates to.

In the absence of this supporting document the individual receivable account for A J Holland has been found in the sales ledger, to investigate which transactions are being paid and to ensure that the correct payment amount has been received.

A J Holland

	£		£
13/05/X2 Invoice 2256	336.67	20/05/X2 Credit 249	54.09
18/05/X2 Invoice 2271	846.23		
20/05/X2 Invoice 2280	447.69		
25/05/X2 Invoice 2288	147.73		

Solution

By a process of trial and error it can be discovered that the invoices that are being paid off are number 2256, 2280 and 2288 less the credit note. It would appear therefore that the payment is for the correct amount although there might be some concern as to why invoice 2271 has not been paid; maybe there is some dispute over the amount of this invoice which should be investigated.

Always check figures carefully as such errors are often easy to miss.

3.5 Checking cheques

When cheques are received in the post it is important that they are checked for their validity, particularly in respect of:

- the date: a cheque can become out of date as it is only valid for 6 months from the date of issue

- the payee's name: should be the same as the one shown on the account the cheque is being paid into

- the words and figures agree; if they disagree the cheque should be returned by the bank for amendment or a new cheque issued

- the cheque is signed.

Test your understanding 3

(a) Today is the 15 March 20X3. Would the cheque below be accepted for payment if it were now presented to the National Bank plc?

(b) Give two reasons for your answer.

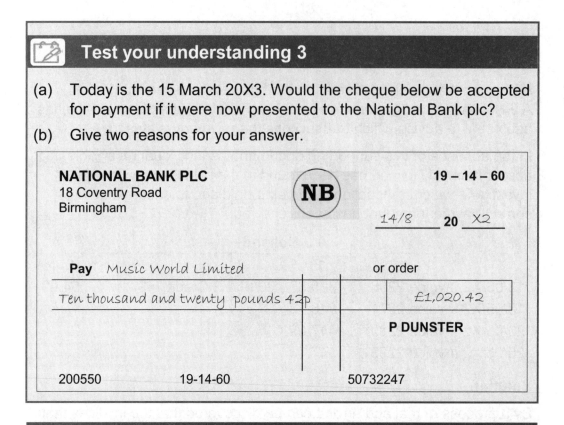

NATIONAL BANK PLC	NB	19 – 14 – 60
18 Coventry Road		
Birmingham		14/8 20 X2

Pay   Music World Limited   or order

Ten thousand and twenty pounds 42p   £1,020.42

                                             P DUNSTER

200550   19-14-60   50732247

---

4 Recording cash receipts and cash payments

4.1 The cash book

The cash book was introduced in chapter 2. It is the book of prime entry for recording receipts and payments.

Definition – The cash book

A cash book is a record of cash receipts and payments that conforms to the double entry system.

An analysed cash book is a cash book with additional columns for analysing principal sources and payments for cash.

There are many different forms of the cash book that you may encounter. As already discussed in chapter 2, Bookkeeping Transactions requires knowledge of a two-column cash book which maintains separate columns for 'bank' and 'cash' transactions for both receipts and payments. You may also hear of a three-column cash book which in addition to a bank and a cash column for receipts and payments would also have a discount column for both receipts and payments.

KAPLAN PUBLISHING

A three-column cash book is not examinable for Bookkeeping Transactions as instead of incorporating discount columns within the cash book, the AAT has set out separate discount day books which we introduced in chapter 2 and also reviewed in chapters 5 and 6.

There are two ways a cash book can be used within the accounting system. As set out in the assessment criteria of Bookkeeping Transactions, you need to be aware that the cash book can be a book of prime entry on its own or it can be a book of prime entry that also forms part of the double entry bookkeeping system.

It will always be made clear if the cash book forms part of the double entry bookkeeping system as well as being a book of prime entry. If this is the case, the impact on the cash or bank account is already dealt with and no separate posting is required to the bank or cash ledger account – as effectively the cash book is forming the ledger account in the general ledger. The cash book as part of the general ledger is reviewed in section 5 of this chapter. The examples we see before then will be where the cash book is a book of prime entry alone.

4.2 Recording cash receipts

We will now review an example for recording cash receipts, which shows how transactions are posted into the cash book and transferred to the appropriate accounts within the general and subsidiary ledgers.

Example 6

The following is an example of the general and sales ledgers, including entries from the sales and sales returns day books. For the purposes of this example, the narratives in the ledger accounts are references to the appropriate day books.

General ledger

Sales

	£		£
		SDB	4,600.00

VAT

	£		£
SRDB	140.00	SDB	805.00

SLCA

	£		£
SDB	5,405.00	SRDB	940.00

Sales returns

	£		£
SRDB	800.00		

Sales ledger

	A				B		
	£		£		£		£
SDB	1,057.50			SDB	1,880.00		

	C		
	£		£
SDB	2,467.50	SRDB	940.00

The following transactions took place:

Receivable A pays £1,057.50

Receivable B pays £1,000.00

Enter this information in the cash receipts book and in the appropriate ledger accounts in the general and subsidiary ledgers.

Solution

The following steps are needed.

Step 1   Enter these transactions in the cash book.

Step 2   Total the cash book and post the totals to the general ledger.

Step 3   Post the individual amounts of cash paid by receivables to the individual accounts in the sales ledger.

Step 1

CASH RECEIPTS BOOK							
Date	Narrative	Ref	Cash £	Bank £	VAT £	Receivables £	Cash sales £
	A			1,057.50	See note 2 – step 2	1,057.50	
	B			1,000.00		1,000.00	
Totals				2,057.50		2,057.50	

Step 2

We have brought forward the balances from the general ledger in the earlier example and now post the cash received book (CRB) totals to the general ledger.

General ledger

Sales

	£		£
		SLCA	4,600.00

VAT

	£		£
SLCA	140.00	SLCA	805.00

SLCA

	£		£
Sales & VAT	5,405.00	Sales returns & VAT	940.00
		Bank	2057.50

Sales returns

	£		£
SLCA	800.00		

Bank

	£		£
SLCA	2,057.50		

Note 1: We have posted the total of the SLCA column of the CRB to the sales ledger control account. This is the same as the total column in this example, but in more complex examples it may not be. The entry to the sales ledger control account is a credit entry as this is reducing the amount owed by our receivables.

Note 2: A common confusion is for people to wonder about the VAT – surely some of the money paid by A and B is actually paying the VAT part of the invoice. Yes it is, but we have already accounted for this VAT element when we entered the invoices themselves into the ledger accounts via the sales day book.

The total of the invoices in the SDB were debited to the SLCA and the VAT and sales were the corresponding credits. We therefore now post the total cash including VAT to the sales ledger control account but nothing is posted to the VAT account as this has already been done when dealing with the invoices.

Note 3: This is now the full double entry for the cash received completed.

Debit   Bank account (cash receipts book)

Credit   Sales ledger control account (receivables)

We have credited the sales ledger control account and the debit entry is posted to the bank account as the cash receipts book does not form part of the double entry system.

Note: if the cash receipts book was not only a day book but also formed part of the double entry bookkeeping system, the entry in the cash receipts book itself is the related debit entry. In this case there would be no need for any further debit entry to a separate cash/bank ledger account.

Step 3

We have brought forward the balance from the sales ledger in the earlier example and now post the cash received to the individual sales ledger accounts. Again, as with the sales ledger control account, this is a credit entry in each case as the cash received is reducing the amount owed by each receivable.

		A				B	
	£		£		£		£
b/d	1,057.50	CRB	1,057.50	b/d	1,880.00	CRB	1,000.00

		C	
	£		£
b/d	2,467.50	SRDB	940.00

4.3   Prompt payment discounts allowed to customers

Prompt payment discounts have already been considered in chapter 5. However we shall now look at this in more detail using an example to show how the transactions are entered into the day books and ledger accounts.

Example 7

The sales day book with prompt payment discounts.

Consider the following sales transactions made by Roberts Metals.

Customer	Sales value (ex VAT)	Trade discount	Net sales value	VAT	Total
	£	£	£	£	£
A	1,000	10%	900	180	1,080
B	2,000	20%	1,600	320	1,920
C	3,000	30%	2,100	420	2,520

In addition to the trade discount, customer A has been offered an additional 5% discount if he pays his invoice within 5 days.

Enter this information in the sales day book and ledger accounts.

Solution

Recording the invoice

The following steps are needed.

Step 1 Write up the sales day book.

Step 2 Post the totals to the accounts in the general ledger.

Step 3 Post the individual invoices to the sales ledger.

At the point of issuing the invoice it is not known if the prompt payment discount will be taken or not. It simply does not impact the invoice amounts at the point of making the sale.

Step 1

SALES DAY BOOK						
Date	Customer	Reference	Invoice number	Total £	VAT £	Sales £
	A			1,080	180	900
	B			1,920	320	1,600
	C			2,520	420	2,100
			TOTALS	5,520	920	4,600

Step 2

Sales				VAT			
£		£		£		£	
		SLCA	4,600			SLCA	920

SLCA			
£		£	
Sales & VAT	5,520		

Step 3

A				B			
£		£		£		£	
SDB	1,080			SDB	1,920		

C			
£		£	
SDB	2,520		

Recording the cash received

Customer A pays within the required time for the discount allowed. Details of the payments from customers A and B are below:

Customer A: Payment £1,026 (see working 1)

Customer B: Payment £1,000

Working 1:

Discounted sales price £900 × 95% = £855

VAT on discounted price £855 × 20% = £171

Total payment £1,026

The adjustment to the balance of customer A due to the prompt payment discount being taken will be made by issuing a credit note – recorded in the discounts allowed day book. The cash receipts for customers A and B will be recorded in the cash receipts book.

CASH RECEIPTS BOOK

Date	Narrative	Ref	Cash £	Bank £	VAT £	Receivables £	Cash sales £
	A			1,026	See note 2 – step 2	1,026	
	B			1,000		1,000	
Totals				2,026		2,026	

The deduction to the value of the original net amount and the VAT amount, by issuing a credit note, will now be entered into the discounts allowed day book.

The discount offered to A was 5%. This equates to a deduction from the original net price of £45.00 and a reduction to the VAT amount of £9.00 – in total the discount reducing A's receivable balance will be £54.00. The credit note for receivable A has been entered into the discounts allowed book below:

DISCOUNTS ALLOWED DAY BOOK

Date	Narrative	Reference	Total £	VAT £	Net £
	A		54	9	45
Totals			54	9	45

Step 3 – Posting the cash book and discount allowed book totals

The totals are posted as follows to the general ledger.

Sales				VAT			
£		£		£		£	
	SLCA	4,600	SLCA		9	SLCA	920

SLCA				Discount allowed			
	£		£		£		£
Sales & VAT	5,520	Bank	2,026	SLCA	45		
		Disc. allowed & VAT	54				

The discount allowed figure in the discount allowed book is entered into the ledger accounts as follows:

The gross amount (inclusive of VAT) is credited to the SLCA, to acknowledge a reduction to the receivable balance.

The net amount (exclusive of VAT) is debited to the discount allowed ledger account, to recognise the expense to the business of allowing the customer the discount.

The VAT amount is debited to the VAT ledger account recognising that due to the net price of the goods being reduced, the amount of VAT recoverable on that sale is now less.

If the cash book only acts as a book of prime entry rather than also being part of the double entry bookkeeping system, a debit entry to the bank or cash ledger account would also be seen here.

Step 4 – Posting to the sales ledger

	A				B		
	£		£		£		£
SDB	1,080	CRB	1,026	SDB	1,920	CRB	1,000
		Disc. all.	54			c/d	920
	1,080		1,080		1,920		1,920
				b/d	920		

	C	
	£	£
SDB	2,520	

✐ Test your understanding 4

Your organisation receives a number of cheques from receivables through the post each day. The amounts received in payment have been recorded in the cash receipts book. Some of the receivables (G Hunt and J Dent) were in receipt of discounts after taking advantage of prompt payment discounts that had been offered. These discounts have been recorded in the discounts allowed day book.

The organisation also makes some sales to non-credit customers each day which include VAT at the standard rate of 20% and are paid for by cheque.

Today's date is 28 April 20X1 and the cash receipts book and the discounts allowed book are as follows:

CASH RECEIPTS BOOK							
Date	Narrative	Ref	Cash £	Bank £	VAT £	Receivables £	Cash sales £
28/4/X1	G Hunt	SL04		114		114	
	L Tessa	SL15		110		110	
	J Dent	SL17		342		342	
	F Trainer	SL21		97		97	
	A Winter	SL09		105		105	
	Non-credit sales			120	20		100
Totals				888	20	768	100

DISCOUNTS ALLOWED DAY BOOK					
Date	Narrative	Reference	Total £	VAT £	Net £
28/4/X1	G Hunt – SL04	CN658	6	1	5
	J Dent – SL17	CN659	18	3	15
Totals			24	4	20

Required:

Show what the entries in the sales ledger will be:

Account name	Amount £	Dr ✓	Cr ✓

Show what the entries will be in the general ledger for the cash receipts book totals:

Account name	Amount £	Dr ✓	Cr ✓

Show what the entries will be in the general ledger for the discount allowed book totals:

Account name	Amount £	Dr ✓	Cr ✓

4.4 Recording cash payments

We will now review an example for recording cash payments which shows how transactions are posted into the cash book and transferred to the appropriate accounts within the general and subsidiary ledgers.

Example 8

Parma Products buys goods for resale from two suppliers on credit. The business buys £1,000 + VAT at 20% of goods from X and £3,000 + VAT at 20% of goods from Y. Parma receives an invoice and pays £500 + VAT at 20% rent to their landlord via bank transfer. Parma also pays X's invoice in full by cheque. Enter these transactions in the accounts of Parma Products. The rent invoice is not entered in the PDB.

Solution

Step 1 Enter the invoices for goods in the PDB.

PURCHASES DAY BOOK						
Date	Supplier	Reference	Invoice number	Total £	VAT £	Purchases £
	X			1,200	200	1,000
	Y			3,600	600	3,000
			TOTALS	4,800	800	4,000

Step 2 Enter the totals of the PDB in the general ledger.

Purchases

	£		£
PLCA	4,000		

VAT

	£		£
PLCA	800		

PLCA

	£		£
		Purchases & VAT	4,800

Step 3 Enter the cash paid in the analysed cash payments book.

CASH PAYMENTS BOOK								
Date	Narrative	Reference	Cash £	Bank £	VAT £	Payables £	Rent £	Admin £
	X			1,200		1,200		
	Rent			600	100		500	
Totals				1,800	100	1,200	500	

Note that the VAT on the payment to the credit suppliers has already been accounted for in the general ledger via the entries in the purchases day book. However, the rent invoice was not entered in the PDB so the VAT has to be entered in the VAT column of the cash book from where it will be posted to the VAT account (see Step 4).

Step 4 Post the cash paid totals from the cash book to the general ledger.

Purchases

	£		£
PLCA	4,000		

VAT

	£		£
PLCA	800		
Bank	100		

PLCA

	£		£
Bank	1,200	Purchases & VAT	4,800

Rent

	£		£
Bank	500		

Note 1: All the VAT paid is now debited to the VAT account. You must make sure that you understand how VAT can be posted via the PDB and via the cash book.

Note 2: All of the entries (payables, VAT and rent) made from the cash payments book are debit entries. The credit entry is the total of the cash payments (£1,800) which would be credited to the bank ledger account.

Step 5: Enter the amounts in the purchases ledger.

X

	£		£
CPB	1,200	PDB	1,200

Y

	£		£
		PDB	3,600

The entries to the purchases ledger from the cash payments book are debit entries in the individual payable accounts as the payment means that less is owed to the payable.

4.5   Prompt payment discounts received from suppliers

Prompt payment discounts from suppliers are a tricky complication that we were introduced to in chapter 6. We shall now review an example.

 Example 9

Consider a business run by Francis which buys goods costing £2,000 + VAT from Z. Z offers a 5% settlement discount if Francis pays within 10 days. Francis does pay within 10 days.

Enter these new transactions in the books of Francis.

Solution

Step 1   Calculate the value of the invoice.

	£
Cost of goods	2,000
VAT (2,000 × 20%)	400
Total invoice value	2,400

Step 2   Enter the invoice from Z in the purchases day book.

PURCHASES DAY BOOK						
Date	Supplier	Reference	Invoice number	Total £	VAT £	Purchases £
	Z			2,400	400	2,000
			TOTALS	2,400	400	2,000

Step 3   Enter the totals of the purchases day book in the general ledger.

Purchases

	£			£
PLCA	2,000			

VAT

	£		£
PLCA	400		

PLCA

	£		£
		Purchases & VAT	2,400

Step 4   Calculate the cash paid by Francis.

	£
Cost of goods	2,000
5% prompt payment discount	(100)
	1,900
VAT (2,000 – (5% × 2,000)) × 20%	380
Total cash paid	2,280

Step 5   Enter the cash paid in the analysed cash payments book and the discount received in the discounts received day book.

CASH PAYMENTS BOOK

Date	Narrative	Reference	Cash £	Bank £	VAT £	Payables £	Rent £
	Z			2,280		2,280	
		TOTALS		2,280		2,280	

DISCOUNTS RECEIVED DAY BOOK

Date	Narrative	Reference	Total £	VAT £	Net £
	Z		120	20	100
Totals			120	20	100

Step 6   Post the cash payments book and discounts received day book totals to the general ledger.

Purchases

	£		£
PLCA	2,000		

VAT

	£		£
PLCA	400	PLCA	20

PLCA

	£		£
Bank	2,280	Purchases & VAT	2,400
Discount received & VAT	120		

Discount received

	£		£
		PLCA	100

Bank

	£		£
		PLCA	2,280

 Test your understanding 5

Given below is the cash payments book and discounts received day book for a business.

CASH PAYMENTS BOOK							
Date	Details	Cheque no	Code	Bank £	PLCA £	Cash purchases £	VAT £
12/3	Homer Ltd	03648	PL12	176.40	176.40		
	Forker & Co	03649	PL07	285.18	285.18		
	Purchases	03650		342.00		285.00	57.00
	Print Ass.	03651	PL08	190.45	190.45		
	ABG Ltd	03652	PL02	220.67	220.67		
	Purchases	03653		198.00		165.00	33.00
	G Greg	03654	PL19	67.89	67.89		
				1,480.59	940.59	450.00	90.00

DISCOUNTS RECEIVED DAY BOOK					
Date	Narrative	Reference	Total £	VAT £	Net £
12/3	Homer Ltd	CN897	3.60	0.60	3.00
	Forker & Co	CN898	8.82	1.47	7.35
Totals			12.42	2.07	10.35

Required:

Show what the entries in the purchases ledger will be:

Account name	Amount £	Dr ✓	Cr ✓

Show what the entries will be in the general ledger for the cash payments book totals:

Account name	Amount £	Dr ✓	Cr ✓

Show what the entries will be in the general ledger for the discounts received day book totals:

Account name	Amount £	Dr ✓	Cr ✓

5 The cash book as part of the general ledger

5.1 Introduction

The Bookkeeping Transactions assessment may show the cashbook as a ledger account format. This indicates the cashbook forms part of the general ledger, with the entries being one side of the double entry required within the general ledger. Therefore a typical assessment requirement will be to complete the other side of the entry within the general ledger, and to update the individual accounts in the subsidiary ledger.

Example 10

Date	Detail	Bank £	Date	Detail	Bank £
30/6/X9	Bal b/d	16,173	30/6/X9	Plant & machinery	25,500
30/6/X9	Receivable A	13,200	30/6/X9	Loan repayment	1,500
			30/6/X9	Motor expenses	1,440
			30/6/X9	Bal c/d	933
		29,373			**29,373**

We need to appreciate that the bank account has already been completed with one side of the entry, and the other side of the entry is all that is required in order to complete the double entry postings.

Postings to general ledger (ignoring VAT)

Account	Amount	Dr or Cr
SLCA	13,200	Cr
Plant and machinery	25,500	Dr
Loan	1,500	Dr
Motor expenses	1,440	Dr

Postings to the sales ledger

Account	Amount	Dr or Cr
Receivable A account	13,200	Cr

Test your understanding 6

Date	Detail	Bank £	Date	Detail	VAT £	Bank £
30/6/X9	Bal b/d	24,067	30/6/X9	Motor vehicles		20,000
30/6/X9	Bal c/d	2,913	30/6/X9	Motor expenses	80	480
			30/6/X9	Payable B		6,500
		26,980			**80**	**26,980**
			1/7/X9	Bal b/d		2,913

What are the postings to the general and purchases ledgers?

 Example 11

You may be asked to only record transactions for one side of the cash book.

Cash book – debit side

Details	Bank £
Balance b/d	2,568
Edwards Ltd	3,864

(a)   Record the entry into the sales ledger.

(b)   Record the entry within the general ledger.

Solution

The cash book has already been completed with one side (debit side) of the entries. The other side (credit side) is all that is required in order to complete the double entry postings.

(a)   **Sales ledger**

Details	Amount £	Debit/Credit
Edwards Ltd	3,864	Credit

(b)   **General ledger**

Details	Amount £	Debit/Credit
Sales ledger control account	3,864	Credit

Test your understanding 7

Cashbook – credit side

Details	VAT £	Bank £
Motor expenses	60	360
Wages		4,785

Record the THREE transactions within the general ledger.

Details	Amount £	Debit/Credit

6 Petty cash

6.1 Introduction

 Definition – Petty cash

Petty cash is the small amount of cash that most businesses hold in order to make small cash payments, such as payment for coffee and milk for the staff kitchen.

6.2 Petty cash box

Holding cash on business premises is a security risk and therefore it is important the petty cash is secure. It should be kept in a locked petty cash box and usually this itself will be held in the safe. Only the person responsible for the petty cash should have access to the petty cash box.

6.3 Payment of petty cash

Petty cash is usually reimbursed to employees who have already incurred a small cash expense on behalf of the business. These payments should only be made for valid business expenses. For this reason, the petty cashier should only pay out to the employee on receipt of an authorised petty cash voucher and, where appropriate, VAT receipt.

 Definition – Petty cash voucher

A petty cash voucher is an internal document that details the business expenditure an employee has incurred out of his own money.

This voucher must be authorised by an appropriate person before any amounts can be paid to that employee out of the petty cash box.

A typical petty cash voucher is shown below:

Signature
of person
authorising
voucher

Details of
expenditure
including
the date
and the
nature of
the
expense

Signature of
claimant

Sequent
vouche
numbe

Total paid
to
employee

PETTY CASH VOUCHER

Authorised by	Received by	No 4173	
F R Clarke	L Kent		
Date	Description	Amount	
4 April 20X1	Train Fare	12	50
Total		12	50

6.4 Maintaining petty cash records

Upon the petty cash vouchers being received and the employees being reimbursed, the details are recorded in the petty cash book. In Chapter 2 we were briefly introduced to the petty cash book as a book of prime entry. The Bookkeeping Transactions assessment requires you to be able to make entries into the petty cash book.

6.5   Writing up the petty cash book

When cash is paid into the petty cash book, this will be recorded on the receipts side (debit side) of the petty cash book.

Each petty cash voucher will then in turn be written up in the petty cash book on the payments side.

To ensure no vouchers have been mislaid, petty cash vouchers are pre-numbered sequentially. Each voucher is then entered into the petty cash book in the correct order, with each item of expenditure being recorded in the correct expense analysis column.

 Example 12

A business has just started to run a petty cash system with an amount of £100. £100 is withdrawn from the bank account and paid into the petty cash box on 3 April 20X1.

During the first week the following authorised petty cash vouchers were paid. These transactions will now be recorded in the petty cash book.

PETTY CASH VOUCHER				
Authorised by T Smedley	*Received by* P Lannall		*No* 0001	
Date	*Description*		*Amount*	
3 April 20X1	Tea/coffee/milk		4	73
	Total		4	73

PETTY CASH VOUCHER				
Authorised by T Smedley	*Received by* R Sellers		*No* 0002	
Date	*Description*		*Amount*	
3 April 20X1	Train fare		14	90
	Total		14	90

PETTY CASH VOUCHER

Authorised by T Smedley	Received by F Dorne	No	0003	
Date	Description		Amount	
4 April 20X1	Stationery		4	00
	VAT		0	80
	Total		4	80

PETTY CASH VOUCHER

Authorised by T Smedley	Received by P Dent	No	0004	
Date	Description		Amount	
5 April 20X1	Postage costs		16	35
	Total		16	35

PETTY CASH VOUCHER

Authorised by T Smedley	Received by H Polly	No	0005	
Date	Description		Amount	
7 April 20X1	Train fare		15	30
	Total		15	30

PETTY CASH VOUCHER			
Authorised by T Smedley	Received by P Lannall	No	0006
Date	Description		Amount
8 April 20X1	Milk/biscuits		3	85
		Total	3	85

Solution

Petty cash book											
Receipts			**Payments**								
Date	Narrative	Total	Date	Narrative	Voucher no	Total	Postage	Travel	Tea & coffee	Sundry	VAT
20X1		£	20X1			£	£	£	£	£	£
03/04	Bank	100.00	03/04	Tea/coffee	0001	4.73			4.73		
			03/04	Train fare	0002	14.90		14.90			
			04/04	Stationery	0003	4.80				4.00	0.80
			05/04	Postage	0004	16.35	16.35				
			07/04	Train fare	0005	15.30		15.30			
			08/04	Milk/biscuits	0006	3.85			3.85		

6.6 The imprest system

Many businesses use the imprest system for petty cash. Using an imprest system makes petty cash easier to control and therefore reduces the possibility of error and fraud.

The business decides on a fixed amount of petty cash (the imprest) which is just large enough to cover normal petty cash requirements for a period (usually a week). This amount of petty cash is withdrawn from the bank.

Claims are paid out of petty cash by a voucher being completed for each amount of petty cash paid out. The vouchers are kept in the petty cash box so that the amount of cash held decreases and is replaced by vouchers.

At any given time, the total contents of the box (i.e. petty cash plus amounts withdrawn represented by vouchers) should equal the amount of the imprest.

At the end of the period, a cheque is drawn for the total of the vouchers which restores the petty cash float to the amount of the imprest. The vouchers are removed from the petty cash box and filed.

Example 13

The imprest amount for a petty cash system is £150, which is the amount paid into the petty cash box on 1 November. At the end of the week the total of the vouchers in the petty cash box is £125.05. How much cash is required in order to replenish the petty cash box to the imprest amount?

Solution

£125.05, the amount paid out on the basis of the petty cash vouchers.

6.7 Non-imprest petty cash system

An imprest petty cash system as in the previous example is the most common method of dealing with and controlling petty cash. However some businesses may use a non-imprest system. This might be where a set amount of cash is withdrawn each week and paid into the petty cash box no matter what the level of expenditure in that week.

For example it may be an organisation's policy to cash a cheque for £50 each Monday morning for use as petty cash for the week. The danger here is either that petty cash requirements are more than £50 in the week in which case the petty cash box will run out of money. Alternatively week after week expenditure is significantly less than £50 each week, leading to a large amount of cash building up in the petty cash box.

6.8 Posting the petty cash book

Once the petty cash book has been written up, we must now post the totals of the petty cash book to the general ledger accounts.

The petty cash book can be a book of prime entry alone, or a book of prime entry that also forms part of the double entry bookkeeping system.

6.9 Posting the petty cash receipt

The receipt into the petty cash box has come from cash being withdrawn from the bank account. This will have been done by writing out a cheque for cash and withdrawing this from the bank. Therefore the cheque should be recorded in the cash payments book as a payment when the cash payments book is written up.

The receipt of the cash into the petty cash box is recorded in the receipts side of the petty cash book, i.e. the debit side.

6.10 Posting the petty cash payments – the petty cash book as part of the double entry bookkeeping system

We will consider an example where the petty cash book is part of the double entry bookkeeping system as well as being a book of prime entry.

 Example 14

A petty cash book is give below. This is to be posted to the general ledger accounts.

Petty cash book											
Receipts			Payments								
Date	Narrative	Total	Date	Narrative	Voucher no	Total	Postage	Travel	Tea & coffee	Sundry	VAT
20X1		£	20X1			£	£	£	£	£	£
20/08	Bal b/d	100.00	20/08	Tea/coffee	0001	13.68			13.68		
20/08	Bank	50.00	21/08	Train fare	0002	6.80		6.80			
			21/08	Stationery	0003	19.20				16.00	3.20
			22/08	Postage	0004	16.35	16.35				
			23/08	Train fare	0005	15.30		15.30			
			24/08	Milk/biscuits	0006	3.85			3.85		

Solution

Step 1 Each of the columns in the petty cash payments side must be totalled.

The accuracy of your totalling should be checked by ensuring that all of the analysis column totals add back to the total of the 'total' column in the petty cash book payments side.

Petty cash book											
Receipts			Payments								
Date	Narrative	Total	Date	Narrative	Voucher no	Total	Postage	Travel	Tea & coffee	Sundry	VAT
20X1		£	20X1			£	£	£	£	£	£
20/08	Bal b/d	100.00	20/08	Tea/coffee	0001	13.68			13.68		
20/08	Bank	50.00	21/08	Train fare	0002	6.80		6.80			
			21/08	Stationery	0003	19.20				16.00	3.20
			22/08	Postage	0004	16.35	16.35				
			23/08	Train fare	0005	15.30		15.30			
			24/08	Milk/biscuits	0006	3.85			3.85		
				Bal c/d		74.82					
		150.00				150.00	16.35	22.10	17.53	16.00	3.20

Step 2 Each of the analysis column totals must now be entered into the general ledger accounts as debit entries.

VAT account

	£		£
Petty cash book (PCB)	3.20		

The entry has come from the petty cash book and this is the reference – this is now shortened to PCB.

Postage account

	£		£
PCB	16.35		

Travel account

	£		£
PCB	22.10		

Tea and coffee account

	£		£
PCB	17.53		

Sundry expenses account

	£		£
PCB	16.00		

Bank account

	£		£
		PCB	50.00

There is no need for an entry to the petty cash control account as the petty cash book acts as the general ledger account and the closing balance on the account is taken from it when the trial balance is prepared.

6.11 Posting the petty cash payments – the petty cash book not part of the double entry bookkeeping system

When the petty cash book is not part of the double entry system, the accounting entries must show the impact on the expense accounts, the VAT account and the petty cash control account.

In the event of there being a top up to the petty cash, a separate entry will be required. We would need to show the money being withdrawn from the bank and deposited into petty cash.

We will now consider the earlier illustration to review the general ledger postings required when the petty cash book is not part of the double entry accounting system.

 Example 15

A petty cash book is give below. This is to be posted to the general ledger accounts.

Petty cash book										
Receipts			Payments							
Date	Narrative	Total	Date	Narrative	Voucher no	Total	Postage	Travel	Tea & coffee	Sundry	VAT
20X1		£	20X1			£	£	£	£	£	£
20/08	Bal b/d	100.00	20/08	Tea/coffee	0001	13.68			13.68		
20/08	Bank	50.00	21/08	Train fare	0002	6.80		6.80			
			21/08	Stationery	0003	19.20				16.00	3.20
			22/08	Postage	0004	16.35	16.35				
			23/08	Train fare	0005	15.30		15.30			
			24/08	Milk/biscuits	0006	3.85			3.85		

Solution

Step 1   Each of the columns in the petty cash payments side must be totalled.

The accuracy of your totalling should be checked by ensuring that all of the analysis column totals add back to the total of the 'total' column in the petty cash book payments side.

Petty cash book											
Receipts			Payments								
Date	Narrative	Total	Date	Narrative	Voucher no	Total	Postage	Travel	Tea & coffee	Sundry	VAT
20X1		£	20X1			£	£	£	£	£	£
20/08	Bal b/d	100.00	20/08	Tea/coffee	0001	13.68			13.68		
20/08	Bank	50.00	21/08	Train fare	0002	6.80		6.80			
			21/08	Stationery	0003	19.20				16.00	3.20
			22/08	Postage	0004	16.35	16.35				
			23/08	Train fare	0005	15.30		15.30			
			24/08	Milk/biscuits	0006	3.85			3.85		
		150.00				75.18	16.35	22.10	17.53	16.00	3.20

Check the totals:

	£
Postage	16.35
Travel	22.10
Tea and coffee	17.53
Sundry	16.00
VAT	3.20
	75.18

We have been told that the petty cash book is not part of the double entry accounting system. The expense accounts of postage, travel, tea and coffee, sundry along with the VAT account will be debited, the corresponding impact on the petty cash control account will be to credit it (to reduce the balance) by the amount in total that has been paid out.

Remember the account name in the general ledger should always match the analysis column headings in the petty cash-book and not the description of the expense given in the 'Details' column.

We must also record the impact of the top-up to the petty cash from the bank account. This will be shown as a credit from the bank ledger account and a debit to the petty cash control account.

Step 2   We will now make the entries required into the general ledger accounts.

VAT account

	£		£
Petty cash book (PCB)	3.20		

The entry has come from the petty cash book and this is the reference – this is now shortened to PCB.

Postage account

	£		£
PCB	16.35		

Travel account

	£		£
PCB	22.10		

Tea and coffee account

	£		£
PCB	17.53		

Sundry expenses account

	£		£
PCB	16.00		

Bank account

	£		£
		PCB	50.00

Petty cash control

	£		£
Balance b/d	100.00	PCB	75.18
Bank	50.00		

Test your understanding 8

Summary of petty cash vouchers in hand at 31 October 20X7

Date	Description	Total £	VAT included £
1/10	Envelopes (Administration)	19.72	3.28
4/10	Cleaner (Administration)	8.75	
6/10	Food for staff lunch (Marketing)	17.13	
6/10	Taxi fares (Marketing)	16.23	
6/10	Rail fares (Marketing)	43.75	
10/10	Postage (Administration)	4.60	
15/10	Tea and coffee (Production)	4.39	
17/10	Light bulbs and refuse sacks (Distribution)	8.47	1.41
20/10	Flowers for reception (Administration)	21.23	
26/10	Cleaner (Administration)	8.75	

(a) Write up the payments side of the petty cash book for October 20X7 from the information given.

You should allocate a sequential voucher number to each entry in the petty cash book. The last voucher number to be allocated in September was 6578.

Use the blank petty cash book provided.

(b) Total each of the columns in the petty cash book and cross-cast them.

(c) Post the totals to the general ledger accounts given.

PETTY CASH BOOK – PAYMENTS

Date	Voucher no	Total	Production	Distribu-tion	Marketing	Administration	VAT
		£	£	£	£	£	£

Production expenses account

£		£

Distribution expenses account

£		£

Marketing expenses account

£		£

Administration expenses account

£		£

VAT account

£		£

6.12 Reconciling the petty cash

We saw earlier in the chapter that when an imprest system is being used for petty cash then at any point in time the amount of cash in the petty cash box plus the total of the vouchers in the petty cash box should equal the imprest amount.

At regular intervals, usually at the end of each week, this check will be carried out.

6.13 Procedure for reconciling the petty cash box

The total amount of cash in the petty cash box will be counted. The vouchers that have been paid during the week are also in the petty cash box and they must also be totalled.

When the amount of cash is added to the total of the vouchers in the box they should equal the imprest amount.

The petty cash vouchers for the week will then be removed from the box and filed. The petty cash will then be topped up by the value of the vouchers to bring the petty cash back up to the imprest level.

Example 16

The amount of cash remaining in a petty cash box at the end of a week is as follows:

Notes/coins	Quantity
£10	1
£5	2
£2	3
£1	7
50p	9
20p	10
10p	15
5p	7
2p	16
1p	23

The imprest amount is £100 and the vouchers in the petty cash box at the end of the week are as follows:

PETTY CASH VOUCHER				
Authorised by C Alexi	Received by P Trant		No	0467
Date	Description			Amount
4 May 20X3	Window cleaner		15	00
		Total	15	00

PETTY CASH VOUCHER			
Authorised by C Alexi	Received by F Saint	No	0468
Date	Description	Amount	
5 May 20X3	Train fare	9	80
	Total	9	80

PETTY CASH VOUCHER			
Authorised by C Alexi	Received by A Paul	No	0469
Date	Description	Amount	
5 May 20X3	Stationery	8	00
	VAT	1	60
	Total	9	60

PETTY CASH VOUCHER			
Authorised by C Alexi	Received by P Peters	No	0470
Date	Description	Amount	
7 May 20X3	Postage	6	80
	Total	6	80

PETTY CASH VOUCHER			
Authorised by C Alexi	Received by C Ralph	No	0471
Date	Description	Amount	
5 May 20X3	Train fare	16	90
	Total	16	90

The cash and vouchers in the petty cash box at the end of the week are to be reconciled.

Solution

The petty cash must be totalled:

Notes/coins	Quantity	Amount £
£10	1	10.00
£5	2	10.00
£2	3	6.00
£1	7	7.00
50p	9	4.50
20p	10	2.00
10p	15	1.50
5p	7	0.35
2p	16	0.32
1p	23	0.23
		41.90

Now the vouchers must be totalled.

	£
0467	15.00
0468	9.80
0469	9.60
0470	6.80
0471	16.90
	58.10

Finally, total the cash and the vouchers to ensure that they add back to the imprest amount.

	£
Cash	41.90
Vouchers	58.10
	100.00

6.14 Possible causes of difference

If there is more cash in the petty cash box than the balance on the petty cash control account this could be due to an error in writing up the petty cash book as more has been recorded in payments than has actually been paid out. In this case the entries in the petty cash book should be checked to the underlying petty cash vouchers to discover the error.

If there is less cash in the petty cash box than the balance on the petty cash control account this could also be due to an error in writing up the petty cash book as this time less payments have been recorded in the petty cash control account than were actually made. This may be due to a petty cash voucher having been omitted from the petty cash book and therefore again the underlying petty cash vouchers should all be checked to their entries in the petty cash book.

If no accounting errors or posting errors can be found then the cause is likely to be one of the following:

- an error has been made in paying a petty cash voucher and more money was handed out than was recorded on the voucher

- cash has been paid out of the petty cash box without a supporting voucher

- cash could have been stolen from the petty cash box.

In such cases the matter should be investigated and security of the petty cash and petty cash procedures improved.

 Test your understanding 9

Your business runs a petty cash box based upon an imprest amount of £60. This morning you have emptied the petty cash box and found the following notes, coins and vouchers.

Notes
£5 × 2

Coins
£1 × 3
50p × 5
20p × 4
10p × 6
5p × 7
2p × 10
1p × 8

Vouchers	£
2143	10.56
2144	3.30
2145	9.80
2146	8.44
2147	2.62
2148	6.31
2149	1.44

You are required to reconcile the cash and the vouchers in the petty cash box.

7   Additional test your understandings

Test your understanding 10

You work in the accounts department of Farmhouse Pickles Ltd and given below are two receivables' accounts from the sales ledger.

	Grant & Co			SL07
		£		£
1 April	Balance b/d	337.69	12 April SRDB – 0335	38.70
4 April	SDB 32656	150.58	20 April CRB	330.94
18 April	SDB 32671	179.52	20 April DAB – discount allowed	6.75
25 April	SDB 32689	94.36	24 April SRDB – 0346	17.65

	Mitchell Partners			SL10
		£		£
1 April	Balance b/d	180.46	12 April SRDB – 0344	66.89
7 April	SDB 32662	441.57	21 April CRB	613.58
20 April	SDB 32669	274.57	21 April DAB – discount allowed	8.45

Required:

Prepare statements to be sent to each of these customers at the end of April 20X1 on the blank statements provided.

To:

FARMHOUSE
PICKLES
LTD

225 School Lane
Weymouth
Dorset
WE36 5NR
Tel: 0261 480444
Fax: 0261 480555
Date:

STATEMENT

Date	Transaction	Debit £	Credit £	Balance £

May we remind you that our credit terms are 30 days

FARMHOUSE PICKLES LTD

225 School Lane
Weymouth
Dorset
WE36 5NR
Tel: 0261 480444
Fax: 0261 480555
Date:

To:

STATEMENT

Date	Transaction	Debit £	Credit £	Balance £

May we remind you that our credit terms are 30 days

Test your understanding 11

Shown below is a customer's account from the sales ledger of Ryan's Toy Shop Ltd, along with a statement of account to be sent to that customer.

Arnold's Toys Ltd

Dr				Cr			
Date	Transaction	£		Date	Transaction	£	
19/11	Invoice 2195	118	08	20/11	Credit note 2198	323	60
20/11	Invoice 2198	2,201	95	22/11	Cheque	118	08
				22/11	Balance c/d	1,878	35
		2,320	03			2,320	03
23/11	Balance b/d	1,878	35				

Required:

Complete the statement of account below.

Ryan's Toy Shop LTD						
125 Finchley Way Bristol BS1 4PL Tel: 01272 200299						
STATEMENT OF ACCOUNT						
Customer name: Arnold's Toys Ltd						
Customer address: 14 High Street, Bristol, BS2 5FL						

Statement date 1st December		**Amount**		**Balance**	
Date	**Transaction**	**£**	**p**	**£**	**P**

Test your understanding 12

Simon Harris is a self-employed accountant who has a number of clients who all pay by cheque. Today's date is 5 May 20X1 and in the last week he has received the following cheques.

Required:

Inspect each one carefully to ensure that it is valid and make a note of any problems you find.

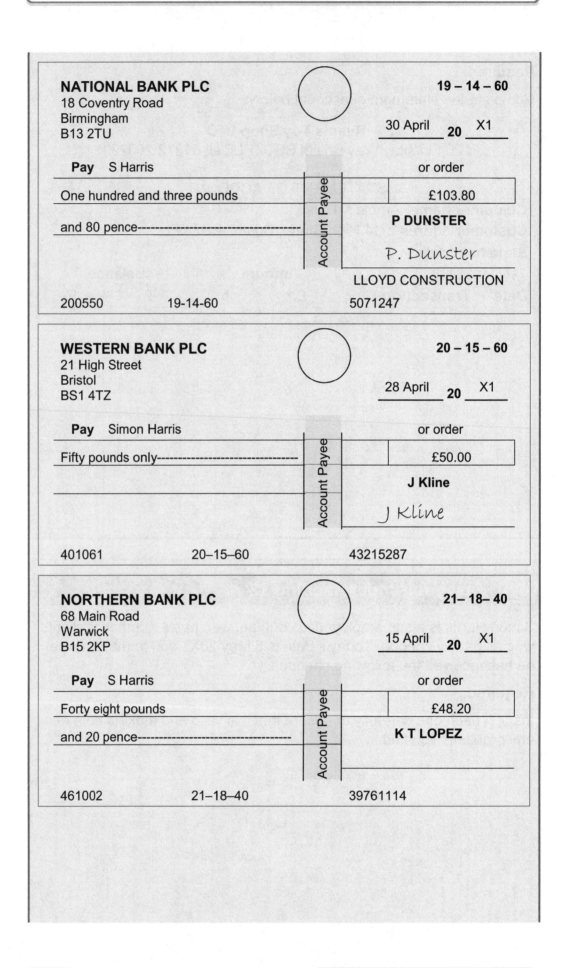

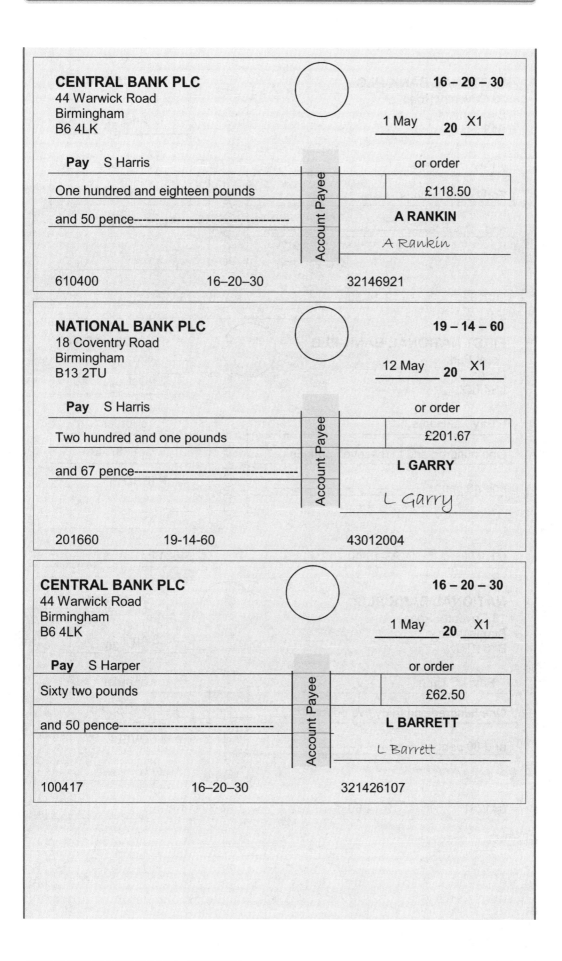

CENTRAL BANK PLC
44 Warwick Road
Birmingham
B6 4LK

16 – 20 – 30

1 May 20 X1

Pay S Harris

or order

One hundred and eighteen pounds

£118.50

and 50 pence-------------------------------------

A RANKIN

A Rankin

Account Payee

610400   16–20–30   32146921

NATIONAL BANK PLC
18 Coventry Road
Birmingham
B13 2TU

19 – 14 – 60

12 May 20 X1

Pay S Harris

or order

Two hundred and one pounds

£201.67

and 67 pence-------------------------------------

L GARRY

L Garry

Account Payee

201660   19-14-60   43012004

CENTRAL BANK PLC
44 Warwick Road
Birmingham
B6 4LK

16 – 20 – 30

1 May 20 X1

Pay S Harper

or order

Sixty two pounds

£62.50

and 50 pence------------------------------------

L BARRETT

L Barrett

Account Payee

100417   16–20–30   321426107

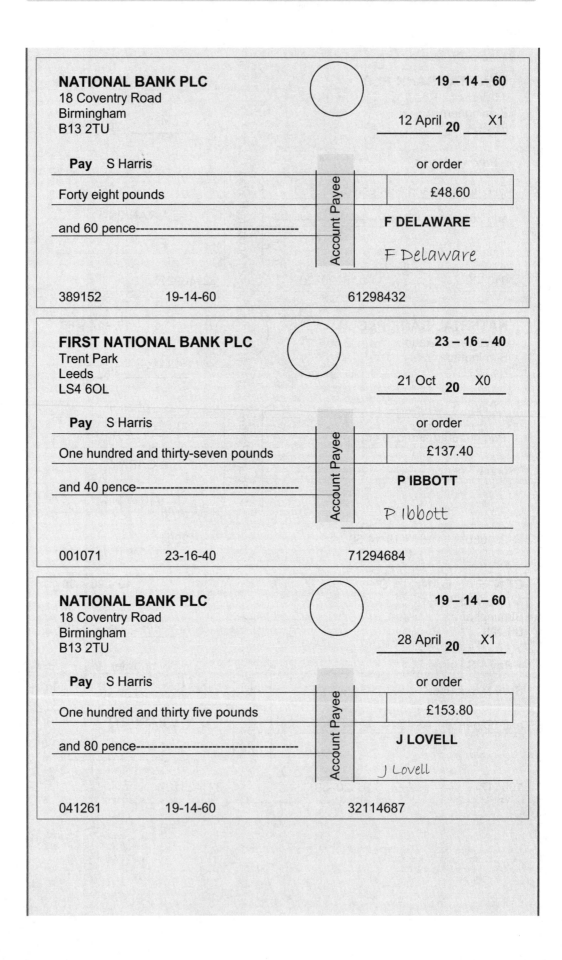

NATIONAL BANK PLC
18 Coventry Road
Birmingham
B13 2TU

19 – 14 – 60

12 April 20 X1

Pay S Harris   or order

Forty eight pounds   £48.60

and 60 pence-------------------------------------   **F DELAWARE**

F Delaware

Account Payee

389152   19-14-60   61298432

FIRST NATIONAL BANK PLC
Trent Park
Leeds
LS4 6OL

23 – 16 – 40

21 Oct 20 X0

Pay S Harris   or order

One hundred and thirty-seven pounds   £137.40

and 40 pence-------------------------------------   **P IBBOTT**

P Ibbott

Account Payee

001071   23-16-40   71294684

NATIONAL BANK PLC
18 Coventry Road
Birmingham
B13 2TU

19 – 14 – 60

28 April 20 X1

Pay S Harris   or order

One hundred and thirty five pounds   £153.80

and 80 pence-------------------------------------   **J LOVELL**

J Lovell

Account Payee

041261   19-14-60   32114687

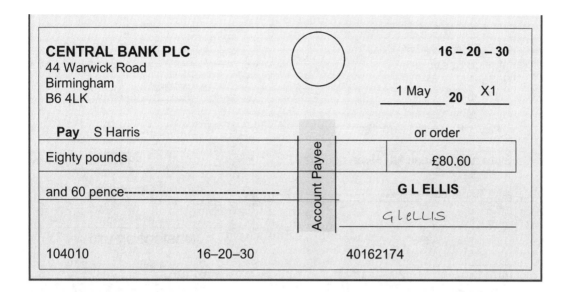

CENTRAL BANK PLC		16 – 20 – 30
44 Warwick Road		
Birmingham		
B6 4LK		1 May 20 X1

Pay   S Harris   or order

Eighty pounds   £80.60

and 60 pence------------------------------------   **G L ELLIS**

G l eLLIS

104010   16–20–30   40162174

Test your understanding 13

You work for Keyboard Supplies. Today's date is 12 May 20X1 and the following five cheques have arrived in this morning's post. You have found the invoices that these payments relate to – these are also given.

Required:

Check each receipt is correct and make a note of any problems you find.

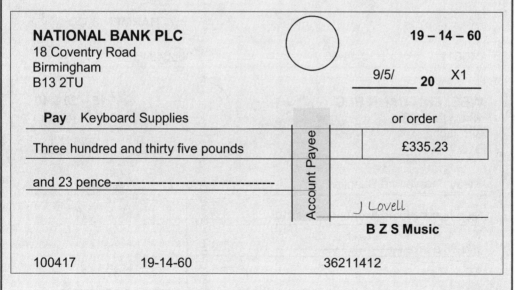

NATIONAL BANK PLC		19 – 14 – 60
18 Coventry Road		
Birmingham		
B13 2TU		9/5/ 20 X1

Pay   Keyboard Supplies   or order

Three hundred and thirty five pounds   £335.23

and 23 pence---

J Lovell

B Z S Music

100417   19-14-60   36211412

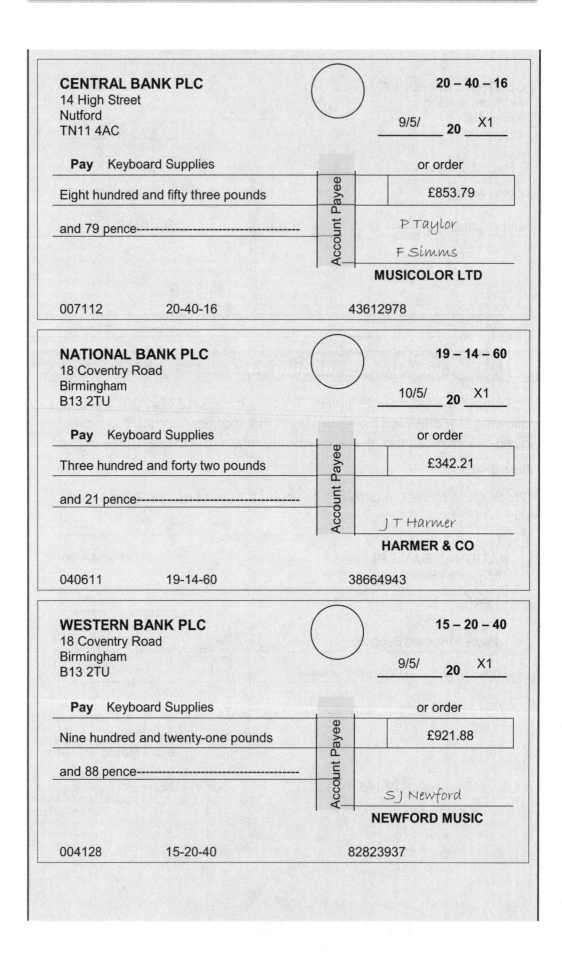

CENTRAL BANK PLC
14 High Street
Nutford
TN11 4AC

20 – 40 – 16

9/5/ 20 X1

Pay Keyboard Supplies   or order

Eight hundred and fifty three pounds   £853.79

and 79 pence-------------------------------------

P Taylor

F Simms

MUSICOLOR LTD

Account Payee

007112   20-40-16   43612978

NATIONAL BANK PLC
18 Coventry Road
Birmingham
B13 2TU

19 – 14 – 60

10/5/ 20 X1

Pay Keyboard Supplies   or order

Three hundred and forty two pounds   £342.21

and 21 pence-------------------------------------

J T Harmer

HARMER & CO

Account Payee

040611   19-14-60   38664943

WESTERN BANK PLC
18 Coventry Road
Birmingham
B13 2TU

15 – 20 – 40

9/5/ 20 X1

Pay Keyboard Supplies   or order

Nine hundred and twenty-one pounds   £921.88

and 88 pence-------------------------------------

S J Newford

NEWFORD MUSIC

Account Payee

004128   15-20-40   82823937

FIRST NATIONAL BANK PLC
Main Square
Nottingham
NT2 4XY

20 – 14 – 60

10/5/ **20** X1

| Pay | Keyboard Supplies | | or order |

Four hundred and thirty eight pounds

Account Payee

£438.06

and 6 pence-------------------------------------

T Gilchrist

Trent Music

201067   20-14-60   67112604

INVOICE

Keyboard Supplies

Invoice to:
BZS Music
42 Westhill
Nutford TN11 3PQ

Trench Park Estate
Fieldham
Sussex TN21 4AF
Tel: 01829 654545
Fax: 01829 654646

Deliver to:

Invoice no:	06180
Tax point:	3 May 20X1
VAT reg:	466 1128 30
Your reference:	SL01
Purchase order no:	77147

Code	Description	Quantity	VAT rate %	Unit price £	Amount excl of VAT £
B4012	Bento Keyboard	2	20	180.00	360.00
					360.00
Trade discount 20%					72.00
					288.00
VAT					57.60
Total amount payable					345.60

Deduct discount of 3% if paid within 10 days, net 30 days

INVOICE

Invoice to:
Musicolor Ltd
23 High Street
Nutford TN11 4 TZ

Keyboard Supplies
Trench Park Estate
Fieldham
Sussex TN21 4AF
Tel: 01829 654545
Fax: 01829 654646

Deliver to:

As above

Invoice no:	06176
Tax point:	1 May 20X1
VAT reg:	466 1128 30
Your reference:	SL06
Purchase order no:	6362

Code	Description	Quantity	VAT rate %	Unit price £	Amount excl of VAT £
Z4600	Zanni Keyboard	3	20	185.00	555.00
A4802	Atol Keyboard	2	20	130.00	260.00
					815.00
Trade discount 10%					81.50
					733.50
VAT					146.70
Total amount payable					880.20

Prompt payment discount of 3% if paid within 5 days, net 30 days

INVOICE

Keyboard Supplies

Invoice to:
Harmer & Co
1 Acre Street
Nutford TN11 0HA

Trench Park Estate
Fieldham
Sussex TN21 4AF
Tel: 01829 654545
Fax: 01829 654646

Deliver to:

As above

Invoice no:	06183
Tax point:	3 May 20X1
VAT reg no:	466 1128 30
Your reference:	SL17
Purchase order no:	047786

Code	Description	Quantity	VAT rate %	Unit price £	Amount excl of VAT £
G4326	Garland Keyboard	3	20	98.00	294.00
					294.00

VAT	58.80
Total amount payable	352.80

Prompt payment discount of 3% if paid within 10 days, net 30 days

INVOICE

Invoice to:
Newford Music
32/34 Main Street
Welland
Sussex TN4 6BD

Keyboard Supplies
Trench Park Estate
Fieldham
Sussex TN21 4AF
Tel: 01829 654545
Fax: 01829 654646

Deliver to:

As above

Invoice no:	06171
Tax point:	30 April 20X1
VAT reg :	466 1128 30
Your reference:	SL18
Purchase order no:	47202

Code	Description	Quantity	VAT rate %	Unit price £	Amount excl of VAT £
Z4406	Zanni Keyboard	6	20	165.00	990.00
					990.00
Trade discount 20%					198.00
					792.00
VAT					158.40
Total amount payable					950.40

Prompt payment discount of 3% if paid within 5 days, net
30 days

INVOICE

Keyboard Supplies

Invoice to:
Trent Music
Trent House
Main Street
Fieldham TN21 6ZF

Trench Park Estate
Fieldham
Sussex TN21 4AF
Tel: 01829 654545
Fax: 01829 654646

Deliver to:

Invoice no:	06184
Tax point:	3 May 20X1
VAT reg :	466 1128 30
Your reference:	SL41
Purchase order no:	93754

Code	Description	Quantity	VAT rate %	Unit price £	Amount excl of VAT £
G4030	Garland Keyboard	4	20	105.00	420.00
					420.00
Trade discount 10%					42.00
					378.00
VAT					75.60
Total amount payable					453.60

Prompt payment discount of 3% if paid within 10 days, net 30 days

Test your understanding 14

Ellis Electricals makes the following credit sales to A and B giving a 20% trade discount plus a 5% prompt payment discount if customers pay their invoices within 5 days.

	Customer A £	Customer B £
Sales value	1,000	4,000
Trade discount (20%)	200	800
	——	——
Net sales value	800	3,200
VAT (calculated on the net sales value after deducting the trade discount)		
Customer A: (800 × 20%)	160	
Customer B: (3,200 × 20%)		640
	——	——
Total invoice value	960	3,840
	——	——

Ellis Electricals also makes a cash sale to C for £300 plus VAT at 20%.

Prompt payment discount is only deducted upon the receivable making payment within the discount period.

Customer A pays his invoice in full within 5 days and takes the prompt payment discount. Customer B pays £2,000 on account.

Task

Write up the sales day book, the cash receipts book and the discounts allowed book and post the entries to the general and sales ledgers.

Test your understanding 15

Given below is the debit side of the cash book and the discount allowed book completed for transactions that took place on 15 May:

CASH BOOK – DEBIT SIDE			
Date	Narrative	SL Code	Bank £
20X1			
15/5	McCaul & Partners	M04	117.60
	P Martin	M02	232.80
	F Little	L03	93.12
			443.52

DISCOUNTS ALLOWED BOOK					
Date	Customer	SL Code	Total £	VAT £	Net £
20X1					
15/5	McCaul & Partners	M04	2.40	0.40	2.00
	P Martin	M02	7.20	1.20	6.00
	F Little	L03	2.88	0.48	2.40
			12.48	2.08	10.40

Required:

Show what the entries in the sales ledger will be:

Account name	Amount £	Dr ✓	Cr ✓

Show what the entries in the general ledger will be:

Account name	Amount £	Dr ✓	Cr ✓

Test your understanding 16

Given below are three invoices received by Nethan Builders that are to be paid today, 18 May 20X1. It is the business policy to take advantage of any prompt payments discounts possible.

You are required to complete a remittance advice for each payment. The last cheque used was number 200549.

INVOICE

Invoice to:
Nethan Builders
Brecon House
Stamford Road
Manchester
M16 4PL

Building Contract Supplies
Unit 15
Royal Estate
Manchester
M13 2EF
Tel: 0161 562 3041
Fax: 0161 562 3042

Deliver to:
As above

Invoice no:	07742
Tax point:	8 May 20X1
VAT reg no:	776 4983 06

Code	Description	Quantity	VAT rate %	Unit price £	Amount excl of VAT £
SDGSL6	SDGS Softwood 47 × 225 mm	20.5 m	20	8.30	170.15
					170.15
VAT					34.03
Total amount payable					204.18

Prompt payment discount of 1½% if paid within 14 days

INVOICE

Jenson Ltd
30 Longfield Park, Kingsway
M45 2TP
Tel: 0161 511 4666
Fax: 0161 511 4777

Invoice to:
Nethan Builders
Brecon House
Stamford Road
Manchester
M16 4PL

Deliver to:
As above

Invoice no:	47811
Tax point:	5 May 20X1
VAT reg no:	641 3229 45
Purchase order no:	7174

Code	Description	Quantity	VAT rate %	Unit price £	Amount excl of VAT £
PL432115	Door Lining set 32 × 115 mm	6	20	30.25	181.50
					181.50
Trade discount 15%					27.22
					154.28
VAT					30.85
Total amount payable					185.13

Prompt payment discount of 3% if paid within 10 days

INVOICE

Magnum Supplies
140/150 Park Estate
Manchester
M20 6EG
Tel: 0161 561 3202
Fax: 0161 561 3200

Invoice to:
Nethan Builders
Brecon House
Stamford Road
Manchester
M16 4PL

Deliver to:
As above

Invoice no:	077422
Tax point:	11 May 20X1
VAT reg no:	611 4337 90

Code	Description	Quantity	VAT rate %	Unit price £	Amount excl of VAT £
BH47732	House Bricks – Red	600	20	1.24	744.00
					744.00
Trade discount 15%					111.60
					632.40
VAT					126.48
Total amount payable					758.88

Prompt payment discount of 2% if paid within 10 days

REMITTANCE ADVICE

To:

Nethan Builders
Brecon House
Stamford House
Manchester
M16 4PL

Tel:	0161 521 6411
Fax:	0161 530 6412
VAT reg:	471 3860 42
Date:	

Date	Invoice no	Amount £	Discount taken £	Paid £

Total paid	£
Cheque no	

REMITTANCE ADVICE

To:

Nethan Builders
Brecon House
Stamford House
Manchester
M16 4PL

Tel:	0161 521 6411
Fax:	0161 530 6412
VAT reg:	471 3860 42
Date:	

Date	Invoice no	Amount £	Discount taken £	Paid £

Total paid	£
Cheque no	

	REMITTANCE ADVICE			
To:		Nethan Builders Brecon House Stamford House Manchester M16 4PL Tel: 0161 521 6411 Fax: 0161 530 6412 VAT reg: 471 3860 42 Date:		

Date	Invoice no	Amount £	Discount taken £	Paid £

Total paid   £

Cheque no

Test your understanding 17

Given below is a business' petty cash book for the week.

Petty cash book											
Receipts			Payments								
Date	Narrative	Total	Date	Details	Voucher no	Amount	Postage	Staff welfare	Station-ery	Travel expenses	VAT
						£	£	£	£	£	£
5/1/X1	Bal b/d	150.00	12/1/X1	Postage	03526	13.68	13.68				
				Staff welfare	03527	25.00		25.00			
				Stationery	03528	15.12			12.60		2.52
				Taxi fare	03529	12.25				10.21	2.04
				Staff welfare	03530	6.40		6.40			
				Postage	03531	12.57	12.57				
				Rail fare	03532	6.80				6.80	
				Stationery	03533	8.16			6.80		1.36
				Taxi fare	03534	19.20				16.00	3.20
				Bal c/d		30.82					
						150.00	26.25	31.40	19.40	33.01	9.12

Required:

NB: The petty cash book also forms part of the general ledger. Show what the entries in the general ledger will be:

Account name	Amount £	Dr ✓	Cr ✓

Test your understanding 18

Given below is a completed petty cash book for transactions that took place on 12 April 20X1:

	Petty cash book										
Receipts			Payments								
Date	Narrative	Total	Date	Narrative	Voucher no	Total	Postage	Staff welfare	Stationery	Travel expenses	VAT
						£	£	£	£	£	£
12/04	Bal b/d	100.00	12/04	Coffee/milk	2534	4.68		4.68			
				Postage	2535	13.26	13.26				
				Stationery	2536	10.48			8.74		1.74
				Taxi fare	2537	15.32				12.77	2.55
				Postage	2538	6.75	6.75				
				Train fare	2539	7.40				7.40	
				Stationery	2540	3.94			3.29		0.65
				Bal c/d		38.17					
						100.00	20.01	4.68	12.03	20.17	4.94

Required:

Post the required entries to the general ledger accounts:

Postage

	£		£
Balance b/d	231.67		

Staff welfare

	£		£
Balance b/d	334.78		

Stationery

	£		£
Balance b/d	53.36		

Travel expenses

	£		£
Balance b/d	579.03		

VAT account

	£		£
		Balance b/d	967.44

Test your understanding 19

A business runs its petty cash on an imprest system with an imprest amount of £100 per week.

At the end of the week ending 22 May 20X1 the vouchers in the petty cash box were:

Voucher no	£
02634	13.73
02635	8.91
02636	10.57
02637	3.21
02638	11.30
02639	14.66

The cash remaining in the petty cash box was made up as follows:

£10 note	1
£5 note	2
£2 coin	3
£1 coin	7
50p coin	5
20p coin	4
10p coin	1
5p coin	2
2p coin	3
1p coin	6

You are required to reconcile the petty cash in the box to the vouchers in the box at 22 May 20X1 and if it does not reconcile to suggest reasons for the difference.

8 Summary

This chapter has reviewed over all aspects of making and receiving payments. The previous chapters have taken us through making credit sales and credit purchases, the documents and processes involved and how to record these transactions in the general and subsidiary ledgers.

In this chapter we have completed the sales and purchases cycle by reviewing the purpose and content of statements of accounts for receivables and from payables, what a remittance advice is and how to enter transactions into the cash books and discounts day book and make entries from those day books to the general and subsidiary ledgers. Finally, the chapter reviewed the maintenance of a petty cash system.

Test your understanding answers

 Test your understanding 1

Thames Traders

To: Jack Johnson

Date: 31 May 20X6:

STATEMENT

Date	Transaction	Debit £	Credit £	Balance £
03 May	Inv 1848	38.79		38.79
07 May	Inv 1863	50.70		89.49
08 May	CN 446		12.40	77.09
10 May	Inv 1870	80.52		157.61
15 May	Payment		77.09	80.52
18 May	Inv 1881	42.40		122.92
23 May	Inv 1892	61.20		184.12
24 May	CN 458		16.50	167.62
30 May	Inv 1904	27.65		195.27

May we remind you that our credit terms are 30 days

 Test your understanding 2

False. A remittance advice is a slip that the customer can send back to the supplier with his payment to identify what the payment is for.

Test your understanding 3

(a) No

(b) Any two from the following:

(i) The cheque has not been signed.

(ii) The cheque is out of date.

(iii) The words and figures on the cheque are not the same.

Test your understanding 4

The entries in the sales ledger will be:

Account name	Amount £	Dr ✓	Cr ✓
G Hunt	114		✓
L Tessa	110		✓
J Dent	342		✓
F Trainer	97		✓
A Winter	105		✓
G Hunt	6		✓
J Dent	18		✓

The entries in the general ledger for the cash receipts book will be:

Account name	Amount £	Dr ✓	Cr ✓
Bank	888	✓	
Sales ledger control account (receivables)	768		✓
Sales	100		✓
VAT	20		✓

The entries in the general ledger for the discounts allowed book will be:

Account name	Amount £	Dr ✓	Cr ✓
Discounts allowed	20	✓	
VAT	4	✓	
Sales ledger control account (receivables)	24		✓

Test your understanding 5

The entries in the purchases ledger will be:

Account name	Amount £	Dr ✓	Cr ✓
Homer Ltd	176.40	✓	
Forker & Co	285.18	✓	
Print Ass.	190.45	✓	
ABG Ltd	220.67	✓	
G Greg	67.89	✓	
Homer Ltd	3.60	✓	
Forker & Co	8.82	✓	

The above entries in the purchases ledger are for the cash payments made and the discounts received from the suppliers.

The entries in the general ledger for the cash payments book will be:

Account name	Amount £	Dr ✓	Cr ✓
Bank	1480.59		✓
PLCA	940.59	✓	
Purchases	450.00	✓	
VAT	90.00	✓	

The entries in the general ledger for the discounts received day book will be:

Account name	Amount £	Dr ✓	Cr ✓
Discounts received	10.35		✓
VAT	2.07		✓
PLCA	12.42	✓	

Test your understanding 6

Postings to general ledger

Account	Amount	Dr or Cr
Motor vehicle	20,000	Dr
Motor expenses	400	Dr
VAT	80	Dr
PLCA	6,500	Dr

Postings to the purchases ledger

Account	Amount	Dr or Cr
Payable B account	6,500	Dr

Test your understanding 7

Details	Amount £	Debit/Credit
Motor expenses	300	Debit
VAT	60	Debit
Wages	4,785	Debit

Test your understanding 8

(a), (b)

Date	Voucher no	Total £		Production £		Distribution £		Marketing £		Administration £		VAT £	
01/10/X7	6579	19	72							16	44	3	28
04/10/X7	6580	8	75							8	75		
06/10/X7	6581	17	13					17	13				
06/10/X7	6582	16	23					16	23				
06/10/X7	6583	43	75					43	75				
10/10/X7	6584	4	60							4	60		
15/10/X7	6585	4	39	4	39								
17/10/X7	6586	8	47			7	06					1	41
20/10/X7	6587	21	23							21	23		
26/10/X7	6588	8	75							8	75		
		153	02	4	39	7	06	77	11	59	77	4	69

PETTY CASH BOOK – PAYMENTS

(c)

Production expenses account

	£		£
PCB	4.39		

Distribution expenses account

	£		£
PCB	7.06		

Marketing expenses account

	£		£
PCB	77.11		

Administration expenses account

	£		£
PCB	59.77		

VAT account

	£		£
PCB	4.69		

Test your understanding 9

Notes and coins

	£	£
£5 × 2	10.00	
£1 × 3	3.00	
50p × 5	2.50	
20p × 4	0.80	
10p × 6	0.60	
5p × 7	0.35	
2p × 10	0.20	
1p × 8	0.08	
		17.53

Vouchers

	£	£
2143	10.56	
2144	3.30	
2145	9.80	
2146	8.44	
2147	2.62	
2148	6.31	
2149	1.44	
		42.47
Imprest amount		60.00

Test your understanding 10

To: Grant & Co

FARMHOUSE PICKLES LTD

225 School Lane
Weymouth
Dorset
WE36 5NR
Tel: 0261 480444
Fax: 0261 480555
Date: 30 April 20X1

STATEMENT

Date	Transaction	Debit £	Credit £	Balance £
1 April	Opening balance			337.69
4 April	Inv 32656	150.58		488.27
12 April	Credit 0335		38.70	449.57
18 April	Inv 32671	179.52		629.09
20 April	Payment		330.94	298.15
20 April	Discount		6.75	291.40
24 April	Credit 0346		17.65	273.75
25 April	Inv 32689	94.36		368.11

May we remind you that our credit terms are 30 days

FARMHOUSE PICKLES LTD

225 School Lane
Weymouth
Dorset
WE36 5NR
Tel: 0261 480444
Fax: 0261 480555
Date: 30 April 20X1

To: Mitchell Partners

STATEMENT

Date	Transaction	Debit £	Credit £	Balance £
1 April	Opening balance			180.46
7 April	Inv 32662	441.57		622.03
12 April	Credit 0344		66.89	555.14
20 April	Inv 32669	274.57		829.71
21 April	Payment		613.58	216.13
21 April	Discount		8.45	207.68

May we remind you that our credit terms are 30 days

 Test your understanding 11

Ryan's Toy Shop LTD
125 Finchley Way Bristol BS1 4PL Tel: 01272 200299

STATEMENT OF ACCOUNT

Customer name Arnold's Toys Ltd
Customer address 14 High Street, Bristol, BS2 5FL

Statement date 1st December		Amount		Balance	
Date	**Transaction**	**£**	**p**	**£**	**p**
19/11	Invoice 2195	118	08	118	08
20/11	Invoice 2198	2,201	95	2,320	03
20/11	Credit note 2198	323	60	1,996	43
22/11	Cheque	118	08	1,878	35
				1,878	35

Test your understanding 12

The following problems exist on the cheques received:

Cheque from K T Lopez – not signed

Cheque from L Garry – post dated

Cheque from L Barrett – made out to wrong name

Cheque from P Ibbott – more than six months old

Cheque from J Lovell – discrepancy between words and figures.

 Test your understanding 13

Cheque from BZS Music – prompt payment discount of £10.37 has been taken – this is valid.

Cheque from Musicolor Ltd – prompt payment discount of £26.41 has been taken – but is not valid as the cheque has been received after 5 days from the invoice date. However, in the interest of good customer relations, perhaps the discount should be granted but the customer should be informed and reminded of the prompt payment discount terms.

Cheque from Harmer & Co – prompt payment discount of £10.59 has been taken – this is valid.

Cheque from Newford Music – prompt payment discount of £28.52 has been taken – this is not valid as the receipt is too late to claim the discount. Again the discount might be granted in the interest of good customer relations but the customer should be informed and reminded of the prompt payment discount terms.

Cheque from Trent Music – prompt payment discount of £15.54 has been taken – however it should have been £13.61 (3% × £453.60). Customer should be informed of the error.

Test your understanding 14

Step 1

Write up the sales day book.

SALES DAY BOOK				
Date	Customer	Total £	VAT £	Sales £
	A	960.00	160.00	800.00
	B	3,840.00	640.00	3,200.00
		4,800.00	800.00	4,000.00

Step 2

Write up the cash receipts book and the discounts allowed book.

CASH RECEIPTS BOOK					
Date	Customer	Total £	VAT £	SLCA £	Cash sales
	A (W)	912.00		912.00	
	B	2,000.00		2,000.00	
	C	360.00	60.00		300.00
		3,272.00	60.00	2,912.00	300.00

DISCOUNTS ALLOWED BOOK				
Date	Customer	Total £	VAT £	Net £
	A (W)	48.00	8.00	40.00
		48.00	8.00	40.00

Working:

Cash paid by A:

	£
Sale value net of VAT	800.00
Less: prompt payment discount (£800 × 5%)	(40.00)
	760.00
VAT (760 × 20%)	152.00
	912.00

The prompt payment discount is:
Net £800 × 5% = £40
VAT £160 × 5% = £8
Gross £48

Step 3

Post the totals to the general ledger. Note that for this example the source of the data (day book references have been used for the narrative), the opposite account posted to is also acceptable.

Sales				VAT			
£		£		£		£	
		SDB	4,000.00	DAB	8.00	SDB	800.00
		CRB	300.00			CRB	60.00

SLCA				Discount allowed			
£		£		£		£	
SDB	4,800.00	CRB	2,912.00	DAB	40.00		
		DAB	48.00				

Step 4

Post individual amounts for the SDB and CRB to the sales ledger.

A				B			
£		£		£		£	
SDB	960.00	CRB	912.00	SDB	3,840.00		2,000.00
		DAB	48.00				

📝 Test your understanding 15

The entries in the sales ledger will be:

Account name	Amount £	Dr ✓	Cr ✓
McCaul & Partners	117.60		✓
P Martin	232.80		✓
F Little	93.12		✓
McCaul & Partners	2.40		✓
P Martin	7.20		✓
F Little	2.88		✓

Show what the entries in the general ledger will be:

Account name	Amount £	Dr ✓	Cr ✓
Discounts allowed	10.40	✓	
VAT	2.08	✓	
Sales ledger control account	12.48		✓
Sales ledger control account	443.52		✓

Test your understanding 16

REMITTANCE ADVICE

To:

Building Contract Supplies
Unit 15 Royal Estate
Manchester
M13 2EF

Nethan Builders
Brecon House
Stamford House
Manchester
M16 4PL

Tel:	0161 521 6411
Fax:	0161 530 6412
VAT reg:	471 3860 42
Date:	18 May 20X1

Date	Invoice no	Amount £	Discount taken £	Paid £
8 May 20X1	07742	204.18	3.06	201.12

Total paid	£201.12
Cheque no	200550

REMITTANCE ADVICE

To:

Jenson Ltd
30 Longfield Park
Kingsway
M45 2TP

Nethan Builders
Brecon House
Stamford House
Manchester
M16 4PL

Tel: 0161 521 6411
Fax: 0161 530 6412
VAT reg: 471 3860 42
Date: 18 May 20X1

Date	Invoice no	Amount £	Discount taken £	Paid £
5 May 20X1	47811	185.13		185.13

	Total paid	£185.13
	Cheque no	200551

REMITTANCE ADVICE

To:

Magnum Supplies
140/150 Park Estate
Manchester
M20 6EG

Nethan Builders
Brecon House
Stamford House
Manchester
M16 4PL

Tel: 0161 521 6411
Fax: 0161 530 6412
VAT reg: 471 3860 42
Date: 18 May 20X1

Date	Invoice no	Amount £	Discount taken £	Paid £
11 May 20X1	077422	758.88	15.18	743.70

	Total paid	£743.70
	Cheque no	200552

Test your understanding 17

The entries in the general ledger will be:

Account name	Amount £	Dr ✓	Cr ✓
Postage	26.25	✓	
Staff welfare	31.40	✓	
Stationery	19.40	✓	
Travel expenses	33.01	✓	
VAT	9.12	✓	

Test your understanding 18

Postage

	£		£
Balance b/d	231.67		
PCB	20.01		

Staff welfare

	£		£
Balance b/d	334.78		
PCB	4.68		

Stationery

	£		£
Balance b/d	53.36		
PCB	12.03		

Travel expenses

	£		£
Balance b/d	579.03		
PCB	20.17		

VAT account

	£		£
PCB	4.94	Balance b/d	967.44

Test your understanding 19

Voucher total

	£
02634	13.73
02635	8.91
02636	10.57
02637	3.21
02638	11.30
02639	14.66
	62.38

Cash total

		£
£10 note	1	10.00
£5 note	2	10.00
£2 coin	3	6.00
£1 coin	7	7.00
50p coin	5	2.50
20p coin	4	0.80
10p coin	1	0.10
5p coin	2	0.10
2p coin	3	0.06
1p coin	6	0.06
		36.62

Reconciliation of cash and vouchers at 22 May 20X1

	£
Voucher total	62.38
Cash total	36.62
	99.00

The reconciliation shows that there is £1 missing. More cash has been paid out of the petty cash box than is supported by the petty cash vouchers. This could be due to a number of reasons:

- A petty cash claim was made out for, say, £11.30 but mistakenly the amount given to the employee was £12.30.

- An employee borrowed £1 from the petty cash box for business expenses and this has not been recorded on a petty cash voucher.

- £1 has been stolen from the petty cash box.

MOCK ASSESSMENT

1 Mock Assessment Questions

Each task is independent.

You must complete all tasks.

Task 1.1 (12 marks)

A sales invoice is being prepared for goods supplied, as shown in the customer order below:

Customer order

ELA Ltd
Order number 154
Please supply: 14 June 20XX
10 units of product VC
@ £40.00 each less 5% trade discount

(a)   Calculate the amounts (pounds and pence) to be included on the invoice: (4 marks)

	£
Net amount before discount	
Net amount after discount	
VAT	
Total	

(b)   What will be the amounts entered in the sales day book when the invoice in (a) is prepared? (3 marks)

Sales day book

Date 20XX	Details	Invoice number	Total £	VAT £	Net £
14 June	ELA Ltd	314			

A cheque for £995 has been received from ELA Ltd which incorrectly states is in full settlement of their account as at 31 May 20XX. The customer's account in the sales ledger is shown below:

ELA Ltd

Date 20XX	Details	Amount £	Date 20XX	Details	Amount £
1 May	Bal b/f	900	4 May	Bank	900
5 May	Invoice 200	600	6 May	Credit note 34	12
10 May	Invoice 232	1,010	18 May	Credit note 39	300
12 May	Invoice 237	532			
29 May	Invoice 289	285			

(c) Show which THREE transactions are still outstanding by circling the relevant transactions shown below: (3 marks)

Transactions

Bal b/f   Credit note 39

                      Invoice 289

         Credit note 34

Bank   Invoice 237

               Invoice 232

                      Invoice 200

A quotation to supply goods for £2,440 plus VAT has been sent to ELA Ltd offering a prompt payment discount of 3% for payment within 5 days of the invoice date.

(d) What will be the amount ELA Ltd will pay if they purchase the goods and pay within 5 days of the invoice date? (2 marks)

£

Task 1.2 (9 marks)

The invoice and purchase order below relate to goods received from LGJ Ltd.

Invoice:

```
                        LGJ Ltd
            VAT registration 369 4577 00
                 Invoice number 231
To: T Blossom        5 May 20XX
                                              £

200 product code 156CC @ £1.50 each         300
VAT @ 20%                                     60
                                        _____
Total                                        360
Terms: 30 days
```

Purchase order:

```
              T Blossom
          Order number 756
                   4 May 20XX
Please supply:
200 units of product 156CC
@ £1.70 each less 5% trade
discount
Terms: 30 days
```

(a) Identify any discrepancies on the invoice by placing a tick in the appropriate box in the table set out below: (4 marks)

	Correctly shown on invoice	Not shown on invoice	Incorrectly shown on invoice
Product code			
Unit price			
Terms of payment			
Trade discount			

The invoice below has been received from Carrera Ltd.

Invoice:

Carrera Ltd

VAT registration 446 4482 01

Invoice number 54879

To: T Blossom   15 May 20XX

	£
350 product code 546TC @ £1.25 each	437.50
VAT @ 20%	87.50
Total	525.00

Terms: Net monthly account

(b)   Record the invoice in the appropriate day book by: (5 marks)

- Inserting the correct day book title (in the first row):

Select from: sales day book, purchases day book, discounts allowed day book, discounts received day book, sales returns day book, purchases returns day book.

- Inserting the correct details:

Select from: Carrera Ltd, T Blossom

- Making the necessary entries.

Date 20XX	Details	Invoice number	Total £	VAT £	Net £
15 May		54879			

Task 1.3 (9 marks)

Shown below is a statement of account received from a credit supplier, Spence & Co and the supplier's account as shown in the purchases ledger of Alfie Electricals.

<table>
<tr><td colspan="6" align="center">**Spence & Co**</td></tr>
<tr><td colspan="6" align="center">**42 Armour Lane, Kilwinning, KA16 7YH**</td></tr>
<tr><td colspan="6">To: Alfie Electricals</td></tr>
<tr><td colspan="6">1 Albert Street</td></tr>
<tr><td colspan="6">Edinburgh, EH1 4BH</td></tr>
<tr><td colspan="6" align="center">STATEMENT OF ACCOUNT</td></tr>
<tr><td>Date
20X2</td><td>Invoice
number</td><td>Details</td><td>Invoice
amount
£</td><td>Cheque
amount
£</td><td>Balance
£</td></tr>
<tr><td>1 Oct</td><td>232</td><td>Goods</td><td>900</td><td></td><td>900</td></tr>
<tr><td>5 Nov</td><td>248</td><td>Goods</td><td>400</td><td></td><td>1,300</td></tr>
<tr><td>6 Nov</td><td>269</td><td>Goods</td><td>300</td><td></td><td>1,600</td></tr>
<tr><td>23 Nov</td><td>–</td><td>Cheque</td><td></td><td>900</td><td>700</td></tr>
<tr><td>26 Nov</td><td>299</td><td>Goods</td><td>100</td><td></td><td>800</td></tr>
</table>

Spence & Co

Date 20X2	Details	Amount £	Date 20X2	Details	Amount £
23 Nov	Bank	900	1 Oct	Purchases	900
26 Nov	Bank	700	5 Nov	Purchases	400
			6 Nov	Purchases	300

(a) Which item is missing from the statement of account from Spence & Co and which item is missing from the supplier account in Alfie Electricals? (3 marks)

Item missing from the statement of account from Spence & Co:

Select your account name from the following list: Invoice 232, Invoice 248, Invoice 269, Invoice 299, Cheque for £700, Cheque for £900

Item missing from the supplier account in Alfie Electricals purchases ledger:

Select your account name from the following list: Invoice 232, Invoice 248, Invoice 269, Invoice 299, Cheque for £700, Cheque for £900

(b)   Assuming any differences between the statement of account from Spence & Co and the supplier account in Alfie Electricals purchases ledger are simply due to omission errors, what is the amount owing to Spence & Co? (1 mark)

£

This is the account of RR & Co in the purchases ledger and a credit note that has been received from the supplier but not yet entered into their account.

RR & Co

Date 20X2	Details	Amount £	Date 20X2	Details	Amount £
3 Nov	Bank	1,500	1 Nov	Balance b/f	1,840
3 Nov	Credit note 50	100	3 Nov	Invoice 134	550
			4 Nov	Invoice 148	700
			5 Nov	Invoice 176	860

Credit note:

RR & Co

VAT registration 432 4577 00

Credit note number 56

To: Alfie Electricals   6 November 20XX

For return of goods on invoice 132

	£
10 product code A132 @ £20 each	200
VAT @ 20%	40
Total	240
Terms: 30 days	

(c) What will be the amount owed to RR & Co once the credit note has been entered into their account? (1 mark)

£

The two invoices below were received on 7 November from credit suppliers who offer prompt payment discounts.

Invoices:

Hudson & Co	
VAT registration 446 4852 01	
Invoice number 15963	
To: Alfie Electricals 6 November 20XX	
	£
10 product code 517 @ £63.50 each	635.00
VAT @ 20%	127.00
	———
Total	762.00

Terms: 3% prompt payment discount if payment is received within 5 days of the invoice date.

Marsh & Co	
VAT registration 446 4982 01	
Invoice number 986	
To: Alfie Electricals 6 November 20XX	
	£
32 product code 121 @ £57.25 each	1,832.00
VAT @ 20%	366.40
	———
Total	2,198.40

Terms: 2.5% prompt payment discount if payment is received within 10 days of the invoice date.

(d) Calculate the amount to be paid to each supplier if the prompt payment discount is taken and show the date by which the supplier should receive the payment. (4 marks)

Supplier	£	Date by which the payment should be received by the supplier
Hudson & Co		
Marsh & Co		

Task 1.4 (15 marks)

There are five payments to be entered in Adams & Son's cash-book.

Receipts

Received cash with thanks for goods bought.	Received cash with thanks for goods bought.	Received cash with thanks for goods bought.
From Adams & Son, a customer without a credit account.	From Adams & Son, a customer without a credit account.	From Adams & Son, a customer without a credit account.
Net £400	Net £320	Net £350
VAT £80	VAT £64	(No VAT)
Total £480	Total £384	
Johnson Ltd	*A Alpha*	*Bond's*

Cheque book counterfoils

ABC Ltd (Purchase ledger account ABC006)	Twilight (Purchase ledger account TWI001)
£2,000	£240
000123	000124

(a) Enter the details from the three receipts and two cheque book stubs into the credit side of the cash-book shown below and total each column. (7 marks)

Cash-book – credit side

Details	Cash	Bank	VAT	Payables	Cash purchases
Balance b/f					
Johnson Ltd					
A Alpha					
Bond's					
ABC Ltd					
Twilight					
Total					

There are two cheques from credit customers to be entered in Adam & Son's cash book:

Rhoda Ring   £560

Reef   £210

(b) Enter the above details into the debit side of the cash-book and total each column. (6 marks)

Cash book – debit side

Details	Cash	Bank	Receivables
Balance b/f	1,500	11,710	
Rhoda Ring			
Reef			
Total			

(c) Using your answers to (a) and (b) above, calculate the cash balance. (1 mark)

£

Using your answers to (a) and (b) above, calculate the bank balance. Use a minus sign if your calculations indicate an overdrawn balance, e.g. –123 (1 mark)

£

Task 1.5 (15 marks)

This is an extract of the petty cash book containing transactions for the month of June made by an organisation. The organisation maintains an imprest system level of £200.00 on the last day of each month.

Date	Details	Amount £	Date	Details	Amount £	VAT £	Carriage and postage £	Travel £	Office Expenses £
1 Jun	Bal b/f	200.00	5 Jun	Mick Ltd	24.00	4.00		20.00	
			17 Jun	R Walsh	22.80	3.80	19.00		
			21 Jun	Office Supplies Ltd	26.40	4.40			22.00
			28 Jun	Stationery Stop	20.88	3.48			17.40

(a) What will be the entry in the petty cash book to restore to the imprest level on 30th June? (3 marks)

Details	Amount £	Debit ✓	Credit ✓

Details picklist: Amount, Balance b/d, Balance c/d, Cash from bank

(b) What will be the entry in the petty cash book to record the closing balance on 30th June after the imprest level has been restored? (3 marks)

Details	Amount £	Debit ✓	Credit ✓

Details picklist: Amount, Balance b/d, Balance c/d, Cash from bank

(c) What will be the total of the Office Expenses column in the petty cash book? (1 mark)

£ [   ]

It is now 3rd July and the petty cash vouchers below require entry into the petty cash book:

Petty cash voucher 285	Petty cash voucher 286
3rd July	3rd July
Your Office – A4 paper 5 × 500 sheets	Speedy Delivery – Courier services
£13.50 including VAT	£27.50 plus VAT

(d) What will be the total, VAT and net amounts to be entered into the petty cash book? (6 marks)

Petty cash voucher number	Total £	VAT £	Net £
285			
286			

(e) What analysis columns in the petty cash book will be used to record the net amounts of the petty cash payments detailed in (d)? (2 marks)

Petty cash voucher number	Analysis column
285	
286	

Analysis column picklist: Amount, Carriage and postage, Office expenses, Travel, VAT

Task 1.6 (12 marks)

These are the totals of the discounts allowed day book at the end of the month.

Details	Total £	VAT £	Net £
Totals	600	100	500

(a)   What will be the entries in the general ledger? (9 marks)

Account name	Amount £	Debit ✓	Credit ✓

Select your account name from the following list: Discounts allowed, Discounts received, Purchases, Purchases ledger control, Purchases returns, Sales, Sales ledger control, Sales returns, VAT

One of the entries in the discounts allowed day book is for a credit note sent to Johnson Cooper for £60 plus VAT.

(b)   What will be the entry in the sales ledger? (3 marks)

Account name	Amount £	Debit ✓	Credit ✓

Select your account name from the following list: Discounts allowed, Discounts received, Johnson Cooper, Purchases, Purchases ledger control, Purchases returns, Sales, Sales ledger control, Sales returns, VAT

Task 1.7 (12 marks)

The following transactions all took place on 31 December and have been entered in the cash-book as shown below – the debit side and credit side have been shown separately. No entries have yet been made in the ledgers.

Cash-book – Debit side

Date 20X1	Details	Bank £
31 Dec	Balance b/f	3,110
31 Dec	Paul Bros (trade receivable)	500

Cash-book – Credit side

Date 20X1	Details	VAT £	Bank £
31 Dec	Office expenses	30	180
31 Dec	Travel expenses		48

What will be the entries in the general ledger? (12 marks)

Select your account name from the following list: Balance b/f, Bank, Entertainment, Insurance, Office expenses, Purchases ledger control, Sales ledger control, Travel expenses, VAT

Account name	Amount £	Debit ✓	Credit ✓

Task 1.8 (12 marks)

The following two accounts are in the general ledger of Brooklyn Boats at the close of day on 31 December.

Motor vehicles

Date 20XX	Details	Amount £	Date 20XX	Details	Amount £
01 Dec	Balance b/f	12,500			
12 Dec	Bank	7,000			

Loan from the bank

Date 20XX	Details	Amount £	Date 20XX	Details	Amount £
5 Dec	Bank	500	1 Dec	Bal b/f	10,000

(a) What will be the balance brought down at 1 January on each account. (4 marks)

Account name	Balance b/d at 1 January £	Debit ✓	Credit ✓
Motor vehicles			
Loan from the bank			

(b) The following account is in the general ledger of ABC Ltd at the close of day on 31 December.

Complete the account below by:

- Inserting the balance carried down together with date and details.

- Inserting the totals.

- Inserting the balance brought down together with date and details. (8 marks)

Electricity

Date 20XX	Details	Amount £	Date 20XX	Details	Amount £
01 Dec	Balance b/f	870			
12 Dec	Bank	350			
	Total			**Total**	

Picklist: Balance b/d, Balance c/d, Bank, Closing balance, Opening balance, Purchases ledger control

Task 1.9 (12 marks)

Below is a partially prepared trial balance as at 31st December 20XX.

(a) Insert the total of the debit and credit columns of the partially prepared trial balance. (2 marks)

Account name	Debit £	Credit £
Sales revenue		646,818
Sales returns	135,629	
Purchases	273,937	
Purchases returns		1,348
Discounts received		1,700
Discounts allowed	2,340	
Wages	152,099	
Motor expenses	2,853	
Office sundries	14,579	
Rent and rates	7,345	
Advertising	1,452	
Totals		

The remainder of the balances have now been extracted from the accounting records.

(b) Complete the trial balance by transferring the relevant amounts to the debit or credit column. Do not enter a zero in the unused cells. (10 marks)

General ledger	£
Inventory	28,814
Sales ledger control	172,696
Purchases ledger control	75,987
VAT owed to tax authorities	63,252
Capital	28,352
Hotel expenses	1,785
Motor vehicles	?
Bank loan	?

Other balances	£
Petty cash book	200
Cash book	10,222

The account balances for motor vehicles and the bank loan were missed from the general ledger accounts' listing above, however the ledger accounts have been provided below:

Motor vehicles

Date 20XX	Details	Amount £	Date 20XX	Details	Amount £
1 Dec	Bal b/f	20,500	31 Dec	Bal c/d	30,927
5 Dec	Bank	10,427			
		30,927			30,927

Bank loan

Date 20XX	Details	Amount £	Date 20XX	Details	Amount £
28 Dec	Bank	579	1 Dec	Bal b/f	18,000
31 Dec	Bal c/d	17,421			
		18,000			18,000

Account name	Debit £	Credit £
Motor vehicles		
Inventory		
Bank		
Petty cash control		
Sales ledger control		
Purchases ledger control		
VAT owed to tax authorities		
Capital		
Bank loan		
Sales revenue		646,818
Sales returns	135,629	
Purchases	273,937	
Purchases returns		1,348
Discounts received		1,700
Discounts allowed	2,340	
Wages	152,099	
Motor expenses	2,853	
Office sundries	14,579	
Rent and rates	7,345	
Advertising	1,452	
Hotel expenses		

Task 1.10 (12 marks)

Earl & Robinson, code all purchase invoices with a supplier code AND a general ledger code. A selection of the codes used is given below.

Supplier	Supplier account code
Alpha Ltd	ALP21
Burton Products	BUR14
Cuddington Couriers	CUD22
Farrah Ltd	FAR13
Jacob Brothers	JAC17

Item	General ledger code
Pasta	GL12
Tomatoes	GL14
Herbs	GL21
Cheese	GL23
Wine	GL34

This is an invoice received from a supplier.

Jacob Brothers **19 Clough Road, Sale M34 5HY** **VAT Registration No. 349 2354 13**

Earl & Robinson

42 Maple Street
Audenshaw, M11 2SQ   20 March 20X2

500 ....Tins of tomatoes @ £0.15 each   £75

VAT   £15

Total   £90

(a)   Select which codes would be used to code this invoice. (2 marks)

Supplier account code	Select your account code from the following list: ALP21, BUR14, CUD22, FAR13, JAC17, GL12, GL14, GL21, GL23, GL34
General ledger code	Select your account code from the following list: ALP21, BUR14, CUD22, FAR13, JAC17, GL12, GL14, GL21, GL23, GL34

One customer has been offered a prompt payment discount for payment within 5 days.

(b) Show what TWO actions should be taken if the customer does pay within 5 days. (2 marks)

Action	✓
Issue a credit note for the discount taken plus VAT.	
Issue a new invoice for the amount paid.	
Change the amounts of the original invoice.	
Record the amount received in the appropriate day books and ledgers.	

A business has the following assets and liabilities.

Assets and liabilities	£
Land & Buildings	545,000
Cash at bank	12,547
Loan from bank	25,879
Plant & Machinery	35,489
Receivables	24,056
Payables	17,697

(c) Show the accounting equation by inserting the appropriate figures. Enter all figures as positive values. (3 marks)

Assets £	Liabilities £	Capital £

(d) Select one option in each instance below to show whether the item will be capital expenditure, revenue expenditure, capital income or revenue income. (5 marks)

Item	Capital expenditure	Revenue expenditure	Capital income	Revenue income
Purchase of stationery				
Receipts from cash sales				
Receipt from sale of machinery				
Purchase of additional machinery				
Payment of rates				

2 Mock Assessment Answers

Task 1.1 (12 marks)

(a) Calculate the amounts (pounds and pence) to be included on the invoice: (4 marks)

	£
Net amount before discount	400.00
Net amount after discount	380.00
VAT	76.00
Total	456.00

(b) What will be the amounts entered in the sales day book when the invoice in (a) is prepared? (3 marks)

Sales day book

Date 20XX	Details	Invoice number	Total £	VAT £	Net £
14 June	ELA Ltd	314	456.00	76.00	380.00

(c) Show which THREE transactions are still outstanding by circling the relevant transactions shown below: (3 marks)

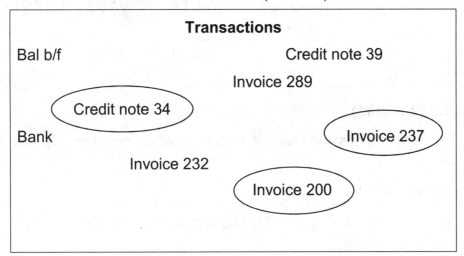

(d) What will be the amount ELA Ltd will pay if they purchase the goods and pay within 5 days of the invoice date? (2 marks)

£2,840.16

Task 1.2 (9 marks)

(a)   Identify any discrepancies on the invoice by placing a tick in the appropriate box in the table set out below: (4 marks)

	Correctly shown on invoice	Not shown on invoice	Incorrectly shown on invoice
Product code	✓		
Unit price			✓
Terms of payment	✓		
Trade discount		✓	

(b)   Record the invoice in the appropriate day book by: (5 marks)

- Inserting the correct day book title (in the first row):

Select from: sales day book, purchases day book, discounts allowed day book, discounts received day book, sales returns day book, purchases returns day book

- Inserting the correct details:

Select from: Carrera Ltd, T Blossom

- Making the necessary entries.

Purchases day book					
Date 20XX	Details	Invoice number	Total £	VAT £	Net £
15 May	Carrera Ltd	54879	525.00	87.50	437.50

Task 1.3 (9 marks)

(a)   Which item is missing from the statement of account from Spence & Co?

Cheque for £700

Which item is missing from the supplier account in Alfie Electricals purchases ledger?

Invoice 299

(b) Assuming any differences between the statement of account from Spence & Co and the supplier account in Alfie Electricals purchases ledger are simply due to omission errors, what is the amount owing to Spence & Co?

£100

(c) What will be the amount owed to RR & Co once the credit note has been entered into their account? (1 mark)

£2,110

(d) Calculate the amount to be paid to each supplier if the prompt payment discount is taken and show the date by which the supplier should receive the payment. (4 marks)

Supplier	£	Date by which the payment should be received by the supplier
Hudson & Co	739.14	11 November 20XX
Marsh & Co	2143.44	16 November 20XX

Task 1.4 (15 marks)

(a) Enter the details from the three receipts and two cheque book stubs into the credit side of the cash-book shown below and total each column. (7 marks)

Cash-book – credit side

Details	Cash	Bank	VAT	Payables	Cash purchases
Balance b/f					
Johnson Ltd	480		80		400
A Alpha	384		64		320
Bond's	350		–		350
ABC Ltd		2,000		2,000	
Twilight		240		240	
Total	1,214	2,240	144	2,240	1,070

There are two cheques from credit customers to be entered in Adam & Son's cash book:

Rhoda Ring   £560

Reef   £210

(b) Enter the above details into the debit side of the cash-book and total each column. (6 marks)

Cash book – debit side

Details	Cash	Bank	Receivables
Balance b/f	1,500	11,710	
Rhoda Ring		560	560
Reef		210	210
Total	1,500	12,480	770

(c) Using your answers to (a) and (b) above, calculate the cash balance. (1 mark)

£286

Using your answers to (a) and (b) above, calculate the bank balance. Use a minus sign if your calculations indicate an overdrawn balance, e.g. –123 (1 mark)

£10,240

Task 1.5 (15 marks)

(a) What will be the entry in the petty cash book to restore to the imprest level on 30th June? (3 marks)

Details	Amount £	Debit ✓	Credit ✓
Cash from bank	94.08	✓	

(b) What will be the entry in the petty cash book to record the closing balance on 30th June after the imprest level has been restored? (3 marks)

Details	Amount £	Debit ✓	Credit ✓
Balance c/d	200.00		✓

(c) What will be the total of the Office Expenses column in the petty cash book? (1 mark)

£39.40

(d)   What will be the total, VAT and net amounts to be entered into the petty cash book? (6 marks)

Petty cash voucher number	Total £	VAT £	Net £
285	13.50	2.25	11.25
286	33.00	5.50	27.50

(e)   What analysis columns in the petty cash book will be used to record the net amounts of the petty cash payments detailed in (d)?
(2 marks)

Petty cash voucher number	Analysis column
285	Office expenses
286	Carriage and postage

Task 1.6 (12 marks)

(a)   What will be the entries in the general ledger? (9 marks)

Account name	Amount £	Debit ✔	Credit ✔
Discounts allowed	500	✔	
VAT	100	✔	
Sales ledger control	600		✔

(b)   What will be the entry in the sales ledger? (3 marks)

Account name	Amount £	Debit ✔	Credit ✔
Johnson Cooper	72		✔

Task 1.7 (12 marks)

What will be the entries in the general ledger? (12 marks)

Account name	Amount £	Debit ✓	Credit ✓
Sales ledger control	500		✓
Office expenses	150	✓	
VAT	30	✓	
Travel expenses	48	✓	

Task 1.8 (12 marks)

(a) What will be the balance brought down at 1 January on each account. (4 marks)

Account name	Balance b/d at 1 January £	Debit ✓	Credit ✓
Motor vehicles	19,500	✓	
Loan from the bank	9,500		✓

(b) The following account is in the general ledger of ABC Ltd at the close of day on 31 December.

Complete the account below by:

- Inserting the balance carried down together with date and details.

- Inserting the totals.

- Inserting the balance brought down together with date and details. (8 marks)

Electricity

Date 20XX	Details	Amount £	Date 20XX	Details	Amount £
01 Dec	Balance b/f	870	31 Dec	Balance c/d	1,220
12 Dec	Bank	350			
	Total	1,220		**Total**	1,220
1 Jan	Balance b/d	1,220			

Task 1.9 (12 marks)

(a)   Insert the total of the debit and credit columns of the partially
prepared trial balance. (2 marks)

Account name	Debit £	Credit £
Sales revenue		646,818
Sales returns	135,629	
Purchases	273,937	
Purchases returns		1,348
Discounts received		1,700
Discounts allowed	2,340	
Wages	152,099	
Motor expenses	2,853	
Office sundries	14,579	
Rent and rates	7,345	
Advertising	1,452	
Totals	590,234	649,866

(b)   Complete the trial balance by transferring the relevant amounts to the debit or credit column. Do not enter a zero in the unused cells. (10 marks)

Account name	Debit £	Credit £
Motor vehicles	30,927	
Inventory	28,814	
Bank	10,222	
Petty cash control	200	
Sales ledger control	172,696	
Purchases ledger control		75,987
VAT owed to tax authorities		63,252
Capital		28,352
Bank loan		17,421
Sales revenue		646,818
Sales returns	135,629	
Purchases	273,937	
Purchases returns		1,348
Discounts received		1,700
Discounts allowed	2,340	
Wages	152,099	
Motor expenses	2,853	
Office sundries	14,579	
Rent and rates	7,345	
Advertising	1,452	
Hotel expenses	1,785	

NB Although it is not a requirement of the question, the accuracy of the trial balance can be tested by ensuring both the totals of the debit and credit columns agree. In this task both the debit and credit columns total £834,878.

Task 1.10 (12 marks)

(a) Select which codes would be used to code this invoice. (2 marks)

Supplier account code – JAC 17

General ledger code – GL14

(b) Show what TWO actions should be taken if the customer does pay within 5 days. (2 marks)

Action	✓
Issue a credit note for the discount taken plus VAT.	✓
Issue a new invoice for the amount paid.	
Change the amounts of the original invoice.	
Record the amount received in the appropriate day books and ledgers.	✓

(c) Show the accounting equation by inserting the appropriate figures. Enter all figures as positive values. (3 marks)

Assets £	Liabilities £	Capital £
617,092	43,576	573,516

(d) Select one option in each instance below to show whether the item will be capital expenditure, revenue expenditure, capital income or revenue income. (5 marks)

Item	Capital expenditure	Revenue expenditure	Capital income	Revenue income
Purchase of stationery		✓		
Receipts from cash sales				✓
Receipt from sale of machinery			✓	
Purchase of additional machinery	✓			
Payment of rates		✓		

KAPLAN PUBLISHING

INDEX

Advanced Diploma Synoptic

Workbook

Sheriden Amos

Published by Osborne Books Limited
Tel 01905 748071
Email books@osbornebooks.co.uk
Website www.osbornebooks.co.uk

Design by Laura Ingham

Printed by CPI Group (UK) Limited, Croydon, CR0 4YY, on environmentally friendly, acid-free paper from managed forests.

British Library Cataloguing in Publication Data
A catalogue record for this book is available from the British Library

ISBN 978-1-911681-02-1

Contents

Introduction

Qualifications covered

This book has been written specifically to cover the AAT Synoptic Assessment, which is mandatory for the following qualifications:

- AAT Advanced Diploma in Accounting – Level 3
- AAT Advanced Diploma in Accounting at SCQF Level 6

This book provides four full Practice Assessments to prepare students for the Computer-Based Synoptic Assessment. Further details of the content and structure of the book are shown on page 1.

Osborne Study and Revision Materials

Our materials are tailored to the needs of students studying this unit and revising for the assessment. They include:

- **Tutorials:** paperback books with practice activities
- **Wise Guides:** pocket-sized spiral bound revision cards
- **Student Zone:** access to Osborne Books online resources
- **Osborne Books App:** Osborne Books ebooks for mobiles and tablets

Visit www.osbornebooks.co.uk for details of study and revision resources and access to online material.

HOW TO USE THIS SYNOPTIC ASSESSMENT WORKBOOK

INTRODUCTION

The AAT Advanced Diploma in Accounting covers a range of complex accounting tasks, including maintaining cost accounting records and the preparation of reports and returns. It comprises the following four mandatory units:

- Advanced Bookkeeping*
- Final Accounts Preparation*
- Management Accounting: Costing*
- Ethics for Accountants

All of the units within this Advanced Diploma in Accounting are mandatory. Three units are assessed individually in end-of-unit assessments (in the bulleted list above these are indicated with an *). This qualification also includes a synoptic assessment that students sit towards the end of the qualification, which draws on and assesses knowledge and understanding from across all units in the qualification – except Spreadsheets for Accounting and Indirect Tax.

Students must successfully complete all three of the unit assessments, the synoptic assessment, Spreadsheets for Accounting and Indirect Tax to achieve the qualification.

synoptic assessment coverage

One of the units in this qualification is only assessed through the synoptic assessment. This is Ethics for Accountants. However, the synoptic assessment for the Advanced Diploma in Accounting covers four of the mandatory units and has six assessment objectives (AO). These are detailed as follows:

AO1   Demonstrate an understanding of the relevance of the ethical code for accountants, the need to act ethically in a given situation and the appropriate action to take in reporting questionable behaviour.

AO2   Prepare accounting records and respond to errors, omissions and other concerns in accordance with accounting and ethical principles and relevant regulations.

AO3   Demonstrate an understanding of the inter-relationship between the financial accounting and management accounting systems of an organisation and how they can be used to support managers in decision-making.

AO4   Apply ethical and accounting principles when preparing final accounts for different types of organisation, develop ethical courses of action and communicate relevant information effectively.

AO5   Analyse, interpret and report management accounting data.

AO6   Prepare financial accounting information, comprising extended trial balances and final accounts for sole traders and partnerships.

synoptic assessment structure

The synoptic assessment for the Advanced Diploma in Accounting is a computer-based assessment that is partially computer-marked and partially human-marked. The live synoptic assessment is a total of 2 hours and 30 minutes.

what this book contains

This book provides four full Practice Synoptic Assessments to prepare students for the live Computer-Based Synoptic Assessment. They are based directly on the structure, style and content of the sample assessment material provided by the AAT at www.aat.org.uk.

The AAT sample assessment material provides a breakdown of the marks allocated to each task. This helps students to appreciate the relative importance of each task in the assessment and to plan how long to spend on each task. The Practice Synoptic Assessments in this book also show the mark allocation for each task.

Suggested answers to the Practice Synoptic Assessments are set out in this book.

The AAT recommends that students complete all other assessments before attempting the synoptic assessment and there are restrictions in place to prevent premature scheduling of the synoptic assessment. It is suggested that in order to gain maximum benefit from this book students should not attempt these Practice Synoptic Assessments until they have studied all four units and completed the three unit assessments.

Practice synoptic assessment 1

assessment information

Read the scenario carefully before attempting the questions.

Complete all 6 tasks.

Tasks 1 to 6 require you to write your answers in this book.

The total number of marks for this assessment is 80.

Task 3 and Task 4 require extended writing as part of your responses to these questions. You should make sure you allow adequate time to complete these tasks.

Where the date is relevant, it is given in the task data.

Both minus signs and brackets can be used to indicate negative numbers unless task instructions say otherwise.

advice

Read each question carefully before you start to answer it.

Attempt all questions.

You will have 2 hours and 30 minutes to answer all parts of the assessment.

scenario background

Task 1 is based on a work-based scenario separate to the rest of the assessment.

Tasks 2 to 6 are based on the workplace scenario for First Class Flooring.

You are Jo Bradley, a part-qualified accountant who works at First Class Flooring, a partnership making and selling wooden flooring to retailers. The partners, George Walker and Janek Bach, have worked together for many years.

You are responsible for all aspects of accounting and bookkeeping.

Task 1: 15 marks

This task is based on a different workplace scenario to the rest of the assessment.

Bill is an accountant who works for Artons Limited, a large business with a large number of employees. He has just employed Sarah, a part-qualified accountant.

Sarah has been discussing her understanding of the Code of Ethics with Bill.

(a)   Are the following statements true or false?

Statement	True	False
'I will not have to keep so up to date with the latest accounting regulations once I have qualified'		
'I am never allowed to share information I have learned through my job with anyone else'		

(2 marks)

(b)   Show whether the ethical code requires Sarah to take the following actions in order to act in line with the principle of professional behaviour.

Action	Required	Not Required
Comply with all laws that affect Artons Limited		
Report misreporting of information by the Finance Director		

(2 marks)

(c)   Sarah reported being sick one day last week and did not come to work. However, a colleague of Bill's saw her at a local event during that day, with a group of her friends.

Which fundamental principle has Sarah breached?

(a) Integrity	
(b) Professional competence and due care	
(c) Objectivity	

(1 mark)

(d)   When confronted with her breach, Sarah commented that the Sales Director was claiming for petrol on expenses for a car which is not his. Therefore she thought her behaviour was acceptable.

Indicate whether the following statements are true or false.

Statement	True	False
The Sales Director's behaviour indicates unethical leadership of the organisation		
The values and ethics of the Directors will influence the values and actions of staff		

(2 marks)

(e)   Sarah has committed other ethical breaches and is now facing disciplinary action by Artons Limited.

State the action that each organisation below may take against Sarah.

The AAT [may / may not] expel Sarah from the AAT as a result of disciplinary procedures.

Artons Limited [may / may not] bring disciplinary procedures against Sarah.

The National Crime Agency [may / may not] bring disciplinary procedures against Sarah.

(3 marks)

(f)   Syed is an accountant who works for Bodmin Limited reporting to Mo, who is also an accountant. Syed has discovered that Bodmin Limited have been illegally polluting a local stream with waste from their plant. Mo is aware of the pollution, as are the Directors, and has told Syed to ignore it.

What action must Syed now take?

(a)	Inform the directors of the pollution and say that it should stop	
(b)	Follow the internal procedures within Bodmin Limited for reporting unethical behaviour	
(c)	Ignore it	

(2 marks)

(g)   Syed is considering 'whistleblowing' about the pollution to the Environment Agency.

Under what circumstances will Syed be protected from dismissal if he whistleblows?

Circumstance	Protected	Not protected
Syed believes the disclosure to be true		
Syed does not act in good faith		
Syed believes the evidence will be concealed or destroyed		

(3 marks)

Scenario Background (for Tasks 2 – 6)

You are Jo Bradley, a part-qualified accountant who works at First Class Flooring, a partnership making and selling wooden flooring to retailers. The partners, George Walker and Janek Bach, have worked together for many years.

You are responsible for all aspects of accounting and bookkeeping.

Task 2: 12 marks

This task is based on the workplace scenario for First Class Flooring.

Today's date is 15 September 20-9.

You are raising an invoice for a customer that needs to be completed.

To: Flooring Perfection Ltd Wye Valley Road Hereford HE4 2TE	From: First Class Flooring Unit 15 Holwick Industrial Estate Holwick Loop Rd Nottingham NG4 2AB	Invoice Date: 15 September 20-9	Invoice number: 206157
Purchase Order: 6543	Delivery Date: 14 September 20-9		
Description	**Quantity**	**Per Unit** £	£
Product 7987: Oak 2.4m x 100mm x 200mm	100	25.58	2,558.00
		VAT at 20%	
		Total	
VAT Registration number 789 165 078			

(a)   Calculate the VAT to include on this invoice.

£ [   ]

(1 mark)

(b)   Calculate the invoice total.

£ [   ]

(1 mark)

You discover that in the last three months, the Sales Clerk at First Class Flooring, Janet Moran, has raised several invoices for flooring for two employees and has not included any VAT on the sales. This means that the VAT is understated by a significant amount. When you go to discuss the issue with her, she states that she 'thought sales to employees were not VATable' and will 'tell the partners that you told her to treat the sales this way for VAT purposes' as she does not want to lose her job.

(c) Which ethical principles are being broken by Janet Moran? Tick **all** that apply.

(a) Professional competence and due care	
(b) Professional behaviour	
(c) Confidentiality	

(1 mark)

You investigate further and find out that the employees who purchased the flooring were both related to Janet Moran. You now consider it to be deliberate.

(d) Applying the conceptual framework from the ethical code, which one of the following describes the situation faced by Janet Moran when charging VAT on sales to relatives?

(a) A familiarity threat to objectivity	
(b) A self review threat to integrity	
(c) An intimidation threat to professional competence and due care	

(1 mark)

(e) What action should you take?

(a) Send a Suspicious Activity Report to the National Crime Agency	
(b) Tell George and Janek about your concerns	

(1 mark)

(f) Enter each of the figures below into the appropriate place in the statement of profit or loss. You are told products are priced to give a gross profit margin of 20%. Closing inventory equals 30% of the month's sales.

116,856   23,371   93,485   85,548   −35,057

Statement of profit or loss for the period ended 30 September

	£	£
Sales revenue		
Opening inventory		
Purchases		
Less closing inventory		
Cost of sales		
Gross profit		

(3 marks)

(g) Calculate the missing figure for opening inventory.

£ ☐

(1 mark)

(h) Which **one** of the following will have been accounted for in the **purchases figure?**

(a)	Purchase returns	
(b)	Discounts received	
(c)	Discounts allowed	

(1 mark)

(i) Complete the following statement for allowance for doubtful debts.

When the allowance for doubtful debts is increased, there will always / sometimes / never be a negative effect on profit.

(2 marks)

Task 3: 13 marks

(a) You have been informed by George that there is a shortage of prime oak, width 180mm; for this month – only 7000m is available. The production team must choose how much of the two products to produce, the information for which is given below.

	Product 5467	**Product 7685**
Sales price per pack	£75.00	£96.00
Direct materials cost per pack £	£20.00	£36.00
Direct labour per pack £	£25.00	£20.00
Materials per pack in metres	10m	10m
Amount required	500 packs	500 packs

Explain which product should be made and show your workings.

(4 marks)

(b) Identify which of the following is the correct journal for recording the direct labour for this month. Choose **one** option.

Dr Wages control Cr Production	
Dr Production Cr Wages expense	
Dr Production Cr Wages control	
Dr Wages expense Cr Production	

(1 mark)

(c)   Today's date is 28 February 20-9. From the cost accounting records you can see First Class Flooring held 1,000m of 220mm prime oak at the start of February. The cost of the oak was £8,000. In February 20-9, the following movements took place:

12 February – purchased 500 metres for £4,150

18 February – issued 800 metres

22 February – purchased 1,167 metres for £9,920

First Class Flooring use the Average cost (AVCO) method to value inventory. George and Janek would like to know the value of this inventory at the end of February.

(i)   Calculate the value of issues to production in February 20-9 to the nearest £.

£ ⬚

(1 mark)

(ii)   Calculate the value of inventory held on 28 February 20-9 to the nearest £.

£ ⬚

(2 marks)

(d)   Oak prices are increasing and, as a result, the partners are considering changing the method of valuing inventory to the FIFO method.

Explain the effect of changing from Average Cost to FIFO on the **value of issues to production** and **month end inventory value** when prices are rising. Use the information and answers in part (c) to illustrate your answer. You must show any further workings.

(4 marks)

(e)   George and Janek think moving to FIFO will give a higher profit figure for the financial statements at the end of 20-9. Based on your answer in (d), which costing method for valuing inventory will give higher profits in the year end financial statements? Choose **one** option.

First In First Out (FIFO)	
Average Cost	

(1 mark)

Task 4: 15 marks

George and Janek have recently reviewed the service provided by the payroll bureau and have decided to set up an internal payroll in First Class Flooring. They have asked you to find a suitable package and look at running the payroll within the next two months. They have offered you a substantial pay rise for performing these additional duties. You have no experience of payroll but you were hoping for a pay rise as you are in the process of buying your first house.

(a) Describe **two** threats to your ethical principles.

(2 marks)

(b) Describe **two** actions you could take to remain ethical.

(2 marks)

(c)   You have been asked by George and Janek to consider how they could make the business more sustainable.

Give **one** reason why sustainability would be important to First Class Flooring.

(1 mark)

(d)   George Walker has sent you the following email:

EMAIL
To: Jo Bradley **From:** George Walker **Date:** 1 December 20-9 **Subject:** Re – Final Accounts
Hi Jo, I am looking to invest in some new equipment and the bank have asked for a set of accounts, 'produced on the usual going concern basis' and I have no idea what they mean! Could you explain the following: (1)   What is a going concern? Why is it important? (2)   Why should the accounts be produced on this basis? How would they be different if the going concern concept was not used? (3)   Could we send the bank the management accounts, instead of the final year end figures and if not, why not? Many thanks George

Write an email to George explaining the points raised in the above email.

EMAIL

To: George Walker
From: Jo Bradley
Date: 3 December 20-9
Subject: Re – Going Concern and Final Accounts

(10 marks)

Task 5: 12 marks

First Class Flooring are producing a budget for the next quarter ending 31 March 20-9 and would like to know how much profit they might make at different levels of output.

(a) Complete the table for the two alternative levels of output:

	Current budget **7,000**	Option 1 **8,000**	Option 2 **9,000**
Sales	£770,000		
Direct materials	£380,100		
Direct labour	£119,000		
Variable production overheads	£71,400		
Fixed production overheads	£70,000		
Non-production overheads	£80,000		
Operating profit	£49,500		

(7 marks)

(b) George and Janek now consider 8,000 units the most likely level of output for the next quarter and would like you to produce some cost-profit analysis on this.

(i) Calculate the fixed cost per unit for an output of 8,000 units to the nearest penny.

£ [   ]   (1 mark)

(ii) Calculate the variable cost per unit to the nearest penny.

£ [   ]   (1 mark)

(iii) Calculate the contribution per unit to the nearest penny.

£ [   ]   (1 mark)

(iv) Calculate the break-even revenue to the nearest £.

£ [   ]   (1 mark)

(v) Calculate the margin of safety % to one decimal place, based on an output of 8,000 units.

[   ] %.   (1 mark)

Task 6: 13 marks

Today's date is 18 February 20-9. You are now preparing the final accounts for First Class Flooring for the year ended 31 December 20-8.

The statement of profit or loss for First Class Flooring shows a profit for the year ended 31 December 20-8 of £159,950.

The business is still operated as a partnership.

You are given the following information:

- George is entitled to a salary of £20,000 per annum. Janek earns no salary.

- Interest on capital has been calculated as £3,877 for George and £3,743 for Janek.

- George has taken drawings of £56,200 over the year, and Janek has taken £62,200.

- Interest on drawings has been calculated at £600 for George and £720 for Janek for the year ended 31 December 20-8.

- The residual profit after adjustments is shared between George and Janek in the ratio 2:3.

You are required to prepare the appropriation account and current accounts for First Class Flooring for the year ended 31 December 20-8.

(a) Complete the partnership appropriation account in accordance with the partnership agreement for the year ended 31 December 20-8.

Show your answers as positive and to the nearest whole pound. There does not need to be an entry for every space.

(7 marks)

Partnership appropriation statement for year ended 31 December 20-8

	Total £	George £	Janek £
Profit for the year			
Add			
Total			
Less appropriation of profits			
Total			
Profit available for distribution			
Profit share			
George			
Janek			
Total profit distributed			

(b) Complete the current accounts for the two partners as at 31 December 20-8 in accordance with the partnership agreement

(6 marks)

Partnership current accounts for year ended 31 December 20-8

	George Debit	Janek Debit		George Credit	Janek Credit
			Balance b/d	£7,500	£9,600
Total					

Practice synoptic assessment 2

assessment information

Read the scenario carefully before attempting the questions.

Complete all 6 tasks.

Tasks 1 to 6 require you to write your answers in this book.

The total number of marks for this assessment is 80.

Task 3 and Task 4 require extended writing as part of your responses to these questions. You should make sure you allow adequate time to complete these tasks.

Where the date is relevant, it is given in the task data.

Both minus signs and brackets can be used to indicate negative numbers unless task instructions say otherwise.

advice

Read each question carefully before you start to answer it.

Attempt all questions.

You will have 2 hours and 30 minutes to answer all parts of the assessment.

scenario background

Task 1 is based on a work-based scenario separate to the rest of the assessment.

Tasks 2 to 6 are based on the workplace scenario for Catering for Occasions.

You are Tim Oakley, a part-qualified accountant who works for Amy Cox, a sole trader. She runs Catering for Occasions, a catering business, which has been operating for many years.

You are responsible for all aspects of accounting and bookkeeping.

Task 1: 15 marks

This task is based on a workplace scenario separate to the rest of the assessment.

Alek is an accountant who works in practice at Able and Best, a medium-sized accountancy practice. A client recently made the following statements to him, stating her beliefs on Alek's duties as an AAT member.

(a)   Are these statements true or false?

Statement	True	False
You have to do whatever I tell you in my accounts, as I am your client		
You have to keep to rules, which tell you how to behave ethically in every situation		

(2 marks)

(b)   In the following situations, identify whether Alek does or does not comply with the principle of objectivity.

Situation	Comply	Not Comply
Alek produced the financial statements for his sister-in-law's business. He has known his sister-in-law for several years		
Alek accepts a meal for his family for free from a local client who owns a restaurant		

(2 marks)

(c)   Alek's colleague, Monica, stated to Mr Able, one of the partners, that she had completed a tax return for a client, Rushwick and Co, when she had not.

Which fundamental ethical principle did Monica breach?

(a) Confidentiality	
(b) Integrity	
(c) Objectivity	

(1 mark)

(d)   Alek provides bookkeeping services, including raising invoices, to People First, a small recruitment agency. The business has a March year end. The owners have asked Alek to date several invoices as April, when the sales occurred in March, to reduce the tax bill for this year.

What should Alek do? Tick **all** that apply.

Action	Tick to do
Agree with the client and record the accounts in April	
Inform his manager	
Document the request on People First's file	
Report People First to the National Crime Agency (NCA)	

(3 marks)

(e)   Fruity Fruits Limited, a local fruit farm, is using Able and Best to process its payroll. It pays the National Minimum Wage to its pickers and charges them significantly above market rent to live in caravans on site.

Which of the following statements are true?

Statement	True	False
By paying the National Minimum Wage, rather than the living wage, Fruity Fruits is acting ethically.		
Charging high rents to the pickers raises doubts about Fruity Fruits Limited's ethical approach to business		

(2 marks)

(f) Alek has been given a new client and has discovered they are improperly accounting for VAT and so underpaying VAT to HMRC. He has spoken to them and suggested they disclose the error immediately. They have refused to do so.

What does Alek need to do next? Tick **all** that apply.

Action	
(a) Tell the client he will be reporting them to HMRC	
(b) Make a Suspicious Activity Report to the Money Laundering Reporting Officer	

(2 marks)

(g) Alek has now inadvertently become involved in money laundering with a client, Patios and Paving. Complete the following statement.

If Alek informs Patios and Paving he is going to report them for ⎢ money laundering / tax evasion ⎢ he will be guilty of ⎢ tipping off / whistle blowing ⎢ and will be ⎢covered under protected disclosure /

⎢ liable to be prosecuted ⎢ .

(3 marks)

> **Scenario Background (for Tasks 2 – 6)**
>
> You are Tim Oakley, a part-qualified accountant who bookkeeps for Amy Cox, a sole trader. She runs Catering for Occasions, a catering business, which has been operating for many years.
>
> You are responsible for all aspects of accounting and bookkeeping.

Task 2: 12 marks

You have been reviewing Amy's expenses for the year and have realised that she has claimed VAT on entertaining several important regular corporate clients last quarter. The entertaining amount claimed is £1,260, including VAT. Claiming VAT on entertaining expenses is not allowed.

(a)   What will the journal be to correct this error?

Select the General ledger code from the following: Entertaining, VAT control a/c, Bank, Drawings

General ledger code	Dr £	Cr £

(2 marks)

(b)   As a result of the adjustment in part (a), what will the impact on the profit for the year be?

Choose **one** option.

(a)	Increase the profit	
(b)	Decrease the profit	
(c)	No change to the profit	

(1 mark)

Amy Cox has been approached by a client, Ted, who has suggested he pay Amy in cash. He suggested no invoice be raised for the catering for his birthday party, so he could pay a lower price and he would save the VAT. He also pointed out that Amy will save the tax on the profit.

Amy has told your colleague, Sarah, who also works in accounts, that she intends to do this and has promised to share the saving in tax with her.

(c) Applying the ethical framework from the ethical code, which of the following describes the situation faced by Sarah? Choose **one** option.

(a) A self-review threat to objectivity	
(b) An intimidation threat to objectivity	
(c) A self-interest threat to objectivity	

(1 mark)

You conclude that the deliberate misrecording of sales is unethical behaviour by Sarah.

(d) What should your action be regarding Sarah?

(a) Send a Suspicious Activity Report to the National Crime Agency	
(b) Discuss the situation with Sarah and try to persuade her to report the sale correctly	

(1 mark)

Amy is looking at expanding into providing a bar service as part of her business. She has suggested that you look into the matter for her with a view to helping her work through the paperwork and apply for the licence, as you are good at rules and regulations. She thinks she will be licensed within two months and wants to offer it as a service to her clients now. You have no experience of licence applications.

(e) What action should you take?

(a) Resign from Catering for Occasions	
(b) Agree to help her but suggest she does not advertise it yet	
(c) Decline the work and suggest she contact a local specialist in licence applications	

(1 mark)

You are working through the trial balance and have a suspense account balance of £350 cr. You have found the following errors, which you must correct:

- Payment of a miscellaneous food invoice for £172 posted as a credit to the bank, with no corresponding debit.

- The equipment balance is shown correctly on the general ledger as £5,545 but has been transferred to the trial balance as £5,145.

(f)   What is the balance on the suspense account once these adjustments have been made? Complete the amount and choose Dr or Cr.

	Dr / Cr

(2 marks)

(g)   If corrected, what error could now clear the suspense account?

(a)	A wages payment was recorded in the wages control account but not in the cashbook	
(b)	A sale was recorded in the sales account but not in the sales ledger control account	

(1 mark)

As part of the year end procedures you are completing the bank reconciliation as at 31 December 20-4. You have compared the cash book with the bank statement and found the following issues:

(h)   Which **two** of the following items require the cash book to be updated?

(a)	A faster payment of £375 has been recorded in the cash book as £275	
(b)	A cheque paid to a supplier for £500 has cleared the bank on 5 January 20-5	
(c)	Overdraft charges of £57 have not been entered into the cash book	
(d)	A customer remittance was received dated 30 December 20-4, which has been entered into the cash book. The receipt has not yet been received	

(2 marks)

(i)   Amy is unclear why you reconcile the bank account to the cash book every month.

Choose **one** reason.

(a) To keep track of the bank balance each period	
(b) To make sure the bank is applying the correct bank charges	
(c) To ensure the cash book accurately reflects the bank transactions of the business	

(1 mark)

Task 3: 13 marks

(a)   Amy uses absorption costing when pricing each job.

Her estimated fixed overheads for the year ended 31 December 20-5 are:

	Budget, £
Rent	4,000
Rates	1,000
Insurance	1,000
Marketing	1,000
Total fixed overheads	7,000

She expects to cater 250 events, using 5,000 labour hours.

(i)   Calculate the fixed overhead absorption rate per labour hour used to price each job to the nearest penny.

£ [   ]   (1 mark)

(ii)   Amy is using the fixed overhead rate to quote for a job. Complete the job quotation, using the fixed overhead rate calculated in part (i).

Quotation for Hanson's birthday party (50 people)

	£
Direct materials (£20 per head)	
Direct labour	
- 5 waiting staff 6 hrs each @ £12 per hour	
- 1 supervisor 6 hrs @ £16 per hour	
- 2 chefs 12 hours each @ £15 per hour	
Variable overheads (£3.50 per person)	
Fixed overheads absorption rate (based on labour hours)	
Total cost	
Markup (20%)	
Price for party	

(6 marks)

(b) On 1 July 20-5, Amy was informed of a rent review, effective from 1 September 20-5. Amy made rent payments in advance during 20-5 as follows:

1 January 20-5 £1,000

2 April 20-5 £1,000

30 June 20-5 £1,000

2 October 20-5 £1,000

The new rent was agreed at £5,200 per annum on 1 February 20-6 and was backdated to 1 September 20-5.

(i) Calculate the rent payable amount to include in the financial statements for the year ended 31 December 20-5.

£ [   ]   (1 mark)

(ii) Complete the journal to record the rent adjustment for the rental increase in the year ended 31 December 20-5.

Select the account name from the following list: Accrued expenses, prepaid expenses, rent payable, rental income

Account name	£	£

(2 marks)

(iii) Explain the impact of the rent increase on the profit for the year ended 31 December 20-5 and the overhead absorption rate calculation for 20-6. Use information from parts (a) and (b), along with your answers. You must show your workings.

(3 marks)

Task 4: 15 marks

When Amy is catering for events, she employs waiting staff to serve at the event. Waiting staff are all casually employed and you process the payroll for them. You have discovered during your work that Amy is including tips given to waiting staff as part of their minimum wage, which is incorrect. Without these, the staff would be earning below minimum wage.

You have discussed this with Amy and she stated that the staff wages were a very high proportion of her costs and she would reduce her profits significantly if she were to pay them more. She has suggested that the business would not continue to trade if she had to change the wage rates.

(a) Explain the **two** threats to ethical principles that you face.

(2 marks)

(b) Explain the actions you must now take, including any information you must record and any advice you might seek.

(2 marks)

(c) Amy has asked you to help promote and uphold sustainability in Catering for Occasions.

State why, as an accountant, you have a professional duty to uphold sustainability as part of your role.

(1 mark)

Amy Cox is considering trading as a limited company but is unsure what this means and how it will affect the way she runs the business.

(d)   Write an email to Amy covering the following areas:

   (1)   State the ownership and reporting requirements of each type of business

   (2)   Explain the accounts regulations covering a sole trader and a limited company

   (3)   State one advantage of becoming a limited company

EMAIL

To: Amy Cox

From: Tim Oakley

Date: 12 January 20-5

Subject: Sole Trader or Limited Company

(10 marks)

Task 5: 12 marks

Amy would like you to produce a variance analysis for the year ended 31 December 20-4. Some of the information has been collected and summarised. You must now complete the variances column.

(a) Complete the analysis below, calculating the variances. Show adverse variances as negative using a minus sign.

Operating statement for year ended 31 December 20-4

	Budget, £	Actual, £	Variance, £
Revenue	100,600	106,250	
Direct materials	35,730	42,302	
Direct labour	30,700	34,250	
Variable overheads	6,000	6,700	
Fixed overheads	7,000	7,400	
Total cost	79,430	90,652	
Operating profit	21,170	15,598	

(5 marks)

(b) What reason could have caused the revenue variance? Choose **one** option.

The actual price per customer is lower than budgeted.	
An unplanned price increase was implemented during the year.	
Customers purchased less food than expected.	

(1 mark)

(c) What reason could have caused the fixed overheads variance? Choose **one** option.

A rent increase was not budgeted for.	
More waiting staff were used than planned.	
Catering equipment was hired for a specific catering job.	

(1 mark)

(d) Today's date is 2nd February 20-5.

Amy has asked you to produce a budget for year ending 31 December 20-5, based on the actual figures for year ended 31 December 20-4. Amy catered for 250 events in 20-4 and expects to cater for 260 in 20-5. The following amendments are also required:

- Sales price increase of 2%

- Direct materials cost increase of 1%

Complete the budgeted operating statement below. Enter all numbers as positive to the nearest £.

Budgeted operating statement for year ended 31 December 20-5

	Actual 20-4 £	Budget 20-5 £
Revenue	106,250	112,710
Direct materials	42,302	44,434
Direct labour	34,250	35,620
Variable overheads	6,700	6,968
Fixed overheads	7,400	8,200
Total cost	90,652	95,222
Operating profit	15,598	17,488

(5 marks)

Task 6: 13 marks

You are now preparing the final accounts for Catering for Occasions for the year ended 31 December 20-5.

Your next task is to complete the extended trial balance, which you started but did not finish. An extract is shown below.

(a) **(i)** Extend the entries for the highlighted items into the appropriate SPL/SFP columns in the extract of the extended trial balance shown below.

(5 marks)

(ii) The profit for the year has been calculated correctly as £18,121. Insert this in the relevant place(s) in the extract of the extended trial balance.

(2 marks)

Extract of extended trial balance year ended 31 December 20-5

	Ledger balances		Adjustments		Statement of profit or loss		Statement of financial position	
Account	**Dr**	**Cr**	**Dr**	**Cr**	**Dr**	**Cr**	**Dr**	**Cr**
Cash and bank		25,697						
Value Added Tax		1,363						
Insurance	1,500			500				
Inventory (opening & closing)	3,540		3,097	3,097				
Profit for the year								

(total 7 marks)

When you review the extended trial balance, you realise you have not depreciated the van this year. The van cost £20,000 and was purchased on 1 January 20-0. The residual value was estimated at £2,000 and it has been depreciated on a straight-line basis. The useful life was five years.

(b)   **(i)**   Complete the journal (including narrative) to account for the adjustment that is required. Show your answers to the nearest £.

Date	Account	Dr £	Cr £
Narrative:			

(5 marks)

(ii)   Following the inputting of this journal, calculate the revised profit or loss for the year ended 31 December 20-5. Use a minus sign to indicate a loss.

£ [   ]

(1 mark)

Practice synoptic assessment 3

assessment information

Read the scenario carefully before attempting the questions.

Complete all 6 tasks.

Tasks 1 to 6 require you to write your answers in this book.

The total number of marks for this assessment is 80.

Task 3 and Task 4 require extended writing as part of your responses to these questions. You should make sure you allow adequate time to complete these tasks.

Where the date is relevant, it is given in the task data.

Both minus signs and brackets can be used to indicate negative numbers unless task instructions say otherwise.

advice

Read each question carefully before you start to answer it.

Attempt all questions.

You will have 2 hours and 30 minutes to answer all parts of the assessment.

scenario background

Task 1 is based on a work-based scenario separate to the rest of the assessment.

Tasks 2 to 6 are based on the workplace scenario for Beautiful Tableware.

You are Serena Parry, a part-qualified accountant who works for Beautiful Tableware, a partnership owned by Claire Giles and Jason Taylor, which has been operating for many years and produces stoneware dishes for cooking and serving food in.

You are responsible for all aspects of accounting and bookkeeping.

Task 1: 15 marks

This task is based on a workplace scenario separate to the rest of the assessment.

Daisy is an accountant who works in practice at Martin, Plum and Holsworth, a medium-sized accountancy practice. A new employee, Brian, has asked Daisy to clarify his understanding of the Code of Ethics.

(a)   Are these statements true or false?

Statement	True	False
How I behave in my personal life is not important to the AAT, as I only need to comply with the Code of Ethics at work		
If I have an ethical problem, I need to use a methodical approach to resolve it		

(2 marks)

(b)   In the following situations, identify whether Daisy does or does not comply with the principle of professional competence and due care.

Situation	Comply	Not Comply
Daisy completes the VAT return for a client who sells and buys overseas, when she has no experience of imports and exports		
Daisy attends a training course on new International Accounting Standards		

(2 marks)

(c)   Daisy has accepted two tickets to a show in London, plus a night in a hotel, from one of her clients, as a 'thank you' on completion of their accounts.

Which fundamental ethical principle did Daisy breach?

(a) Objectivity	
(b) Professional behaviour	
(c) Integrity	

(1 mark)

(d)   A few months ago, Daisy went to work for a client, Fantastic Floors Limited, to help them while the Financial Controller was on maternity leave. Whilst there, she set up a new asset register, calculating the depreciation and deciding on the useful lives of various new additions. She is due to work on the year end accounts and part of her work will be to review the asset register.

What ethical threat is Daisy facing to her objectivity?

(a) A self-interest threat	
(b) A familiarity threat	
(c) A self-review threat	

(1 mark)

What actions should Daisy take to safeguard against this threat? Tick **any** that could apply.

Action	Tick to do
Inform the client	
Complete the work, then inform her manager once the accounts are finished	
Inform her manager and request he reviews the work in detail once she has performed it	
Request to be removed from the work for this year end	

(3 marks)

(e)   Daisy has noticed that one of her clients is making large payments to an overseas bank account with no supporting documentation. Daisy is concerned these may be payments to fund terrorism.

What action must Daisy take? Tick **all** that apply.

Action	
(a) Immediately inform Martin, Plum and Holsworth's Money Laundering Officer of her concerns	
(b) Complete a Suspicious Activity Report (SAR) and send it to the National Crime Agency (NCA)	

(2 marks)

(f)   Daisy was working on the most recent corporation tax return for Excellence in Recruitment and noticed that they had incorrectly deducted entertaining expenditure on last year's return.

What action should Daisy take? Tick **one** option.

Action	
Correct the error on this year's return and do not tell anyone	
Advise HMRC of the error without disclosing it to Excellence in Recruitment or Martin, Plum and Holsworth	
Tell Martin, Plum and Holsworth of the error and recommend the error be disclosed to Excellence in Recruitment	

(2 marks)

(g)   Daisy realises she has inadvertently become involved in a money laundering operation for Prestigious Presents Limited.

Complete the following statement:

If Daisy does not tell the MRLO of their money laundering she will be guilty of   an unauthorised

disclosure / failure to disclose / prejudicing an inquiry   and could be imprisoned for up to

five / fourteen years   .

(2 marks)

Scenario background

For Tasks 2 – 6

You are Serena Parry, a part-qualified accountant who works for Beautiful Tableware, a partnership owned by Claire Giles and Jason Taylor, which has been operating for many years and produces stoneware dishes for cooking and serving food in.

You are responsible for all aspects of accounting and bookkeeping.

Task 2: 12 marks

(a)   Whilst reviewing the non-current asset register, you realise that the vehicle cost of a new lorry, purchased on 1 April 20-4, includes a two-year servicing agreement, costing £1,250. What will the journal be to record the servicing agreement correctly?

Select the General ledger code from the following: Vehicles, equipment, cost, vehicles expenses

General ledger code	Dr £	Cr £

(2 marks)

(b)   How much is the adjustment for the servicing agreement for the year ended 31 March 20-5?

£ [   ]

(1 mark)

(c)   Choose the correct treatment for the servicing agreement adjustment for the year ended 31 March 20-5.

Accrual	
Prepayment	

(1 mark)

(d)   As a result of the adjustments in parts (a) to (c), what will the impact on profit for the year be?

Choose **one** option.

Increase in profit	
Decrease in profit	
No change in profit	

(1 mark)

Jason and Claire have been reviewing their suppliers recently and plan to reduce them. They believe this will enable them to build better long-term relationships and give them more price stability. As a result of this, several suppliers are competing to supply the glazing used to finish the stoneware. Your colleague, Daniel Juke, a part-qualified accountant, has been part of the review, and is assessing the glazing suppliers.

You overheard Daniel on the phone yesterday, discussing a trip to see one supplier, Gorgeous Glazing Limited, in Bath. He will stay overnight and will go to a very expensive restaurant for dinner.

(e)   Applying the conceptual framework, from the ethical code, which of the following describes the situation faced by Daniel Juke? Choose **one** option.

(a)	A familiarity threat to professional behaviour	
(b)	A self-interest threat to objectivity	
(c)	A self-review threat to professional competence and due care	

(1 mark)

You have also now found out that he has emailed another supplier's tender to Gorgeous Glazing Limited. You conclude that this is unethical behaviour by Daniel Juke.

(f)   What should you do now? Choose **one** option.

(a)	Tell Jason and Claire about your concerns	
(b)	Report Daniel to the AAT	

(1 mark)

As a result of Daniel's unethical behaviour, he has been dismissed. You are temporarily Beautiful Tableware's only accountant. There is a meeting planned with the bank this afternoon, to finalise a new overdraft facility, which Daniel Juke was negotiating. It is quite complex and you do not believe you are in a position to contribute fully to the meeting. Claire and Jason insist you are present and that the overdraft be signed.

(g)   Which of the following should be your next action? Choose **one** option.

(a)	Request that the visit from the bank be postponed	
(b)	Agree to deal with the bank, in line with Claire and Jason's instruction	
(c)	Phone the bank and discuss the problem with them	

(1 mark)

As a result of Daniel's dismissal, you have been asked to update the asset register for the following disposal. Claire bought a car on 1 April 20-2 for £17,500. It has been depreciated at 25% using the diminishing balance method. The company policy is to charge a full year's depreciation in the year of disposal. The car was sold on 1 January 20-5 for £5,000.

(h) How much is the depreciation on the car when it is sold? Show your answer to **two** decimal places.

(1 mark)

(i) How much is the profit or loss on disposal? Show your answer to **two** decimal places.

(1 mark)

(j) Claire and Jason have asked you why the car is being depreciated.

Which **one** of the following explanations would be suitable?

(a) So the carrying value always equals market value	
(b) To minimise the likelihood of a profit occurring when it is sold	
(c) To apply the accruals concept, matching cost to revenue	

(2 marks)

Task 3: 13 marks

(a)   Beautiful Tableware produces items in batches of 100. In the last production run in March 20-5, the following costs were incurred in the batch of dishes.

	£
Direct materials	1,120
Direct labour	480
Prime cost	**1,600**
Variable production overheads	150
Fixed production overheads	300
Fixed non-production overheads	80
Total costs	**2,130**

At 31 March 20-5, 40 dishes remained in inventory. Beautiful Tableware currently values inventory at full absorption cost.

(i)   Explain how the inventory of unsold dishes is valued differently, depending if absorption or marginal costing is used. You must show your workings.

(4 marks)

(ii)   Explain the effect of using the two different methods mentioned in (i) on the reported profit.

(2 marks)

(b)   Claire is convinced that a quantity of inventory has been lost or stolen during the year ended 31 March 20-5. She asks you to calculate the value of inventory lost or stolen.

Sales are £1,600,000. Opening inventory for the year is £225,000 and actual closing inventory is £188,000. Direct materials, labour and production overhead costs, i.e. purchases, total £1,010,000 and the gross profit margin is 35%.

Calculate the amount of inventory that is lost or stolen during the year. You must show your workings.

(4 marks)

(c)   Claire has been looking at investing in a new kiln and is keen to maximise possible additional income. She requires the project to payback within 3 years.

She has given you some information about three kilns she is considering and you have calculated the net present value and payback for each kiln below.

	Cost	Net present value (6 years) (including purchase cost of kiln)	Payback period
Kiln 1	£28,500	£36,000	2 years 1 month
Kiln 2	£19,500	£45,500	2 years 9 months
Kiln 3	£37,000	£60,000	4 years 2 months

(i)   Which kiln should Claire purchase, based on this information? Choose **one** option.

Kiln 1	
Kiln 2	
Kiln 3	

(1 mark)

(ii)   State the reason for your decision. Choose **one** option.

Claire should purchase the kiln with the highest net present value.	
Claire should purchase the kiln with the highest net present value, which pays back within the required payback period.	
Claire should purchase the kiln with the shortest payback period, which has a positive net present value.	

(2 marks)

Task 4: 15 marks

Claire has been reviewing the year end figures you recently produced for the partners. She wants to move house next year and requires the profits she earns to be above a certain level, to secure the mortgage she needs. As the profit is currently too low, she has asked you to move some expenses into the next year, to increase the profit.

She has told you that Jason is aware of this request and is happy for you to do it. She has offered you a free set of their complete product range to say 'thank you'. The products are very expensive.

(a)   Explain the situation, with reference to the Code of Ethics, and state the **two** threats you face.

(3 marks)

(b)   Set out the actions you must now take, considering both Claire and Jason, to resolve this ethical conflict.

(2 marks)

(c)   Claire and Jason have been discussing setting up a charity, to send simple earthenware pots to India. However, they are not familiar with charities so would like some information on them.

Prepare an email to them setting out:

(1)   A brief description of a charity

(2)   Details of ownership and how the charity is structured and managed

(3)   Liability and taxation

(4)   The regulations that govern a charity

EMAIL

To: Claire Giles; Jason Taylor

From: Serena Parry

Date: 6 April 20-5

Subject: Charity information

(10 marks)

Task 5: 12 marks

Beautiful Tableware has three production departments, Moulding, Glazing and Finishing, and one support department, Stores, which is a cost centre.   Stores supports the three production departments with 60% of its time spent on Moulding, 30% on Glazing and 10% on Finishing.

The budgeted overheads for the year ending 31 March 20-6 are shown below and you have been asked to help apportion them.

Budgeted overhead	
Overhead	**Total cost**
Buildings insurance	£3,300
Depreciation of machinery	£15,000
Lighting and heating	£9,900
Rent and rates	£18,150
Supervisors' salaries	£36,000
Total	£82,350

Department	Floor space (sq metres)	Number of employees	Value of machinery
Moulding	500	5	£35,000
Glazing	150	2	£15,000
Finishing	100	1	£5,000
Stores	75	1	£5,000
	825	9	£60,000

(a)   Complete the missing figures in the following overhead apportionment table. Show your answers to the nearest whole pound. Show deductions as negative.

Select the basis of apportionment from: Floor space (sq metres), Number of employees or Value of machinery.

Budgeted Overheads	Basis of apportionment	Moulding	Glazing	Finishing	Stores	Total
Buildings insurance	Floor space (sq metres)	£2,000	£600	£400	£300	£3,300
Depreciation of machinery	Value of machinery	£8,750	£3,750	£1,250	£1,250	£15,000
Lighting and heating	Floor space (sq metres)	£6,000	£1,800	£1,200	£900	£9,900
Rent and rates						
Supervisors' salaries	Number of employees	£20,000	£8,000	£4,000	£4,000	£36,000
Sub-totals						
Re-apportion Stores						
Total						

(6 marks)

(b) The overheads are to be apportioned on machine hours for moulding and glazing and labour hours for finishing.

	Moulding	Glazing	Finishing
Machine hours	25,100	3,865	200
Labour hours	1,300	750	1,232

(i) Calculate the overhead rate for the moulding department to the nearest penny.

£ [ ]

(1 mark)

(ii) Calculate the overhead rate for the finishing department to the nearest penny.

£ [ ]

(1 mark)

(c) The moulding department works in teams. The basic rate is £15 per hour, and overtime is paid at basic pay + 50%. Beautiful Tableware sets a target for production of each item. A team bonus equal to 10% of basic hourly rate is payable for every equivalent item produced in excess of the target.

The target for April 20-5 was 4,500 units and 4,800 units were produced. Overtime and bonuses are all included as part of direct labour costs.

Complete the table below to calculate the total labour cost for April 20-5.

Description	Hours	£
Basic pay	1,920	
Overtime rate	260	
Total before team bonus	2,180	
Bonus payment		
Total cost including team bonus		

(4 marks)

Task 6: 13 marks

The final accounts for Beautiful Tableware for the year ended 31 March 20-5 show Claire's capital account as £35,000 and Jason's capital account as £25,000. Neither partner has any transactions on these accounts in the current year. Claire and Jason currently share profits in the ratio 3:2 respectively.

They have asked their friend Andrea Summerwell to enter the partnership and the goodwill in the business has been valued at £48,000. Andrea will bring £45,000 of cash into the business as her capital, part of which represents a premium for goodwill. She paid them through the bank on 31 March 20-5. The new profit sharing ratio for Claire, Jason and Andrea will be 3:2:3 respectively.

Claire and Jason have asked you to prepare a statement of their capital accounts, reflecting this change.

You are required to prepare the capital statement for Beautiful Tableware as at 31 March 20-5.

(a) Complete the partnership capital accounts for the year ended 31 March 20-5 and show the balances carried down.

Partnership capital accounts for year ended 31 March 20-5

	Claire Debit £	Jason Debit £	Andrea Debit £		Claire Credit £	Jason Credit £	Andrea Credit £
Goodwill	18,000	12,000	18,000	Balance b/d	35,000	25,000	
Balance c/d	45,800	32,200	27,000	Goodwill	28,800	19,200	
				Bank			45,000
Total	63,800	44,200	45,000		63,800	44,200	45,000

(9 marks)

(b) The current accounts for the year ended 31 March 20-5, after the profit has been distributed, are Claire £14,500 credit and Jason £7,800 debit.

Complete the extract of the statement of financial position below, using your answer from (a). Use minus signs for deductions.

Extract of the statement of financial position

Financed by:	Claire £	Jason £	Andrea £	Total £
Capital account	45,800	32,200	27,000	105,000
Current account	14,500	-7,800		6,700
	60,300	24,400	27,000	111,700

(4 marks)

Practice synoptic assessment 4

assessment information

Read the scenario carefully before attempting the questions.

Complete all 6 tasks.

Tasks 1 to 6 require you to write your answers in this book.

The total number of marks for this assessment is 80.

Task 3 and Task 4 require extended writing as part of your responses to these questions. You should make sure you allow adequate time to complete these tasks.

Where the date is relevant, it is given in the task data.

Both minus signs and brackets can be used to indicate negative numbers unless task instructions say otherwise.

advice

Read each question carefully before you start to answer it.

Attempt all questions.

You will have 2 hours and 30 minutes to answer all parts of the assessment.

scenario background

Task 1 is based on a work-based scenario separate to the rest of the assessment.

Tasks 2 to 6 are based on the workplace scenario for Trendy Togs.

You are Bruno Costa, a part-qualified accountant who works for Luke Graham, a sole trader, who runs Trendy Togs, a clothing business, which has been operating for a couple of years.

You are responsible for all aspects of accounting and bookkeeping.

Task 1: 15 marks

This task is based on a workplace scenario separate to the rest of the assessment.

Paul is an accountant who works in Galvanised Products Limited, a manufacturing business employing many employees. A new employee, Edyta, needs help understanding the Code of Ethics and has asked Paul to help her.

(a)   Are these statements Edyta makes true or false?

Statement	True	False
Galvanised Products Limited's reputation may be damaged if I do not comply with the Code of Ethics		
The Code of Ethics sets out the rules I must apply in my work and personal life		

(2 marks)

(b)   In the following situations, identify whether Edyta does or does not comply with the principle of integrity.

Situation	Comply	Not Comply
Edyta informs her manager she is sick, when she is, in fact, going away for a long weekend		
Edyta made an error on payroll and has not corrected it. She knows the incorrect information is included in the monthly reporting		

(2 marks)

(c)   The sales bonuses are based on paying a fixed percentage of sales made for the month to each sales manager. Historically these have been displayed in the sales office. Edyta has been told by the Financial Controller, Emma, to increase the percentage for two of the four sales managers and to stop displaying the sales totals and bonuses. Edyta has no documentation to support the change.

What fundamental ethical principle did Emma breach?

(a) Integrity	
(b) Objectivity	
(c) Confidentiality	

(1 mark)

(d) Paul is due to be paid a bonus if reported profits are above a certain level. He is aware that a key customer is now unlikely to pay a debt and should provide for it, and profit would therefore be below the level for the bonus.

What threat to Paul's objectivity exists?

(a) A self-review threat	
(b) A self-interest threat	
(c) A familiarity threat	

(1 mark)

What actions should Paul take to safeguard against this threat? Tick **any** that could apply.

Action	Tick to do
Request the Finance Director review the provision for bad and doubtful debts	
Follow the provisioning policy, as set out by the Finance Director	
Request to be removed from the work for this year end	

(3 marks)

(e) Paul has found out that, as part of the production process, some health and safety regulations are being breached.

What action must Paul take? Tick **one** option.

Action	
(a) Discuss the matter with the management of Galvanised Products Limited and request they comply with the health and safety regulations	
(b) Resign	
(c) Report Galvanised Products Limited to the Health and Safety Executive immediately	

(2 marks)

(f)   During his work, Paul has discovered the Purchasing Director is being given sums of money to award contracts to a specific supplier.

What action should Paul take? Tick **one** option.

Action	
(a) Tell the Purchasing Director to stop	
(b) Inform the Managing Director of the Purchasing Director's actions	

(2 marks)

(g)   Paul has subsequently found out that the Managing Director is also taking bribes from several suppliers. He has been told by the Managing Director that he must 'keep quiet' or he will lose his job.

Complete the following statement:

Paul must seek advice | from a colleague / by phoning the AAT's confidential helpline | to determine

what to do next. If he believes the directors will destroy evidence of the bribes, he must make

| a protected disclosure / an unprotected disclosure | to the relevant authority.

(2 marks)

> **Scenario background**
>
> **For Tasks 2 – 6**
>
> You are Bruno Costa, a part-qualified accountant who works for Luke Graham, a sole trader, who runs Trendy Togs, a clothing business, which has been operating for a couple of years.
>
> You are responsible for all aspects of accounting and bookkeeping.

Task 2: 12 marks

As you are reviewing a supplier's account, you realise the VAT on a credit note they sent you is £85.00 when it should be £58.00. Currently the VAT control account includes debit balances totalling £2,135 and credit balances totalling £7,535.

(a)   The amended amount on the VAT control account will be

(1 mark)

(b)   Complete the following statement:

The VAT amount will be | due to / due from | HMRC.

(1 mark)

Luke has asked you why items under £250, such as clothes hangers, are not included in the non-current assets register.

(c)   Choose **one** of the following options to explain why this is the case.

(a) Luke has not asked you to do this. You will include all items from now on	
(b) The principle of materiality means that the users' view of the accounts will not change if small items, such as clothes hangers, are not capitalised	
(c) It is not worth the time and effort to maintain so many items on the non-current asset register	

(1 mark)

Luke Graham has noticed you spend a lot of time reconciling information for the accounts at the end of the month and this means Luke gets information later than he would like. He has asked you why you need to perform so many reconciliations at the end of the month.

(d) Considering the underlying principles of producing accounts and the process of reconciliations, what explanation can you give him? Choose **one** option.

(a) The financial statements must be prepared on an accruals basis	
(b) The financial statements must be prepared on a going concern basis	
(c) The financial statements need to be free from material misstatement	

(1 mark)

You are now preparing the accruals and prepayments for the year ended 31 March 20-6. You have the following information for rent and vehicle costs for the year:

Rent

Rent prepaid 1 April 20-5	£1,750
Rent paid per bank during year	£8,470

A rent invoice for 1 March 20-6 to 31 May 20-6 of £3,090 is not included in the above figures.

Vehicle costs

Vehicle costs accrued 1 April 20-5	£500
Vehicle costs paid per bank during the year	£4,200

Included in the vehicle costs payments is the prepayment for road tax for 1 April – 31 March 20-7 of £256.

(e) What is the profit and loss account charge for rent for the year?

(2 marks)

(f) What is the profit and loss charge for vehicle costs for the year?

(2 marks)

Neil Clines is a builder and he is currently doing some building work for Luke Graham at his home. When you are reviewing the monthly management accounts, you identify an invoice for Neil Clines for building work. You are sure this is not a business purchase, but a personal one.

(g) What action should you take?

(a)	Discuss this transaction with Luke Graham to find out if it is an error	
(b)	Report Luke Graham to HMRC	

(1 mark)

Luke is considering exporting clothes to America. He wants you to set up all the contracts and paperwork. You have no experience in this area.

(h) What actions must you now take? Tick **any** that could apply.

(a)	Explain that you have no experience of doing this to Luke and refuse to do it	
(b)	Suggest Luke discuss this with his accountant	
(c)	Contact the AAT helpline	

(3 marks)

Task 3: 13 marks

Today's date is 30 April 20-6.

(a) In March 20-5 Luke prepared a budget for the sales revenue, costs and profit for the year to 31 March 20-6.

The budget was set at 1,050 customers, purchasing an average of £105 of clothes each. Fixed costs were budgeted to be £34,000 and average variable cost per customer was expected to be £55.

(i) Calculate the number of customers required to break-even to the nearest customer.

	customers	(1 mark)

(ii) Luke considers a target profit of £20,000 should be achievable. How many customers need to purchase clothes from the shop to achieve this?

	customers	(1 mark)

(iii) Luke is considering a price increase. Calculate the average selling price if he applies a markup of 120% to the nearest £.

£ | | (1 mark) |

(b) The following is an extract from Trendy Togs' trial balance at 31 March 20-6.

Account	Ledger balances	
	Dr	Cr
Direct materials (cost of clothes sold)	68,943	
Vehicle at cost	15,000	
Fixtures and fittings at cost	12,600	
Accumulated depreciation – vehicle		12,000
Accumulated depreciation – fixtures and fittings		6,300
Sales ledger control account	22,165	
Sales revenue		135,897
Rent	11,250	
Administrative expenses	2,325	
Distribution costs	8,355	
Wages of store staff (overheads)	14,033	
Depreciation		

Depreciation expenses for the vehicle is calculated as £2,000 and has not yet been entered into the trial balance.

Depreciation on the fixtures and fittings has not been calculated. Trendy Togs' policy is to depreciate fixtures and fittings on a straight-line basis over 10 years, with no residual value.

Using this information and the information from the trial balance, calculate the following actual figures for ALL non-current assets:

(i) Depreciation expense for the year

£ [   ] (1 mark)

(ii) Non-current assets accumulated depreciation as at 31 March 20-6

£ [   ] (1 mark)

(iii) Non-current assets carrying amounts as at 31 March 20-6

£ [   ]

(1 mark)

(iv) What will the accumulated depreciation of non-current assets for the year be? Choose **one** option.

Debit	
Credit	

(1 mark)

(c) Actual customers were 1,235 for the year ended 31 March 20-6. Using the figures from the extract of the trial balance in (b) above:

(i) Calculate the actual contribution for the period.

£ [   ] (1 mark)

(ii) Calculate the actual fixed costs, adjusted for depreciation.

£ [   ] (1 mark)

(iii) Calculate the actual break-even volume, based on the actual figures for year ended 31 March 20-6. Show your workings.

[   ]

(2 marks)

(iv) Explain why the actual break-even point for 20-6 was different to the budgeted break-even point.

[   ]

(2 marks)

Task 4: 15 marks

This task is based on the workplace scenario of Trendy Togs.

Today's date is 30 June 20-6.

Luke is considering reviewing the way he is dealing with his suppliers currently and has discussed it with you. He is planning to inform all the suppliers he will only use them if they give him an immediate 10% price reduction and accept extended payments terms of 60 days, rather than the current 30 days. He knows some suppliers will find it difficult to meet his request. They could experience cash flow and profitability problems as a result of it. His business is making profits and he has no cash flow issues.

He has suggested your fees could be increased if you help him persuade them that it would be in the best interests of the business. If you do not help, he has suggested he will find another bookkeeper.

(a)   Identify and explain the sustainability issues regarding Luke's request.

(3 marks)

(b)   Explain the **two** threats to ethical issues that you face as a result of Luke's request.

(2 marks)

(c)   Identify what actions you can take to remain ethical in this situation.

(2 marks)

Luke is now considering asking a friend to invest some money into the business, so he can expand his product lines and increase sales. He has asked you to explain the difference between trading as a partnership and a sole trader.

(d) Write an email to Luke including:

(1) a description of a partnership and a sole trader

(2) the key differences between a partnership and a sole trader, including management, taxation and liability for debts

(3) one advantage and one disadvantage of operating as a partnership rather than a sole trader

---

EMAIL

To: Luke Graham

From: Bruno Costa

Date: 30 June 20-6

Subject: Partnership vs sole trader

(8 marks)

Task 5: 12 marks

(a)   Luke is considering purchasing a new van, to enable him to expand the business by selling in local markets and at festivals. He has asked you to help prepare a capital investment appraisal for the new van. The van will cost £25,000 and is expected to be used for three years, when it will be sold for an estimated value of £12,700.

He has provided you with the following information:

Year	Forecast profit/loss £	Depreciation £
1	10,600	4,100
2	18,650	4,100
3	20,892	4,100

(i)   Complete the following table, rounding numbers to the nearest whole number.

Year	Net cash flow £	Discount factor	Discounted cash flow £
0	(25,000)	1.000	(25,000)
1		0.893	
2		0.797	
3		0.712	

(6 marks)

(ii)   Calculate the net present value of the investment in the van.

£ [   ]   (1 mark)

(b)   Luke has asked you to prepare a variance analysis, flexing the original budget for 31 March 20-6 for actual customers.

Complete the following table. Show your answers to the nearest £. Adverse variances must be denoted with a minus sign.

	Original budget, £ 1,050 customers	Flexed budget, £	Actual results, £ 1,235 customers	Variance
Sales revenue	110,250		135,897	
Variable costs	57,750		68,943	
Fixed overheads	34,000		39,223	
Operating profit	18,500		27,731	

(5 marks)

Task 6: 13 marks

Today's date is 14 May 20-6.

You are now completing the final accounts for Trendy Togs for the year ended 31 March 20-6.

Trendy Togs has decided to set up an allowance for doubtful debts of 1% of trade receivables.

(a) **(i)** Enter the adjustment for the allowance for doubtful debts into the ledger balances below, rounded to the nearest pound.

(2 marks)

Extract of Ledger Balances for Trendy Togs for Year Ended 31 March 20-6

Account	Ledger balances	
	Dr	**Cr**
Opening inventory	6,000	
Purchases	71,435	
Bank & cash	26,221	
Sales ledger control account	22,165	
Prepayments	545	
Vehicles at cost	15,000	
Fixtures and fittings at cost	12,600	
Depreciation – vehicles		14,000
Depreciation – fixtures and fittings		7,560
Value added tax		14,598
Purchases ledger control		17,912
Accruals		4,500
Capital		22,600
Drawings	24,100	
Sales revenue		135,897
Rent	11,250	
Administrative expenses	2,103	
Distribution costs	8,355	
Wages	14,033	
Allowance for doubtful debts		
Allowance for doubtful debts: adjustment		
Depreciation	3,260	
Closing inventory	8,492	8,492

(ii)   Prior to the adjustment, a profit of £27,953 was calculated. Calculate the new profit, after the adjustment for doubtful debts, to be included on the final trial balance.

£ [   ]

(2 marks)

Your next task is to finish completing the statement of financial position, using the final ledger balances from part (a).

Trendy Togs has a policy of showing trade receivables net of any allowances for doubtful debts.

(b) Complete the missing entries, including the carrying amounts of non-current assets, in the year ended 31 March 20-6. Enter deductions to capital as negative. Enter all other numbers as positive.

(9 marks)

Select the items to include in the statement of financial position from the following list: Accruals, Allowance for doubtful debts, Allowance for doubtful debts: adjustment, Drawings, Fixtures and Fittings, Inventory, Loss for the year, Prepayments, Profit for the year, Purchases, Purchases ledger control account, Sales, Sales ledger control account, Trade receivables, Trade payables, Vehicles.

Trendy Togs Statement of financial position year ended 31 March 20-6

	£	£
Non-current assets		
Current assets		
Inventory	8,492	
Bank & cash	26,221	
Current liabilities		
Trade payables	17,912	
Value added tax	14,598	
Net current assets		
Net assets		
Financed by:	£	£
Capital		
Opening capital		22,600
Subtotal		
Closing capital		

Answers to practice synoptic assessment 1

Task 1: 15 marks

(a)

Statement	True	False
'I will not have to keep so up to date with the latest accounting regulations once I have qualified'		✔
'I am never allowed to share information I have learned through my job with anyone else'		✔

(b)

Action	Required	Not Required
Comply with all laws that affect Artons Limited	✔	
Report misreporting of information by the Finance Director	✔	

(c)   (a)   Integrity

(d)

Statement	True	False
The Sales Director's behaviour indicates unethical leadership of the organisation	✔	
The values and ethics of the Directors will influence the values and actions of staff	✔	

(e)   The AAT **may** expel Sarah from the AAT as a result of disciplinary procedures.

Artons Limited **may** bring disciplinary procedures against Sarah.

The National Crime Agency **may not** bring disciplinary procedures against Sarah.

(f)   (b)   Follow the internal procedures within Bodmin Limited for reporting unethical behaviour

(g)

Circumstance	Protected	Not protected
Syed believes the disclosure to be true	✔	
Syed does not act in good faith		✔
Syed believes the evidence will be concealed or destroyed	✔	

Task 2: 12 marks

(a) £511.60

(b) £3,069.60

(c) (a) Professional competence and due care
(b) Professional behaviour

(d) (a) A familiarity threat to objectivity

(e) (b) Tell George and Janek about your concerns

(f) **Statement of profit or loss for the period ended 30 September**

	£	£
Sales revenue		116,856
Opening inventory		
Purchases	85,548	
Less closing inventory	−35,057	
Cost of sales	93,485	
Gross profit		23,371

(g) £42,994

(h) (a) Purchase returns

(i) When the allowance for doubtful debts is increased, there will **always** be a negative effect on profit.

Task 3: 13 marks

(a) The product which makes the most contribution per metre of oak must be produced first, to maximise the contribution First Class Flooring can earn.

Product 5467 makes a contribution per pack of £30 (£75 – £20 – £25) and uses 10m per pack, so the contribution is £3/m.

Product 7685 makes a contribution per pack of £40 (£96 – £36 – £20) and uses 10m per pack, so the contribution is £4/m.

First Class Flooring should make Product 7685 first. This will use 5000m of oak, producing the full 500 packs. The remaining 2000m should be used to make Product 5467, so 200 packs will be produced.

(b)

Dr Wages control Cr Production	
Dr Production Cr Wages expense	
Dr Production Cr Wages control	✔
Dr Wages expense Cr Production	

(c) **(i)** £6,480

(ii) £15,590

(d)

> *Issues to production*
>
> Under the Average Cost method, the materials issued to production were £6,480.
>
> Using the FIFO method, the issue on 18 February would be made from the inventory held at the start of February. This cost £8 per m (£8,000 / 1,000m). Materials issued to production in February 20-9 would be £6,400 under the FIFO method. This is £80 lower (£6,400 – £6,480) than under the Average Cost method.
>
> *Inventory value*
>
> Under Average Cost, inventory was valued at £15,590 at the end of February 20-9.
>
> Under FIFO, this would be the cost of inventory held at the start of the month (£8,000), plus purchases (£4,150 + £9,920), less the issues to production of £6,400. Inventory held is £15,590, valued under FIFO. This is £80 higher than under the Average Cost method.

(e)

First In First Out (FIFO)	✔
Average Cost	

Task 4: 15 marks

(a)   **Threat 1**

I do not have the appropriate experience to complete the payroll as it is a technical area, so this would be a self-interest threat to my professional competence and due care.

Threat 2

I am facing a self interest threat to my objectivity as I would like a pay rise to help buy my new house.

(b)   **Action 1**

I would tell George and Janek that I do not have the relevant experience and need training to allow me to perform the task. This may take some time to organise.

Action 2

I could ask that their accountant undertake payroll, as they will have the appropriate knowledge.

(c)   It is important for First Class Flooring to take a long-term view, allowing it to meet the needs of the present generation without compromising those of a future generation. As First Class Flooring use natural wood in their products, they should ensure that their wood comes from sustainable sources and does not harm the environment.

(d)

EMAIL

To: George Walker

From: Jo Bradley

Date: 3 December 20-9

Subject: Re – Going Concern and Final Accounts

Dear George

Thank you for your email of 1 December 20-9.

Going concern and production of accounts

This is a fundamental principle when a set of accounts is prepared and it is the assumption that the business will continue to trade for the foreseeable future in its current form.

Assets and liabilities are recorded within the accounts when they are purchased or incurred. The method of valuation will assume that the business will run in its current format, so use the plant and machinery purchased over the course of several years, sell inventory at market rates and collect receivables fully.

If the business were to cease trading the value of these assets would have to be adjusted to reflect this. The plant and machinery would be valued at market value, not cost less depreciation. Inventory would all be valued at net realisable value.

If the business were to cease operating, additional liabilities could require recording eg redundancy payments.

Management accounts vs final accounts

The bank requires a final set of accounts, produced in a partnership format, so they can understand how the business is performing. The final accounts will include any adjustments, such as inventory losses or gains made on an inventory count, and will show a true picture of the financial position and profitability of the business.

Partnership accounts include similar information, so the bank can compare our business with others by using performance indicators and financial ratios, to see if we are well managed or not. As they wish to lend you money for the new equipment they will want to assess whether we will be able to repay the loan.

Management accounts are used to support decisions made by the partners, so can be produced in any format and as often as needed. Partnership accounts will always include a statement of profit or loss and a statement of financial position, in the partnership format, and are produced once a year.

Please let me know if you need any further information.

Best wishes

Jo

Task 5: 12 marks

(a)

	Current budget 7,000	Option 1 8,000	Option 2 9,000
Sales	£770,000	£880,000	£990,000
Direct materials	£380,100	£434,400	£488,700
Direct labour	£119,000	£136,000	£153,000
Variable production overheads	£71,400	£81,600	£91,800
Fixed production overheads	£70,000	£70,000	£70,000
Non-production overheads	£80,000	£80,000	£80,000
Operating profit	£49,500	£78,000	£106,500

(b) **(i)** £18.75 ((£70,000 + £80,000)/ 8,000 units)

(ii) £81.50 ((£434,400 + £136,000 + £81,600) / 8,000 units)

(iii) £28.50 ((£880,000 / 8,000 units) – £81.50/ unit)

(iv) £579,040   (Break-even units = 5,264 units (£70,000 + £80,000) / £28.50, 5,263.16 units rounded up. Sales price per unit = £110 (£880,000 / 8,000 units). Break even revenue = 5,264 units x £110 / unit, £579,040.)

(v) 34.2% ((8,000 units – 5,264 units) / 8,000 units x 100)

Task 6: 13 marks

(a)

Partnership appropriation statement for year ended 31 December 20-8

	Total £	George £	Janek £
Profit for the year	£159,950		
Add			
Interest on drawings	£1,320	£600	£720
Total	£1,320		
Less appropriation of profits			
Salary	£20,000	£20,000	
Interest on capital	£7,620	£3,877	£3,743
Total	£27,620		
Profit available for distribution	£133,650		
Profit share			
George	£53,460		
Janek	£80,190		
Total profit distributed	£133,650		

(b)

Partnership current accounts for year ended 31 December 20-8

	George Debit	Janek Debit		George Credit	Janek Credit
			Balance b/d	£7,500	£9,600
Drawings	£56,200	£62,200	Salary	£20,000	
Interest on drawings	£600	£720	Interest on capital	£3,877	£3,743
			Profit share	£53,460	£80,190
Balance c/d	£28,037	£30,613			
Total	£84,837	£93,533		£84,837	£93,533

Answers to practice synoptic assessment 2

Task 1: 15 marks

(a)

Statement	True	False
You have to do whatever I tell you in my accounts, as I am your client		✔
You have to keep to rules, which tell you how to behave ethically in every situation		✔

(b)

Situation	Comply	Not Comply
Alek produced the financial statements for his sister-in-law's business. He has known his sister-in-law for several years		✔
Alek accepts a meal for his family for free from a local client who owns a restaurant		✔

(c)   (b) Integrity

(d)

Action	Tick to do
Agree with the client and record the accounts in April	
Inform his manager	✔
Document the request on People First's file	✔
Report People First to the National Crime Agency (NCA)	

(e)

Statement	True	False
By paying the National Minimum Wage, rather than the living wage, Fruity Fruits is acting ethically.		✔
Charging high rents to the pickers raises doubts about Fruity Fruits Limited's ethical approach to business	✔	

(f)   (b)   Make a Suspicious Activity Report to the Money Laundering Reporting Officer

(g)   If Alek informs Patios and Paving he is going to report them for **money laundering** he will be guilty of **tipping off** and will be **liable to be prosecuted**.

Task 2: 12 marks

(a)

General ledger code	Dr £	Cr £
Entertaining	210	
VAT control a/c		210

(b)   (b)   Decrease the profit

(c)   (c)   A self-interest threat to objectivity

(d)   (b)   Discuss the situation with Sarah and try to persuade her to report the sale correctly

(e)   (c)   Decline the work and suggest she contact a local specialist in licence applications

(f)   £922 Cr

(g)   (a)   A wages payment was recorded in the wages control account but not in the cashbook

(h)   (a)   A faster payment of £375 has been recorded in the cash book as £275

            (c)   Overdraft charges of £57 have not been entered into the cash book

(i)   (c)   To ensure the cash book accurately reflects the bank transactions of the business

Task 3: 13 marks

(a)   (i)   £1.40

(ii)

Quotation for Hanson's birthday party (50 people)

	£
Direct materials (£20 per head)	1,000
Direct labour	
- 5 waiting staff 6 hrs each @ £12 per hour	360
- 1 supervisor 6 hrs @ £16 per hour	96
- 2 chefs 12 hours each @ £15 per hour	360
Variable overheads (£3.50 per person)	175
Fixed overheads absorption rate ((5 x 6) + 6 + (2 x 12)) x £1.40	84
Total cost	2,075
Markup (20%)	415
Price for party	2,490

(b)   (i)   £4,400

(ii)

Account name	£	£
Rent payable	400	
Accrued expenses		400

(iii)

The rent prior to the increase was £1,000 x 4 quarters, £4,000. The increase of £1,200 (£5,200 – £4,000) applies to a whole year. As it is backdated to September, this needs adjusting, so £1,200 / 12 x 4 months (September to December 20-5) must be accrued for and recorded as an expense in 20-5. This will reduce the profit by £400 in 20-5.

The overhead absorption rate must be recalculated for 20-6, as it must be based on current financial information. The new fixed overhead costs will total £8,200 (rent £5,200 + rates £1,000 + insurance £1,000 + marketing £1,000). If the labour hours worked remain at 5,000 hrs, the overhead absorption rate must be increased to £1.64 per hour (£8,200/ 5,000 hrs), £0.24 higher. This will increase the quoted price on future jobs.

Task 4: 15 marks

(a)   **Threat 1**

I face a familairty threat to my integrity. Amy is breaking the law by including tips as part of the wages payment, to bring it up to the national minimum wage, and is using our relationship to stop me telling the staff.

Threat 2

I face an intimidation threat to my objectivity, as Amy is suggesting if the minimum wage was paid, I would be responsible for the business ceasing to operate.

(b)   As Amy is breaking the law, I am able to break confidentiality and report her to the relevant authorities.

I must record the actions I have taken and conversations I have had to help Amy comply with the legislation.

I could phone the AAT Ethics helpline or, alternatively, seek legal advice prior to reporting this.

(c)   As a professional accountant, I support sustainability, as I have a duty to society as a whole. It is important to take a long-term view and allow the needs of present generations to be met without compromising the ability of future generations to meet their needs.

(d)

EMAIL

To: Amy Cox

From: Tim Oakley

Date: 12 January 20-5

Subject: Sole Trader or Limited Company

Dear Amy,

Further to our conversation yesterday, I set out below the main issues you should consider while you decide if you wish to trade as a limited company:

(1) As a sole trader, you own the business and you must produce a set of accounts to support your annual tax return. I produce these for you and they will only be distributed to people or organisations you choose to give them to, such as HMRC.

If you choose to set up a limited company, you will own shares in the business and you will be the director of it. A limited company must produce a set of accounts at least annually and these will be filed at Companies House, so they will be available to the public.

(2) The accounts currently are produced using general accounting principles and the format can be tailored to meet your needs.

A limited company must produce a set of accounts which comply with accounting standards and regulations and the Companies Act 2006. The accounts format is therefore more defined. This is to ensure suppliers, customers, banks and shareholders can easily understand them and compare them with other businesses. There is a much greater administrative burden on you and this will mean additional costs.

(3) By setting up a limited company you will limit your liability. Currently you are liable for all of the debts of Catering for Occasions. As a shareholder of a limited company you will only be liable up to the value of the investment in the shares you own, as the company is a separate legal entity.

Task 5: 12 marks

(a)

Operating statement for year ended 31 December 20-4

	Budget, £	Actual, £	Variance, £
Revenue	100,600	106,250	5,650
Direct materials	35,730	42,302	−6,572
Direct labour	30,700	34,250	−3,550
Variable overheads	6,000	6,700	−700
Fixed overheads	7,000	7,400	−400
Total cost	79,430	90,652	−11,222
Operating profit	21,170	15,598	−5,572

(b)

The actual price per customer is lower than budgeted.	
An unplanned price increase was implemented during the year.	✔
Customers purchased less food than expected.	

(c)

A rent increase was not budgeted for.	✔
More waiting staff were used than planned.	
Catering equipment was hired for a specific catering job.	

(d)

Budgeted operating statement for year ended 31 December 20-5

	Actual 20-4 £	Budget 20-5 £
Revenue	106,250	112,710
Direct materials	42,302	44,434
Direct labour	34,250	35,620
Variable overheads	6,700	6,968
Fixed overheads	7,400	8,200
Total cost	90,652	95,222
Operating profit	15,598	17,488

Task 6: 13 marks

(a) **(i)** and **(ii)**

Extract of extended trial balance year ended 31 December 20-5

Account	Ledger balances Dr	Ledger balances Cr	Adjustments Dr	Adjustments Cr	Statement of profit or loss Dr	Statement of profit or loss Cr	Statement of financial position Dr	Statement of financial position Cr
Cash and bank		25,697						25,697
Value Added Tax		1,363						1,363
Insurance	1,500			500	1,000			
Inventory (opening & closing)	3,540		3,097	3,097	3,540	3,097	3,097	
Profit for the year					18,121			18,121

(b) **(i)**

Date	Account	Dr £	Cr £
31/12/-5	Depreciation	3,600	
31/12/-5	Accumulated depreciation – van		3,600
Narrative:	Being the depreciation on the van for the year ended 31 December 20-5.		

(ii) £14,521 (£18,121 − £3,600)

Answers to practice synoptic assessment 3

Task 1: 15 marks

(a)

Statement	True	False
How I behave in my personal life is not important to the AAT, as I only need to comply with the Code of Ethics at work		✔
If I have an ethical problem, I need to use a methodical approach to resolve it	✔	

(b)

Situation	Comply	Not Comply
Daisy completes the VAT return for a client who sells and buys overseas, when she has no experience of imports and exports		✔
Daisy attends a training course on new International Accounting Standards	✔	

(c)   (a) Objectivity

(d)   (c) A self-review threat

Action	Tick to do
Inform the client	✔
Complete the work, then inform her manager once the accounts are finished	
Inform her manager and request he reviews the work in detail once she has performed it	✔
Request to be removed from the work for this year end	✔

(e)

Action	
(a) Immediately inform Martin, Plum and Holsworth's Money Laundering Officer of her concerns	✔
(b) Complete a Suspicious Activity Report (SAR) and send it to the National Crime Agency (NCA)	

(f)

Action	
Correct the error on this year's return and do not tell anyone	
Advise HMRC of the error without disclosing it to Excellence in Recruitment or Martin, Plum and Holsworth	
Tell Martin, Plum and Holsworth of the error and recommend the error be disclosed to Excellence in Recruitment	✔

(g) If Daisy does not tell the MRLO of their money laundering she will be guilty of **failure to disclose** and could be imprisoned for up to **five** years.

Task 2: 12 marks

(a)

General ledger code	Dr £	Cr £
Vehicles expenses	1,250	
Vehicles		1,250

(b) £625

(c)

Accrual	
Prepayment	✔

(d)

Increase in profit	
Decrease in profit	✔
No change in profit	

(e) (b) A self-interest threat to objectivity

(f) (a) Tell Jason and Claire about your concerns

(g) (a) Request that the visit from the bank be postponed

(h) 20-2: £17,500.00 x 25% = £4,375.00, carrying value = £17,500.00 – £4,375.00 = £13,125.00

20-3: £13,125.00 x 25% = £3,281.25, carrying value = £13,125.00 – £3,281.25 = £9,843.75

20-4: £9,843.75 x 25% = £2,460.94, carrying value = £9,843.75 – £2,460.94 = £7,382.81

Depreciation = £4,375.00 + £3,281.25 + £2,460.94 = £10,117.19

(i) £5,000.00 – £7,382.81 = £2,382.81 loss

(j) (c) To apply the accruals concept, matching cost to revenue

Task 3: 13 marks

(a)　(i)

> *Marginal costing*
>
> Using marginal costing, only variable costs are included in the value of individual units of inventory. This includes the prime cost – direct materials and direct labour – and the variable production overheads.
>
> Direct labour (£1,120), materials (£480) and variable production overheads (£150), total £1,750 for the batch of 100 dishes.
>
> The inventory value for 40 dishes would be £1,750 / 100 x 40, i.e. £700 using marginal costing.
>
> The fixed production overheads would be charged as a period cost in March 20-5, so are not carried forward in inventory under marginal costing.
>
> *Absorption costing*
>
> Both variable and fixed production costs would be included in inventory. The total cost for 100 dishes using absorption costing is £2,050 (£1,120 + £480 + £150 + £300).
>
> The inventory value for 40 dishes would be £2,050 / 100 x 40 i.e. £820.
>
> Non-production overheads are not included in inventory under either method.

(ii)

> If Claire and Jason use marginal costing for inventory, the inventory value would be £120 lower (£820 – £700) than under absorption costing.
>
> The difference is the fixed production overheads incurred in the year under marginal costing. Under absorption costing, these would be included in inventory and carried forward to the year the dishes are sold in.

(b)

	£	£
Sales		1,600,000
Opening inventory	225,000	
Purchases	1,010,000	
Calculated closing inventory (balancing figure)	(195,000)	
Cost of sales (65% of sales)		1,040,000
Gross profit (35% of sales)		560,000

Calculated closing inventory £195,000 – actual closing inventory £188,000 = £7,000 lost or stolen inventory.

(c)　(i)

Kiln 1	
Kiln 2	✔
Kiln 3	

(ii)

Claire should purchase the kiln with the highest net present value.	
Claire should purchase the kiln with the highest net present value, which pays back within the required payback period.	✔
Claire should purchase the kiln with the shortest payback period, which has a positive net present value.	

Task 4: 15 marks

(a) **Threat 1**

I am facing a self-interest threat to my integrity as I will be dishonestly moving expenses from one year into the next. I will not be behaving professionally, as the information will be used for obtaining a mortgage incorrectly. If this action should be discovered I would bring the accounting profession into disrepute.

Threat 2

I am facing a self-interest threat to my professional competence and due care as Claire has offered me the complete product range if I do it, which is worth a lot of money.

(b) I must explain to Claire that I cannot do this, as it breaches my professional integrity. If she insists that I must, then I will inform Jason of her request.

If both Jason and Claire are unhappy and demand I change the accounts, I will have to resign.

(c)

EMAIL

To: Claire Giles; Jason Taylor

From: Serena Parry

Date: 6 April 20-5

Subject: Charity information

Dear Claire and Jason,

I set out below the information regarding charities you requested:

(1) A charity is an organisation run by trustees, which uses its resources to fund charitable activities under its control. A charity is not expected to make a profit and any surpluses should be kept within the charity.

(2) The trustees manage the charity, where funds will come in and then be distributed for the benefit of the public. The charity will have a trust deed, which sets out the charity's name, object and powers, how to appoint and remove trustees and whom the charity can make distributions to.

(3) If the charity is unincorporated, the trustees will be liable for the debts of the charity. If it is limited, liability will be limited. Charities do not pay tax. If it is a charitable company (with limited liability) it must be registered with Companies House.

(4) The Charities Act is the main regulation that governs charities. Charities must produce accounts under the Statement of Recommended Practice (SORP).

All charities are registered with the Charity Commission, who monitor what they do. Charities submit financial statements to the Charity Commission each year, which are publically available.

Please contact me if you require anything further.

Best wishes

Serena

Task 5: 12 marks

(a)

Budgeted Overheads	Basis of apportionment	Moulding	Glazing	Finishing	Stores	Total
Buildings insurance	Floor space (sq metres)	£2,000	£600	£400	£300	£3,300
Depreciation of machinery	Value of machinery	£8,750	£3,750	£1,250	£1,250	£15,000
Lighting and heating	Floor space (sq metres)	£6,000	£1,800	£1,200	£900	£9,900
Rent and rates	Floor space	11,000	3,300	2,200	1,650	18,150
Supervisors' salaries	Number of employees	£20,000	£8,000	£4,000	£4,000	£36,000
Sub-totals		£47,750	£17,450	£9,050	£8,100	£82,350
Re-apportion Stores		£4,860	£2,430	£810	-£8,100	
Total		£52,610	£19,880	£9,860	0	£82,350

(b)   **(i)**   £2.10 (£52,610 / 25,100 machine hours)

   (ii)   £8.00 (£9,860 / 1,232 labour hours)

(c)

Description	Hours	£
Basic pay	1,920	28,800
Overtime rate	260	5,850
Total before team bonus	2,180	34,650
Bonus payment		450
Total cost including team bonus		35,100

Task 6: 13 marks

(a)

Partnership capital accounts for year ended 31 March 20-5

	Claire Debit £	Jason Debit £	Andrea Debit £		Claire Credit £	Jason Credit £	Andrea Credit £
Goodwill written off	18,000	12,000	18,000	Balance b/d	35,000	25,000	
Balance c/d	45,800	32,200	27,000	Goodwill created	28,800	19,200	
				Bank			45,000
Total	63,800	44,200	45,000		63,800	44,200	45,000

(b)

Extract of the statement of financial position

Financed by:	Claire £	Jason £	Andrea £	Total £
Capital account	45,800	32,200	27,000	105,000
Current account	14,500	−7,800	0	6,700
	60,300	24,400	27,000	111,700

Answers to practice synoptic assessment 4

Task 1: 15 marks

(a)

Statement	True	False
Galvanised Products Limited's reputation may be damaged if I do not comply with the Code of Ethics	✔	
The Code of Ethics sets out the rules I must apply in my work and personal life		✔

(b)

Situation	Comply	Not Comply
Edyta informs her manager she is sick, when she is, in fact, going away for a long weekend		✔
Edyta made an error on payroll and has not corrected it. She knows the incorrect information is included in the monthly reporting		✔

(c)   (a)   Integrity

The sales bonuses are not fair and are no longer being given transparently.

(d)   (b)   A self-interest threat

Action	Tick to do
Request the Finance Director review the provision for bad and doubtful debts	✔
Follow the provisioning policy, as set out by the Finance Director	✔
Request to be removed from the work for this year end	✔

(e)

Action	
(a) Discuss the matter with the management of Galvanised Products Limited and request they comply with the health and safety regulations	✔
(b) Resign	
(c) Report Galvanised Products Limited to the Health and Safety Executive immediately	

(f)

Action	
(a) Tell the Purchasing Director to stop	
(b) Inform the Managing Director of the Purchasing Director's actions	✔

(g)   Paul must seek advice **by phoning the AAT's confidential helpline** to determine what to do next. If he believes the directors will destroy evidence of the bribes, he must make **a protected disclosure** to the relevant authority.

Task 2: 12 marks

(a)   £5373

(b)   The VAT amount will be **due to** HMRC.

(c)   (b)   The principle of materiality means that the users' view of the accounts will not change if small items, such as clothes hangers, are not capitalised

(d)   (c)   The financial statements need to be free from material misstatement

(e)   £1,750 + £8,470 + (£3,090/3) = £11,250

(f)   £4,200 − £500 − £256 = £3,444

(g)   (a)   Discuss this transaction with Luke Graham to find out if it is an error

(h)   (a)   Explain that you have no experience of doing this to Luke and refuse to do it
         (b)   Suggest Luke discuss this with his accountant
         (c)   Contact the AAT helpline

Task 3: 13 marks

(a) **(i)** 680 customers (£34,000 / (£105-£55))

   (ii) 1,080 customers ((£34,000 + £20,000) / (£105-£55))

   (iii) £121 (£55 + (£55 x 120%))

(b) **(i)** £3,260 – fixtures and fittings depreciation of £1,260 (£12,600 / 10 years) + £2,000 for the vehicle

   (ii) £21,560 (£12,000 + £6,300 + £3,260)

   (iii) £6,040 (£15,000 + £12,600 – £21,560)

   (iv) Credit

(c) **(i)** £66,954

   (ii) £39,223 (£11,250 + £2,325 + £8,355 + £14,033 + £3,260)

   (iii)

> The actual break-even volume is 724 (rounded up to the nearest customer).
>
> The actual contribution per customer is £66,954 / 1,235 = £54.21.
>
> The break-even volume is the fixed costs divided by the contribution per customer ie £39,223 / £54.21 = 724 customers rounded up.

   (iv)

> The actual break-even point was 44 more customers than budgeted. This has been affected by the following changes:
>
> The actual contribution per customer was £54.21 (£66,954 / 1,235 customers). Budgeted contribution was £50 (£105 – £55), so actual contribution was £4.21 higher than budgeted.
>
> This is mainly due to the higher average sales price, budgeted as £105, when the actual average sales price was £110.04 (£135,897 / 1,235 customers), £5.04 higher. This is offset by the increase in actual variable cost per unit. The actual variable cost per unit is £55.82 (£68,943 / 1,235), £0.82 (£55.82 – £55) higher than planned.
>
> The higher contribution per customer should have reduced the break-even number of customers. However, the fixed costs were £5,223 (£39,223 – £34,000) higher than budget, increasing the break-even volume required.
>
> *Note: Due to rounding to two decimal places, there is a difference of £0.01 between the sales price per unit (£110.04) and the total of the variable cost per unit (£55.82) and the contribution per unit (£55.21).*
>
> **You are not required to raise all the points to earn full marks.**

Task 4: 15 marks

(a)   Luke's treatment of the suppliers is against the principle of long-term sustainability, as some suppliers may face cash flow and profitability pressures by agreeing to these requests. His request could be detrimental to the long-term prosperity of his business, should he be unable to obtain appropriate quality supplies.

Ethically he should pay a fair price for the goods he purchases and pay for goods on time. By imposing a discount and extending credit terms without consultation and for no reason, he is not behaving in a sustainable manner.

(b)   **Threat 1**

I am facing a self-interest threat to my objectivity, as my fees rely on supporting Luke in this unethical, unsustainable behaviour.

Threat 2

I am also facing an intimidation threat because Luke is suggesting he will find another bookkeeper, so I will lose his fee income.

(c)   I can tell Luke that he is acting unethically and suggest he consider the long-term implications of his actions. I can tell him I will not help him to persuade the suppliers to comply with his request.

If Luke continues to implement his new policy, I may need to resign as his bookkeeper.

(d)

EMAIL

To: Luke Graham

From: Bruno Costa

Date: 30 June 20-6

Subject: Partnership vs sole trader

Hello Luke

Thank you for your email dated 30 June 20-6.

(1) Partnerships are formed between two or more people, whereas a sole trader is just you, continuing to trade as you are.

(2) A partnership will either be governed by an agreement you draw up with your partner or, if there is no agreement, by the Partnership Act 1890.

There will be another person to assist in managing the business, to give continuity for holidays or sickness.

Each partner will be liable for the debts of the whole business, unless it is set up as a Limited Liability Partnership. As a sole trader you are currently just responsible for the transactions you enter into yourself.

In a partnership, you will have an agreed share of the profits and will pay income tax on this amount. As a sole trader you are taxed on all the profits of the business.

(3) One advantage would be that you have access to the additional capital you want to expand your business.

One disadvantage would be that you would be liable for any decisions made for the business by your partner.

Please contact me if you require any further information.

Best wishes

Bruno

Task 5: 12 marks

(a)   **(i)**

Year	Net cash flow £	Discount factor	Discounted cash flow £
0	(25,000)	1.000	(25,000)
1	14,700	0.893	13,127
2	22,750	0.797	18,132
3	37,692	0.712	26,837

(ii)   £33,096

(b)

	Original budget, £ 1,050 customers	Flexed budget, £	Actual results, £ 1,235 customers	Variance
Sales revenue	110,250	129,675	135,897	6,222
Variable costs	57,750	67,925	68,943	−1,018
Fixed overheads	34,000	34,000	39,223	−5,223
Operating profit	18,500	27,750	27,731	−19

Task 6: 13 marks

(a)   (i)

Extract of Ledger Balances for Trendy Togs for Year Ended 31 March 20-6

Account	Ledger balances	
	Dr	Cr
Opening inventory	6,000	
Purchases	71,435	
Bank & cash	26,221	
Sales ledger control account	22,165	
Prepayments	545	
Vehicle at cost	15,000	
Fixtures and fittings at cost	12,600	
Depreciation – vehicles		14,000
Depreciation – fixtures and fittings		7,560
Value added tax		14,598
Purchases ledger control		17,912
Accruals		4,500
Capital		22,600
Drawings	24,100	
Sales revenue		135,897
Rent	11,250	
Administrative expenses	2,103	
Distribution costs	8,355	
Wages	14,033	
Allowance for doubtful debts		222
Allowance for doubtful debts: adjustment	222	
Depreciation	3,260	
Closing inventory	8,492	8,492

(ii)   £27,731

(b)

Trendy Togs Statement of financial position year ended 31 March 20-6

	£	£
Non-current assets		
Vehicles		1,000
Fixtures and Fittings		5,040
		6,040
Current assets		
Inventory	8,492	
Trade receivables	21,943	
Prepayments	545	
Bank & cash	26,221	
		57,201
Current liabilities		
Trade payables	17,912	
Accruals	4,500	
Value added tax	14,598	
		37,010
Net current assets		20,191
Net assets		26,231
Financed by:	£	£
Capital		
Opening capital		22,600
Profit for the year		27,731
Subtotal		50,331
Drawings		−24,100
Closing capital		26,231

for your notes

for your notes

for your notes